Juan in a Hundred

Juan in a Hundred

The Representation of Latinos on Network News

BY OTTO SANTA ANA

University of Texas Press ◆ Austin

Requests for permission to reproduce material from this work should be sent to:
    Permissions
    University of Texas Press
    P.O. Box 7819
    Austin, TX 78713-7819
    www.utexas.edu/utpress/about/bpermission.html

♾ The paper used in this book meets the minimum requirements of ANSI/NISO
Z39.48-1992 (R1997) (Permanence of Paper).

Library of Congress Cataloging-in-Publication Data
Santa Ana, Otto, 1954–
Juan in a hundred : the representation of Latinos on network news / by Otto
Santa Ana.
        p.   cm.
    Includes bibliographical references and index.
    ISBN 978-0-292-74260-4 (cloth : alk. paper)
    ISBN 978-0-292-74374-8 (pbk. : alk. paper)
    1. Hispanic Americans—Press coverage—United States.   2. Hispanic Americans
on television.   3. Television broadcasting of news—United States.   I. Title.
    PN1992.8.H54S36   2012
    305.868'073—dc23   2011048867

doi:10.7560/742604

To Thelma
I am the moth; you are the Moon

Contents

Acknowledgments

Juan in a Hundred was conceived in 2005 during an incredibly energizing set of conversations with my dear friend, Federico Subervi. From the mid-1980s onward, Federico has written extensively about the state of television network news reporting on Latinos, so in 2004 the National Association of Hispanic Journalists (NAHJ) commissioned him to undertake the *Brown Out Report*, a then-yearly survey of the news coverage about Latinos. When Federico invited me to participate, I was thrilled! We had regularly commiserated on the absence of substantive scholarship on network television news reporting on Latinos. By combining Federico's broad knowledge of the field with a multimodal expansion of the critical cognitive metaphor work I had recently completed for *Brown Tide Rising*, we thought we could complete a book in 12 months. Crazy! Our plan morphed into two books, *The Mass Media and Latino Politics* (Subervi 2008) and the volume you hold in your hands. Without Federico's vision and steady encouragement throughout the years, *Juan in a Hundred* would never have been.

After the idea was born, I engaged my UCLA students to explore the multimodal semiotics of television news imaging. Their observations and ideas quickly shattered all the simplistic preconceptions with which I had begun, and their dynamism kept moving the project forward. I list the individuals with whom I worked most closely in endnote 3 of Chapter 1. They kept me honest, focused, and sane as we labored over both the oversimplifications and the falsehoods (some glaring, some subtle) about Latinos and other Americans that aired on the 2004 network evening news.

I enjoyed substantial material support from those who believed in me and my project. Several people helped me borrow video recordings of the ABC, NBC, CBS, and CNN evening newscasts from the Vanderbilt Television News Archive: Federico Subervi; Joe Torres, former NAHJ deputy director for policy and programs; and Ivan Román, former NAHJ executive director. VTNA executive director Marshall Breeding took special interest in my research. I received funding from the good folks at the University of California Institute for Mexico and the United States in 2005, and a Faculty Research Grant in 2006 from the UCLA Academic Senate Council on Research. In 2011, UCLA dean of the College of Arts and Sciences Alessandro Duranti provided subvention funds. The work could not have been completed without their support.

My nearly completed manuscript was stolen in late 2008 when thieves broke into my home and took my laptop and most of the backups, leaving all the charging cords. My luck changed the following year, when President Obama nominated my wife, Thelma Meléndez de Santa Ana, to join his administration. With the blessing of UCLA provost Scott Waugh, UCLA acting dean of the College of Arts and Sciences Reynaldo Macías, and my department chair, Professor Alicia Gaspar de Alba, I moved to Washington with Thelma. Reynaldo, first as dean and later as my departmental colleague, made every effort to reduce the distance that I sometimes felt from my home campus. My new department chair, Professor Abel Valenzuela, and the new UCLA dean of the College of Arts and Sciences, Alessandro Duranti, both supported a second year of leave. I am particularly indebted to Alessandro. In a new role with a daunting learning curve, Alessandro remained the scholar, sustaining an academic dialogue with me that advanced my work. He also smoothed over the mounting administrative challenges that I faced working at a distance from my home campus. With the help of all my UCLA colleagues, I finished *Juan in a Hundred* in Washington.

In Washington I served as visiting professor at the University of the District of Columbia. Former UDC trustee Fernando J. Barrueta, UDC provost Graeme Baxter, and former UDC College of Arts and Sciences dean Rachel Petty were extraordinarily supportive of my scholarship. I became friends with UDC professor Guy F. Shroyer, who read the first full draft of *Juan in a Hundred*; the volume only profited from Guy's apt suggestions. The executive director of the University of California Washington Center, Bruce Cain, lent me an office. I am grateful to Professor Cain, as well as UCWC's Professors James Desveaux and Rodger Rak, for their hospitality.

One of my deepest debts is to Amelia Tseng, Georgetown University graduate student, who edited my sprawling and overwritten manuscript. It had been accepted for publication with the proviso that I cut over 10% of the text. I just couldn't, so I turned to Amelia. A capable and always sensitive editor, she trimmed with surgical precision. *Juan in a Hundred* reads better due to Amelia's global stylistic changes. I looked forward to her always intelligent ideas on content changes, where she clarified terminology and semantic model descriptions.

Deep thanks go to my friend Theresa J. May, editor-in-chief at the University of Texas Press; the editorial board; Sue Carter, my copy editor; and especially the two external readers, who both offered solid, challenging critiques of the manuscript. Insofar as I was able to address their ideas, the book was improved.

I presented parts of my analysis over the years at several venues: in 2006 at the 51st Journalism Association of California Community Colleges, and at the Learning Institute for Working Journalists, the latter held at the University of Arizona; in 2007 at the Dilemmas of Democracy Conference of Loyola Marymount University; in 2008 at the American Anthropological Association meetings, at the UCSC Latinos in a Global Context seminar, and to the Department of Linguistics at UC Davis; in 2009 as a Conferencia Magistral at the annual Feria Internacional del Libro, held in Guadalajara, Mexico; and in 2011 at the UCLA Graduate Student Conference. I want to thank all the conveners and participants for their time and ideas.

The views and opinions expressed here are my own; they do not necessarily represent those of anyone mentioned above, or any institution with which I have been affiliated. I am responsible for all misstatements.

Finally I dedicate this book to my bride of eighteen years, Thelma Meléndez de Santa Ana, whose love sustains me. Thelma is my morning inspiration to push forward, my Happy Hour partner to celebrate successes, and my evening solace when life squeezes too hard. I could not be a happy man without her.

Transcription and Semiotic Conventions

- Quoted text is set in "quotation marks" (except for block quotations, which are indented, no quotation marks).
- Italics are used to indicate spoken text. Example: "*We're not criminals.*"
- Underline is used to indicate emphasis in spoken text. Example: "*Many conservative allies of the President who oppose any legalization for undocumented workers said they felt <u>betrayed</u> by Mr. Bush.*"
- Boldface is used to indicate paralinguistics (gestures or body language) accompanying spoken text. Example: The camera provides a medium close-up of Colorado representative Tom Tancredo, who jabs a newspaper, underscoring his opposition to the measure as he reads aloud the *Denver Post* headline while tapping on the paper in a three three-beat cadence: "*Bush Plan*: **lets illegals stay**."
- Translations are set in single quotes, e.g., *loco*, 'crazy.'
- Metaphors and their source and target semantic domains are set in SMALL CAPS.

Prologue: Studying the Network News Coverage on Latinos

For 50 years network television news programs have been America's most important source of understanding the nation and the world. Even today the nation assumes that network news reporting, with its very sophisticated use of technology, provides an authoritative daily accounting of America's unfolding reality. Since Latinos constitute the nation's fastest growing and largest minority group, in this book I explore how well the network news portrays them.

In 2004 the four top American networks (ABC, CBS, NBC, and CNN) broadcast over 12,000 separate stories on their evening news programs. Less than 1% of these stories addressed Latino issues. Given that Latinos comprised 14% of the United States population at the time, the nation's understanding of Latinos from network news programs was and remains wholly inadequate. This 1:100 ratio has not changed in the last 15 years; thus this study of network news programs will remain germane for the foreseeable future. Moreover, the news about Latinos is not only scarce, but too often it also misrepresents this heterogeneous people. Two or three times a week an often muddled message is broadcast to millions of American network news viewers—who tend to accept the message as trustworthy and accurate.

In *Juan in a Hundred*, I explore the network television news images with three increasingly focused studies. The first presents the panorama of a year's news coverage about Latinos. The second study is a series of close semiotic readings of a representative sample of those news stories about Latinos. The final study develops a cognitive model explaining how audiences make meaning out of television news broadcasts. These studies represent three distinct ways to understand the character of today's network news discourse. The findings are at times disheartening, but I do not simply criticize; I also put forward three sets of constructive recommendations for journalists.

In Chapter 1, the frequencies of news stories for four networks over an entire year are presented to reveal the full range and depth of network reporting, Latino and otherwise. I compare the patterns of the total 12,140 news stories to the subsets of stories involving Latinos, women, and other minorities. The finding is predictable: only a handful of Latino topics are aired, which restricts the information about Latinos that reaches news viewers. From this, I identify the two criteria that made a Latino event newsworthy in 2004: either it was an "inside-the-Beltway" topic, or it was a story about death and mayhem. It follows that the networks materially still did not consider Latinos to be an integral part of the American social fabric. After a literature review that addresses the implications of these findings, I demonstrate that better news coverage is possible. I offer a set of newsworthy Latino stories that were not televised in 2004, but which would have been consistent with the overall network coverage patterns.

In Section I, starting with Chapter 2, I shift methodologies entirely. I offer a series of 45 close readings of a representative sample of the original 118 Latino news stories. This includes the 10 principal Latino topics found in the network news, and consists of news briefs, breaking stories, and feature stories, as well as regular and investigative reports. I employ a set of semiotic concepts to distinguish the multimodal signs (visual, graphic, text, spoken, audio) that projected the specific Latino imagery of each news story. These semiotic concepts are drawn from several disciplines: visual art iconography, critical social semiotics, and cultural and media studies. With them, I present the multimodal imagery and messaging with which our nation makes sense of Latinos.

This approach exposes the techniques that the networks use as they construct Latino images for national consumption and edification. I note considerable unevenness of news reporting within and across the networks. There are a few superb reports—and many news stories displaying astonishing ignorance about Latinos. But almost every network story is polished with a glossy veneer of high production values that can divert viewers from such inadequacies.

A focus on semiotics reveals visual and other nontext representation. I find, for example, that while network newsrooms take care to balance the spoken reporting of politically contentious topics, they often pay little attention to balancing visual signs. In one news brief, for example, the news writers balance spoken text about unauthorized immigrants by using both *undocumented* and *illegal*—terms with quite different values. The

12 accompanying visual signs, however, all ascribe criminality to the immigrants. Thus this news story only superficially took a neutral political stance. These five chapters reveal other semiotic patterns that are rarely taken into account in journalistic content analyses.

Chapter 2 explores a few of the inside-the-Beltway stories that dominated network news coverage in 2004, including the domestic terrorism case of José Padilla, reporting on two White House appointees, and the 2004 presidential bid to garner Latino votes. Chapter 3 reviews a set of news briefs and feature stories, including stories about Latinos' impact on the national economy, Latino health care stories, entertainment stories centered on Latinos, public education, and Latinos in sports and in the Iraq War. In 2004, immigration was the major domestic news topic, so it is treated in three chapters. Chapter 4 covers Caribbean immigrant stories; Chapter 5 reviews key policy stories; and Chapter 6 covers feature-length stories about Mexican immigrants.

In Section II, I shift once more, from description to explanation. On the basis of the foregoing case studies, I develop a testable cognitive model of how viewers make meaning out of television news stories, based on Michel Foucault's theorizing about history and Hayden White's theorizing on writing history. I use this model to analyze the previously described immigration news stories, including both highly accomplished stories that succeed at opening up the world to their audience and less successful stories that restrict viewers' understanding of the world and their place in it.

In Chapter 7, I propose a cognitive model that explicitly maps out the process by which network news consumers create interpretations out of the multimodal stimuli of television news stories. The model has two challenges: how to incorporate into one interpretive framework different modes of lower-order signs (visual, nonspoken audio, graphic, and spoken) and how to deal with higher-order semantics. For the first challenge, I adapt the cognitive science scholarship on "concept blending" developed by Gilles Fauconnier and Mark Turner. To deal with the second, I enlist the aid of venerable humanist theories that offer insight into the nature of complex higher-order meanings. I draw on rhetorician Calvin McGee's influential theory on ideographs, a small set of everyday words that are higher-order abstractions of values that guide normative public commitments. I also recruit the still compelling visual semiotics of Roland Barthes. He posited a small set of higher-order semiotic signs, each a "repository of a rarefied meaning" that can invoke a society's historical dreams, fears, and values. However, this model fails to capture the dynamic meanings that viewers can draw from the televised news. Thus I propose taking one more step.

In Chapter 8, the final substantive chapter, I integrate narrative into the cognitive model to deal with dynamic interpretation. Here I draw on Northrop Frye's concept of archetypes, a small set of story types that have been used across time and that define societal values. In a similar vein, Barthes aptly called his own higher-order signs "myths." I argue that while the network news proffers a somewhat extensive set of images of Latinos, the set of story types on which the pieces are based is exceedingly small, and viewers tacitly link these story types to deeply held American social values. Crucially, narrative theorists argue that a mere fragment of the story type can signal the whole archetype; in Barthes' terms, even an "evaporated" scrap of a lower-order sign can invoke the myth. With this addition, this cross-disciplinary model begins to explain how network news viewers compose their (albeit limited) understandings about Latinos, and how news reporting sustains the nation's sociocultural and political values.

This model building will allow future scholars to inductively determine the finite set of story types underlying Latino news stories. The take-away for journalists may be more controversial. Objectivity has been the key criterion of American journalism for nearly 100 years. I propose a new criterion for professional news writing—narrative—and recommend that journalists demote objectivity to a second-level tenet, alongside fact checking and concise writing, to achieve greater journalistic fairness.

Juan in a Hundred

CHAPTER 1

What US Latino Stories
Make the Network News?

*The press may exercise more clout in what it omits than in what it
disseminates.*
—MICHAEL SCHUDSON[1]

Every night, CNN, ABC, NBC, and CBS broadcast television news reports
about the nation to millions of viewers.[2] These networks inform the viewer
about issues dealing with the economy, foreign relations, health care, the
weather—just about every important topic. The US viewing public tends to
accept the networks' reporting as legitimate and trustworthy. My research
team[3] and I begin by asking: *How well does network television represent US
Latinos on the evening news?*[4] To develop a solid answer I draw on a full
year of news stories from these four networks. Since I worked from an effectively complete 2004 corpus, we can inductively specify the reasoning
behind network story selection. So we will also answer the question: *On
what basis do network newsrooms select Latino news stories for broadcast?* I
will start with a brief summary of the findings of this chapter.

Major Findings of Chapter

On June 14, 2004, anchor Tom Brokaw reported on the *NBC Evening News*
a milestone for the country. Hispanics had "surged" to become the largest
minority group in the nation, with over 39.3 million people. In spite of the
increasing prominence of this group, most serious students of television
news expect little reporting on US Latinos, but the utter lack of representation is still astonishing. Less than 1% (0.79%) of the year's 12,000 news stories about US Latinos were broadcast in 2004. The disparity is troubling,

since Latinos made up over 14% of the total US population. Moreover, immigration was the topic of 22% of these few stories, at a time when immigration policy was not the momentous national issue that it would become in subsequent years. Thus, while network news severely underrepresents US Latinos, one aspect of their numbers is overrepresented. The nation's portrait of US Latinos is thus distorted. Yet, for all the attention focused on immigration as a problem, later chapters of this book will demonstrate that network news reporting gives comparatively little attention to the root causes of immigration, thus failing to edify the nation about this crucial consequence of globalization. More generally, the scope of Latino news topics was so narrow that over 70% of all US Latino stories aired on network evening news involved Washington "Beltway" politics. This further distortion of the nation's view of Latinos is not due to a lack of newsworthy material. At the end of the chapter, I demonstrate that many interesting and important Latino stories appeared in print news that would have given the national television network news audience a more well-rounded understanding about Latinos.

Sources and Method

To undertake this book I did not merely sample some portion of the networks' broadcast news stories. I included every NBC, CBS, ABC, and CNN evening news story broadcast during 2004 that was available in the Vanderbilt Television News Archive (VTNA).[5] This allows us to offer a panoramic overview of Latino representation on network news.

We first asked what would provide the best network news coverage of Latinos. One utopian answer would be numerical parity. Numerical parity means 14% of network news stories would be about Latinos, since Latinos made up 14% of the nation, and the nation would obtain a terrific understanding of the Latino populations. In a similar manner, topic parity would mean the distribution of story topics presented on network news would be mirrored in Latino news stories.

Some readers might dismiss these evaluative measures because they believe raw numbers of television stories are a poor measure of representation. Nevertheless, parity comparisons will reveal the relative visibility of minority groups on television network news. We begin with VTNA's aggregate set of news stories ($n = 12{,}140$) for the four networks for the year 2004. We amplified the index of the VTNA with two complementary procedures in order to determine how many subpopulations of ethnic, racial, and gender groupings had been mentioned in news stories, and what story topics were covered. The first procedure was a computer tabulation. In spite of reduced expectations, our team was frankly surprised at the extremely low numbers of news stories that were tagged with this computer algorithm. Therefore, we undertook a second, computer-assisted procedure using a keyword search to expand the list of stories. In the case of women, for example, a researcher first marked any story title or abstract that referenced any of the words (such as *woman, female, girl,* and attendant plurals) by which that subpopulation is known. She also conducted keyword searches of common Spanish-language surnames, which turned up more stories on Attorney General Alberto Gonzales, and of well-known US Latinos who have English surnames, such as then governor of New Mexico Bill Richardson.[6] She also sought the names of popular artists such as Daddy Yankee and J-Lo in order to locate additional news stories pertaining to US Latinos in news archive records that lacked other references to these subgroups. We designed our two procedures to overselect, rather than underselect, Latino stories, so our findings do not diminish the overall numbers of Latino stories vis-à-vis the aggregate.[7]

Numerical Parity

Table 1.1 displays number of news stories by subpopulation. As expected, the story count did not achieve numerical parity with the nation's subgroups. In fact, the subpopulation news item numbers were so small that we were able to inspect many full sets of stories item by item. For example, American Indians comprise nine-tenths of 1% of the nation's population, but were depicted in 12 stories, or 0.1% (one-tenth of a percent) of the aggregate news stories. The networks represented Asian Americans even more poorly, with a total of 13 stories (0.11% of aggregate) for a group that comprises 3.6% of the nation's population. Meanwhile, the 2000 census listed US Latinos as the largest minority population in the country, but Latinos make the network news much less frequently than the next largest minority group, African Americans, who were represented in 5.68% of the aggregate of news stories.[8]

The numbers of news stories about women was also limited. Although they constitute just under 51% of the US population, women were represented in just 13.66% ($n = 1,658$) of the network news stories. Since we tagged gender, nationality, and ethnicity, we noted that women of color (Asian American, African American, and Latina) appeared even more

Table 1.1. News story numerical representation of select subgroups

Subpopulation	Story count	% aggregate	% population
Aggregate	12,140	100.00	100.0
Women	1,658	13.66	50.9
African American	689	5.68	12.3
US Latino	96	0.79	14.1
Asian American	13	0.11	3.6
American Indian	12	0.10	0.9

Source: US Census 2000 (www.census.gov/prod/2001pubs/c2kbr01-5.pdf, c2kbr01-9.pdf, and c2kbr01-1.pdf; retrieved 27 July 2006).

rarely on network news. The great majority of stories about women involved White women. The exception was Condoleezza Rice, who at the start of 2004 was US national security advisor and who later in the year became secretary of state. When we exclude references to her, women of color appeared a total of 13 times. The bottom line is that the face of the nation presented by network news does not reflect the gender or racial complexion of twenty-first century America. As student researcher Serena Villalba quipped: if the evening news is accurate, all American women are White, all African Americans are famous, all Latinos are immigrants, and American Indians and Asian Americans hardly exist at all.

Table 1.2 provides numbers and percentages for the Latin American "cluster." A cluster is a collection of subpopulations. This one includes US Latinos and non-US Latin Americans.[9] Latinos are made up of a number of communities and populations, and our conventions allowed a story to be listed under more than one subpopulation. Hence a story can be listed, for example, as referring both to Women and to Mexicans, or pertain to a number of subpopulations in the Latin American rubric.[10] The Minority category in Table 1.2 refers to stories in which ethnicity or nationality was mentioned in the archive abstract, but not specified. Once again, our tagging procedures were designed to err in the direction of overrepresentation. Using the most inclusive set of criteria, we found that 471 (3.88%) of the 2004 sample of network evening news stories pertained to Latinos, including both US Latinos and Latin Americans.

In spite of very generous count assumptions, the number of stories in the Latin American cluster of subpopulations is derisory (just under 4%).

Latinos made up about 14% of the US population, so if we combine this subpopulation with all Latin American cluster stories together, the smallest gap we can estimate is less than one-third of numerical parity. However, this estimation includes stories about non-US Latinos, and because of non-mutually exclusive categories, some stories were counted more than once. When we exclude stories about non-US Latinos, our total is 96 stories, less than 1% (0.79%) of the aggregate. Thus US Latinos are not shown to national viewing audiences at anywhere near their proportion of the US population. In 2004, they appeared once in every 11 broadcasts. To approximate numerical parity, Latinos would have to appear in nearly two news stories (1.6) per broadcast day.

In the subsequent chapters, I will combine in the total Latino stories all network news stories about US immigration policy, whether or not reference is made to US Latinos. This raises the figure for all 2004 Latino news stories to 118. After considering other classifications of the Latino news stories, we chose this grouping. A problem that compounds the paucity

Table 1.2. US Latino and Latin American story count
(Latin American cluster)

Latino & Latin American	Story Count	% of 471	% of 12,140
Haitian	126	26.75	1.04
Cuban	110	23.35	0.91
US Latino	96	20.38	0.79
Mexican	46	9.77	0.38
Dominican	18	3.82	0.15
Caribbean	12	2.55	0.10
Minority	15	3.18	0.12
Chilean	12	2.55	0.10
Puerto Rican	10	2.12	0.08
Venezuelan	8	1.70	0.07
Honduran	5	1.06	0.04
Central American	4	0.85	0.03
Guatemalan	4	0.85	0.03
Nicaraguan	2	0.42	0.02
Costa Rican	1	0.21	0.01
Panamanian	1	0.21	0.01
Salvadoran	1	0.21	0.01
Totals	471	100.00	3.88

of Latino news stories is the networks' failure to distinguish among non-Caribbean Latino communities. In 2004, Caribbean coverage was comparatively ample, which allows viewers to distinguish Cuban, Dominican, and Puerto Rican communities. However, the networks rarely distinguish Mexican-origin, Central American–origin, and other Latino communities. Network journalists regularly failed to make two basic distinctions: generation (immigrant, first US born, later generations) and legal status (unauthorized or authorized immigrant), although these factors account for major differences in the economic, educational, political, electoral, and cultural life patterning among the various Latino communities. In the following chapters we will note network reporting failures that stem from viewing Latinos as an undifferentiated group. As a result, the American public also tends to consider all non-Caribbean Latinos to be unauthorized Mexican immigrants. In this book each of these 118 news stories about Latinos will be identified by story number. (See the Appendix for a thumbnail summary of each of the 118 stories.)

In terms of news story counts, the networks have failed their Fourth Estate responsibility to establish a full and adequate picture of the nation and world. The Fourth Estate is an Enlightenment argument that a free and independent press strengthens a nation's democracy by keeping its citizenry informed on crucial matters. US journalists for over 100 years have expressly claimed this role for themselves, and have been buttressed by First Amendment guarantees of press freedom. However, raw numbers indicate that the networks have failed to keep Americans informed about the increasingly important US Latino communities. Proportional representation is evidently not the logic at work in network news programming; we will begin to discern its logic when we explore the distribution of news content in the next section.

Topic Parity

Another way to optimally represent US Latinos would be with a similar topic distribution to that found within the aggregate 12,140 stories from 2004. However, given the low number of stories in the Latin American cluster, topic parity simply cannot be achieved. Consequently we modified our query to ask: *What were the topics that captured the attention of network news programmers?*

We begin by describing the subject matter, or groupings of topics, of our nearly comprehensive general sample. These were tabulated to come

Table 1.3. Aggregate news story subject matter distribution

Subject matter groupings	Story count	% of 12,140	Story topics (only a sampling)
War	3,278	27	9/11, Iraq, terrorism, Afghanistan, CIA
US politics & policy	2,748	23	Presidential campaign, George Bush, Congress, Supreme Court, health, Medicare, Social Security, gay marriage, public education
Domestic US subject matter	1,277	11	States, religion, crime, immigration, African Americans, historical events
World affairs	1,186	10	Middle East, Europe, Asia, Haiti, Sudan
Business & technology	1,040	9	Economy, business, internet, technology, space, environment
Weather & natural disasters	566	5	Weather, hurricanes, earthquakes, floods
Human interest	546	4	Holidays, obituaries, animals, former presidents
Sports	514	4	Sports
Entertainment	475	4	Television, movies, music, photography
Consumer	391	3	Gasoline prices, consumer products, airport safety
Other	102	1	Miscellaneous
Totals	12,140	100	

up with a ranking of the most frequent topics. This listing of most frequent topics came to more than 1,000 items, which could not be easily interpreted. Even a ranking of the most frequent 100 stories turned out to be cumbersome.[11] Most students of television news will recognize the pattern of topic groupings in Table 1.3.[12] Broadly speaking, in 2004 the Iraq war (27%) and US politics and policy (23%) made up half of all news stories. All other non-war world affairs stories as a subject matter grouping made up

Table 1.4. Caribbean cluster topic distribution

Principal story topics of the Caribbean cluster	Count	% of 276	% of 12,140
Haitian unrest	95	34.42	0.78
Guantánamo Bay	69	25.00	0.57
Weather & natural disasters	68	24.64	0.56
Cuba/US relations	14	5.07	0.12
Immigration	11	3.99	0.09
Sports	5	1.80	0.04
Health	3	1.09	0.02
Other	11	3.99	0.09
Total	276	100.00	2.27

10% of the total. Business and technology stories made up another 9% of all items.[13] Another way to summarize the stories is to divide them in two: domestic topics comprised just over one-third of all news; the other two-thirds covered the wars in Iraq and Afghanistan, other world topics, and US politics and policies.

Given these preliminaries, we will now evaluate the topic patterns for key clusters of US Latino and Latin American subpopulations. We begin with the Caribbean story cluster.[14] A noticeable feature of Table 1.2, apart from the counts, is the proportional abundance of Caribbean stories, with stories about Haiti and Cuba taking up over 50% of all US Latino and Latin American stories. In contrast, Mexican stories registered a comparatively small 10%, 46 out of a total of 471 stories in the Latin American cluster.

In regard to the Caribbean story topic distribution, shown in Table 1.4, the major topics of the year were Haitian unrest, as well as the US prison in Guantánamo Bay, in Cuba. In 2004 the people of Haiti suffered political strife when numerous, persistent demonstrators demanded the removal of President Jean-Bertrand Aristide. In response the president called in the army, and hundreds were killed, which led to more demonstrations and violence. Finally, the US military intervened, and in the end, Aristide left the country. These four months of political upheaval were covered on a nearly daily basis by the networks. To add to the misery, the worst hurricane season on record pummeled Haiti, with 3,000 deaths as a result of Hurricane Jeanne alone.

As for Cuban-based stories, two-thirds of the stories focused on the Guantánamo Bay prison facility, which houses detainees designated as "enemy combatants" by the Bush administration. Friction between the US and Cuban governments, along with hurricanes, accounted for another 27% of stories.[15]

From this review, it is evident that US news coverage follows federal government involvement and interests. To make further sense of the news coverage, let us compare the topics of the Caribbean events and the topics of the Latin American cluster. Since the Latin American cluster patterns are so polarized, we venture to explain the patterning of network television evening news for these stories.

Criteria for Latino Story Newsworthiness

Two newsworthiness criteria are involved for either a US Latino or Latin American story to be aired on a US television network. First and foremost, the story must involve dramatic political events that directly involve Washington politics. If it doesn't, it is unlikely to be broadcast. Our results reconfirm much empirical research on US journalism.[16] The second criterion is that the story involve a human calamity or natural disaster. The second criterion is invoked for all domestic communities, not just Latinos. See Table 1.5.

These criteria capture the distribution of the most distinctive Latino topic, immigration—the largest topic of the Latin American story cluster. Immigration ranked 95th among the aggregate of 12,140 stories, with less

Table 1.5. Topic distribution of Latin American cluster

Principal story topics of the Latin American cluster	Count	% of 471	% of 12,140
Haitian unrest	101	21.44	0.83
Weather & natural disasters	86	18.26	0.71
Guantánamo Bay	73	15.50	0.60
Immigration	59	12.53	0.49
2004 presidential campaign	28	5.94	0.23
Sports	16	3.40	0.13
Cuba/US relations	15	3.18	0.12
Iraq	15	3.18	0.12
Other	78	16.56	0.64
Total	471	100.00	3.88

than two-tenths of a percent (.13%, $n = 16$) of the total.[17] On the other hand, in Table 1.5 it ranked fourth (12.5%) in the Latin American cluster of 471 stories, behind stories on Haitian political unrest, natural disasters, and post–September 11 foreign policy. The preponderance of these news items is the reason the news media, and hence the public, perceive that immigration is a Latino topic.[18]

Immigration also predominates in the Central American story cluster (not reproduced here), where it is the most frequent news topic, making up 33% of all stories.[19] The networks aired stories about US agents using torture techniques, and it happened that Central American victims of torture were interviewed about their experiences. Our two newsworthiness criteria account for the presence of immigration stories and the absence of other Central American story topics that might otherwise be considered newsworthy. For example, in January 2004 no networks reported that Nobel Peace Prize winner Rigoberta Menchu accepted a position in the new government of Guatemala's incoming president, Oscar Berger, where she would oversee their nation's compliance with the United Nations–brokered peace accords that ended its 36-year civil war. Nor did US network news viewers learn, half a year later, that President Berger reduced the size of the army by more than 50%.[20] Historical events that do not involve the two aforementioned criteria are not considered newsworthy.

Finally, in Table 1.6 we provide all story topics of US Latinos in order to display the lumpiness of television news coverage. Two topics dominate 40% of stories: the presidential campaign and immigration. No other Latino topic breaks into double figures except sports, an entertainment topic. In the aggregate, by contrast, the presidential campaign was also the most frequent story, but at a far less dominating 18%, and the immigration topic contributed less than 1% to the aggregate.[21] Again, immigration is defined as a US Latino issue. A few more contrasts between Latino and aggregate topic frequencies in Table 1.6 make these disparities clearer. The fourth most frequent Latino topic is education, at about 7%. In contrast, in the aggregate, education stories do not break 1% (0.6%). Notice that if we combine the relatively high-ranking Latino story topics, Attorney General Alberto Gonzales and President George Bush, the combination makes up nearly 12% of the Latino total. However, the Gonzales story frequency does not even break into the top 100 stories in the aggregate, and Bush (excluding the election campaign, Iraq war, and other defined topics) comes in at less than 3% (2.2%).

We can now refine our description of the patterning of US Latino news

Table 1.6. Topic distribution of US Latino stories

US Latino story topics	Count	% of 96	% of 12,140
Presidential campaign	26	27.08	0.21
Immigration	22	22.92	0.18
Sports	10	10.42	0.08
Education	7	7.29	0.06
Alberto Gonzales	6	6.25	0.05
Bush	5	5.21	0.04
California	3	3.13	0.02
Cuba/US relations	3	3.13	0.02
Iraq	3	3.13	0.02
Health	2	2.08	0.02
Human interest	2	2.08	0.02
Terrorism	2	2.08	0.02
Weather & natural disasters	2	2.08	0.02
Obituaries	1	1.04	0.01
Racism	1	1.04	0.01
Television	1	1.04	0.01
Total	96	100.00	0.79

item selection in 2004. First, the calamities criterion accounted for just over 2% of the 96 stories. However, the Washington Beltway relevance criterion for Latino newsworthiness captured over 73% of all US Latino stories. Thus we observe that news selection of Latino stories to be aired on the network evening news overwhelmingly prefers Washington, DC, politics. The Latino topics that fit this criterion, described in Table 1.6, include the presidential campaign, immigration, education, Alberto Gonzales, George Bush, Cuba/US relations, Iraq, terrorism, and all three stories about California politics.

To add to this skewing, very often Latinos are only tangentially related to the main topic of the story. For example, a US Latino/California news story briefly cited Fabian Nuñez, then speaker of the California Assembly, during multiple-story celebrity coverage of Arnold Schwarzenegger's first days as governor. In another US Latino story about a decision to close libraries in Salinas, California, Chicano author Gary Soto received cursory mention and far less airtime than John Steinbeck, another Salinas-born author.

Effects of Misrepresenting Latinos on Television News

The effects of underrepresentation and misrepresentation of Latinos on network television news has been documented much more thoroughly now than when Félix Gutiérrez called for research in the late 1970s, and when Federico Subervi repeated the call a dozen years ago.[22] For television, there are now studies of Latinos in prime-time programming,[23] in commercials,[24] in reality-based programs,[25] in cable programming; on Latinos' access to television production;[26] and on Latino subjectivity in news programs.[27] Poindexter et al. (2003) found Latinos to be "virtually invisible as anchors, reporters, and subjects," and "rarely" interviewed as news sources in local newscasts.

Television rarely shows Latinos to be full subjects in the news or other programming; the result is that two-dimensional renderings of Latinos predominate, and television viewers judge Latinos as a group accordingly. For example, in a statistical analysis of prime-time entertainment programming in 1997, Mastro and Robinson (2000) found that police were significantly more likely to be shown using excessive force when perpetrators were young racial minorities. Mastro and Robinson note that a broad base of research indicates that such negative stereotypical depictions have a significant detrimental impact.[28] Repeatedly showing violent acts against Latinos on television across genres tends to normalize such violent behavior in the eyes of viewers. For example, on the police program *Cops*, Oliver found that Whites were more likely to be portrayed as police officers than criminal suspects, while Latinos were more likely to be portrayed as criminal suspects than as police officers. Moreover, Oliver noted that police officers physically assaulted Latinos who had been arrested more frequently than they assaulted arrested Whites. In this hybrid of news and entertainment programming, both the story staging and the camera work mimic a television news format, which heightens viewer perceptions of authenticity.[29] However, such "reality-based" program should be called "stereotype-based." Skeptics might discount the relevance of *Cops* to the study of network television news coverage and imagery,[30] but Dixon and his collaborators have conducted a series of television news studies demonstrating that such two-dimensional portrayals are not limited to popular entertainment programming.[31]

Dixon and Linz studied Latino representation in a random sample of Southern California local television news programs in the late 1990s. Comparing television news to official crime statistics drawn from the California Department of Justice, they found that Whites were overrepresented as victims, while Latinos were largely absent on television news. Studying intergroup representations (e.g., White vs. Black or Black vs. Latino, etc.), they found that Whites were more likely than Latinos to be portrayed as victims of crime. In "inter-role" television news representations (e.g., perpetrator vs. victim), Latinos were more likely to be portrayed as lawbreakers than as crime victims, whereas Whites were significantly more likely to be portrayed as defenders than as lawbreakers. Whites therefore appear to be overrepresented and Latinos underrepresented as homicide victims on television news, and Whites are overrepresented as law defenders.[32] Further, in a 2006 random sample of local Los Angeles television news programming, Dixon and Azocar found that Latino juveniles were significantly more likely to be portrayed as perpetrators than White juvenile lawbreakers.[33]

Mastro has explored the effects of Latino criminality stereotyping.[34] With increased exposure to televised stereotyping, Whites evaluated Latinos in greater accordance with the negative racial stereotypes broadcast by television and tended to accept the stereotypes. Mastro, Behm-Morawitz, and Ortiz also found that real-world perceptions of US Latinos respond closely to television consumption rates: increased television exposure to negative portrayals of Latinos leads to more negative opinions.[35]

Others have also focused on television's ability to influence the host society's perception of minorities. For example, in the 1980s Faber, O'Guinn, and Meyer compared Latino and White beliefs about the adequacy of televised minority character portrayals.[36] They found that White respondents who were heavy viewers tended to believe that television portrayed Latinos fairly, while Latinos disagreed. In sum, the preponderance of research indicates that stereotypical television depictions tend to reify misleading beliefs about Latinos in the eyes of viewers.

Dimming Aura of Network Journalism

No one will disagree that the purveyors of network news were indifferent to the lives of women and minority populations 60 years ago.[37] But one might ask why network newsrooms have failed to correct the inadequacies of the 1950s. Faber and his colleagues offer a partial reason: few Latinos have been network television news executives. A broader explanation is that when the Big Three networks perfected television's technology in the 1960s, with free access to public airwaves, they became an oligarchy.[38] For 20 years—the so-called golden age of network news—they entertained their captive audiences with news programming of global scope and unprecedented visual immediacy. However, when further technology allowed viewers to roam, the networks were slow to change their winning formula. The golden age of television news ended when real competition brought about a steep viewership decline. Their competitors include cable television,[39] the internet, partisan commentators such as O'Reilly, Hannity, Olbermann, and Dobbs, and television news satirists Colbert and Stewart.

This decline accelerated as changing national demographics made standard network news fare increasingly nonrepresentative. Suro reported on Latino attitudes toward news media preferences, finding that nearly half of the adult Latino population draw on both mainstream English-language and Spanish-language news media.[40] Suro also found that the language in which Latinos get their news significantly influences their opinions on domestic and international political issues, since Spanish-language media groups offer viewers more pro-Latino news framings. Finally, Suro found that Latinos have strong views about the roles the news media play in society, reaffirming the twenty-five-year-old observation of Faber, O'Guinn, and Meyer that Latinos believe English-language media contribute to a negative image of Latinos among English-speaking Americans. Insofar as new media sources continue to emerge and mainstream English-language network news offerings fail to address the interests of the Latino market and an ever more diverse US viewing public, network news programming will become increasingly irrelevant and less dominant.

It would be one thing if US journalism professed no guiding directive beyond the profit motive. However, American journalism has an important responsibility to help safeguard the nation's democracy by providing the electorate with accurate information about the state of the nation and reliable depictions of daily events.[41] As part of its Fourth Estate[42] responsibilities, television news in particular should strive to depict the various US Latino populations as a significant portion of the body politic. Otherwise the electorate, which depends on television news to form its views, will not be equipped to address contentious issues that it associates with this population.

Individual journalists no doubt acknowledge this failing, and call for executives to recognize the networks' failure to accurately represent the Latino communities and their political issues. Some skeptics may dismiss the industry's responsibility, but prominent media scholar Michael Schudson notes the "public aura" of television news: "When the media offer the public an item of news, they confer on it public legitimacy. What is amplified in popular media, first of all, is subject matter." Speaking about the moment when the BBC stopped being a governmental mouthpiece, Schudson notes that the BBC developed "an irreverence toward authority as broadcasters began to speak on behalf of the general public."[43] He goes on to say that the network

> is a . . . moral organization. A news story . . . is not like an advertisement, the self-interested purpose of which one can presume. It is not like a public relations event, which is suspect on its face. It is a declaration . . . by news professionals that an event is noteworthy. . . . Frequency of mention indicates *how* noteworthy . . . and viewers understand . . . this calibration of importance.[44]

The public aura projects national importance and validates stories deemed newsworthy. Stories passed over by the networks are not validated. The news media have, in Schudson's words, the ability to "publicly include,"[45] but as the findings of this chapter demonstrate, they also have the ability to publicly exclude. Schudson claims that national news is "more comprehensive and credible"[46] than it was years ago; our research demonstrates that it continues to underreport US Latino issues in both breadth and depth.[47]

The public aura of network news has dimmed. For one thing, a more diverse and discerning national audience is increasingly indifferent to the monochromatic broadcasts of formulaic news drawn from few sources. In our nearly comprehensive study of a recent year of network news, the single major finding is their gross disregard of Latinos.

Latino Stories the Networks Ignored

We asked, *What other Latino stories were newsworthy?* In the final section of this chapter, we address this question. Television network news programmers had many opportunities to report on newsworthy topics about the nation's 39.3 million Latinos. Such stories would have made a striking difference in the public images and public views of Latinos. Without diminishing the business and journalistic challenges that television news programmers face, I will demonstrate that the television network status quo constitutes national erasure of Latinos and perpetuates bias.

I will compare the 2004 networks news stories that were broadcast to other newsworthy Latino stories that the networks chose not to broadcast in 2004. To locate the stories that television networks failed to report, we reviewed the nation's newspapers. Two student researchers were independently given the same task. Each spent an afternoon using the LexisNexis search engine to locate local and national newspaper articles about Latinos that satisfied one criterion: the topic of the story was required to match the categories for the aggregate, namely the subject matter of Table 1.3. As it turned out, our researchers did not have to scour for relevant news stories about Latinos. Each researcher easily tracked down journalistically compelling stories that would have deepened the nation's understanding of Latinos, had the television network newsroom broadcast them to their audience. In this section we present a typical sample of each news topic.

The most reported issue on television in 2004 was the Iraq War. The television networks included a good number of patriotic pieces, such as heartrending stories of Latino soldiers like Lance Corporal Jose Gutierrez, one of the first soldiers to die in the war (#33). The networks also aired much lighter stories about Latino soldiers, such as story #56, about a Latino who is a gentle Mr. Mom at home and an intimidating drill sergeant at work. In subsequent chapters we will analyze the semiotic content of these and 43 other television news stories.

However, the television network news did not cover war stories involving Latino immigrant soldiers whose intense desire to become part of the US fabric was frustrated. In contrast, some newspapers reported on the difficulties Latino veterans faced when they sought US citizenship.[48] One person whose story appeared in print is Pfc. Juan Escalante. In his hometown he "enlisted by showing a fake green card he bought for $50." The army wanted him to become a citizen because he had proved to be "a valuable soldier who risked his life in a war zone." Sadly, even as one branch of government sought to make Escalante a citizen, another was taking steps to deport his parents.[49] An even more poignant newspaper story reported that after Angela Cabral lost her soldier son in Iraq, she faced deportation.[50]

The runner-up television news story of 2004 was the presidential election. While we noted a good deal of pre-election news speculation about the "Latino vote,"[51] we had to go to newspapers to find the actual Latino voter count. No network followed up with these figures: "'Latinos registered and cast their ballots in record numbers . . . a significant milestone,' said Antonio González, president of William C. Velásquez Institute. Latinos accounted for 7.59 million votes cast. . . . Importantly, 81.5 percent of registered Latinos voted."[52] The television news silence regarding the actual Latino voter count is telling, since in this election cycle news pundits bemoaned the vanishing American voter.[53] A related issue was whether Latinos voted for Bush or Kerry: newspaper readers learned that both political parties claimed success at attracting the perceived last big voter bloc, while television viewers did not.[54] Another fascinating news angle was the debate of Latino political scientists about the national implications of the Latino voter turnout. However, the television networks showed no interest in the political power of nearly 40 million people, only in the election itself.

Another regular topic on the television evening news was health and health care. In 2004 the networks aired over 600 such stories. Yet, coverage of Latino health was nearly nonexistent. Only one health-related network news story about the uninsured, #47, dealt with Latinos. In it, one person stood in for the diverse experiences of 39.9 million US Latinos. The other health news story, #80, will be shown in Chapter 3 to have misrepresented a Latino medical concern. Network news did not broach any aspect of the chronic diseases plaguing Latino communities, such as AIDS, diabetes, alcoholism, cancer, heart disease, or obesity.

The absence of health-related television news stories on Latinos was apparently due to network indifference, not deficiency. To demonstrate this, from a good number of newsworthy newspaper articles, we will mention just three. The first reported on storefront clinics that serve the Latino population with unlicensed, traditional Mexican care.[55] The second newspaper story found that living in a neighborhood among other Mexican Americans afforded elderly residents greater protection against stroke, cancer, and hip fractures.[56] Finally, the third print media article noted a significant and growing shortfall of Latino medical professionals for this growing population:

"Latinos accounted for more than 12 percent of the U.S. population in 2002, but only 2 percent of the nation's registered nurses, 3.4 percent of its psychologists, and 3.5 percent of its physicians . . . Minority populations are growing at a tremendous pace, but they remain seriously underrepresented in the health-care professions," said [the author of] the National Academies' Institute of Medicine 2004 report on Racial Disparities in Health Care.[57]

The information in this single quote provides more information than a year of network television news reporting on Latino health issues.

Another national issue covered by the television network news was public education. The networks aired almost 50 education stories in 2004. If the news editors had chosen to elaborate on Latino education concerns, the network news audience's understanding of Latinos would have become more nuanced. For example, in 2004 over 45 million people spoke a language other than English at home, comprising almost 18% of the total US population. This multilingualism was reflected in a school population of over 2 million English-language learners, mainly Latino students.[58] We chose this topic in part because during the presidential campaign John Kerry attacked George Bush's major public education initiative, No Child Left Behind, which reorganized pedagogy and language assessment for English-language learners and other students across the country. Thus, adequate pedagogies for and assessment of these students are crucial national issues. However, English-language learners were referred to only once, and bilingual education was never mentioned in our inclusive database of 12,140 network television news stories.

Moreover, the 2004 education stories on network television were placating rather than provocative. On the fiftieth anniversary of the *Brown v. Board of Education* ruling, school resegregation was the topic of a single network story, #51. However, the story did not explore its causes. One newspaper aptly described this as the ongoing "hyper-segregation" of public schools.[59] A newsworthy debate would have asked whether vouchers or sustained court intervention would better foster public school student success,[60] but the newsroom did not offer this to its viewing audience.

On a related topic, when discussing affirmative action, television network news frequently points to Attorney General Alberto Gonzales (#100 to #104) or Secretary of State Condoleezza Rice, but does not mention affirmative action's original design, namely to root out institutional racism. Gonzales and Rice should rightly be considered a special, separate class of Americans, along with other celebrities such as athletes and entertainers. In the context of affirmative action, when the networks simply refer to a high-achieving and high-profile minority individual, they imply that racism today is no longer widespread and institutionalized, but localized in a few disreputable individuals with serious personality failings.[61] In contrast to the networks' failure to name White racism, several newspapers pointed out chronic racism in professions such as medicine and law,[62] and the increasingly high hurdles confronting students of color.[63] Lastly, while television news repeatedly observed the fifth anniversary of the suburban rampage at Columbine High, neither the rise of urban school violence[64] nor the provocative issue of Black/Brown racial conflict in public high schools[65] was considered newsworthy.

Crime was another recurring issue on the national agenda. We have already noted that the misrepresentation of Latinos in crime stories reinforces false views about US Latinos, for example, that they are more likely than Whites to be criminals. The National Council of La Raza (NCLR) assessed the facts and expressly called this myth "a travesty of justice." In 2004 the NCLR reported the unjust "overrepresentation of the nation's largest minority at every stage of the criminal justice system from police stops to penitentiary and parole."[66] This authoritative report, which challenged this nationally accepted belief, received no network airtime. Instead, NBC chose to dedicate its prime news time to extensive coverage of one despondent Latino with marital problems who briefly took a hostage in Los Angeles (#95). NCLR and other Latino advocacy organizations regularly challenge national orthodoxies about Latinos. Their claims invite greater news coverage, and news editors and directors should not dismiss them.

While many television news stories about the US economy were aired, only one, #27, addressed the Latino contribution to the economy. As will be discussed in a later chapter, the television story misrepresents the newspaper article on which it is based. Many pertinent stories which should have piqued the interest of networks were not broadcast. In 2004, 1.5 million Latino families fulfilled all but one requirement to be a home buyer: legal status. The National Association of Hispanic Real Estate Professionals (NAHREP), an 18,000-member trade association, estimated that serving these families would generate $44 billion for the US economy.[67]

A less controversial but still newsworthy issue is lower rates of homeownership among US Latinos generally. In 2004 the NAHREP estimated that Latinos would account for 31% of the nation's household growth between 2000 and 2010, making them the fastest growing minority group; 84% of Latino renters "strongly" desired to buy a home and 55% planned on buying in the next five years.[68] A community advocate argued that since homeownership is "the first step to wealth creation for a family . . . policy-makers . . . and business leaders [should] find new and innovative ways to reach this market and help bridge the home buying information gap."[69] These and many more economic topics were available to the networks as opportunities to present Latinos as communities woven into the US fabric.

Other economic topics included the growing power of the immigrant labor movement, primarily unauthorized Latino workers;[70] the role of Latino entrepreneurs in creating wealth and jobs for the nation;[71] and one human interest story about the upsurge of Latino restaurants and food products, driving double-digit growth of Mexican-style cheeses in Wisconsin's $20.6 billion dairy industry.[72]

In 2004 network television news aired 89 stories about Ronald Reagan's death. This blanket television coverage did not include a single Latino assessment. In contrast, one mainstream Spanish-language newspaper alone provided three divergent critical appraisals by Latinos.[73] And, among the 144 obituaries broadcast on the evening news during the year, not one prominent Latino was mentioned. We take the opportunity to commemorate the 2004 passing of four extraordinary Latinos whose deaths went unnoticed by the television news audience.

In 2004, Gloria Anzaldúa died. This Chicana lesbian author raised the profile of the literature of all US women of color. As a philosopher, Anzaldúa expanded the idea of international and transnational borders of consciousness, a notion she helped define.[74] Her renowned *Borderlands/ la Frontera: The New Mestiza* made several national lists of the 100 best books of the century.

Another important Latino who passed away in 2004 was the nation's first Latino federal judge, Reynaldo Garza.[75] In 1976, President Jimmy Carter asked Garza to become US attorney general. Although Garza declined for family reasons, had he accepted, he would have become the first Chicano to serve as a US cabinet official.

Frank del Olmo, arguably the most influential Latino journalist in the nation, also passed away in 2004. This Pulitzer Prize–winning editor, columnist, and reporter for the *Los Angeles Times* was known nationally for his sharp insights into Latino issues.[76]

Finally, we commemorate Pedro Pietri, the Nuyorican poet. Reverend Pietri was best known for *Puerto Rican Obituary*, his 1973 epic poem depicting the lives of five Puerto Ricans and their unfulfilled American dreams.[77] The poem begins as follows:

PUERTO RICAN OBITUARY
They worked
They were always on time
They were never late
They never spoke back
when they were insulted
They worked
They never took days off
that were not on the calendar
They never went on strike
without permission
They worked
ten days a week
and were only paid for five

They worked
They worked
They worked
and they died
They died broke
They died owing
They died never knowing
what the front entrance
of the first national city bank looks like.[78]

In commemorating Pietri's death, the editors of the journal *Monthly Review* said that his "power, insight, and message . . . continue to resonate among activists and dreamers all over the world."[79] The lives of these and other exceptional Latinas and Latinos deserve a national tribute, if only in a 20-second network television news segment. Ignoring these literary and political figures perpetuates the false impression that among 40 million US Latinos, there are no individuals of note.

To conclude, newspapers reported on every Latino-related topic that the network evening news aired in 2004. The newspapers often covered these topics with greater depth. In contrast, the network news aired only a fraction of the Latino-related topics that newspapers published. This is not to say that networks should cover Latinos as thoroughly as print news, but that the scarcity of television network news stories about Latinos is not due to the absence of newsworthy items.

When Latinos were depicted on the network news broadcasts, the story almost always involved Washington politics. Still, the most telling network news failure was the disproportional paucity of Latino stories. Even a modest effort to bridge this gap would be a noteworthy improvement. The current coverage, which has not changed significantly since 2004, is so limited that it cannot display Latino diversity, and thus it sustains biased viewpoints. While network officials might claim that progress is being made, at the rate of change of the past 15 years, even modest approximation of parity will not occur in our children's lifetimes.

Now that I have provided an overview of the narrow and shallow network news coverage of Latinos, in the next five chapters we will examine in detail the images of Latinos as portrayed by the 2004 network news. I will introduce new analytic tools that reveal the multimodal semiotic messages of 45 individual stories. Some of the news stories are journalistic jewels; many are mediocre; a few are dreadful. We will see how network representation can perpetuate uninformed views leading to Latino stereotypes. These stories regularly display impeccable production values and, at times, astonishing technical virtuosity. However, we will see that too often they don't get the facts right. Others seem to flaunt a willful ignorance of the nation's rapidly changing Latino communities. If network editors do not rapidly respond to the increasingly important role that Latino communities play in the nation, their long-vaunted network evening news programming will be relegated to the status of a cultural relic.

SEMIOTIC ANALYSES OF NETWORK NEWS STORIES ABOUT LATINOS

The pretense of looking at the world directly . . . seeing others as they really are when only God is looking . . . is itself a rhetorical strategy.
—CLIFFORD GEERTZ[1]

Network television news presents a broadcast journalistic version of the day's events, not the events themselves. However, network anchors rarely qualify their news stories with a phrase such as "as far as we can tell." On the contrary, news stories are executed via methods that urge viewers to accept the stories as slices of reality. News teams work to "create an impression that real people then take to be real, and to which they respond [accordingly] in their lives."[2] Viewers accept the verisimilitude of news stories because they are familiar with the source or comfortable with the news anchor's semiotic style. Network anchors expressly avow the veracity of their programs with their personal sign-offs, such as Walter Cronkite's "That's the way it is" or Dan Rather's "That's part of our world tonight." Of course many reports, such as of a car accident, lend themselves to fact-filled, less interpretive reporting. On the other hand, events that involve nation, citizenship, and identity are politicized, and so news stories about Latinos and other minorities are inescapably political. These observations lead us to ask: *What is the major-network journalistic portrait of Latinos?*

When presented with this question, people often express surprise that news is not a mirror of reality. They ask: What makes up these media products? How are they made? To explain the journalistic enterprise, scholars have used a variety of images, each of which highlights one or another aspect of the whole. The factory metaphor characterizes news stories as "depletable consumer" products that are manufactured.[3] Joseph Gripsup offers a medical metaphor: news stories regulate and maintain the health of the social network.[4]

In contrast, Hartley says the news is a textual system in which network news stories conform to culturally established news genres. Each story is composed of meaning units, rhetorical forms, and discursive structures that give it meaning within US public culture. To mix metaphors, the evening news is a multivitamin made up of the textual elements our society uses in its everyday functions. This discursive matrix creates and sustains our understanding of social relations. In the early twenty-first century, our complex society suffers if each of us does not ingest a similar daily discursive vitamin.[5] In this five-chapter section, we describe a portion of the meaning compounds used to formulate the political concepts that make up the news about Latinos.

Sources of News Media Power

Our discursive analysis rests on Michael Schudson's sociological scaffolding of the news. He writes that mass media news is "a dominant force in the public construction of common experience and a popular sense of what is real and important,"[6] describing the source of news media power with a pair of complementary social theory frameworks. Schudson posits that the first is the "public sphere," which Jürgen Habermas posited is a "public conversation" based on rationality that has been in place since the eighteenth century. For Habermas, newspapers were the "preeminent institution" for Europeans to construct a more rational, enlightened society that was striving to distance itself from the dogma-driven feudalism of the past.[7] As increasingly more members of society participated in the public sphere, collective feelings of European national consciousness developed. The second aspect of Schudson's framework, which draws from Benedict Anderson's powerful writing, is the "imagined community" of millions of strangers who experience a shared orientation and affiliation.[8] Newspaper reading for Anderson was a key element in developing this community of sentiment and became an "extraordinary mass ceremony."[9] This broadly shared interaction of people through news media created a common emotional identity. As media technologies became more powerful, so did media's capacity to create common identities.

The social theory frameworks that Schudson offers, however, do not address the discursive power of mass media. While he frequently refers to the social ritual of consuming news media products, Schudson does not cite discursive theories of society and has expressed skepticism about the constitutive power of discursive practices.[10] To fill this gap, I turn to Michel Foucault, who, using the term *discourse*, theorized that discursive practice reveals the social relations constituted in everyday social interaction.[11] Foucault's notion of discourse is well exemplified in the daily streams of news reporting that we channel through our remote controls. For a nation of television viewers this reporting is one prime source of constituent narratives about "the world," "the nation," and "the city"—that is to say, the discourses that construct social roles and relations. In the same way that discourses are more than talk, news stories are more than journalistic lists of facts; they are social practices within social orders with which individuals engage. People learn to function in society by engaging these discourses and the image-defined characteristics that are set up in news narratives.

When people enact these discursive practices, they tend to accept the ideology of the standing social order, namely the institutional practices that sustain and legitimize prevailing power relations. As people live their lives, they enact the discourse practices associated with their subject positions, namely the legitimated roles that society allots to individuals that provide them identity and standing.[12] *Subject positions* defined by these discursive practices confine the lives of both the powerful and the weak, in terms of knowledge and beliefs, social relationships, and social identity. Thus when people go about their daily tasks, they take for granted and experience as natural a good deal about the sources of oppression that are articulated in all parts of society.

In this five-chapter section I will discuss 45 news stories as case studies of the networks' portraiture of Latinos and Latino political issues. In these case studies, I will refer to the political stance taken by the newsroom, anchors, and correspondents. Sometimes it seems that the newsroom deliberately builds these stances into their stories, and sometimes the political stance is likely an unconscious part of standard cultural expression. Journalists and the consumers of network news often use the term *ideology* to refer to the political stances articulated in news stories.[13] Since the news is produced, viewed, and evaluated one story at a time, political stances are relevant to this discussion.

However, my larger objective is to explain the construction and reinforcement of the nation's standing social order regarding Latinos. I will compile evidence that television news is a crucial stream of American societal discourse about Latinos, and begin to explore what Hayden White called discursive meaning production[14] in television network news reporting.[15]

Method: Selecting 45 Stories

The next five chapters examine the social semiotic structures, news content, and sociopolitical slants of 45 of the 118 stories with content about Latino individuals, communities, or Latino-related topics that aired to vast network audiences in 2004.[16] My research team[17] and I selected these 45 stories with a mind to include the range of network news item types: news briefs, short news stories, feature-length stories, and multisegment news reports, as well as a representative range of network news story content. We subjected each story to a critical intentional and symptomatic reading of its possible projected social and political meanings. By *intentional*, I mean that we sought the meanings that the news team intended to convey; by *symptomatic*, that we tried to decode the news team's unacknowledged understandings of the topic of the news within its cultural context.[18] To conduct these readings we applied a combination of cultural and media study tools[19] and social semiotics[20] to the rich multimodal displays composed by network news teams and editors. The operative assumption is that all aspects of network news stories are intentionally composed. Even particular camera shots can evoke meaning for viewers, such as when a shot from below amplifies the size and "presence" of a person, or when a shot from above takes away from the person's stature. In this way I hope to make explicit meanings that are subtly portrayed and hence potentially compelling projections of so-called facts. By identifying the meaning-making combinations of multimodal signs, we can explore the connotations implied by or presumptions underlying these signs. Each of the five following chapters provides scene-by-scene reviews of each story, peeling apart the multiple layers of meaning-making signs, to offer a multimodal textual analysis of the claims regularly repeated in news stories.

The selection of our sample was the first step in our method. To select the stories for detailed interpretive analysis, the author and at least one student researcher sat together to watch each of the 118 stories.[21] See the Appendix for a description of each story. For our semiotic analysis we included stories covering the 10 major topics for Latino news stories. We originally planned to analyze three news items per topic to sample the range of story types. However, given the small total, the networks rarely covered some topics, while other topics were more complex. We chose to add more news stories to our sample to be sure that we addressed news story complexity. If we had chosen a more limited sample, a critic might charge that we were "cherry-picking" exemplars of our predetermined thesis.[22] On the contrary, we did not begin with a thesis, only with a critical perspective, and ended up sampling over one-third of the total 118 news stories to provide sufficient breadth of coverage.[23]

To begin the analysis, we watched each story a few times without taking notes. We then broke down each story into its basic unit: the camera shot. A shot is a section of film or its digital equivalent exposed during a single take.[24] The shots fall into groups, or scenes, that make up the phrasing of the story.[25] While the 5-shot story structure is taught in many broadcast journalism schools, the format of these news stories generally had three parts: an opening, the body, and a closing scene. In the opening scene, which is made up of one or more camera shots, the network news anchor introduces the news story. The body of the story typically contains at least one other scene of a news correspondent narrating the story. In the final scene, the anchor closes the story. The exception to this three-part format is the news brief, in which the anchor reports the entire news item.

We approached each story with the premise that the newsroom personnel purposefully selected, edited, and arranged each camera shot, ambient sound, photo, and full or partial screen graphic to tell a story. A screen graphic is a multimedia composition of words, images, and sounds that opens on the screen, employing the complete range of image- and sound-altering effects, colorful backgrounds and textures, masks, filters, and lighting effects as well as vector and other kinds of artwork to contribute to the story. These windows can fill or take up a portion of the television screen.

Newsrooms manipulate their viewers' responses with sophisticated techniques. For one, their cameras can introduce an individual in various ways, from a full-body shot to an extreme close-up. Then the cameras can contextualize the subject with other methods ranging from point-of-view to zooming, each evoking distinct responses.

Network news stories are visually rich. The 118 Latino news stories in our sample had an average of 24 camera shots. Even a "news brief," in which the anchor both introduces and reports the story in less than 30 seconds, can be composed of one or two scenes, a dozen camera shots, and complexly composed graphic inserts. In addition to news briefs, there are regular news reports (which the anchor introduces and a correspondent reports) as well as feature-length news stories that might involve multiple correspondents or dozens of scenes.

Regarding multimodal semiotics, we identified the videographic, news story, and human body conventions that became evident throughout the investigation,[26] and asked specifically if stereotyping was evident. Following the social semiotic method, we also asked about the structure of the signs. For example, we looked to see if the major signs of a particular story were set in opposition (such as good/evil), or whether clusters of similar or related signs converged (such as speaking of subjects with infant metaphors while video-recording them from a camera angle that diminishes their physical presence). We also asked what connotations followed from the sign structure and other semiotic features of each story. Once we attended to the semiotic composition of a story, we could see what had been implied and what had been omitted. Articulating a news story's exclusions often revealed the precepts on which it was based.

We confirmed the observations of many journalism scholars that network news now blends many features of the entertainment genre, creating so-called soft news programming.[27] The once discrete entertainment and news formats are now combined in content and form, in an effort to keep the audience's attention and to retain market share. One attention-grabbing technique we will address in the following chapters is digital media modification and complexifying of images.

Finally, a key communication theory concept that we will discuss involves the anchor's role in the news story. Frequently, the anchor "frames" the story. In communication studies framing has been frequently discussed, yet it remains weakly theorized. In a news story, for example, a sudden death can be framed in multiple ways. It can be a mystery, a fulfilled life, or tragic destiny. The individual can be depersonalized or rendered with a variety of attributes. The viewer is quite likely to accept the framing as appropriate and, if there is no irregularity, will not be skeptical about the story's framing. In communication studies, the news frame has been described with a wide range of terms, such as organizational principle or idea, thematic unit, symbolic device, schema, or discursive cue. Newsrooms draw on several kinds of semiotic devices to frame a news story. When discussing newspapers, Tankard listed 11 framing mechanisms, or focal points, to identify frames.[28] His list can be readily transposed to television news stories: headlines and kickers; subheads; photographs; photo captions; leads; selection of sources and quotes; pull quotes; logos; statistics, charts, and graphs; and concluding statements. Gamson and Modigliani pointed to five framing devices "used to create an *image* of the subject matter,"[29] namely metaphors, as well as exemplars, catchphrases, depictions, and visual images. These are all conceptual image-making devices, and so they are different ways to express metaphors, which by definition create mental images. While the frame may be abstract, news material items that signal frames can be located in visual, audio, or graphic modalities. In my work, I employ Robert Entman's definition of framing:

Essentially [it] involves selection and salience. To frame is to select some aspects of a perceived reality and make them more salient in a communicating text, in such a way as to promote a particular problem definition, causal interpretation, moral evaluation, and/or treatment recommendation for the item described.[30]

In the news stories we studied, news correspondents framed the news story as frequently as anchors did. Particularly effective and informative news stories were often framed with a succession of different images which offered multiple ways to consider the subject matter. In our study we noted each framing in each story, and asked ourselves if the news report composition emphasized some aspect of the story and what was omitted. Moreover, we kept track of other aspects or individuals in the story, apart from its framing and reframing.

Thus in the next five chapters I provide a series of close readings of individual news stories. Each analysis is my interpretation of the multimodal messaging as well as the substantive characteristics of the network news story. These stories fall into subsets which are covered in different chapters. In Chapter 2 I explore a portion of the Beltway topics that were the most frequent network news stories about Latinos. These are topics directly involving the federal government and national and international politics. In Chapter 3 I sample a set of the news briefs and feature stories. Features are stories of ongoing interest, such as health or popular music, which may not involve national policy. In these two chapters we review the 10 major Latino topics covered in 2004 by network news: stories about José Padilla (the Chicago native who became known as the "dirty bomber"), two Latino White House cabinet nominees, Latinos and the 2004 presidential campaign, the impact of Latinos on the national economy, Latino health care, entertainment politics involving Latinos, Latinos in public education, Latino soldiers in the Iraq War, and Latinos in sports. I discuss immigration policy reporting in the final three chapters of this section, since it was the major Latino domestic network news topic of 2004. News stories about Caribbean immigrants make up Chapter 4, immigration policy stories are discussed in Chapter 5, and feature-length news stories about Mexican immigrants are addressed in Chapter 6.

CHAPTER 2

Inside-the-Beltway Stories

Every shortcoming of American governance, in foreign relations and domestic affairs, is related in some fashion to the knowledge deficit of the American public.
—SUSAN JACOBY[1]

We begin our close readings of network news stories about Latinos with the stories that made up the majority of the Latino news, the "inside-the-Beltway" stories.[2] Three topics will be addressed: a Latino man who was accused of being a domestic terrorist, two Latinos who served in the Bush administration, and political campaigning for the Latino vote in the 2004 presidential election.[3] Throughout the book we will distinguish the various semiotic modes of television news signs with certain conventions (see the list of transcription and semiotic conventions at the front of the book).

José Padilla: Citizen Terrorist or Simply Terrorist?

Seven of the 118 Latino-centered stories of 2004 involved José Padilla, a Chicago native who was arrested in the wake of the September 11, 2001, catastrophe. The Bush administration officially designated him an "enemy combatant" under the Patriot Act after saying he was working with al-Qaeda.[4] This controversial act suspended Padilla's legal rights as a citizen, including habeas corpus. At the start of 2004 Padilla had already been held incommunicado for over 20 months without being charged with a crime and without legal counsel. As will be shown below, the news media typically exhaustively cover the life of similarly notorious individuals. However, none of these seven news stories explored Padilla's personal background, even when it was implicated in the government's case, or the broader implications of the "enemy combatant" designation for him and American society. Instead, network news editors focused on legal case specifics. In this chapter, we will discuss two news stories about Padilla. Each covered a different episode of his life as an "enemy combatant."

CNN News Brief, #2

On January 7, 2004, CNN anchor Aaron Brown delivered a 2-scene, 3-shot news brief (#2). While quickly running down the news events of the day, Brown succinctly framed the story as an aberrant legal case.

> *A few other stories making news around the country starting with a US citizen suspected of plotting with al-Qaeda to explode a dirty bomb. The Justice Department said today it will ask the US Supreme Court to throw out a lower court ruling that requires the release of José Padilla from military custody. He was arrested 20 months ago, designated an enemy combatant. He has not been charged. He has not been allowed to see a lawyer or anyone else.*

In this brief, Brown passes over the circumstances of a citizen denied civil rights. Instead he says Padilla was *"suspected of plotting with al-Qaeda to explode a dirty bomb."* Brown's verbal framing of the news story is visually reinforced in Scene 2 with a text caption, "Padilla Case," which does not refer to Padilla as a citizen. The CNN newsroom emphasized the legal precedent, not a citizen's experience in the custody of US military authorities.

Scene 1 shows Padilla's close-up "mug shot" behind Aaron Brown. Over several years of coverage of Padilla, all network news editors modified this single photo with various editing tools. Repeatedly the photo was altered digitally to reinforce a wannabe terrorist image by adding dramatic photo contrasts, exposure, and saturation levels. CNN avoided this temptation; its digital image appeared to project a strong, calm gaze from Padilla. Consequently the viewer's visual attention was drawn to Padilla's gaze and away from Aaron Brown, creating an interesting visual semiotic tension as the CNN anchor and Padilla momentarily vied to engage the television news viewer.[5]

In Scene 2 Aaron Brown's voice redirects audience attention by speaking of *"military custody"* and by reiterating that Padilla has been *"designated an enemy combatant"* who has not been *"allowed to see a lawyer or anyone else."*[6] By describing rather than identifying the habeas corpus issue, the CNN anchor could more easily purport to be maintaining journalistic objectivity without having to expand on Padilla's legal situation.[7] Moreover, Padilla's personal plight is not developed at all.

The CNN news brief about this Latino man accused of being a terrorist was immediately followed by another news brief about US soldiers returning from Iraq to their loved ones. CNN's sequencing of news items reinforced its presumption of Padilla's guilt, juxtaposing this Latino man, who purportedly joined Islamic militants to destroy America, with families in uniform who were defending America from those same Islamic enemies.

During the years that Padilla was in the news, his exceptional status did not lead to background news reports, as other notorious news makers generally arouse. It may have been that the networks consented to an undisclosed Bush administration directive to not cover the Padilla story as they would other newsworthy topics. Other factors might also have been involved. In the end, no investigative journalism on Padilla, as an individual, aired on the television news in 2004.

Likewise, little on Padilla's background appeared on the nation's newsstands. A search of Chicago newspapers (*Tribune, Daily Herald,* and *Sun Times*) from his 8 May 2002 arrest to early 2004 revealed minimal coverage, despite the importance of his case and the severity of the accusations against him. The *Chicago Tribune* archives had no articles on him. The *Daily Herald* provided brief articles about Padilla's trial, but they do not elaborate on his background except to say he is a citizen. The *Sun Times* articles include one entitled "Padilla's Past" (12 June 2002) that offered a chronology. An 11 June 2002 *Sun Times* article entitled "A couple years back I knew he entered a cult" offered a brief line of testimony of those who knew him, describing him as "a nice kid as comfortable with a softball as with a school textbook," and revealing his nickname, *Pucho,* 'Pudgy.' These newspaper articles also highlighted his criminal record and gang involvement, referring to him as "the homegrown terrorist" before the 2004 federal indictment was handed down. Consequently, network news viewers and newspapers readers never obtained any sense of Padilla's humanity; to the American public, he was a terrorist.

CBS News Report, #60

Padilla was indicted in June. The Bush administration had been forced to set out its indictment in order to thwart a succession of legal appeals that had been successfully moving toward restoring Padilla's legal rights as a citizen. CBS's Dan Rather anchored a 6-scene, 16-shot news story about

Padilla, #60. The news story begins with a standard medium close-up camera shot of the news anchor at his desk.[8] Anchor room sets are typically decorated in cool or neutral colors, which soothe viewers while conveying a professional air. In contrast to this calm setting, an over-the-shoulder graphic insert appears behind Dan Rather featuring a US flag background, over which the news story title "Terror Plots" is written in bright red letters. Dan Rather succinctly opens the story, saying: *"The US Justice Department tried today to explain and justify holding a US citizen without charge as a, quote, 'enemy combatant,'"* for a *"series of terrorist attacks the man allegedly was plotting against the United States."* He does not uncritically accept the controversial descriptor *"enemy combatant."* Instead, he sets it off with the word *quote* and pauses briefly before and after stating it. The anchor also emphasizes two words, *tried* and *allegedly*. When Dan Rather stresses these qualifiers, he underscores that Padilla has only been indicted. In contrast to Rather's neutral presentation, with its implied questioning of the enemy combatant status, the visual graphic behind the anchor associates Padilla with terror, and the words and visuals in the next six scenes declare Padilla guilty as charged.

CBS correspondent James Stewart begins by narrating the following voice-over:

> *Pounded by the US military in Afghanistan and running for their own lives, al-Qaeda members reportedly approved a desperate counterattack shortly after 9/11, when two men, including former Chicago gang-member-turned-terrorist José Padilla, approached them with a daring plan.*

In contrast to Dan Rather's careful qualification, Stewart's voice-over carries on for two active verb clauses before inserting a single understated qualifier: *"reportedly."* The next four scenes build a visual narrative that overwhelms Stewart's minimal verbal proviso about Padilla's guilt. Stewart's report of the Justice Department's indictment is visually reinforced with video of Taliban positions in Afghanistan being bombed; of New Yorkers fleeing the collapsing Twin Towers during the 9/11 attack; and of two images of Padilla wearing a *keffiyeh*, or Arab headdress. In these two never-before-broadcast photos he does not wear it as a neck scarf, as European youth do to signal their raffish fashion sense, but as a headdress, as an Arab might.[9] In post-9/11 America, this clothing signaled disloyalty to many of the nation's news viewers. However, CBS did not let its viewers know when the photos were taken.

The next scene, Scene 3, presents a stark contrast between two political positions. On the one hand, viewers see a prosecuting attorney, the official government spokesperson. He stands bolt-upright at a podium with key symbols of US justice: the nation's flag and the Justice Department emblem. His clean-shaven appearance and dark suit complement his spit-and-polish authoritative image. The next scenes bespeak considerable time and resources on the part of the CBS newsroom to create a visually powerful narrative to complement the government's case.

Scene 4 presents viewers with a full-screen graphic captioned "Padilla Plot." This caption remains throughout the next six consecutive camera shots, which are shaded in red, connoting danger.[10] A vivid red background reveals a rotating globe of the world, with the infamous mug shot of Padilla fading into the center. Meanwhile the words "TERROR THREAT," in all capital red letters, appear behind Padilla's image. This time, the mug shot has been digitally enhanced with a mirroring reflection that both highlights his facial features and through visual reduplication suggests deceit. Now that Padilla has been characterized as a menacing terrorist and disloyal citizen, his portrait slides to the left side of the screen, where it remains while a slide presentation of key elements of the Justice Department's indictment open up on the right side of the television screen.

Stewart's voice-over then states: "*The Justice Department released details of the Padilla plot today following criticism they have held him without charges for over two years.*" Stewart does not say who has been expressing this criticism, assigning no agency to the criticism and thus diffusing it. The voice-over continues, presenting the prosecutor's allegations as facts:

- "*the Justice Department released details of the Padilla plot*"
- "*al-Qaeda decided Padilla's plan to set off a nuclear bomb*"
- "*ordered him to blow up apartment buildings and hotels instead using natural gas lines*"
- "*Padilla's first partner in the nuclear bomb plan . . .*"

The claims are reinforced with multiple visuals, rendered with red background and lettering. The effect is to intensify and lend greater credibility to the prosecutor's claims.

Scene 4 continues with a sequence of shots that dynamically display Padilla's alleged actions to viewers: the text "US Citizen" flashes on the screen against the background image of an airliner taking off; the lights of an airport landing site serve as backdrop to "*arrested in May 2002 in Chicago O'Hare Airport*"; a third shot of the airplane crossing the screen in background appears with the text "*$10,000 in cash*" and "*e-mail addresses and* *phone numbers of al-Qaeda handlers."* The fourth background is a video clip of marching Islamic soldiers. The militants can be heard chanting and can be seen firing AK-47s into the air in this highly textured news report. The text "Nuclear Bomb" then appears, followed by a voice-over stating that al-Qaeda leaders judged Padilla's nuclear bomb plot to be *"not feasible."* Although these were allegations, not established facts, the network's multimodal enactment forcefully corroborates the legal indictment with its visual narrative.

Graphics flashing on the screen reinforce Stewart's voice-over, which continues to lay out the indictment. With an unemotional, matter-of-fact tone, Stewart states that Padilla plotted mass death in downtown Chicago as the camera pans apartment buildings; the graphics are overlaid with text: *"Blow up apartment buildings and hotels"* with *"natural gas lines."* His narrative continues, with a corresponding sixth graphic, a computer-generated drawing of a pointed bomb with tail fins. It is marked with a nuclear radiation logo, as text describes al-Qaeda's purported directive: *"Explore constructing a dirty bomb."*

In the seventh graphic, Padilla's alleged accomplice, *"Shukrijumah,"* is referred to. Adnan Shukrijumah's mug shot first appears to the right of Padilla's photo, then is moved to cover Padilla's photo. This visually merges the images of the Latino and Arab men, semiotically blending their identities and symbolically uniting their actions and culpability. All the while the red background globe rotates, and each time it displays the Middle East the text flashes *"Still at large"* and *"Presumed planning strike against US."* Taken together, the CBS images support without qualification the claims of the prosecuting attorney.

Scene 5 returns to the Justice Department pressroom, where the official continues to set out the indictment. In the final scene, CBS correspondent James Stewart is seen at last in a mid-shot in which he summarizes his single news framing: that Padilla is a *"gang member turned terrorist."* To this point, CBS has dramatically staged the government allegations with no mention of Padilla's defense, so it does not merely report on the accusations, it presents them as truth.

Only at the end of the report does Stewart mention a significant complication: *"Officials haven't figured out what to do with Padilla yet."* Here the CBS correspondent's tightly scripted reporting suddenly becomes vague. He does not specify which officials are baffled by which aspects of Padilla's situation. Stewart therefore muddles a clear-cut controversy: whether or not the government can deny Padilla his legal rights as a citizen. Nor does Stewart note that the only apparent reason the Justice Department officials have formally indicted Padilla at this moment is to derail an impending strong legal challenge to his indefinite detention without charge. CBS viewers therefore likely remembered the dramatically described allegations against Padilla, not the unmentioned Patriot Act controversy.[11] The suspension of civil rights was apparently not a newsworthy story angle for this citizen, whom the CBS newsroom depicted as a Latino *"former gang member."* Nor did the network accord Padilla our nation's judicial presumption of innocence until proven guilty. CBS correspondent James Stewart's story depicted Padilla as a criminal with all the semiotic tools of the network news on the day of the indictment, before he stood before a judge to be acquitted or condemned.[12] CBS network news expressly failed to evaluate the legitimacy of the government's claims against Padilla or to investigate the person behind the mug shot.[13]

Stewart's extensive report did not present all the issues involved in the Padilla case. CBS did not present Padilla's point of view or offer a counterpoint to the government's indictment. CBS and the other networks had already sustained two years of indifference to Padilla's personal life, even though he was the first citizen since Timothy McVeigh whom the news media vigorously identified as a homegrown terrorist. More broadly, no human interest stories in 2004 were televised about Padilla; the networks evinced no curiosity about the young Latino man from Chicago. In the news stories broadcast nationally about Padilla in 2004, the networks painted him with the same brush as Osama bin Laden and Ayman al-Zawahiri.

Reporting on Padilla differed from that for other homegrown militants. In 2002 the nation learned about John Walker Lindh, a young American linked to a radical Islamist organization. Lindh actually admitted carrying a gun alongside the Taliban after being captured at an Afghanistan camp in which a CIA agent was killed. News organizations fell over themselves covering all aspects of Lindh's life and character. Lindh's legal treatment also contrasts with Padilla: he was allowed all due legal process. Lindh was criminally charged in a civilian court, reached a plea agreement with prosecutors in July 2002, and is now serving his sentence.[14]

On the day of Padilla's indictment, CBS news broadcast a technically well-crafted news story presenting Padilla as guilty of all charges. Its visual narrative sequencing, color, graphics, and text worked hand-in-hand to dramatize the correspondent's voice-over report of Justice Department accusations. The network newsroom chose not to articulate Padilla's defense in any way, thus forfeiting journalistic balance. The visually arresting result illustrates the power of coordinated multimodal meaning making.

The CBS story projected the prosecutor's allegations as facts, framing Padilla as an international terrorist, not as a citizen charged with a crime.

Latinos in the White House

In this section we address the network news representation of the elevation of US Latinos to the highest levels of government. In November 2004, President Bush nominated two Latinos to fill White House cabinet positions, Alberto Gonzales as attorney general and Carlos Gutierrez as commerce secretary.

The Vanderbilt Television News Archive recorded five stories on November 10 reporting on the appointment of Alberto Gonzales. ABC, NBC, and CBS each aired a story, and CNN broadcast two stories. The importance of this cabinet position and the controversies that immediately surrounded Bush's choice are indicated by comparatively extensive coverage, totaling 122 camera shots, or almost 25 shots per story. In contrast, ABC, CBS, CNN, and NBC covered the November 29 Gutierrez nomination with coverage averaging three shots per story.

ABC: Alberto Gonzales Nominated Attorney General, #100

In the 6-scene, 26-shot ABC story on Gonzales, Peter Jennings in a standard anchor shot announces Bush's nominee for attorney general: "*President Bush made some history today. He nominated a Hispanic Texan to be attorney general.*" Behind Jennings, Alberto Gonzales is portrayed in a prominent photo insert between two unidentified robed judges with the caption: "The President's Choice." Jennings continues: "*His confirmation is almost certain, though there will be some questions.*" Thus in this balanced opening, Jennings does not frame Gonzales' confirmation as a surprise, and he foreshadows the concerns that would be voiced.

Scene 2 frames the Gonzales nomination as an affirmative action appointment, alternating shots of the president and Gonzales. As Bush leads Gonzales into the White House Roosevelt Room, the voice-over states: "*To fill one of the toughest jobs in the administration*" the president chose "*anything but a country club Republican.*" The ABC newsroom thus contrasted the president's privileged background and Gonzales' humble origins. In keeping with Bush's remarks about Gonzales, the story structure speaks to Bush's charitable character in nominating a modest, respectful minority candidate over others. By referring not to Gonzales' credentials, only his personal relationship to the president, the newsroom implies that other candidates have superior qualifications.

The visuals reinforce this framing. ABC presents Bush's own description of Gonzales—rather than reporting the story independently.[15] When Bush states that Gonzales was raised in a two-bedroom house with seven brothers and sisters, ABC provides an image of a modest house. Another presidential close-up follows in which Bush switches languages to refer to Gonzales' parents, "*Pablo y Maria*," who "*instilled reverence, integrity, and personal responsibility*" in their son (in spite of their precarious lives as migrant workers, ABC adds). When Gonzales is seen making some remarks, ABC reinforces its framing by choosing images (illustrating Gonzales' references) that present him echoing his president's characterization. In a 2-shot, with Gonzales at the podium and Bush standing beside him, Gonzales states: "*Within the Hispanic community there is a shared hope for an opportunity to succeed: 'Just give me a chance to prove myself.' That is the common prayer for those in my community.*" As will be noted throughout the book, a 2-shot is a camera shot of two individuals. Two-shots semiotically tie individuals into a closer relationship, in this case referencing the friendship of the president and Gonzales.

Strikingly, ABC provides a contrast in Scene 3, with images of a shackled prisoner. The voice-over indicates that civil rights advocates have questioned Gonzales' legal opinions. For example, they point to the treatment of prisoners taken in Iraq, which ABC reinforces with an image of a military prison, followed by a graphic: an enlarged overlaid excerpt from Gonzales' memo: "*the Geneva conventions may not be appropriate in dealing with terrorists.*" A series of photographs of Abu Ghraib follow, referencing the April 2004 discovery of maltreatment of Iraqi prisoners in US custody who were found to have been subjected to sexual and other humiliating treatment by their US guards, in contravention to both US and international military policy. This is followed by a shot of Bush and Gonzales shaking hands, as a voice-over states that the Democrats will confirm Bush's nomination. At this point, before the 2004 midterm elections, Bush's poll numbers were high enough that he could dismiss any protests. Republicans had a majority in both the House and the Senate, so the Democrats chose not to mount a vocal but vain opposition to the appointment. The scene ends with a ranking Democrat member of the Judiciary Committee confirming the voice-over. The clear implication is that Gonzales' liabilities will not get in the way of Bush's choice, since the Democratic opposition is so weak. However, ABC and the other networks do not explore Gonzales' hinted-at liabilities.

To this point, three-quarters through the story, ABC has offered no indication of Gonzales' qualifications other than a brief mention that he is the president's legal counsel. His formal credentials, such as a Harvard law degree and his term as a Texas state Supreme Court justice, have not been mentioned. This frames Gonzales as one of Bush's inner circle.

Next, two scenes reveal that Gonzales' legal qualifications warrant serious consideration for the US Supreme Court, but his less-than-staunch conservative political viewpoints put him at odds with Bush's constituent base. A representative of Focus on Family, a socially conservative organization, comments on Gonzales as viewers see a computer graphic of a medical clinic overlaid with a title: *"Gonzales' record: Abortion,"* and the text, *"Upheld right of minor to have abortion without parents' consent."* Next, a pair of classroom shots with students of color appear, with two successive captions reiterated in a voice-over: *"Gonzales' Record: Affirmative Action"* and *"Conservatives disliked his views on programs for minorities."* Finally, ABC correspondent John Cochran restates the criticism far more bluntly: *"Some conservatives are relieved that Gonzales is going to the Justice Department. One conservative said he'd cause a lot less trouble there than he would at the Supreme Court."*

In the final shot, the correspondent lists the problems requiring Gonzales' immediate attention, all pertaining to Bush's response to the events of 9/11. B-roll imagery[16] complements the voice-over: incomplete computer systems overhauls, the apparent weakness of domestic security systems, treatment of "enemy combatant" prisoners in the Guantánamo Bay detention camp, and the implementation of the Patriot Act. Jennings sums it up: *"How will Mr. Gonzales balance national security with personal liberties?"*

Overall, this ABC news story employed standard television videographic techniques. The content, however, deserves comment. The ABC narrative framed the story as an affirmative action hire in which the president picked a loyal Hispanic subordinate to be the nation's attorney general. This framing underplayed both the nominee's credentials and the keystone role of this judiciary position in the federal government. ABC discussed the important issues that the Iraq War and Patriot Act had placed on the attorney general's table. The network indirectly expressed the civil liberty concerns with Gonzales' selection. Conservatives, on the other hand, were allowed to voice their views, which were then legitimated by the ABC correspondent's reiteration. Regarding the second issue, the network newsroom chose not to inform its viewers about the crucial place of the US attorney general in the federal government—that while serving at the pleasure of the president, the attorney general must also be able to face down his or her boss by setting down firm constitutional limits on presidential actions. ABC news failed to point out that Bush's naming of an in-debted friend to this position compromised the Justice Department's independence and strengthened an already powerful wartime executive.

CNN: Carlos Gutierrez Nominated Commerce Secretary, #112

As in the Gonzales news story, the framing rather than the videographics deserves comment. CNN's 1-shot news brief of November 29 explicitly articulates a standard form of the American Dream narrative. It offers a profile middle close-up of the president at the podium with the nominee, Carlos Miguel Gutierrez, at his side, zooming into a close-up 2-shot of Bush and Gutierrez. With CNN's trademark dramatic music in the background, anchor Aaron Brown provides the voice-over:

> President Bush today nominated Carlos Gutierrez to be the new secretary of commerce. He's a great story, Mr. Gutierrez—a Cuban-born American, currently the CEO at Kellogg. He started driving a truck for the company back in 1975, selling cereal from a van in Mexico City. At a news conference, the president said Mr. Gutierrez is a perfect example of the American Dream.

In this story CNN sets up a standard announcement of a high political appointment, but CNN's newsroom, like ABC in the Gonzales appointment, chose to accept the president's account of his selection at face value. The ABC, CBS, and NBC stories on Gutierrez' nomination did not stray from the presidential narrative, either.[17]

Gutierrez' achievements are remarkable; he was Kellogg's youngest and also its first Latino CEO. However, CNN failed to mention the backstory of Gutierrez' rise to power, so CNN could recite the familiar fable of the American Dream.

Gutierrez is the son of a Cuban plantation owner who left in the wake of the Cuban Revolution: "In a country run into poverty by the corrupt regime of dictator Fulgencio Batista, the Gutierrezes enjoyed a relatively idyllic life." The family suffered some adversity on their move to the US: "The transition was a blow to the family, long used to both great wealth and influence in their homeland. For a while they lived in a hotel in Miami. It was there that six-year-old Gutierrez learned English from a bellhop."[18] Gutierrez later attended the elite Instituto Tecnológico de Monterrey, Mexico's top private business school. As the CNN story noted, Gutierrez did a brief stint as a delivery truck driver. But he was never a blue-collar working stiff pulling down minimum wage. He indeed rose to CEO by the time he was

50, but CNN failed to mention that he did not start at the bottom, but as a corporate management trainee. Gutierrez' life is a riches-to-riches story, not the Horatio Alger story that CNN presented.

In sum, the network news represented Latinos in the White House in 2004 in terms of well-worn affirmative action and American Dream frames. In the case of the secretary of commerce, a more accurate characterization of his life would not have diminished Gutierrez' successes—but it would have rendered impossible CNN's use of the American Dream fable. In the case of Gonzales, ABC could have taken a more critical view of Gonzales' nomination, since the post requires the personal fortitude to tell your boss to cease and desist.[19] As the proverbial fourth branch of government, the press could have pointed out to the US public that the problems within the Justice Department cited in the news story were consequences of Bush's policy making after 9/11. The networks are responsible for articulating the possible consequences of a given appointment to the public.

Presidential Campaign for Latino Voters

The 2004 US presidential campaign, which resulted in the reelection of George W. Bush, received substantial network news coverage. As election day approached, the networks aired multiple stories daily on this topic. Consequently, there was some spillover of Latino news stories as news editors sought new tie-ins to the daily campaign reports. Twenty-six of the 118 Latino news stories in 2004 addressed Latino voters and the presidential campaign. We reviewed all of these stories and will provide analyses of four stories, in chronological order, to follow the twists of the campaign history. In these stories, with one exception, videographics took a backseat to story writing. For the most part, the Latino campaign stories were not visually arresting, apart from the news story series graphics, which were used for all campaign stories. Nor were the compositions of the stories very complex. However, their success at covering the politics of increasing Latino voting power runs the gamut from excellent to ugly.

One leitmotif of network coverage on Latino individuals and communities was the repeated introduction of Latinos as political newcomers. Early in the election year, ABC's Peter Jennings introduced Latinos as potentially influential voters: "Where the candidates decide to campaign in the last 24 hours [before Super Tuesday] is a matter of important strategy. All but one of the . . . candidates has made the decision to speak before a Latino group in Phoenix" (#10). Six months later Kerry and Bush were the two sole contenders, and Tom Brokaw of NBC, in #82, again emphasized the novelty of Latino voters when he opened by saying, "*We're going to be taking a look at different groups of voters who could make a big difference in this close election. Tonight, Hispanic voters, the fastest-growing group in the country.*"

A second recurring theme was network ambivalence about the relevance of Latinos themselves to electoral news stories. For example, ABC found it unnecessary to mention the name of the Latino national organization[20] from which all the Democratic candidates sought an endorsement. Key Latino political actors were treated with similar indifference, identified vaguely as "Latino political advocate," in one instance, instead of by the person's affiliation. In another story NBC editors chose not to identify Antonio González, of the Southwest Voter Registration Education Project, who, despite his often-lauded role as director of the country's largest Latino voter registration group,[21] was not provided with a caption during his 5-shot commentary. Thus, these newsrooms effectively diminished the importance of Latino national organizations, political leaders, and analysts.[22] We now turn to the analyses of four news stories.

ABC: Speaking Spanish Garners Latino Votes, #10

One ABC 6-scene, 20-shot feature-length story exhibited high production values that camouflaged general ignorance about Latino culture. The story begins with a mortifying shot of candidate Wesley Clark at a campaign stop trying to demonstrate that he's got the rhythm of Mariachi music. He apparently does not know that this particular melody is not dance music; he is conspicuously the only one bouncing up and down, looking awkward in a crowd of Latinos.[23] The musician closest to him can be seen trying to avert her eyes. Two video clips follow. One is John Kerry speaking in Spanish on a television commercial. The other shows Howard Dean stating the one Spanish political phrase that monolingual English-speaking candidates can utter without bungling. Ill at ease, glancing from side to side and nervously rubbing his nose, he says: "*Sí se puede.*" Still, his Mexican American audience responds with a cheer.

Framing these uncontextualized visuals, ABC correspondent Susan Snow refers to language use: "*It has almost become a campaign requirement: appealing to Latinos in español.*" These clips of the candidates mangling a Spanish political slogan make for comic sound bites, at least among the bilingual portion of the national audience. However, ABC editors made no effort to debunk the assumption that voicing a brief Spanish phrase is all you need to win over Latino voters.

After her dubious claim about the vote-getting value of speaking Spanish, in Scene 3 Snow follows with an insightful statement by NCLR's Clarissa Martínez about the importance of the Latino vote in "*battleground states.*" Martínez, state policy and advocacy director for the National Council of La Raza, is vaguely identified as a "Latino political advocate," and Snow does not explore her comment. Instead, she addresses the challenge both political parties would face with the Latino vote. The scene ends with a quip by South Tucson planning director Richard Salaz: "*We don't know how to get to us.*" Again, Snow does not follow up on Salaz' incisive observation about (Latino) Democrats to ask what might bring out more Latino voters.

Rather, she returns to the language theme to wrap up her story. Once again viewers see Wesley Clark, this time declaring: "*I'm one tough hombre. And I can stand against George W. Bush.*"[24] This is followed by a shot of Bush, who stammers: "*Bienvenidos. Mi casa es su casa,*" and receives a subdued response from the Latino crowd. As the camera pulls in to a closer shot of Bush, Snow cites an unnamed analyst's prediction that Latinos are as likely to vote Democrat as Republican.[25] This is followed by the final shot: John Kerry at an African American voter forum quipping, "*I thought for a White guy, I showed rhythm.*" To this Snow counters: "*Maybe Kerry better learn to dance Mariachi.*"

ABC's Snow could have explored the ways in which Latinos, like other groups in the country, are divided on political issues. She completely failed to mention the issues that set the candidates apart, and which are as important to Latinos as to other voters, such as the war, education, and health care. Instead she chose to reinforce a stereotype about Latino voter immaturity: just speak Spanish to them and they'll vote for you.

While John Kerry's comments are tongue-in-cheek, Snow's tone does not acknowledge the irony.[26] Indeed, her implied claim that the candidate who speaks more Spanish gets more of the Latino vote is expressed in both the first and last scenes of her news story. When mixed with the leitmotifs of network news coverage of Latinos, Snow's comments provoke a symptomatic reading that Spanish-speaking Latinos are not real Americans, since they speak Spanish.[27] ABC's national news correspondent displays very limited substantive knowledge about the diversity of Latino politics. Like the hapless General Clark, she believes that all Mariachi music is dance music.

NBC: Rejecting a Latino Voter Myth, #82

NBC's 4-scene, 29-shot story echoes the ABC story in its initial focus on language, with shots of Bush and Kerry speaking Spanish, but the story then focuses on how the contending parties are courting Latino voters in this close campaign. Reporting from a Bush campaign rally in Albuquerque, New Mexico, correspondent David Gregory states: "*Ground Zero in this year's fight for Hispanic voters is the Southwest.*" He follows with clips that illustrate the "air war" of rival high-quality Spanish-language television ads aimed at Latino voters. He undermines the Latino-bloc stereotype as he states, "*Coming from diverse backgrounds, Hispanics don't always vote as a bloc. Still, they make up the fastest-growing voting group in the country.*"

Gregory next offers a standard compare-and-contrast report. He first points to Republican efforts to "*target first-generation Hispanic voters who are in sync with the president on issues like abortion and gay marriage.*" Gregory then describes Democrats, who "*feel they have an edge on the economy and on an issue critical to Hispanics.*" The issue is education, and Gregory follows up with commentary from Roberto Suro, who authoritatively declares: "*In one survey after another, Latinos absolutely say that education is their top issue.*"[28]

Gregory is then shown in an Arizona grocery store, where he asks Latino shoppers which election day issues are on their minds: "*The war in Iraq,*" says Francisco Medina. "*I can put myself in the shoes of those guys, brothers and husbands and wives, that they lost their loved ones over there. I don't see justification for it.*" Rosa Martínez says she has not made up her mind who to support: "*I'm waiting for the debates and looking forward to seeing what they have to offer.*" Thus, though this NBC news story begins with Spanish-language appeals, Gregory goes on to complicate this monofocus, showing the political agency of actual Latinos as individuals.

NBC: Latino Voters in Western States, #90

Two weeks before the election, NBC ran another feature-length story (6 scenes, 46 shots); anchor Tom Brokaw reported on the influence Latino voters have in several western swing states. Brokaw opens the report:

> *There are other battlegrounds, smaller states are in play. Here in the American West, the Latino or Hispanic vote is changing the landscape, particularly in Nevada, New Mexico, Arizona, and Colorado—what used to be solid Ronald Reagan country. Now Nevada and New Mexico are rated toss-ups, Colorado and Arizona just leaning Bush.*

Brokaw first reports on Nevada, illustrating its fast growth and its vibrant economy with numerous visually appealing and diverse images of Latinos: "*Since the year 2000, Nevada has added almost 100,000 Latinos to its pop-*

ulation, and registered Democrats now outnumber Republicans. Nevada's five electoral votes could be a jackpot in this presidential election." Brokaw then turns to the race in New Mexico, with its five electoral votes, noting: *"Bush lost New Mexico in 2000 by only 366 votes. This time it's expected to be just about as close."* NBC thus explicitly references the potential influence of Latino voters.

Brokaw then interviews New Mexico governor Bill Richardson, who undercuts the stereotype of an undifferentiated Latino bloc:

> *For the young Hispanics, it's not just immigration and civil rights, it's education, health care, entrepreneurship, home ownership. We believe that by dealing with those issues, instead of just treating Hispanics like an interest group, we [Democrats] can get them.*

In Brokaw's next interview, political scientist Christine Sierra continues the focus on issues: *"Latino families are saying, 'Wait a minute. Let's talk substance. We're important. Show us what you're going to be able to do for us.'"* The interview scene wraps up with a young Latino voter registration volunteer, who says: *"It's a big election coming up, and we're the ones who are going to decide who's going to be the next president of the United States."*

Brokaw ends this news story with a voice-over contradicting the Latino-bloc stereotype, as viewers see young Latino families and children playing in a park. Brokaw states, *"Call them Hispanics or call them Latinos, but in this election year, call them important and even more important in elections to come."* While both NBC and ABC newsrooms display professional video polish in these two reports on Latino voters, correspondent Gregory's inquiry into Latino views offered NBC viewers solid content, whereas ABC's Snow only restated stereotypes.

ABC: Candidates Appear on *Sábado Gigante*, #97

Finally, on the last weekend of the campaign, ABC ran its last story on Latinos and the election. Peter Jennings begins the 5-scene, 18-shot feature-length story:

> *We're going to take a minute to focus on a television event that demonstrates the closeness of the election and the power of a minority group. Tomorrow, both candidates will appear on Spanish-language television. That's how important Latino voters are now. And what a program it is! On Univision: the enormously popular Sábado Gigante.*

This is followed by a full-screen graphic opening of *Sábado Gigante*, showing a dynamic, colorful, swirling shot with multiple frames of El Chacal de la Trompeta, 'Jackal of the Trumpet,' a hooded personage that looks like an executioner, dressed in black, complete with robe trimmed with gold. He plays a trumpet as he zooms in and out of focus and then sinks below the television frame.[29] A woman then appears, singing in front of a vibrant blue-and-purple background. This image is replaced with a quick shot of the master of ceremonies of *Sábado Gigante*, Don Francisco, aptly dressed as a circus ringmaster with a top hat. Then there is a shot of a woman. El Chacal pops up beside her and blows her off-screen with a trumpet blast that spouts glitter. The "Univision TV" logo appears at bottom left. The glitter blurs to reveal Don Francisco, holding his top hat as dancers twirl in the background. Firecrackers burst as a large gold text ("SÁBADO GIGANTE") rises to the top center of the screen. This logo is still visible at center as the camera zooms in and the graphic shrinks. The graphics give way to a panning shot of the studio audience. Then we see Don Francisco on stage holding a microphone as tall women dressed in bikinis and high heels preen beside him.

Jennings' voice-over proclaims: "*Oh, yes! This is what you're missing!*"

On stage, a scantily clad woman dances with a man in a tuxedo. The camera closes in on the dancers; the man is gyrating wildly—another parody. The camera then pans across the studio audience, who claps rhythmically for another dancing woman. Jennings picks it up again: "*But if you want to reach 3 million Latinos on Saturday night, este es el lugar. This is the place to be.*"

In contrast to the other network's relatively staid news reports, ABC presents the carnivalesque *Sábado Gigante*. The presumed point of the story is that four years previously, Don Francisco was rebuffed when he sought Bush and Gore, the 2000 presidential candidates, for his show. Jennings continues, "*Then 6 million Latinos voted. This time, it was easy.*"

As the tumultuous imagery ends, Jennings concludes the report by returning to its initial assertion: "*Latinos, if they vote, will make a significant difference in several battleground states, including Florida, Wisconsin, and certainly, New Mexico.*"

The ABC newsroom exploited the burlesque so enthusiastically that its viewers became unwitting voyeurs. When ABC lifted the skirts of the *Sábado Gigante* carnival tent, it did not intend to raise the audience's opinion of Latinos, much less offer insight into the Latino electorate. The association between the carnival and Latino voting was not incidental: Don Francisco, his bikini-clad entourage, El Chacal, and the gyrating dancer are semiotically linked to Latino voters. Behind this gaudy display of the Latin exotic, Jennings emphasized the conditional of his assertion: "*if they vote*." His point: not only are Latinos unfit to vote; they might not bother to do it. ABC chose to not offer a serious report on this crucial electoral reality[30] and also passed over a pertinent query about the wider electorate that could have used the same visual hook: Why did Bush and Kerry both seek appearances on *Sábado Gigante*, as well as on *Oprah* and *The Tonight Show*?[31] On election eve, this question would have made for a nation-unifying story. Another question that ABC did not explore was why the American voting public now insists on identifying with its leaders. Had it chosen to address that question, the ABC audience might have seen the similarities, not the differences, among the viewers of *Sábado Gigante* and the viewers of *Saturday Night Live*, NBC's long-running late-night live comedy show.

The networks offered good, bad, and ugly news stories about the electoral power of Latinos in 2004. The first ABC story we reviewed reiterated an old myth that the Spanish-speaking candidate garners the most Latino votes. This story also revealed the correspondent's broad ignorance of Latino politics. The story began and ended with the myth, while significant and informative issues about Latinos were left undeveloped. The ABC story's false allusions were contested by the first NBC report, which was effective in part because it did not depend on a single story frame to create a narrative. The NBC story began by addressing an issue apparently salient to monolingual English-speaking Americans: the use of Spanish among candidates. It then presented a respected Latino pollster, who expressly rejected the Latino voting-bloc myth. Finally, it built its content when the NBC correspondent interviewed actual Latinos, a network first in 2004. The second NBC story also displayed high journalistic quality. It addressed the topic of Latino voters' role in presidential battleground states that ABC originally failed to explore. Most saliently, the correspondent sought out Latino political and academic experts for their opinions. Attentive NBC audiences would have learned that Latino voters had concerns very similar to their own.

In 2004, NBC broadcast the best-informed Beltway news stories about Latinos to its national audience. ABC's final news story, on *Sábado Gigante*, could have been a memorable hook to inform its viewership about the cross-language phenomenon of soft-news programming. However, ABC made no visual comparison to *Saturday Night Live*, another popular program that, at its best, subverts everyday American life with irreverent humor. The ABC newsroom demonstrated a low opinion of its audience's political sophistication. ABC emphasized the exotic and kept its audience at arm's length from the voting communities of Latinos across the country, who are more likely to gather their opinions from Oprah than from Don Francisco.[32]

Conclusion

Among the most memorable 2004 Beltway news stories addressing Latino issues were CBS's visually rich and compelling indictment of José Padilla, CNN's rags-to-riches story of Commerce Secretary Gutierrez, and ABC's story about *Sábado Gigante*, the Spanish-language variety show. The networks' powerful videographic tools can be used to reinforce a narrative, as in the Padilla indictment story. However, a news story can still be very satisfying, that is to say, memorable and distinctive, without recourse to television's graphic arts, as with the news report about the nomination of Alberto Gonzales as US attorney general. Satisfying narratives share several features. The framing of the story is not complicated and most often can be stated as a metaphor: PADILLA AS TERRORIST, GONZALES AS DEVOTEE, GUTIERREZ AS HORATIO ALGER, LATINOS AS EXOTIC. These frames make the news story narratives easy to recognize. If they are news briefs, the stories are as coherent as they are succinct. When of extended length, the stories are well-composed and consistent narratives. They are not written to convince the skeptics in their audience, but to stay on point. Such stories vex the critical thinker, since they do not edify; they are designed to affirm the viewer's preconceptions. The framing metaphors foreground certain features and background other features. For example, in the PADILLA AS TERRORIST metaphor and frame, the "enemy combatant" in an international war is foregrounded, while other elements of the individual's circumstances that may be quite important are backgrounded, such as his US citizenship. These simple metaphor-based frames often evoke allusions that carry significant political and ideological meaning.

While the aforementioned stories were entertaining, they were among the least enlightening Beltway stories, for the very reasons that they are successful as simple narratives. The principal opposition that television news stories must engage is, on the one hand, the goal of broadcasting visually and narrativistically engaging stories, and on the other, the goal of presenting new concepts and content to the network news audience. Stories that strove to edify, such as the NBC stories on what political issues concern Latinos in the presidential election, were not composed with a single restrictive frame, but with multiple frames. Complex stories make greater demands on news writers to sustain a coherent narrative line, and on news audiences because they are more nuanced and thus more difficult to process.

In the next chapter we analyze stories about Latinos in two kinds of news programming: news briefs and news features.

CHAPTER 3

News Briefs and Feature Stories

Economic Impact of Latinos
NBC News Brief on Jobs, #27

Network news stories about Latinos rarely diverge from a small set of top-ics, and the frames used to narrate the facts are seldom original. As was shown in Chapter 1, while network stories about the US economy consti-tuted 9% of all reports, only one news brief ran about Latinos and the US economy, #27. On February 22, NBC offered a 1-shot, 27-second summary of Miriam Jordan's *Wall Street Journal* article.[1] In the standard medium close-up shot of the NBC anchor, viewers see a graphic insert in the upper-right corner of the television screen. The *Wall Street Journal* logo appears in the corner just as the story begins, quickly replaced by the story title "Hispanic Jobs" superimposed on a photograph of a street scene including two men of color. With this backdrop, anchor John Seigenthaler gives his 72-word report:

> *A new trend in the American workforce. Hispanics are taking a large share of the new jobs created in the US economy . . . The number of Hispanics with jobs increased to almost 660,000 in the last year, while only 371,000 non-Hispanics found work. Most of the new jobs were in construction and services.*

Word choice is particularly crucial in news briefs, since the whole story is said in a matter of seconds. NBC did not use the semantically unmarked verb *get*, but framed the story with the word *take*. This implies that Latino workers seized more than their fair share of all new employment. In this case, NBC wording was drawn from the lead sentence of the original *Wall Street Journal* article.[2]

However, after invoking the authority of the *Wall Street Journal*, NBC editors chose to omit key information from the well-written article, portraying a monolith of Latinos competing unfairly against all other Americans, or against an implied White majority. Given that immigration had become the major domestic issue involving Latinos in 2004, NBC was irresponsible on two counts. First, it did not differentiate between citizens and noncitizens. In contrast, the *Wall Street Journal* writer distinguished between the two, noting: "the number of foreign-born Latinos who found work was nearly 10 times that of the number of second-generation U.S. Hispanics."[3] Moreover, NBC editors misled viewers about the affected sectors of the economy. The visual image projected behind Seigenthaler, of two men, including a Latino in suit and tie, referred to white-collar sectors. The actual jobs were difficult, seasonal, often dead-end jobs in the construction sector. To illustrate the nature of these jobs, the *Wall Street Journal* article described Jorge Alberto's work as

> pushing a cart through the muddy lot where he and five other Hispanic men are laying a foundation for a house. Immigrants such as Mr. Alberto, whose five siblings in Guatemala depend on his monthly $200 remittance to survive, tend to take jobs that others would shun.

This is followed by quotes from the Kansas City Home Builders Association vice president: "A lot of folks don't want to work in construction. It's hot in the summer and it's cold in the winter. Hispanics have kept our industry going." The article concludes: "Hispanics with deeper roots in the U.S. . . . faced the same employment hurdles that non-Hispanics do."[4] Television news report writing must be both succinct and exacting, but NBC omitted key qualifications, which let its national audience come away with the idea that Latinos as a monolithic group were seizing more than their share of white-collar jobs. We move now from Latino stories about economics to stories about Latino health and medicine.

Health of Latinos
CBS News Brief on Strokes, #80

While health accounted for 5% of all network evening news stories in 2004, this topic accounted for just 2 of the 118 stories designated as predominantly Latino. On August 9, CBS ran a story entitled "Stroke Risk." In this 1-shot, 44-word news brief, the anchor is seen in the standard medium close-up camera shot with a graphic insert over his shoulder in the upper-right portion of the screen. The graphic shows a transparent human head revealing a detailed image of the brain, as well as a caduceus, the emblem of medicine, to signal a medical news story. CBS anchor Scott Pelley states:

> And another medical story today, researchers have pinpointed a *serious* stroke risk for **Mexican-American** men. *It appears they have a much higher risk than other groups of men and* **double** *the normal risk in their* <u>40s</u> *and 50s. The study did not determine why.*

Pelley relates the story with a lot of visual expression. To stress the severity of his message, he emphasizes the word *serious*, raises his eyebrows and emphasizes the word *double*, and emphasizes the word *40s*. This last expression signals the risk for relatively young men. The text of his report unnecessarily scared millions because it characterized the stroke risk as endangering all, rather than a narrow subset, of Mexican American men. With even fewer words, Pelley might have said: "And another medical story today, researchers have pinpointed why some Mexican American men have double the risk of a serious stroke than Whites. A genetic predisposition to diabetes seems to make them more vulnerable to strokes." This rendition would have conveyed precise information without needless sensationalism. Moreover, with fewer than 100 words, the CBS story could have been far more informative, as was a print story on the same study:

> Lead researcher Lewis Morgenstern hopes that these findings about higher stroke risk will prompt their doctors to help Latino men to learn more. He said: "Stroke is arguably the most preventable and most treatable of all catastrophic conditions, and we need to help people recognize their higher risk and take control of their destiny, especially as the Latino population grows and ages."[5]

By investing a few more seconds, CBS could have made this story illuminating, instead of merely frightening.

CBS Investigative Report: Hospitals Price-Gouging Latinos, #47

The other 2004 Latino health story ran on CBS on April 25 in a feature-length piece called "Sunday Cover." This was a 10-scene, 45-shot exposé on hospital price-gouging practices and prominently featured Latinos throughout as full subjects, namely people who can be discerned as unique individuals, with distinctive personal histories, sets of interests, and the ability and opportunity to speak for themselves. The scalar quality of *subjectivity*, a social psychology notion regarding the representation of the humanity of individuals and groups of people, involves three elements: expressions of human cognition, expressions of human motive, and expressions of human emotional affect. These elements express the quality of human portrayals of individuals who are registered by television viewers when depicted on network news stories.[6] In Scene 1, CBS's John Roberts reports on purported abuse of uninsured patients forced to pay more than their share for health care. In Scene 2, viewers have over nine camera shots of the main subject of the story, Pascual Rivera, auto mechanic and uninsured hospital patient. Each shot is composed to portray him with ample subjectivity. The scene shows Rivera shrugging his shoulders as he says that he does not speak English well and, consequently, cannot defend himself. He is depicted as a hardworking and respectable immigrant. Another shot then sets up his adversary, the hospital, first with an exterior shot of the hospital, then a close-up of its banner: "The Greatest Health Care Workers."

Next, Rivera is shown working in his shop in a scene overlaid by a series of graphics of hospital bills taking up much of the television screen, followed by another bill covering most of the screen. An insert pans forward to show the figure: "$29,754.00," with a voice-over stating, "*a startling bill of nearly $30,000 for the lab work.*" This multimodal feature presentation, intensifying visuals and an oral voice-over, was particularly effective since it mimicked the heightened reaction of someone receiving an unexpectedly big bill.

After several more shots of Rivera working, the scene ends with a medium close-up shot of Rivera saying that the hospital's collection agency insisted on immediate full payment even after he offered to borrow the difference. Scene 3 generalizes Rivera's plight with a view of a busy sidewalk filled with pedestrians, with Roberts' voice-over: "*It's a familiar story about the country's almost 40 million uninsured.*" With a close-up, Scene 4 introduces K. B. Forbes, an advocate for the uninsured. In this scene, Forbes speaks to Reina Morillo in what looks like her living room. A close-up of Forbes' hands shows him filling out forms as the voice-over cites "*exploding numbers of uninsured minorities like Rivera who are often billed four to five times what hospitals bill insured patients for the same procedures.*" The camera pans to a close-up of Morillo's hospital bill, with "$9,788.21" visible, and Morillo relating her story in Spanish to Forbes while he holds a tape recorder. Morillo was charged $70,000 to treat a kidney stone. The scene ends with a close shot of K. B. Forbes, who says: *"Hospitals make gobs of money by sucking up the hard-earned assets of uninsured people who are not poor enough to qualify for charity care or Medicaid."*

Scene 5 provides several shots of doctors in operating rooms, accompanied by reporter Roberts' voice-over: *"The American Hospital Association shares Forbes' concern, but says uninsured patients take a tremendous toll on hospitals' bottom lines—$22 billion worth in the last year alone."* This claim is patently unfair, since some individuals are overcharged off-set other people's bills. Still, this claim might be confirmed, since in Scene 6 viewers see the spokesperson for the AHA, Carmela Coyle, in a standard medium close-up shot with the association's large emblem in the background. However, she side-steps the price-gouging issue, saying: *"The problem we have [is] a growing number"* of uninsured people. The Capitol building is shown as she impugns government regulations. Roberts' words support Coyle's contention that the AHA blames the federal government. However, CBS newsroom editors failed to show Coyle responding to the key question that Roberts must have asked: Why are some uninsured people billed more than people who are insured?

Instead, the aggrieved are carefully presented, and Forbes is allowed to directly refute Coyle: *"The bottom line is [hospitals] have to stop this immoral and egregious behavior. Period."* While Forbes is more effective than Coyle because he speaks directly to Roberts' question, it is not clear that CBS offered Coyle a full opportunity to respond to this claim. Coyle did not directly counter Forbes, which made her statements seem beside the point.

Scene 8 shows Pascual Rivera, the auto mechanic and victim of hospital overcharging, addressing congressional staffers. Rivera, tieless and dressed in a shirt and modest sweater, appears nervous as he reads from index cards. Forbes, in suit and tie, assists Rivera at the podium. Forbes is depicted heroically; he was able to eliminate Rivera's bill. The scene ends with the triumphant Forbes and Rivera walking in a hallway after the congressional hearing. In the final scene, CBS correspondent Roberts concludes that hospitals admit taking unfair advantage of uninsured patients: *"the government has now lined up against the American Hospital Association, arguing that in fact there is no federal regulation prohibiting discounts to the uninsured."*

However, this rhetorical coup de grace is phrased oddly. The term *discount* suggests that the government had a two-tiered system allowing hospitals to charge one rate to uninsured individuals and a discount rate to insured patients, but other interpretations may apply, because CBS's investigative report does not provide a straight answer from either the hospitals or the government on the overcharging issue. CBS merely implies that the hospitals are guilty, relying on a complacent audience who will not scrutinize the evidence of its investigative report.[7]

Politics of Entertainment

ABC: Visas Denied to Cuban Musicians, #13

Moving away from medical news stories, I will comment on four entertainment news stories about Latinos, beginning with two about Cubans. The first story is the final segment of the February 7 ABC evening news program, #13. Anchor Bob Woodruff introduces the 11-scene, 22-shot story by framing it as follows:

> *Finally tonight, the Grammy-nominated musicians who will <u>not</u> be part of tomorrow night's big bash in Los Angeles.*[8] *Far from the red carpet, superstar jams, and glittering parties are some Cuban entertainers who find themselves stuck in Havana because the US government won't let them in.*

This entertainment orientation is sustained throughout the story. The ABC audience is introduced to the celebrated Cuban musician Ibrahim Ferrer, performing with captioned lyrics, "Havana is burning, is burning / Hey there, little fire," with a voice-over describing Ferrer as the star of a movie, *The Buena Vista Social Club*, and as an exceptional musician who has performed in Carnegie Hall.[9] This is followed with an interview of Ferrer in his modest Havana home, decorated with silk sunflowers and a wall photo of a child and two dogs. He begins: "*Me siento inconforme . . . ,*" but ABC correspondent Judy Muller's voice-over obliterates the rest of his statement.

Ferrer's statement about the visa denial decision can be translated as 'I disagree . . .' However, ABC's audience only learns about the musician's emotions, not his opinions, because Muller's translation is 'I am unhappy.' Thus the US audience is prevented from hearing what Ferrer, whose music articulates political imagery, has to say about this international political action.

The audience learns that other Cuban musical groups invited to the Grammy award ceremony have also been denied travel visas. In this scene ABC sets up a familiar opposition: an individual versus arbitrary government policy. Against the background of a full-screen graphic of the US Department of Justice Immigration and Naturalization Service insignia and the text of the key legal passage,[10] Muller states, "*an immigration law allows the president to bar anyone deemed detrimental to the interests of the United States*"; she further notes that the Justice Department has declined further comment.

In the next scene, American guitarist and music producer Ry Cooder explains what this exclusion means to the nation: "*the loss of enjoyment, the loss of an aesthetic, the loss of the wisdom of these people.*" Cooder's focus on entertainment rather than cultural politics fits Muller's framing of the news event.[11] Muller then turns to spokespeople for two political groups, the conservative Lexington Institute and the Cuban American National Foundation, both of whom express mixed feelings about this politically motivated decision.

In the following scene, Ferrer's extended comments are once again slashed: "*One's struggles, one's ideas, one's music is very much related to one's country.*" Muller ends her piece by making the injustice explicit, saying: "*When the Grammy for best tropical Latin album is announced tomorrow, no one will be there to accept. The Cubans were the only ones nominated.*" Anchor Woodruff then closes the program by saying: "*In this political season, the politics of music. And that's our report on World News Tonight this Saturday.*"

While Woodruff characterized the story as one about the politics of music, ABC's framing was designed for entertainment news, not political news. At its most poignant, the story frames a conflict between Cuban individuals and the US government. Rather than exploring US relations with Cuba, ABC relied on the usual anti-Castro organizations' spokespeople, who make predictable comments in keeping with their political stances.

Another road not taken was the politics of Latin American music. Ferrer was well placed and appeared disposed to speak on this issue. However, ABC again punted, instead employing stock footage of the Cuban's musicianship to present an *Entertainment Tonight*–type story, as well as cutting Ferrer off when he began to comment.[12] ABC failed to present the political engagement of Latin American musicians, which would have required expanding the image of musicians beyond the simple personae of mere entertainment figures.

Multiple News Briefs on Defecting Cuban Dancers

On November 15, ABC's Peter Jennings delivered a 2-scene, 4-shot news brief on a request for political asylum by a troop of 44 Cuban musicians on tour in Las Vegas (#106). In the first scene, the camera pans across a crowd of men and women in black suits standing outside of a Las Vegas court-house. Jennings' voice-over articulates the presumed question: *"Who are these people?"* Then he characterizes this event as *"one of the largest mass defections ever by the Cubans. They're being allowed to stay in this country until they are granted citizenship—in a year's time."*

A good deal of television news presentation depends on oral delivery, but when Jennings emphasized the word *the* in the phrase *"the Cubans,"* he likely evoked a range of connotations among his audience that, at mini-mum, distinguished Cubans from other asylum seekers. To his credit, Jen-nings did not implicitly judge the merit of the dancers' request, instead framing the event in terms of its size. Indeed, in voice-over he paused after *"citizenship"* and before *"in a year's time,"* which referred to the US dou-ble standard in which Cubans are automatically designated to be politi-cal refugees, and after one year are granted US citizenship. In contrast, most other Latin American immigrants are deemed unwanted economic migrants.[13]

It is illuminating to contrast the renditions by other networks of the same news item. CNN's Aaron Brown reported on it in #107: *"A group of visiting Cuban entertainers tonight have reason to say, 'Viva Las Vegas!' They defected, 43 of them. Seven others did so in Berlin. Seems to be a pat-tern."* The CNN anchor's deadpan delivery implies that, given any oppor-tunity, many more Cubans would seek to escape Castro's repression.

NBC anchor Brian Williams reported on the same event in #108. He ap-pears with an over-the-shoulder graphic insert of the US and Cuban flags colliding in starbursts behind the words "Cuban Defections." Williams of-fers more information in his news brief, which emphasizes the size of the Cuban defection:

> *This next item sounds like a throw-back to the old Cold War days but it hap-pened today: Forty-three members of a Cuban dance troupe performing at the Stardust Casino in Las Vegas defected, one of the biggest mass defections of entertainers from a communist nation ever.... They said they did it because they'd be forced to quit performing if they returned to Havana. So far, there's been no reaction from Fidel Castro's government.*

If we presume that these news briefs presented all the pertinent infor-mation about the Cuban dancer defection, the asylum seekers made no po-litical statement. Had they done so, the networks would presumably have reported it in greater detail. Each network framed the story in terms of im-migration policy, with discernible political differences. ABC hinted at inequitable designations that favor one group; NBC implied that some of the dancers were motivated by money; and CNN's succinct report registered the formulaic narrative CUBA AS TYRANNY.

CBS: "A Day without a Mexican," #49

We move now to two stories about Mexicans. In the first, CBS anchor Dan Rather opened an 8-scene, 44-shot news story about the movie "*A Day without a Mexican*," saying the "*controversy [is] aimed at Californians who complain about undocumented Mexican immigrants.*" Dan Rather frames this story professionally, avoiding any political positioning on immigration policy.

The next scene comprises a series of 15 short clips from the movie trailer, which CBS video editors have spliced together to give a sample of the topics addressed in the movie. Beginning with a Los Angeles skyline at dawn, viewers see brown-skinned workers plucking chickens, laboring in a field, adeptly slicing tomatoes in a kitchen, or walking along the broad sidewalks of a Los Angeles boulevard. More unexpectedly, a leaf blower rotates on its axis on a suburban walkway, propelled by the blowing air as if the gardener using it has suddenly disappeared. And then, a bit of satire: a lowrider car with hydraulics hopping down a street—with no driver. The film's voice-over despairs: "*We have lost our Mexicans.*" Rather characterizes this as the "*provocative premise*" of this "*satirical mockumentary.*"

Scene 3 is an interview with Mexican-born filmmakers Sergio Arau and Yareli Arizmendi. In voice-over, CBS correspondent Bill Whitaker states that the film is a "*response to recent legislative attempts to cut services to undocumented workers,*" as the camera moves from Arizmendi in slow upward pan to the film poster. The poster portrays a mustached man in a sombrero; "MISSING: JOSE" is its caption. Arizmendi states that the film's premise is that immigrants and their labor are taken for granted: "*How do you make the invisible visible? You take them away.*" More quick clips (from agricultural workers to California lieutenant governor Cruz Bustamante) illustrate the film's premise.

In the next scene CBS points out that the film has provoked controversy that is splitting the Latino community, as well as the rest of the country, citing a Latina who called for the removal of what she found to be an offensive Los Angeles billboard ad for the movie. In Scene 6, CBS correspondent Whitaker presents a businessman with a clear stake in continued immigration. At the prospect of losing his Mexican workers, the Anglo-American restaurant owner says, "*It would close me down. It would crip-*

ple the whole economy in the state of California. I have no doubt it would." A series of quick video clips present a number of Latino men and women who state what their jobs are, from meter reader to city attorney, while in voice-over Whitaker reports that Latinos make up a third of California's population.

The next scene offers a satiric clip from the film depicting desperate border patrol agents (whose jobs have been eliminated) joyfully embracing the first immigrants they encounter. CBS juxtaposes this love-fest with a shot and statement by Congressman Tom Tancredo, who is noted for his anti-immigrant stance: *"the trouble with the movie is that it makes light of a weighty problem: illegal immigration . . . It costs American taxpayers billions of dollars every year to have cheap labor."*[14] Tancredo emphasizes the word *cheap* and then becomes a voice-over, which CBS contrasts with an image of an agricultural worker on a tractor, undermining Tancredo's criticism. Whitaker allows the filmmaker the final word, summing it up as a *"very serious comedy [that] may make you laugh until it hurts."*

While Dan Rather carefully remains neutral, the CBS correspondent allows the filmmakers to frame the news story with the film's energetic style and visual richness and make their political statement. The network newsroom built on the film's visual effects in a manner that undermined Tancredo's counterpoint. The story also worked against stereotype, as it depicted the diversity of Latino people across all sectors of the California economy and society.

CBS: Reality Show *¡Gana la Verde!,* #87

Dan Rather also anchored CBS's 5-scene, 49-shot story about a *"controversial"* reality show with skyrocketing ratings. He framed the story with reference to Arnold Schwarzenegger, who was about to keynote the 2004 Republican National Convention. Rather states that the governor *"will talk about his immigrant experience and will say he wants others to enjoy the opportunities he has had."* However, Rather continues, it is *"doubtful [that] reality television is what [Schwarzenegger] had in mind for what seems to be a shot at the American Dream."*

In Scene 2 the CBS voice-over introduces the Spanish-language game show, characterized by Rather as *"the Spanish-language version of Fear Factor,"* the notorious NBC game show in which contestants competed in outrageous events. The news story continues with a rapid succession of images drawn from the introductory sequence of the cable channel game show in question: *¡Gana la Verde!,* 'Win the Green!' A man jumps from one semi-truck to another as the two barrel down a highway neck and neck; another eats a black scorpion with a knife and fork; a woman grapples with a male Mexican wrestler; and an image of the infamous freeway warning sign of a family crossing appears. *La Verde* refers to the "Green Card," the colloquial term for the coveted US resident alien card, which gives noncitizens permission to permanently reside and work in the United States.

The next scene shows an outraged immigration attorney criticizing the show, blinking with agitation as he says that *¡Gana la Verde!* exploits vulnerable participants for cheap entertainment and cannot deliver a resident alien card to the winning contestant. The camera then turns to the show's creator, Lenard Liberman, who arrogantly responds: *"Contestants are never promised an actual Green Card. Winners get one year of legal services by immigration lawyers"*:

> So what are we telling people? That I can give José a year's worth of Armani clothes and dress him for success for a year, but if I want to give José legal representation for a year and help improve his life and make him a real success, they have a problem with that.

Thus Liberman signals his scorn for the immigrants he exploits, racializing them by referring to them with a single given name.[15]

In Scene 5 the CBS correspondent is shown outside a US government building, stating that Homeland Security has a problem with *¡Gana la Verde!* because it falsely implies that a Green Card can be easily and quickly attained. In voice-over, he informs viewers that getting legal status to work in this country takes years, and that people do foolhardy things on the game show, such as riding rodeo bulls. In addition to physical injury, appearing on this television program poses further risk, a voice-over reports, if contestants are identified by Homeland Security. CBS follows with shots of Elda, a woman contestant riding an inner tube behind a speeding powerboat, followed by a medium close-up shot of her acknowledging the deportation risk. As viewers watch her eat an earthworm taco, in voice-over Elda says: *"You can change your visa status from the student visa to a work visa, and maybe file for permanent residency. But that doesn't guarantee that you are going to be able to do all of that in one year."*

With *¡Gana la Verde!* CBS found what newsroom producers would consider the perfect news story about Latinos, namely, one that both generates voyeuristic interest and works a new angle on the unauthorized immigration issue. CBS introduced its news viewers to yet another bizarre reality show with titillating visuals, leaving the correspondent to point out the show's many ironies: a well-spoken English-speaking immigrant cheer-fully risks life, limb, and deportation for the slenderest possibility of le-galized status; Homeland Security and a pro-immigrant Latino attorney become allies as they both disparage the show; and a vast and complicit Spanish-speaking audience, which gave *¡Gana la Verde!* its strong ratings, allows the show's creator, a cynical opportunist, to exploit immigrants.

In this news story, Elda was so telegenic and articulate that she garnered a significant amount of subjectivity. For an unauthorized immigrant, this is an exceptional, nearly unique moment in a year of network news pro-grams. Even so, the CBS audience probably thought of her as yet another crazy person willing to publicly take senseless chances for an improbable prize and 15 minutes of dubious fame.

Latinos and Public Education

Fifty public education stories were among the 12,140 broadcast by the four network evening news programs in 2004, of which a substantial propor-tion (7 out of 118) made the Latino story subset. However, the topics ad-dressed in these stories are circumscribed. We did not find, and presume that the networks did not consider newsworthy, the crucial issues in La-tino public education, such as the exclusion of Latino cultures and lan-guage in schools, the systemic failure of public education to provide proper programs for Latino student achievement, the institutional indifference to Latino dropouts (who should be called "push-outs"), the dearth of certi-fied teachers in classrooms with high proportions of Latino students, the national specter of high-stakes testing, or the pedagogic consequences of enacting antibilingual education referenda in California in 1998 and Ar-izona in 2003. Not even the dramatic Black/Brown tensions in inner-city schools were sufficiently entertaining or otherwise newsworthy to draw network interest. Instead, viewers saw Latino education stories with con-ventional frames of reference.

CBS: Increasingly Segregated Schools, #51

One example was a May 17 CBS story which commemorated the anniver-sary of the US Supreme Court decision repudiating the hypocritical "sepa-rate but equal" doctrine of the 1896 *Plessy v. Ferguson* case. Dan Rather an-chors, but does not frame, this 7-scene, 34-shot story, as the camera shifts to the "Inside Story" logo, a magnifying glass signaling a deeper investigation of the issues. Rather states that "*half a century after the Brown [v. School Board of Topeka Kansas] decision, the legacy of the high court ruling is reflected in what has changed in America, and what has not.*" His phrasing questions the assumption that equity in education has advanced in the subsequent 50 years. The story then reports on a change in the busing policy at Illinois' second largest school district, U-46.[16] A school board decision there purportedly would have created greater racial segregation in a school district of "nearly 40,000 students, half of whom are minority and one-third of whom come from lower-income families,"[17] in the name of neighborhood schooling.[18] However, as will be shown, CBS correspondent Cynthia Bowers did not dig down to the real story: the failure to address the educational needs of a changing population of schoolchildren.

Scene 2 shows a series of schoolroom shots of Latino children. The teacher's Spanish instructions are drowned out by Bowers' voice-over: "*The neighborhood around Huff Elementary is almost entirely Hispanic.*" While Bowers states that the elementary school classrooms are more "diverse," a shot of a homogeneous class, with only one White child amid Latino students, does not confirm her claim (unless by "diverse" she means a Latino, or non-White, population).

In Scene 3, Huff Elementary's principal, Luís Cabrera, responds to the off-camera query about the percentage of students who don't have English as a first language: "*62% now, and next year close to 87%.*" In Scene 4 the report shifts to busing, providing five camera shots of kids waiting to be picked up after school, kids boarding buses, and buses moving in a parking lot. The correspondent's voice-over clarifies that the district's "*voluntary busing program*" will end next year, without explaining that in this context "*voluntary*" means the district was not under a federal court order to desegregate, and for many years had mixed children of different races in classes. The current school board changed this priority, as stated delicately by Assistant Superintendent Lalo Ponce: "*We redrew the boundaries so that they could attend schools that were closer to their homes and in their neighborhoods.*" However, Bowers interviewed no board member for the camera, and the viewing audience soon learns that local politics are divided on the issue.

In Scene 5, as the correspondent and mayor of the town walk together in a 2-shot, viewers hear in a voice-over: "*The mayor worries that this move will isolate the Latino community.*" The mayor then bluntly states that the board is "*turning back the clock in really a perverse way.*" With a shot of children boarding buses, the correspondent states: "*These days residential segregation has replaced the racial segregation the Brown decision out-*

lawed." Two photos punctuate her statement: one of an all-White classroom of the 1950s, and a 1943 shot of an all-Black classroom.

Bowers stands in a law office in Scene 6, dressed far more formally than in the previous scene. Backed by this visual display of authority, she offers an extended description of the demographic changes in schools nationally, stating with candor that effective resegregation of all public school children leads to greater disparities in Latino student education:[19]

> *Fifty-seven percent of Latino kids go to schools that are predominately Latino—where the ratios of teachers and per-pupil spending are lower. This indicates that White communities receive the majority of money and that White students' superior education comes at the expense of Black and Brown schoolchildren.*

The result, Bower notes, is that "*nationally one-third of Latino children drop out before graduation.*" The economic statement hits the bull's-eye, but the CBS newsroom chooses not to pursue the issue, instead running a vague quote by Harvard University educational rights expert Gary Orfield: "*We have an underdeveloped country that is threatening our future right inside this country.*" CBS thus passes over the key issue of funding.

The final scene returns to Principal Cabrera interacting with elementary schoolchildren in staged shots, panning between the principal and his students. Cabrera's last words reflect his position as the top school site administrator: "*It's just accelerating what's going to happen anyways.*" Bowers does not accept this claim, concluding in voice-over that such actions will "*take schools right back to where they were in 1954,*" as three vintage clips show Black children writing and working in segregated classrooms.

CBS respected the principal's awkward political position: he had to represent and articulate school board policy.[20] However, the CBS news team did not dig into Bower's opening about inequitable funding, falling back on the traditional statements about busing. Moreover, the CBS audience did not hear from the Latino parents, whose children will be most affected by the policy change.

The backstory is crucial. Federal courts never imposed busing on U-46 to remedy racial segregation. The school board of the 1960s mandated busing so that Black and White children could grow up together. In the ensuing years, an influx of immigrant Latino children complicated the district's demographics. Meanwhile, residential resegregation continued apace, making busing a less effective desegregation remedy, and administrators used it to integrate Latino students whose home language was not

English by mixing them with White students. Since proactively addressing the needs of Latino students in other ways would redirect resources away from the children of (non-Latino) voting constituencies, the elected school board avoided more politically daring actions that would have addressed the curricular needs of Latino immigrant students.

The busing/redistricting plan exacerbated Latino parent concerns. At the time of the CBS news story, talk of a lawsuit was in the air.[21] After the plan was implemented in 2005, parents filed a lawsuit claiming it "discriminate[d] against students with limited English proficiencies—particularly Hispanics" by "forc[ing] certain students to remain in classes serving [other] students with limited proficiency in English." The petitioners also alleged that the "district [was] forcing families to either send their children to schools outside their neighborhoods to receive services for English-language learners or give up those services entirely."[22]

By excluding such background information, readily available in local newspapers, the CBS "in-depth" story did not probe past the predictable. It allowed its audience to sustain commonly held falsehoods, such as the fiction that desegregation refers only to White and Black students, and did not explore the motives of advocates for "neighborhood schools."[23]

Across the country, Latino schoolchildren pose significant challenges for school leaders, such as the so-called achievement gap, in which Latinos (and African American students) in urban schools perform much more poorly than middle-class suburban public school students.[24] Then there are curricular issues. For example, the average public school teacher is not trained to help Latino students advance academically when these children don't arrive at school speaking English; and nationally Latinos comprise 60% of English-language learners.[25] Moreover, there are more fundamental social issues, such as financing public education at a time when an aging electorate no longer sends its own children to public schools. Because CBS sidestepped the key point that public education issues involving Latinos (whose numbers now make them the largest subgroup of children in the nation's schools) cannot be viewed through the conventional Black/White lens, its in-depth report failed to break the surface.

NBC/Telemundo: DREAM Act Students, #57

After George W. Bush announced his intent to overhaul the national immigration policy in early 2004, immigration became the nation's most pressing domestic policy concern. In late spring, when young people in caps and gowns traditionally appear, a perennial human interest story (a "pegged" feature story)[26] dovetailed with the immigration policy issue. On May 23 NBC anchor John Seigenthaler introduced a 6-scene, 32-shot story by saying:

> High school graduates around the country will be receiving their diplomas in the next few weeks, among them an estimated 65,000 who are illegal immigrants. For many of them graduation day could mark the end of their education and their time in the United States. But a new and controversial bill pending in Congress could change that.[27]

Although he uses the term *illegal*, Seigenthaler balances his framing by referring to these apprehensive students with the same terms as those used to refer to other graduating seniors.[28]

Scene 2 offers 10 shots of a mock high school graduation ceremony. The NBC audience hears a few shaky notes of an amateur solo of the "Star-Spangled Banner" and a speaker proclaiming *"Welcome Graduating Class of 2004!"* to youthful cheers. The camera pans back to a sign on the podium reading "United We DREAM," which fades to a series of shots of marching students in caps and gowns, an audience of mortarboards, and close-ups of 18-year-olds in gowns. Another earnest young student appears at the podium but is not heard. Telemundo correspondent Lori Montenegro's voice-over frames these images:

> A member of Congress as keynote speaker and a valedictorian address— it has all the pomp of a high school graduation. But these 65 students from around the country are not here to graduate but to protest. As children of illegal immigrants they face a future clouded by legal roadblocks and possible deportation.

The Telemundo correspondent accepts this political protest framing, articulating the students' demands to a national audience while dressed in graduation robes and mortarboards.

Scene 3 offers a tight close-up shot of US representative Lucille Roybal-Allard with the Capitol building and a waving American flag as backdrop; she says: *"We are talking about innocent children."* The representative's view is clear: immigration policy unjustly affects children who entered this country without US authorization through no fault of their own. Placing the Capitol behind Roybal-Allard adds force to her claim, while the reference to children effectively elicits viewer sympathy. The Telemundo newsroom thus arranged for Roybal-Allard to rearticulate the students' framing of the news story.

Next an extreme wide shot captures the whole ceremony with the Capitol building in the background; the correspondent voice-over states that the students' hopes *"rest with a bill in Congress called the 'DREAM Act,'"* as student protesters in flowing robes appear. The scene culminates with the students tossing their mortarboards into the air as the voice-over continues: *"a proposal allowing them to earn a legal residency by either serving in the US military or attending college."*

By using the verb *earn*, not *demand*, the students are portrayed as appealing for justice, not demanding it. The legislation's title also suggests that the federal law contradicts higher American values of opportunity for all those striving to better themselves. Telemundo correspondent Lori Montenegro and her crew presented the human face of these protesters, and presented their cause as deserving of understanding and sympathy.

Scene 4 gives viewers their first view of Montenegro, as she describes the politics of the DREAM Act. In Shot 2 she presents an opponent, Dan Stein, who represents the Federation for American Immigration Reform (FAIR). He hesitantly states: *"The DREAM Act is—is a backdoor amnesty program. It's an effort to try to find a way of giving people Green Cards if they have been enrolled in public schools."* Stein does not refer to the students as students or children, but as adults. His facial expression indicates he is uncomfortable. Viewers are immediately shown Stein's foil in Scene 5, a zoom-in on 15-year-old Griselda López of South Carolina, walking out of a high school. Several shots follow of López, first as a babe in arms (she was brought to the US at age two) and ending with images of her multiple Presidential Scholar Awards. She is shown walking the halls of Congress, and Montenegro's voice-over says: *"for Griselda it's a simple matter of justice that has brought her here to Washington to lobby Congress."* In a close-up, Griselda speaks eloquently on her own behalf: *"I would want them to be compassionate of my situation, but what I'm really looking for here is for people to do what is right."* She speaks a dialect of Southern English without a trace of a Spanish accent. Telemundo's news team has contrasted the personal plight of a praiseworthy young woman with Stein's callousness. The final scene returns to DREAM Act students' Washington demonstration, as the Telemundo correspondent connects their plight to the American ideal of fairness, saying that students used *"lessons learned from their high school civics books to present petitions carrying 100,000 signatures to the Education Department, hoping the DREAM Act can soon become a reality."*

This visually and rhetorically powerful story frames the protesters' call for legislative change as a plea for justice. While a congresswoman characterizes the students as children innocent of crime, the Telemundo correspondent contrasts the upbeat qualities of an exemplary student with a mean-spirited FAIR representative. The NBC news team marshaled its many resources to present unauthorized students in a positive light, thus supporting their call to be granted citizenship.

We turn now to a pair of news stories on Latino soldiers.

Iraq War Latino Soldiers

CNN: Death of a Green Card Soldier, #33

On a Saturday evening broadcast, CNN's Carol Li sits away from her anchor's desk, in low light evoking a somber ambiance. A CNN graphic takes up half the background behind her; the other half is a projection screen stating, "IRAQ: A US Marine's Story" over a portrait of a soldier in battle gear, his face darkened, and a geopolitical map of Iraq. The CNN title and subtitle read: "A Marine's Story: Life and Death in Service to His Country" at the bottom of the television screen.

Li's opening statement for this 6-scene, 42-shot story narrows the scope of viewer attention: "*Some people think that wars begin with fighter jets taking off, tanks rolling across the desert, and political announcements on television. But for soldiers, war begins when their comrades die.*" With her professional voice cracking emotionally right on cue, Li reduces the scale of the Iraq War to one person, "*a US Marine who was among the first to fall.*" On the one-year anniversary of the Iraq War, CNN chooses an emotionally compelling, rather than geopolitical, story.

A rapid succession of 14 close-up shots concentrating on one family reinforces the emotional impact of the story in Scene 2. It opens with a shot of a suburban house, followed by an extreme close-up of a somber foster mother, a year after her stepson's death. She begins by recalling when officers came to the front door: "*They didn't have to tell me. I knew that one of the two casualties of that day—one of them, was my son.*" CNN correspondent Frank Buckley then announces, "*Lance Corporal Jose Gutierrez was killed in action in one of the first engagements of the war,*" as viewers witness the solemnity of the funeral. A sequence of three increasingly closer shots of Gutierrez, in his formal military portrait, dissolves into a second, brief image of Marine pallbearers marching with a casket. In turn this image dissolves into a medium close-up of his foster sister asking: "*Why him? And why at the beginning?*" Her image then dissolves into footage of pall-bearers and Gutierrez' family, dressed in black, embracing at his funeral. At this moment any mention of Iraq civilian casualties, geopolitical eventualities, and Beltway politics would be unthinkably disrespectful.

Buckley's voice-over offers that "*Marine Corps officials later confirmed that Gutierrez was killed by friendly fire,*" as viewers see a close-up and then extreme close-up of Gutierrez' formal portrait. He adds, "*His family members accept that as an accident of war. And they are proud of how Gutierrez came to fight as a US Marine because he wasn't even from the United States.*" With this statement CNN relieves the US and impressionable viewers of responsibility for his pointless death.

CNN follows with a very brief shot of Ingracia Paz, Gutierrez' biological sister, who a year after his death remains visibly affected. The CNN clip airs only the briefest portion of her statement, "*because he came to give his life to a country that's not his.*" It is not clear what off-camera question elicited her response.[29] In the rapid flow of imagery, viewers might think she supports CNN's framing, namely that Gutierrez' family is uniformly proud and accepts his death as an "accident of war." However, Paz' statement is too short to corroborate CNN's portrayal of "Life and Death in Service to His Country."

The scene ends with an over-the-shoulder shot of the assembled family in their California living room, in turn zooming into an image of Gutierrez in combat fatigues, which pans and zooms more tightly on his face. Buckley's voice-over concludes: "*He died far away from both homes.*" After Paz' ambivalence, CNN works hard in the last three shots to reiterate its framing of Gutierrez' death as an act of patriotism.

Scene 3 takes viewers to Guatemala to witness Gutierrez' hard life as an orphan. Quick-shot images of children in a plaza appear as the background for an inserted photo of the Marine as a schoolboy, inviting the viewer to identify with Gutierrez, the boy, as the voice-over states that he "*was poor. At one point, he literally lived on the streets of this city.*" The voice-over continues: "*The story of the boy who made it to America only to die in Iraq was front-page news in Guatemala.*" The seventh shot of this scene displays the front page of the *Prensa Libre* newspaper, featuring a very large photo of the same formal Marine photo, with a Spanish headline reading in translation: "Guatemalan Died in Iraq."[30] To CNN's credit, *Prensa Libre* reporter Luisa Rodríguez is allowed to comment on air that Gutierrez' death was newsworthy in Guatemala on many levels: "For every 10 Guatemalans, 4 have a family in the United States." It is noteworthy that the Guatemalan reporter offers this illuminating fact about Latin American life, not CNN's Buckley.

In the first three shots of Scene 4, CNN quickly relates how Gutierrez came to be in the US. Buckley voice-over: "*He hitchhiked and hopped trains across 2,000 miles to get to the US*"; viewers see distance shots of Guatemalan traffic. Next, complemented by a camera shot of a Covenant House orphanage with a photo insert, this time of Gutierrez as a teenager, Buckley continues, "*As a teenager in the care of Casa Alianza, the Central American branch of Covenant House, someone told him that America was the 'Land of Opportunity.'*" CNN returns to his foster mother for an emotionally appealing statement: "*He came to the United States and he found out that everything that an American social worker in Guatemala had told him was really true. And ever more, he was so grateful.*" The patriotic narrative ends with Buckley's voice-over: "*Joining the Marine Corps was a job, but family members say it was also about serving his new country.*"

In this scene a number of changes and omissions stand out. The CNN subcaption changes from "Life and Death in Service to His Country" to "Gutierrez Became a Citizen Posthumously." At no point does CNN offer any details of Gutierrez' harrowing journey north, which was described by other news sources as "a 3,000-mile trail of tears by foot, tire, and rail. . . . The modern version of an underground railway, and the last leg over the wall." Nor does Buckley mention that Gutierrez was arrested as an unauthorized immigrant, and that he was able to remain in the US only because he said was 16 when he was actually 21 years old. CNN news editors treated these key elements of Gutierrez' personal story as distractions from their narrative of the dead war hero,[31] which was reestablished in the next shot. The CNN caption reverts to "Life and Death in Service to His Country" as his foster mother returns to the screen, before panning across Gutierrez' platoon photo to his foster sister, who states: "*He never forgot where he came from. But at the same time, he gave back to the place that gave him so much.*" Indeed, Gutierrez gave the full measure of devotion to his adopted nation, becoming one of the first soldiers in US uniform to die in Iraq.

Scene 5 juxtaposes infrared combat footage with another extreme close-up of Gutierrez' military portrait, visually reminding viewers of the war that killed this handsome young man. CNN then returns one last time to his foster mother: "*He told me that in the event anything bad happened, he wanted to be buried with his parents, in his homeland.*" The final scene concludes with Buckley's voice-over: "*At this dignified cemetery in Guatemala, there is one US Marine who is finally home.*"

CNN thus commemorates the Iraq War anniversary with a well-designed, visually arresting nationalistic narrative of a grateful immigrant's willing sacrifice in patriotic service to his adopted country. To remain on point with the nationalist framing, CNN passed over readily available information aspects of this young man's ambivalent relationship with the US. Instead it relates a formulaic story in which Gutierrez plays proxy for any dead young soldier, passing over many issues that would enrich its viewers' appreciation of Gutierrez as an individual and the meanings of his death in the context of Latino immigrants and US Latinos.

Several newsworthy issues might have expanded this tribute, including the congressional debate over the honors due to noncitizens who have died in combat wearing a US uniform.[32] Gutierrez' death (and President Bush's highly publicized visit to wounded Green Card soldiers) created political discomfort in Washington among those who publicly praise "our young men and women in uniform," yet also regularly repudiate unauthorized immigrants. "*Isn't it amazing? Those who are not acknowledged as citizens here are the ones doing that hard work for the country,*" said Gutierrez' parish priest, Gustavo Castillo. "*Doing the fighting and risking their lives.*"[33] Since Gutierrez was once "an illegal," these civic hypocrites could take comfort in the general public's short attention span when President Bush granted him US citizenship posthumously.

Among the other issues sparked by Gutierrez' death, but not covered by the networks, was the national double standard in the treatment of the 38,000 "Green Card soldiers" serving in the military in 2004. Many US Latinos also decried the Pentagon's multi-million-dollar recruitment campaign. To attain enlistment goals during an unpopular war, an all-volunteer military targets the nation's most underprivileged youth. Poor, undereducated Latino youth and unauthorized immigrants are among the most susceptible. The Pentagon uses high production value advertising, and in 2003 a record $4 billion marketing budget, to make its case: join the military and you will see the world, escape certain poverty, and serve a cause larger than yourself. Critics point to the class- and race-based prejudice inherent in this system, and the disproportionate casualties suffered by enlisted soldiers treated as "dispensable . . . cannon fodder."[34]

Another issue that could have been part of CNN's coverage was the heated debate ignited by Gutierrez' death in Guatemala, where he was seen as both hero and victim. At the Casa Alianza orphanage where Gutierrez lived, its British-born director, Bruce Harris, said: "Having been for years a throwaway kid, a nothing, the rubbish of society, who are we now to question that he should be called a hero?" At the director's insistence, Gutierrez was buried in the modest cemetery reserved for Casa Alianza street children, rather than in the elegant Guatemalan cemetery where the US government had secured a plot. "It is important for him to be here. It is his home," said Harris. "Not manicured; not nice trees. This is where his people are."[35]

ABC: Sergeant Rafael Peralta, #109

In contrast to CNN's war hero narrative, ABC's 7-scene, 31-shot story of another heroic Green Card soldier presents a notable, nuanced story. Anchor Bob Woodruff, who himself later became a casualty of the Iraq War, begins with the familiar verbal drum roll:

> *Finally tonight, we want to end this Thanksgiving Day broadcast with a story about courage. In every war, there are tales of such stunning bravery that they are told and retold, and eventually become legend. This story happened just 10 days ago in the Iraqi city of Fallujah, where a young Marine literally sacrificed his life for his platoon.*

This opening seems to offer another cookie-cutter patriotic story for Thanksgiving 2004. The impression continues in Scene 2, which begins with a close-up shot of a young Latino Marine in his dress formal photo. Sergeant Rafael Peralta's portrait, surrounded by what might be plastic flowers and a large votive candle, is the center of a family shrine. However, ABC audiences see a price tag on the lit candle, conveying a family's unmindful grief. Two camera shots of a flag-draped casket follow, carried by military pallbearers in a church, complemented by Catholic mass music.

In the next scene, Peralta's sister expresses her personal grief: *"It's just hard . . . 'cause I know he saved a lot of people. And it's something that I should be proud of. But I kinda hurt b'cause I need him. I needed him over here."* Icela's grief is so raw; she starts speaking about her personal loss with Latino-accented English before pulling back into a more standard accent for the camera. In contrast to CNN's graceless editing of Jose Gutierrez' sister, ABC gives Icela full voice. She acknowledges, but cannot accept, Rafael's death as patriotic. ABC thus begins to show its viewers the conflicted feelings of Peralta's family.

In Scene 3 Woodruff briefly describes the events of Peralta's sacrifice. Without exaltation or reference to bravery, Woodruff states:

It happened during the storming of Fallujah. A Marine platoon entered an insurgent safe house, like this one. Sergeant Peralta was in the lead. The insurgents opened fire and tossed a grenade. Peralta was shot in the face. As his platoon mates scrambled to get out, Rafael Peralta pulled the grenade against his body. Moments later, it blew up.

This is accompanied by Iraq War footage that visually recreates the circumstances of Peralta's death. The first clip of soldiers is nearly motionless; a fired bazooka is the sole action. Then viewers follow Marines running through Fallujah streets on the shaking footage of a shoulder-carried camera in a military action. Large-caliber blasts and small rounds of fire send dust rising as Marines enter a concrete-block and corrugated-tin building in an awkwardly positioned third camera shot. The fourth shot shows several soldiers in the lobby of a multistory building, with a lead soldier (like Peralta) kicking down a door. Flying dust obscures this shot, which is composed as dramatically as a Hollywood set, even using searchlights mounted on rifles to dramatically illuminate the room. Viewers then see a two-story apartment from the outside. First one grenade explodes through a window of this building; smoke rising. Then more and more grenades and large artillery fire resound, filling the air with smoke and debris. In the final Iraq scene, we see from a distance a motionless Humvee, from which a single rocket is launched.

The foregoing visual narrative of Peralta's death may have been pieced together from different footage since it features not one but several houses and different incidents. ABC invested significant time to visually illustrate the circumstances of Peralta's death and render the events that are succinctly stated in Woodruff's voice-over. The colors of dissimilar images were uniformly desaturated to create an almost monochrome look, which dramatized the action and set Iraq apart from our everyday technicolor world. The final Iraq image begins to cross-dissolve, but does not disappear behind another photo of Peralta, a relaxed and smiling young man. The visual effect is to leave Peralta in Iraq, forever separated from his family.

Scene 4 begins with a shot of an Anglo-American woman sitting in her Georgia home. Becky Dyer, wife of Peralta platoon mate Brannon Dyer, states, *"They say in the Bible there is no greater love than a man that lays down his life for his friends."* On this Thanksgiving Day, viewers see her prepare a turkey with her mother. The camera then zooms into an extreme close-up of the formal Marine portrait of Brannon Dyer. As the voice-over states, *"Brannon Dyer told reporters in Iraq that Sergeant Peralta saved half his fire team,"* a tight close-up of Peralta cross-dissolves and replaces Dyers' photo. The cross-dissolved photos visually analogize Peralta's self-sacrifice. Becky Dyer reiterates the visual statement twice in this final shot, repeating that Peralta *"made the ultimate sacrifice."*

In Scene 5 the audience hears from the hero's family. Viewers again see the casual photo of Peralta, and a photo store picture where he laughingly lifts a baby in a short-sleeved Marine uniform as the voice-over concisely states: *"Rafael Peralta was born in Mexico. So anxious to be a US Marine, he became one just a day after he got his Green Card."* Viewers then meet Rosa, his mother. Speaking only days after her son's death, she speaks in Spanish in a high voice entirely overcome with emotion. The voice-over translates: *"He never told me he was scared,"* she says. *"He just kept telling me, 'Mom, be brave.'"* While ABC's translation cannot be confirmed, Rosa's grief is unmistakable. The newsroom captures the mother's loss in this shot as she expresses her son's attempts to protect her from the trauma she is experiencing.

The next shot shows a family room where Peralta's siblings are assembled, all dressed in black. The voice-over informs us that on *"the day after his death, each of his three siblings got a letter from him."* The hands of his younger brother are shown in close-up holding sheets of three-ring binder paper and from an over-the-shoulder shot, Ricardo reads aloud: *"If anything happens to me, just remember that I already lived my life to the fullest. And I am happy with what I lived. You, Brother, live your life. Have fun. You still have lots of things to do. Aloha from Fallujah, Iraq."* While Peralta offers fatalistic and fatherly advice, any sentimentality that the letter might produce is quickly erased by Peralta's youngest sister, Karen. She is utterly unimpressed by the media attention.

> *When it's going to be like, one year, or two years, they are going to forget about him. And that's why I mean, right now they are giving medals to my mom and everything. But I know that when it comes to later on, they are going to forget him, they're gonna forget about him.*

Karen's voice-over introduces Scene 6, the funeral scene, which reinforces her comments. As she speaks, viewers see soldiers carrying a flag-draped coffin in a cemetery and her voiced-over comments continue while viewers see soldiers fold the flag above the coffin. The camera then cuts to soldiers firing three rifle volleys, and video of the keening family at graveside, as Icela embraces her crying mother. In voice-over, ABC's anchor gently pushes back against Karen's skepticism: *"But they will not forget."*

Thus ABC editors juxtaposed the Peralta family's tragedy with his heroism. By allowing the dead Marine's sisters to speak out about their personal loss, ABC editors effectively used pathos to avoid sensationalizing his death.

The newsroom then inserts a shot of Becky Dyer rearticulating her sentiments: *"I just want them to know how truly grateful we are and how saddened I am at their loss. And that we are so thankful for what he did."* A wide shot returns to Peralta's funeral; 30 people are gathered around the grieving family. Dyer's comments become a voice-over, set off by mournful graveside wailing that does not trail off as the camera zooms back to place the casket at middle distance in a wide camera shot. Then the ABC anchor concludes: *"A remarkable man. A remarkable family. There are many people who believe that Sergeant Peralta deserves this country's highest honors. That's our report on World News Tonight. For all of us here at ABC news, Happy Thanksgiving."*

Woodruff originally framed Peralta's story as a *"legend,"* a heroic war story broadcast. However, the dictates of news reporting demand family stories on Thanksgiving Day, since the national holiday is a family ritual, not a patriotic one.[36] While the ABC news story is as well written and visually rendered as CNN's Jose Gutierrez story, it sensitively focuses on family, not nationalism. Specific details of Peralta's sacrifice are highlighted. For example, he is portrayed as being more eager to be a Marine than a US citizen. ABC mentions his Mexican nationality matter-of-factly and downplays his Green Card status,[37] deviating from repeated newsprint coverage of Latino soldiers striving to earn US citizenship. Moreover, ABC gently revealed the pain-filled responses and nuanced commentaries of two Marine families on the consequences of war. Through this report, ABC viewers (as citizens of the nation) could share the gratitude that the Dyer family feels for Peralta's sacrifice.[38]

Latinos in Sports

ABC: NFL Marketing to Latinos, #9

Sports stories are a staple of television news, and certain athletic events are extensively covered. For example in 2004 the Super Bowl and the Olympics were both covered extensively, and tie-ins to Latinos gave networks opportunities to spin the same topic in the same way with brown faces. On the weekend of the national professional US football championship game, the Super Bowl, ABC's anchor Bob Woodruff introduced an 8-scene, 34-shot story about the *"NFL's new push for more Latino fans."* He frames the story in terms of big business marketing to a potential consumer group in Houston, where Latinos make up more than a third of the city's population.

After this 1-shot introduction, correspondent Bill Redeker takes viewers into an upper-middle-class family's entertainment room, where he says: *"These are some of the NFL's newest fans and not one of them was born here. Fans who grew up with a different kind of football."* Ten camera shots cut back and forth to give viewers a range of views of at least a dozen Latino guests at a Super Bowl party. The news audience is thus given the idea that the participants' attention is focused on a televised football game (not ABC's cameras) to reinforce how important US football has become to these upper-middle-class men and women, all of whom come from Latin America. The body conventions captured by the news team depict the guests enjoying themselves as football fans: some of the assembled cheer the televised football action, while viewers see sports party props, including beer cans, overstuffed sofas, a pool table, and a big-screen television surrounded by football trophies and bobble heads around a large, well-appointed room.

The economics angle is picked up in Scene 3, with Lino García from ESPN Deportes (ESPN Sports): *"Right now [the Hispanic market is] about 30 million and it's projected to be at about 50 million in the next 15 years. So it is really growing at a very fast clip."* The next scene juxtaposes a quick full-screen shot of the football game and a shot of two ESPN Deportes commentators shouting in harmony: *"49ers al ataque!"* ('49ers on the attack!') with closed-fist choreography of soccer commentators, this time shot on an American football locker room set.

Correspondent Bill Redeker is then shown in Scene 4 with huge multiple screens behind him all turned to a Seahawks football game in an incongruously quiet sports bar. Redeker is dressed down in rolled-up shirtsleeves. With a slow zoom into a medium shot, Redeker informs viewers that the NFL has a *"Hispanic task force"* to bring the game to people across the country. His report becomes a voice-over in the next scene, at a New York Jets football clinic. Viewers see seven shots of Latino children (Black Latino or possibly African American) playing US football. Although this clinic *"hosted 200 Hispanic kids"* to *"teach them how to pass, kick, and scrimmage,"* it is clear the children on camera already know the game. The Jets marketing director explains on camera that the effort is to *"break down those barriers . . . and let them see and feel and touch football in a way that they normally wouldn't get a chance to do.*" Possibly the stadium setting is novel, but since it is likely that urban Latino children have played US football, this mock clinic suggests that the NFL pitched the news story to ABC so the league could promote its signature weekend.

The next scene reveals the New York Jets' purpose, to make these children *"season ticket holding, free-spending fans,"* as viewers see a full-screen graphic of a football game and frenzied fans. The ESPN Deportes spokesperson returns: *"We're talking about a market of over 30 million people in the US, with the buying power of half a trillion dollars."* Redeker's voiceover continues: *"That's a lot of tickets, souvenirs, and beer."* ABC provides its advertiser with a freebie, a partial-screen computer-generated graphic of a Spanish-language beer commercial advertising the Super Bowl. As viewers return to the Latino Super Bowl party for six closing shots, Redeker concludes: *"The marketing seems to be paying off. The NFL says 70% of Hispanic men and a growing number of women now regularly follow football."* Both the network and the league regard Latinos as a homogeneous market for their commodity, as the ABC anchor said in his opening: *"Hispanics are playing into the hands of the National Football League."*

Baseball's A-Rod, #16, #18, #19, #20, #21, #22, #23

Alex Rodriguez, the professional baseball player, received relatively extensive network attention when he was traded to the New York Yankees. Seven news stories covered the financial aspects of his $275 million contract and characterized him as a commodity. This is standard journalistic treatment of professional athletes. His ethnicity is never mentioned, and it could be argued these stories should not be included in any counts. If considered Latino stories, these constitute 6% of all the Latino news stories aired in 2004, which demonstrates the narrow regard Latinos have among the networks.

NBC: Olympic Triple Jumper Becomes Iconic Immigrant, #85

The Olympics are an international competition of superbly gifted and committed athletes. NBC owns the franchise to air Olympic events and uses its news programs to pump up viewer interest by treating the games as a global referendum on US superiority, by reiterating US myths in the same way the Greeks projected their city-state fables onto naked runners

2,000 years ago. Over the span of several weeks in 2004 NBC aired stories on Latino athletes (#84–#86) composed to impose national myths on their brown bodies.[39] We review #85.

With the Olympic flame as his backdrop, NBC's Brian Williams anchors the summer games in Athens, Greece. On August 21 he introduced and framed a 6-scene, 38-shot news story about one contestant's life with the conventional fanfare:

> *Every athlete arrives here with a dream. It's what drives years of rigorous training and keeps hope alive, despite obstacles in the way. But there is a triple jumper here, Yuliana Pérez, going for a gold medal tomorrow. She'd already have a medal if only they gave them out for how people get here.*

Scene 2 begins with a full-screen graphic that labels the national myth Pérez is said to embody, a misty image of the Acropolis and a semitransparent waving Olympic flag combined into a dynamic background for the NBC series entitled "Athens 2004." The story title caption flies in from left and right, "American Dream," as the viewing audience hears a girl giggle in the network's careful juxtaposition of nationhood and youth's sweetness. Viewers see Pérez modestly signing autographs on a warm, tourist-strewn Grecian beach. The autograph seekers may not know who she is, but this staging allows NBC correspondent Kerry Sanders to begin to narrate an Olympian life: "*On a beach in Greece, American triple jumper Yuliana Pérez. Her route here to the games began 6,000 miles away—not in the United States, but in Cuba.*"

Scene 3 consists of 12 successive camera shots panning the urban Havana beach, in contrast to the Grecian beach. NBC video editors treat the Cuban images with an ultraviolet filter, depicting the Caribbean beach in surprisingly unappealing blue tones. Sanders states: "*Her parents fled that communist island in the early '80s during the Mariel Boatlift,*" expressing repugnance by emphasizing *that communist island* and conjuring negative associations of the Cuba of Fidel Castro.

Viewers then see a stock visual from the 1980 Mariel Boatlift. We see an ancient boat overfilled with people. Its name: *God's Mercy.* The next scene continues with stock footage on that boat to reinforce the idea that Cubans were and are desperate to leave their country. These images may also have been ultraviolet filtered, with after-filter red dabbings on clothing, to sustain the cold visual effect of the Cuban images.

Panning up the next image in striking contrast is a full-color image of an Arizona skyline. Viewers learn that Pérez was born in Arizona. "*But then,"* Sanders continues, *"tragedy! Both of her parents were killed. With no family in the United States, the US government sent Yuliana back to Havana to her paternal grandmother."* As Sanders underscores the word *tragedy,* viewers see a key framing shot of Pérez as a pensive adolescent. He fails to mention that Pérez was three years old at the time of her mother's death, so the time frame of the photo does not match the narrated event.[40]

The camera then brings his audience into the very modest working-class Cuban living room of her grandmother. The old woman holds a wallet-sized portrait of the teenage Yuliana. The camera closes in tightly on the photo and her grandmother's broken nails and work-worn hands. Sanders continues: *"Yuliana lived like any other Cuban. She shared a bed with four cousins, had only one pair of shoes. She'd often go barefoot, saving her shoes for athletics."* Sanders implies that Pérez owned in total one pair of shoes, his verbal emphasis on *"barefoot"* implying that all Cubans live in deprivation.[41] In Scene 4 Pérez seems to confirm Sanders' off-camera prompt, saying: *"When you get a pair of shoes in Cuba, you're going to take care of them like your eyes."* In fact, at times she had only one pair of training shoes.[42]

NBC's news video technicians create visual interest from limited materials. From stock footage of urban Havana streets (signaling all things Cuban) and a photo of Pérez (the US athlete) landing a triple jump, her hands in the air, they overlay the photo onto a different photo of a stadium. They then reshoot the photos as video that incrementally zooms in, building dynamic movement and athleticism into the stills.

With the help of 10 camera shots, Sanders then describes Pérez' dilemma. He says, *"Four years ago, the Pan Am Games medal winner was destined for greatness."*[43] From the same pensive profile of the athlete—wearing her Cuban uniform—the camera zooms in to an extreme close-up of medals. The images of her Cuban medals are viewed excessively close, out of focus, as if to efface them.

"That's when she learned the rules." Sanders' voice-over is blunt: *"If she wanted to represent Cuba in the 2000 Games, she'd have to give up her US passport."*[44] Viewers see Cuba's national stadium in Havana, including a Che Guevara billboard. The stadium is seen through a set of window bars, behind which the same pensive athlete image is seen in black and white. This extraordinary composite image pans across the stadium through prison-like bars, presenting Yuliana in a somber, head-down profile. The camera panning left crosses sets of bars to articulate a visual metaphor, CUBA AS PRISON, with Pérez as imprisoned in the Cuban stadium.[45] On camera, Pérez explains: *"I have US citizenship, and I didn't want to give it up. So they kicked me out of the team and the school."* The visual meta-

phor thus guides an interpretation for viewers that Pérez considers Cuba as a penitentiary.

However, other, nontelevised news sources indicate that Pérez has related a more balanced story: "'Cuba was going to give me everything,' she said. 'I was going to finish school. I was going to go to the Olympics. I was going to be set. But when they told me I had to choose, I couldn't do it.'"[46] Pérez thus acknowledged that she would have been able to compete on the Cuba national team at the Sydney Olympics four years earlier had she been willing to give up her US citizenship.[47]

Sanders characterizes Pérez' act as a principled decision that elevates her to Olympian status. Forgoing Cuban athletics (and retaining her dual citizenship) is implicitly presented as evidence of American superiority. *"So Yuliana returned to her birthplace—this American from Cuba—making her way in a new country, working as a waitress."* Sanders also suggests that only the US would make Pérez' Olympic dream come true. However, contrary to NBC's fable, when she left the island Pérez had no plans to compete. She simply wanted to leave Cuba. NBC passed over this crucial detail. A Tucson television station quoted Pérez: "Honestly, I didn't think I would be able to represent anybody in the Olympics. . . . I just wanted to come to the United States so I could have a better life than the one I had in Cuba."[48]

In the next scene she is wearing an apron and pouring coffee in the University of Arkansas Razorback Room. Viewers then see Pérez working out in a gym with the Razorback insignia on the back wall, and Sanders states that she is *"always pushing harder. She trains only with men."* While training with men is a common practice for world-caliber women athletes, per Sanders, it is one more example of Pérez' heroic status.

In Scene 5 once again Pérez walks along a beach in Greece. Her last words finally endorse Sanders' myth-making: *"I'm very, very proud to be representing the United States anywhere I go, because this is the country that actually helped me to pursue my dreams."* The closing camera shots play up the American Dream. In one, she is shown competing, and the final shots pan from the ocean to a close-up profile and finally a low-angle shot of the athlete's profile with the sun behind her.

Just as the NBC anchor introduced Pérez by saying she would have a gold medal *"if only they gave them out for how people get here,"* NBC's news team worked to render dramatic episodes of her life to fit this fable, passing over personal drama that would provide the viewing audience with a more human image of this world-class athlete. The visuals in the last scene were designed to reinforce the celebrity quality that NBC news grants to

Pérez: after being rejected and rejecting the unjust island regime, the athlete embraces our noble nation; in a close-up profile viewers visualize her in tomorrow's competition in a culminating leap that will overcome her personal travails. The final shot renders her in full silhouette, the sun behind her, to demonstrate the fulfillment of a fairy-tale. It is effective visual story making.

Unfortunately, Sanders passed over details that would have made Pérez' story less heroic, but no less newsworthy. When Pérez refused to give up her US citizenship, an argument with her family ensued and she "found herself out on the street." There she met Tom Miller, a Tucson reporter who had once interviewed her. He returned to Cuba with an affidavit to explore her legal records. Armed with documents, she received an application for a US passport from the Swiss embassy and arrived in Tucson with $800 of borrowed money and a backpack. Providence, however, continued to favor Pérez. Tucson social worker Cruz Olivarria took special interest in Pérez and invited her to live in her own home, and Pérez took a job as a waitress.

Pérez thought "her triple jumping career was finished," but as *New York Times* reporter Spousta stated, "Fate threw another thunderbolt." Speaking "only a thimbleful of English," one day Pérez took the wrong bus home. At the end of the route the bus driver, Guillermo Díaz, tried to put the distressed young woman at ease by asking if she'd ever participated in sports. "I asked her if she was any good," Díaz recalled. "She said, 'Yeah, I was pretty good.' I said, 'Really, maybe you can get a scholarship and go to school.' The bus driver noted, 'She had no direction or anything.'"[49]

Díaz introduced her to the sprint coach at Pima Community College and to the Aztecs' head coach, John Radspinner. Pérez told Spousta: "I was praying for the opportunity again—'Oh, God, give me a gift'—because I really love the sport. I was sad because I'll never be what I want to be. Then I get here, and oh, what a beautiful thing." Radspinner recalls that he was awestruck watching Pérez when she returned to the track—and she had not trained for over a year. Pérez later won two junior college national championships running for the Aztecs, which brought her to Athens.[50]

Pérez' luck extended to her adopted family. She told Spousta: Cruz Olivarria "saved my life. At that moment, she did not care what the consequences might be. I believed in her right away. She helps me every way she can, and she has so little herself." The feelings were mutual for Olivarria, who told Spousta: "It was like I knew her forever. I loved her right away as a friend and a daughter. I'm not interested in Yuliana making money from this. I want her to finish school and be the person she wants to be."

Finally, for an individual whose life was strewn with thunderbolt events, the Olympics were not one of them. As the NBC newsroom already knew, Pérez would fail to reach the finals in Athens due to a hamstring injury.[51] She had one consolation. She met with her former Cuban teammates: "It was nice to see them," she said. "And they were happy for me. But not the coaches."[52]

Pérez' life was remade for television. Born in the United States and raised in Cuba, her world-class athleticism and determination allowed her to become part of the Cuban national team, where by all accounts she lived in relative privilege. Contrary to the NBC allegory, Cuba wanted her to be an Olympian. Pérez gave up family, community, and a promising career in Cuban athletics when she chose to not represent Cuba in the Sydney games—exactly what Sanders implies *only* the US offered. NBC's Sanders triple jumps from reporter, to novelist, then to myth-maker[53] as he reworks Pérez' story line, omitting the opportunities that Cuba offered her and the serendipity that brought her to the Grecian beach. To sustain the distorted imagination of the national fairy-tale, NBC rewrote the athlete's biography to portray the USA as the one and only land of opportunity. And in doing so, it passed on the remarkable events of Yuliana Pérez' life.

Summary

We can make four observations about the network television feature stories involving Latinos. The first involves story content. In 2004, network newsrooms at times operated with indifference or ignorance about the diversity of Latino communities and individuals. While the two news briefs discussed were drawn from well-written and detailed print sources, network news writers failed to accurately write the stories. The brief on Latinos' impact on the national economy erroneously presented Latino workers as taking more than their fair share of the nation's jobs. The news brief on hemorrhagic or ischemic strokes was unnecessarily alarming, since it falsely stated that all Latinos were at risk. Full-length news stories also displayed negligence. A news story touting an "In-Depth" byline failed to offer a coherent analysis of the challenges that a growing Latino demographic poses to an urban school district, focusing instead a Black/White binary lens on a multiracial setting and painting a twenty-first-century problem in twentieth-century terms.

Regarding the visual imagery of feature stories, which are composed without the urgency of deadlines, the most visually arresting Latino feature stories were often broadcast with images drawn from other sources rather than in-house imagery. For example, the feature on the Spanish-language reality show took its startling imagery directly from the show's commercials, and the feature on *Day without a Mexican* reworked most of the movie trailer. Once it was clear that the networks drew their visual material from outside sources, I had a hard time finding original visual compositions in other Latino feature stories. Consider the *Sábado Gigante* political news story, which used Spanish-language opening visual sequences from the show. We wonder whether general newsroom indifference to Latinos leads networks to let readily available imagery dictate the selection of Latino feature stories, rather than allowing noteworthy stories to lead to the creation of appropriate visuals.

Notable exceptions to the foregoing were two stories about the death of Green Card soldiers. Both stories were tightly composed and carefully crafted with rich visual imagery. Their high production values no doubt were comparatively costly. The CNN story reported on the one-year anniversary of the death of Jose Gutierrez, employing a template "dead-soldier" plot resolution, namely that his family accepted the higher cause justification. The twist, of course, was that Gutierrez wore the soldier's uniform of his chosen country. CNN excluded any element of Gutierrez' well-documented life that deviated from this patriotic narrative, since the apparent goal of the story was to let the audience feel good about itself on the anniversary of the Iraq War.

ABC also ran a dead "Green Card soldier" story, with another twist: he died to save the lives of fellow soldiers. The story on Rafael Peralta's death was memorable because ABC's correspondent took the time to present each person involved, and the film crew captured enough footage on each member of the two families that the newsroom could narrate a story about the interfamily dynamic created by Peralta's death. ABC presented a complex interwoven narrative of the families of soldiers.

Finally, we note that the networks do not all articulate a single political ideological stance regarding Latino people in their feature stories. For example, CBS ran the story on the movie *A Day without a Mexican* with a decidedly progressive stance, since the correspondent allowed the movie's directors to frame the news story. It also ran a rightist story (to be discussed in the following chapter) on the effects of Arizona's Proposition 200. In another story with multiple ideological stances, CNN ran an exposé on how hospitals abuse uninsured patients through price gouging. This story displayed the full human subjectivity of a number of Latino people. CNN also ran a series of news stories (following chapter) about Phoenix "drop houses" for immigrant smuggling that characterized immigrants in dehumanizing ways.

CHAPTER 4

News Stories about Caribbean Immigrants

Thirty-six of the 118 network television news stories about Latinos (33%) that aired in 2004 dealt with immigration.[1] President Bush turned the national spotlight on immigration on January 7, 2004, when he announced a major White House initiative to bring about comprehensive immigration policy reform. The president ultimately did not send Congress a bill for consideration, but the issue became a major topic of domestic policy in a way that it had not been seen since 1994, when Californians debated Proposition 187, the notorious anti-immigrant referendum. As a result, immigrants became the Latino imagery most frequently broadcast to the nation's news viewers in 2004.

In the next chapters, I look at several aspects of this reporting, to inquire how well network television news performed its role as the Fourth Estate on this vital and controversial issue. In the 1990s, major US newspapers disseminated biased imagery about US Latinos and immigrants.[2] However, for a time after 2004 the nation's newspapers offered their readers a comparatively politically balanced presentation of the immigration debate.[3] More has been written about the coverage of immigration in newspapers than in television news.[4] This chapter presents an analysis of the network coverage of Caribbean stories, beginning with Cuban and following with Dominican immigrants. We will see that the networks frame most stories about unauthorized Caribbean immigrants differently than those about other Latino immigrants.

Cuban Migrants as Refugees

For 50 years, communist Cuba's unwillingness to submit to US capitalist prerogatives has been a thorn in the side of the US government. Washington has isolated this tiny country with a severe economic and diplomatic blockade for more than 50 years. The United Nations regularly condemns the US blockade of Cuba, but an anti-Castro community based in Florida has sustained an effective lobby to maintain the blockade in order to punish Fidel Castro, exacerbating the average Cuban's economic deprivation.[5] Over the years Cubans have left the island by the thousands, originally for political freedom or to save their accumulated fortunes (such as Carlos Gutierrez, #110 to #113), but now mostly as last-ditch efforts to improve desperate economic circumstances. This sad history has led to the evolution of a US immigration policy that sets Cubans apart from other unauthorized Latino immigrants. The US granted wide-ranging political refugee status soon after the communists took over in 1959. More recently, as part of the agreement signed between the two countries following the 1980 Mariel Boatlift,[6] the United States began to admit 20,000 Cuban immigrants yearly, instituting the problematic "wet foot/dry foot" policy. If the United States apprehends unauthorized Cuban migrants on the open ocean, they are deemed economic migrants and can be summarily returned to the island nation. However, a Cuban who succeeds in setting foot on "dry land" can request political asylum, which in one year can lead to permanent residency.[7]

ABC and CBS News Briefs about Cubans Floating on a Buick, #11, #12

The television network news editors cast Cuban migrants as intrepid freedom seekers risking their lives to escape tyranny. The journalists do not inquire into the immigrants' motivation; it seems that economics, rather than politics, forces them off the island. For example, on February 4, 2004, both ABC's Peter Jennings (#11) and CBS' Dan Rather (#12) reported in news briefs on the interdiction of a group of Cubans who attempted to cross the 90-mile Florida straits in a car that was modified for ocean travel.

In a 1-scene, 5-shot news brief, ABC viewers see a set of photos of the incongruous image of two men sitting atop a 1955 Buick Riviera sedan floating in the open ocean. Peter Jennings states:

There's another remarkable picture in the news tonight. Eleven Cubans, including five children, were in this vintage Buick outfitted for a sea voyage to Florida and freedom. Seen here: the US Coast Guard intervening to send them back home. [Photos of the Buick are replaced with footage of another floating car.] Last summer at least two of the same Cubans had tried and failed to make it to the USA in this Chevrolet, a '50s pickup truck outfitted with pontoons.

Jennings' verbal reference to *freedom* is reinforced visually by a small-screen graphic above his shoulder labeled "Freedom Road," showing a Cuban flag partially submerged in ocean waves.

Dan Rather calls this story *"remarkable."* Both CBS's Rather and ABC's Peter Jennings speak with admiration verging on delight. The story drips with pro-US symbolism: audacious immigrants risking their lives to escape the hemisphere's worst dictatorship, arriving in a pre-Castro vintage US car to America's free shores.[8]

ABC News Brief about Mexican Piñata Girl, #105

The delighted response to the Buick story contrasts sharply with the tone of ABC anchor Elizabeth Vargas when she anchored a brief about unauthorized Mexican immigrants, #105. During this 1-scene, 2-shot news brief on November 12, she states:

> *Customs inspectors on the US border with Mexico have made a **shocking** discovery. While inspecting a car, they found a young girl about four or five years old, hidden inside a large piñata.[9] Officials say she was in good health. Her mother and her brother were also hiding in the car. All three have been returned to Mexico."*

Elizabeth Vargas shakes her head in dismay as she emphasizes the term *shocking*, paralinguistically and prosodically reproaching the mother for her reckless behavior. Vargas then follows with a statement of the child's health. In contrast, neither Dan Rather nor Peter Jennings mentioned the well-being of the five children placed at risk on the floating Buick. Nor was the children's welfare a concern in subsequent public discourse about this group of Cuban immigrants[10] (although it should be noted that the welfare of immigrant children is rarely a US public-sphere concern).[11]

Vargas also emphasizes the word *hiding* in order to reinforce the framing of the Mexican mother's action as criminal. Among sympathetic viewers, all immigration stories involving children are poignant and reflect parental desperation. This story does not invite sympathy; the mother is cast as irresponsible. However, little in the Mexican story substantiates Vargas' censure. Indeed, since the child was not injured and a traditional Mexican toy was involved, this story could have been cast as lightheartedly as the Cuban story.[12]

ABC and CBS News Briefs on
Cubans Migrating by Inner Tube, #34, #35

The framing in the piñata story can be compared to the framing in a 4-shot news brief, #34, about a passerby pulling an unconscious woman out of Caribbean waters. The woman is one of three people rescued after floating from Cuba to Florida on inner tubes. Vargas describes it as *"a remarkable scene . . . One woman was rescued off Fort Lauderdale in rough seas."* In #35, CBS anchor John Roberts also assesses the inner-tube crossing as daring, not foolhardy, but reveals the loss of lives: *"Five others who set out with them last week didn't make it."* The networks also framed a mass defection in Las Vegas of Cuban entertainers with no derision toward the Cubans (see Chapter 3).[13]

Dominican Migrants as Victims

While the networks frame Cubans as audacious freedom seekers who will do anything to escape Castro's totalitarianism, in terms of sheer numbers, migrants from noncommunist Caribbean countries have even greater incentive to take to the open sea. In 2003 the US Coast Guard detained 1,378 unauthorized migrants from Cuba and 1,679 from the Dominican Republic.[14] What is more, the numbers were increasing: 5,000 Dominicans tried to make the 60-mile trip in the first eight months of 2004.[15] Since the wet foot/dry foot policy does not apply, one might predict that network policy would reflect government policy and treat Dominicans differently from Cubans.[16] However, the findings were mixed: in the two news stories NBC aired in 2004, Dominican immigrants were framed in terms similar to those used for Cubans. And, while ABC framed a news brief using victim terminology, the newsroom also used criminalizing language in its only feature-length story on the issue.[17]

NBC and ABC News Briefs and NBC Report, #63, #81, #14

On June 16, *NBC Nightly News* anchor Tom Brokaw reported a 2-scene, 4-shot news brief, #63, with footage of the most traumatic moments of a mid-sea midnight Coast Guard encounter with a Dominican *yola*, 'homemade fishing boat.' The 40-foot yola is overloaded with 94 people. Viewers see four clips of Coast Guard spotlight illumination at mid-distance, setting up a dramatic depiction of the arrest/rescue. Viewers cannot make out faces as life preservers are tossed to the boat, which is so packed with people sitting shoulder to shoulder that its rail is perilously close to the waterline in calm seas. In the second shot, the boat capsizes, apparently tipped by anxious, jostling passengers. The next shot shows people flailing desperately in the water; only five or six wear life preservers. The final shot shows many people still thrashing in the water as Brokaw in voice-over states that the rescue took more than two hours and three people died.

While the images are harrowing, Brokaw maintains a restrained tone. He does not verbally dramatize this event, describing the setting as "*very difficult*" instead of *horrific* or other sensationalizing terms. Nor are the Dominicans termed *illegal*, but are referred to as "*passengers*" and "*people*." The visual images could have been sensationalized, but NBC news editors chose to downplay this tragedy.

An August 11 an ABC news brief, #81, covered another Coast Guard rescue of Dominican migrants. In this 5-shot story, anchor Elizabeth Vargas conveys the pathos of the news event. In this 66-word brief, she refers to Dominican "*survivors*" who were "*rescued at sea*," as "*people . . . fleeing dire economic conditions*." Meanwhile, a succession of camera shots builds strong subjectivity of the Dominicans as humans. The first is a grainy blow-up of a wide-shot Coast Guard video of a rocking yola with passengers. The next is a mid-shot of 10 apparently listless Dominicans still in a yola. The camera work is shaky; the boat is lolling in shallow water. Several people next to the boat walk easily through the surf. The final shot, on shore, shows a stout man carrying an emaciated Dominican through a crowd. This last shot reinforces the sense of the migrants' suffering. In the piñata story (#105), Vargas censured a Mexican mother for endangering her child, without mentioning the circumstances that motivated this decision. In the Dominican brief, by contrast, Vargas emphasized the word *dire* to draw sympathy from the ABC audience for these economic refugees.

An earlier story, #14, broadcast on February 10 by NBC, also presented Dominicans in a relatively sympathetic light in a 4-scene, 29-shot "in-depth report." Anchor Brian Williams introduces the story:

> *A new wave of boat people, desperate to reach American soil, posing a real challenge for the US Coast Guard. This time it's a surge of Dominican immigrants trying to flee their depressed homeland, crowding into overloaded and dangerous vessels, hoping for a new start in the US.*

The story opens with a full-screen graphic of clips prefiguring the story's images of people in overcrowded yolas. While Williams uses the standard water metaphors for immigration,[18] he frames the Dominican migrants as people suffering economic privation, not as criminals. Analogously, he frames Coast Guard personnel as rescuers, not policing agents.

In Scene 2, correspondent Mark Potter begins a voice-over description as a series of 18 short video clips render the nighttime setting. A light from a hovering helicopter competes with the full moon to illuminate what turns out to be another tiny boat in the open ocean. Viewers barely discern a small, faint image against the inky darkness:

> *Ninety-one people desperately crammed aboard a 35-foot wooden motorboat, known as a yola, tossed about by 10-foot seas—refugees from the Dominican Republic, where economic problems have become so bad hundreds of people are willing to risk the trip to US shores in Puerto Rico. These migrants were intercepted by the US Coast Guard cutter* Decisive, *their yola in danger of capsizing more than 60 miles from their destination.*

The rough water pitches the small boat, and darkness lit only by spotlights renders this rescue/arrest dramatic. A small Coast Guard boat approaches its larger cutter, carrying some Dominicans; an unconscious woman on a stretcher is lifted from the boat to the larger ship, her hands quivering reflexively. Race is repeatedly visually articulated, as when two White Coast Guard personnel escort a Black Dominican who has been covered with a blanket. Other Coast Guard personnel board the cutter from the boat, followed by Dominicans wearing life jackets. In the pitch dark, the life preservers glow bright red, as a burly White Coast Guard officer calls into a two-way radio: "*Hey Doc! We got another customer for you. Migrant passed out.*" Another uniformed US soldier compassionately cradles a sobbing woman; then we see a Dominican with his hands on his head as he is frisked in the glare of the ship's spotlights. The next shot is a close-up and then extreme close-up of the trembling hand of a woman wearing a medical bracelet. The viewers see hands in surgical gloves attend to her. The doctor speaks on camera saying the woman is simultaneously hypothermic and seasick. The Dominicans are ill-prepared for their journey. In contrast to the Coast Guard personnel, who wear pea jackets, one woman wears a tee shirt and we see a man's bare feet climbing up onto the cutter.

The correspondent's text and the camera's visual imagery depict the migrants' motivation as economic desperation. The Coast Guard personnel are cast as rescuers, not police agents. No reference is made to the Dominicans' legal status. The one police-action image, a man being frisked, is swiftly replaced by close-ups of medical personnel tending to suffering women and men. Although the Dominicans' faces are not seen, the camera shot calls viewers to sympathize with rather than resent them.

Scene 3 begins with a full-screen map of the Dominican Republic and Puerto Rico with a red arrow indicating the migrants' direction across the Mona Passage. This bleeds into a daytime shot seen from the cutter across open ocean, and pans to the correspondent on deck, clinging to the rail in choppy waters.

Scene 4 sustains the original rescue framing with more dramatic images and two brief Coast Guard statements. In three images, the Coast Guard rescues people from at least one overloaded yola. Spotlights from the cutter again light up the night with dramatic images, followed by a medium close-up of the Coast Guard captain describing human desperation and denouncing immigrant smugglers' greed and disregard for human life. Next we see footage of a 40-foot yola that is heartbreakingly overloaded with 245 people. A Coast Guard petty officer says, "*The rail of the boat was only just a few inches above the waterline. Any large wave could have capsized it.*" Images dramatize the successful Coast Guard action: from a spotlighted shot of the silhouette of a Coast Guard boat dramatically tossed in rough seas to a shot of sleeping people on the deck of a cutter. While this is a heroic rescue story with humane renditions of the victims, NBC does not explore the Dominican Republic economic crisis that precipitated the increased exodus. Rather, the NBC visuals and text provide a paternalistic, though sympathetic, view of these Caribbean migrants.

Dominican Migrants as Criminals

ABC In-Depth Story, #74

An ABC news story about the increasing numbers of Dominican migrants illustrates a divergent framing. Anchor Peter Jennings set up, but did not frame, a feature-length story that ran on July 14. A full-screen map opens Scene 1, zooming from the North American continent to the Mona Passage in the Caribbean. Next, Jennings appears in his standard anchor medium close-up, describing an ill-fated incident of a capsized boat that carried many "*people*," and a search for "*survivors.*" He then asks Jeffrey Kofman, his correspondent, "*What's going on here?*"

Scene 2 opens with Coast Guard footage of another night rescue/arrest of a group of Dominicans. In contrast to NBC's unmodified clips, ABC broadcasts blown-up images of terrified people struggling in the water around a capsized yola.[19] Over this dramatic imagery, Kofman says:

The illegal migrants were heading for US territory, the shores of Puerto Rico, when their tiny boat capsized Monday night. This US Coast Guard video shows the rescue. But some passengers drowned before the Coast Guard arrived. Since the beginning of this year, the Coast Guard has been engaged in a dangerous cat-and-mouse game here. Boats carrying illegal migrants are attempting the 60-mile crossing to the US, in record numbers. The rickety wooden boats, called yolas, are crammed to the gunwales with passengers. There were 63 aboard this one. Each person has paid smugglers hundreds of dollars. In small groups, they are ferried to the Coast Guard cutter, processed, and taken back where they came from.

Kofman portrays the Dominicans as criminals by calling them "*illegal migrants*" twice. In one scene we see rescuers struggle valiantly to pull men out of the water. While Kofman calls this Coast Guard action a "*rescue*," he downplays the human aspect by framing the interaction in terms of animal predation or play terms: "a *dangerous cat-and-mouse game.*" He concludes his depiction by referencing a criminal "*interdiction,*" the Coast Guard term for 'arrest,' speaking about the price paid to smugglers and the procedure US officials use to process the rescued people. In contrast with the dramatic zoomed-in footage, this focus on procedure verbally downplays the terror of flailing in the open ocean darkness.

In Scene 5, we see a daylight shot of the correspondent on the deck of a boat with apprehended Dominicans lying asleep. Kofman explicitly frames this story in economic terms. There is an unspoken contrast to Cubans, who as a group are officially refugees, regardless of an individual motive: "*These Dominicans are not political refugees, they are economic refugees. Lured across these dangerous waters by the promise, or at least the hope, of prosperity.*"

Viewers then see a 10-shot scene of the homeland of the economic refugees. He says, "*They are leaving towns like Neches, a poor fishing village where yolas line the shore.*" ABC's viewers see several images illustrating poverty as Kofman speaks of a "*poor fishing village,*" "*a banking scandal,*" and "*a country at the edge of bankruptcy*" where "*the cost of basic food has gone up 300% or more.*" The Neches images were shot during a tropical rainstorm, the color scheme reinforcing images of poverty and despair in dark browns and grays. Kofman's cameraman uses a near close-up to single out a young man who sits in an unfinished shell of a house, answering off-camera questions. Kofman's voice-over points him out with a quote: "*Many, like this young man, want to join family in the US. 'If I had a chance, I would go,' he says. 'There are no jobs here. The situation is very hard.'*" As the young man speaks, viewers see a yola in the background; another shot shows a second yola dragged up to the very porch of the house.

In Scene 7, a grainy black-and-white television screen shows a public service announcement produced by the US government for Dominican television. This announcement is meant to deter people from attempting the Mona Passage crossing. Against a dark background we hear screams of panic-stricken people. Then a man can be seen falling overboard from a boat. As many hands try to reach him, he flails about. A shark—shades of Spielberg—approaches and attacks as a graphic text reads: "Los viajes ilegales son viajes a la muerte" ('Illegal voyages are death voyages'). Kofman's voice-over states: *"This ad is not working. Even those who have been returned home are undeterred."*

In the last scene, Kofman asks five Dominicans: *"How many times have you tried to get to Puerto Rico?"* Expressing no spontaneity, each volunteers the reply Kofman seeks: *"Three times," "Four times," "Twice."* This seemingly choreographed exchange cuts to another question: *"Will you try to take a yola to Puerto Rico again?"* The Dominicans play along, all shouting *"Yes! Of course!"* In the final staged action, with heavy-handed symbolism, on cue the group moves en masse together toward the camera, symbolically converging on American viewers.

Kofman describes all the events within a criminalization frame. While the digitally enhanced Coast Guard rescue footage is dramatic, Kofman's voice-over is not sympathetic, as he glosses over the economic circumstances in the Dominican Republic that create desperation.[20] Dominicans are not political refugees, like Cubans. Kofman echoes US State Department rhetoric; its video and his news reporting are meant to frighten, not inform. He argues for increased policing to reduce immigration, even as the story portrays the failure of same. By portraying the futility of these deterrents, Kofman projects the frustration shared by many Americans at the ineffectiveness of US immigration policy. Neither the sharks nor more American patrols cruising the Mona Passage will discourage the hemisphere's most wretched people.

In the next chapter, I turn to the networks' coverage of immigration policy, starting with the most important federal government event in 2004 regarding Latinos, George W. Bush's major proposal for comprehensive immigration reform. I present three news stories about Bush's January 7 proposal and a small set of stories that were generated almost immediately after his announcement. These stories will be analyzed to determine the degree to which networks' representation of policy differed from their characterizations of flesh-and-blood immigrants.

CHAPTER 5

Immigration Policy Stories

Bush's Immigration Policy Initiative

On January 7, 2004, President Bush announced a major immigration reform initiative in which he used astonishingly compassionate language
when he spoke about immigrants. During a 20-minute speech introduc-
ing his initiative for comprehensive immigration policy, Bush called immigrants "Americans by choice" who are members of families with "talent,
character, and patriotism" and who hold values such as "faith in God, love
of family, hard work, and self-reliance." He further described the United
States as a "welcoming society . . . by tradition and conviction," which is a
"stronger and better nation because of the hard work and the faith and en-
trepreneurial spirit of immigrants."[1]

This was Bush's first major domestic policy initiative of the campaign
year. For some commentators, it was a ploy aimed at increasing his share
of the November Latino vote.[2] Bush's benevolent language certainly infu-
riated political conservatives who wanted to retain control over the national discourse on the immigration policy issue, which disparaged immigrants throughout the twentieth century.[3] This discourse used various
constitutive metaphors over the years to denigrate unauthorized immigrants as a menacing army, a devastating plague, criminals, or otherwise
less-than-human creatures who deserve no better treatment than dogs or
vermin.[4] The president's language inadvertently set off a powder keg of
public apprehension in 2004 about the nation's 8 to 12 million unauthorized immigrants.

While Bush did not submit a bill to Congress before the election, immigration became the major domestic policy topic in the national public
sphere, as in the mid-1990s. On the day of his startling press conference,
each network offered full-length multisegment news reports on the Bush

proposal. We will review three of these network news reports on the same news event to permit network comparisons. While the narrative structures and visual tools used are similar, their ideological foci differ. We start with the most elaborated, the ABC report.

ABC *World News Tonight with Peter Jennings,* #3

Peter Jennings opens the evening program with a three-segment, 30-scene, 44-shot, 5-minute, 30-second report on Bush's announcement. As he looks into the camera his gaze is steady,[5] drawing viewers' attention. Jennings opens with a politically balanced statement about this key political moment:

> *Good evening, everyone. We're going to begin tonight with an issue that has invigorated and troubled the United States since the very beginning: Who has the right to be here? President Bush has proposed today that millions of foreign workers, including millions in the country illegally, should get temporary worker status in the US. It's a complex proposal, now being subjected to public opinion, and soon, by Congress.*

Jennings states that the proposal is complex. The adjectives *invigorated* and *troubled* provide color without framing the controversy. Since the question he poses allows both a legal and human rights interpretation of the political issue, his statement is politically neutral. The next scene is less neutral, opening with a full-screen graphic entitled "Immigration Reform" featuring an image of the continental United States as a somewhat jumbled jigsaw puzzle that symbolizes the national discord on this issue. This visual graphic reinforces Jennings' voice-over:

> *The basics are this: foreign workers, including about 8 million here illegally, will get temporary worker status for three years. Someone in Mexico, for example, would be free to come and go across the border. Illegals already here could work in the open and would get some legal status they do not have now.*

In his verbal description, Jennings refers to unauthorized immigrants with a criminalizing noun, *illegals.* The slides are more neutral. One reads: "Temporary worker status for 8 million people" (not the 12 million figure used by other networks). On the next slide: "some benefits and rights of full citizens," implying an alternate kind of citizenship status.

Correspondent Terry Moran opens Scene 3 by taking viewers outside into the bitter Washington winter for four shots of a street corner in *"Arlington, Virginia, just a few miles from the White House,"* where 10 day laborers bundled against the cold wait for work. Moran uses both key terms that are used by rival partisans to characterize immigrants: *undocumented* and *illegal*. *"Illegal immigrant laborers,"* he says, *"looked for work, and asked for respect."* However, Moran's overall framing does not criminalize; instead he shows the immigrants as people, including a close-up shot of a Latino man speaking English with native fluency: *"We're not criminals. We're not terrorists. We're hard workers."* Moreover, ABC's portrayal of these men waiting in bone-chilling weather for the mere chance to work, as well as Moran's sympathetic tone, offers them the respect they seek.

Then Scene 4 offers a stark contrast when Moran reports that in *"the splendor of the East Room, President Bush made his new immigration proposal, which offers millions of immigrants working here illegally a better life."* ABC allows viewers to see Bush's compassion in close-up as the president states: *"Decent, hard-working people will now be protected by labor laws, with the right to change jobs, earn fair wages, and enjoy the same working conditions that the law requires for American workers."*

This is followed by another full-screen graphic, titled "Immigration Policy," showing Latino meat processors working in hard hats and agricultural workers laboring in a field as the text reads:

- "Undocumented workers"
- "Get legal status for three years"
- "Sponsored by employers"
- "Pay one-time registration fee"
- "Three-year term could be renewed"
- "Required to return home after work expires unless they have earned a Green Card"

These expressions and images emphasize the immigrants' humanity, not their legal status.

Moran reiterates the last point, *"unless they have earned a Green Card through the normal, existing process, which is very difficult to do,"* as a caveat to bracket the arguments of opponents of Bush's initiative. The camera cuts back to Bush in close-up, affirming in voice-over: *"This program expects temporary workers to return permanently to their home countries after their period of work in the United States has expired."* Returning to the full-screen graphic, Moran's voice-over features other elements of Bush's proposal that are meant to induce immigrants to leave the US.

In the transition to Scene 6, Moran introduces opponents of the president's plan: "*Many conservative allies of the president who oppose any legalization for undocumented workers said they felt betrayed by Mr. Bush*" (emphasizing the word *betrayed*). Visuals begin with a shot of a man walking on a sidewalk without a topcoat, shivering in the winter cold. Moran in a voice-over directs our attention to this man, a key anti-immigration advocate who is pointing "*to a headline in his local paper.*" The camera provides a medium close-up of Colorado Representative Tom Tancredo, who jabs a newspaper, underscoring his opposition to the measure as he reads aloud the *Denver Post* headline while tapping on the paper in a three-beat cadence: "Bush Plan: *lets illegals stay*." He reiterates the cadence to continue, "*That is amnesty*." Slowing his tempo, he finishes with the three-beat cadence, "*And you should never, ever, do that from a public policy standpoint. It will only encourage more illegal activity.*" Tancredo's sound bite provides an exceptionally effective reframing of the story. In this way, ABC establishes the fulcrum of debate.

In the final scene of this first news segment, standing outside in the cold outside the White House, Moran provides the backstory on Bush's intent:

> *Early in his administration, immigration reform was a big issue for Mr. Bush. Then, the 9/11 terrorist attacks changed all that, making securing the border the top priority. But now, with an election year beginning, the president is trolling for Hispanic votes. And advocates for immigration reform want to see if he is serious and willing to commit political capital to get this passed, or whether it is just political.*

In reference to Latino votes, Moran uses the term *trolling*, a fishing term meaning 'to pull a baited line through the water.' He also emphasizes the terms *securing* and *serious*, indicating that his sources are skeptical that the administration will draft a bill. Moran offers no opinion as his report ends, but ABC has only begun coverage of this major Latino news event. The camera returns to a mid-shot of the anchor, Peter Jennings, who presents the second segment.

Segment 2 is labeled "A Closer Look." It opens with a shot of Jennings and the same puzzle graphic in the upper-right corner of the screen. He says, "*Let's take a closer look. It's going to be complex. It always is.*" Jennings waxes philosophical to present ABC's moderate political stance on the initiative: "*Thomas Jefferson believed Man had a natural right to live anywhere, and he never wanted to curb immigration, but the Founders generally wanted limits, and the US has had many an immigration crisis.*"

Then Jennings directly interprets Bush's proposal: "*This is not amnesty!*" emphasizing "*not*" with rising intonation and volume, to explicitly rebut the views of Tancredo and other anti-immigrant partisans. As with Moran, a full-screen graphic underscores Jennings' next points: "*For example, if an illegal worker gets temporary status to work, it doesn't automatically mean his family is protected. They may still be illegal.*" Jennings then reappears with the "A Closer Look" title insert, implying that viewers get a deeper understanding of the event as he supplies a third evaluation of Bush's plan: "*Senior Mexican officials tell us it is a step in the right direction, but they know that it may be a struggle to get it approved by Congress.*"

Opening the third reporting segment, and emphasizing the word *huge*, Jennings says unauthorized immigration "*is a huge issue in several states, notably these seven; take a look . . .*" A full-screen graphic of a map of the US appears, labeled "Illegal Immigrants," in which seven states stand out, "*where three-quarters of the illegal undocumented workers live. With more on that, here's Brian Rooney.*" As Jennings ends the second reporting segment, it is clear ABC is attempting to sustain journalistic balance as its anchor, correspondent, and graphics editors refer to and hence frame immigrants both as criminals and as noncriminals.

In Scene 2 of the third segment, viewers see eight shots of day laborers, captioned: "A CLOSER LOOK: Changing the Rules." Several turn away and others walk away from the camera, discomfited by the camera exposing their precarious legal status. In spite of this, Rooney is able to interview two men willing to answer an off-camera query: What is their opinion about the Bush guest worker plan? Close-up video clips allow viewers to see their unscripted responses, voiced in translation by Rooney: one man hopes it will allow unauthorized immigrant workers "*to better our lives,*" while another regrets that he may not be eligible since he has no record of the piece-work he has performed over the years.

In Scene 3 viewers see an older Anglo, captioned "Mark Zwick—Immigrant Advocate." Rooney will offer a center-left opinion about the proposal while repeating the competing framings, "*Some advocates for illegals, or what some call 'undocumented workers,' say the Bush program would help people who need it less.*" Though Rooney uses the term *illegal* as a noun, which immigrant advocates and journalists of color condemn,[6] he also brackets the term *undocumented* in a noun phrase that is intonationally set off from the rest of spoken sentence, marking the ideological divide with linguistic signals. Then, in Scene 4, viewers see a Mexican couple strolling in a Los Angeles park in their Sunday best. Rooney provides a voice-over: "*José and Guadalupe have lived illegally for 15 years, and wouldn't want to* return to Mexico after three years as required by the Bush proposal." Viewers see Guadalupe in close-up in the middle of an extended statement, of which Rooney translates just a bit: "We want our kids to grow up here." ABC thus has provided a range of viewpoints, including those of the immigrants themselves, in spite of its repeated reference to the noun *illegals*.

In Scene 5, the network illustrates how entwined immigrants are in the national economy, with seven shots of immigrant workers, including a shot of the folding of the US flag during the closing ceremonies of the Olympic games. In voice-over, Rooney states, "*In Salt Lake City local officials openly admit the Olympics would have been more difficult and expensive . . . without the cooks, maids, and janitors who were not even supposed to be there.*" Anti-immigrant advocate Tancredo's great fear is articulated, ironically, in a final interview with a Latino civil rights lawyer, who says that the proposal will lead to higher pay and permanent residence in the years to follow, even if the Bush's proposal explicitly avoids such provisions.

Rooney offers the final judgment of the Bush proposal, noting that its success will be determined "*by the workers themselves. Illegal immigrants are wary of government, but they sign up for anything that makes their lives better.*" This three-segment news story offers ABC viewers the two major positions, pro and con, of the Bush proposal. Although ABC prioritizes the legal status of the immigrants in its choice of terms, namely *illegals*, the network also explicitly rejects the extreme anti-immigrant view and repeatedly presents the faces and voices of unauthorized immigrants themselves. It also provides a left-of-center political stance by presenting Zwick, the immigrant rights advocate. Before January 2004, concern about immigration was limited to the border states. That would change over the course of the year. We will now compare other networks' presentations of this reform initiative with the ABC piece.

CNN *NewsNight with Aaron Brown,* #1

CNN's story is similar to the ABC story in its multiple-segment structure and length: 5 scenes and 41 shots, and relatively long at 6 minutes, 31 seconds. In contrast to ABC, CNN begins with a news brief about José Padilla, who is "*suspected of plotting with al-Qaeda to explode a dirty bomb.*" The reference to the Latino, who is an alleged terrorist, sets the emotional tone for CNN's presentation of the (Latino) immigration policy story.

Anchor Aaron Brown begins the immigration story by citing law and economics, rather than culture and race, and focusing on what kind of people constitute the nation's rightful population.

*On now to a fundamental question here at home: who has the right to live
and work in the United States, and by extension benefit from the protections
provided by law. The president today proposed a sweeping plan to revamp the
country's immigration laws, reforms that would allow millions of illegal immigrants to obtain legal status as temporary workers. The president is loath
to call this amnesty, a politically loaded term, but if it isn't amnesty it is very
close. Where jobs and immigrants intersect there's long been a flashpoint in
the country.*

Speaking about *"the right to live and work"* in the nation, Brown presents
the Bush proposal as one creating legal status for *"illegal immigrants"*
through unspecified *"protections provided by law"* that do not exist currently. While citizenship is not explicitly mentioned, the story is thus
framed around legal status, and guides viewers to think that the fundamental issue at stake in this plan is possible US citizenship for people currently unauthorized to be in the country.

ABC's Jennings emphasized that Bush made no provision for citizenship or amnesty in his proposal. CNN's Aaron Brown, on the other hand,
in the first shot of the first scene of his news story, disputes the president's
claim that his proposal makes no provision for amnesty. Even though
Brown notes that the term *amnesty* is *"politically loaded,"* he repeats the
word twice before he rolls out the story. This does more than frame the
story; it preempts judgment on the presidential initiative.

After this partisan beginning, in Scene 2, correspondent John King's
comparatively balanced introduction begins with a mid-shot of the president delivering his address in the White House; the voice-over characterizes the initiative as an *"economic necessity and a compassionate way
to bring to bring millions of illegal immigrants out of hiding."* In close-up,
Bush says: *"We must make our immigration laws more rational and more
humane . . . without jeopardizing the livelihoods of American citizens."*

The next scene is a simple graphic text of key provisions, which appear
as King lists them in a voice-over, followed by images of (highly unlikely)
border crossers, including a young man in what appears to be a dance-
hall white cowboy outfit who carries no bag or luggage, as King continues: *"One instant criticism was that Mr. Bush is offering a reward to lawbreakers."* As in his spot on ABC, Tom Tancredo is then shown using his
signature three-beat cadence, making his sound bite particularly effective:
*"People are here illegally. They **need to be** deported. People who hire them
need to be fined. If they keep doing it they **need to be** sent to jail. It's against
the law."*

Another graphic text slide states, "The White House insists it is not amnesty," as King explains that the initiative is Bush's first major policy initiative of the campaign year, attributing it to *"increasing his share of the critical Hispanic vote."* CNN's political calculation interpretation is visually reinforced by an image of seven podiums on a stage where Democratic presidential candidates will speak, as King states that all *"were quick to criticize it and up the ante,"* namely to increase the political gambit by addressing citizenship. As a third graphic presents a photo insert of Senator John Kerry, King reports that the senator criticizes the proposal because it *"fails by not providing a meaningful path to becoming legal permanent residents."* On another graphic slide, Dick Gephardt says much the same as Kerry. Three shots of faceless Latino men hammering on a roof and shucking oysters are shown as King states, *"Most Democrats favor granting permanent residency to illegal immigrants who pass a criminal background check and prove they have had jobs for at least two years."* In the final shot of the scene, a Chamber of Commerce national spokesman says, *"The reality of it is we're not going to deport all these people. So we have to come up with something to deal with the situation, or we can continue to put our head in the sand,"* asserting the economic angle of this political viewpoint.

In Scene 3 anchor Aaron Brown returns to his opening framing, supported by the story caption "Migrant Headache." Scene 3 consists of a dialogue between Brown and King about congressional response to the initiative, visually alternating between a split-screen shot of both parties and a mid-shot of King when he answers. King notes that House Majority Leader Tom DeLay has *"serious reservations about a plan from the president that Mr. DeLay says 'seems to reward illegal behavior.'"*

At this point Brown abruptly breaks from standard anchor discourse to pose a question to King using political-insider language: *"Where's the juice coming from if there's going to be an organized opposition?"* Juice means 'personal political power or influence.'[7] While visibly surprised, King quickly responds by saying in effect that DeLay could keep the initiative off the legislative calendar: *"Tom DeLay does not say that he will flatly oppose this, but if he does that would be enough juice to block it."* King goes on to cite opposition among Bush's conservative base to regularization of legal status for unauthorized immigrants, and Democratic opposition to a measure that offers no path to permanent legal status for immigrants. Brown then returns to his original frame, saying that permanent legal status is *"what many conservatives worry about. The president says he doesn't want amnesty. He doesn't want permanent legal status for those illegal immigrants."* Finally Brown asks a rhetorical question: Would Bush sign compromise legislation that might include "*blanket amnesty? Would the president sign it even though he opposes it today?*" Brown insinuates that Bush will compromise, expressing conservative anxiety and voicing hostility to any policy initiative leading to permanent legal status for immigrants.

To the CNN newsroom's credit, the following 19-shot second segment of this news story counterbalances Brown's biased reporting. Although the caption "Migrant Headache" remains on screen, Frank Buckley narrates a well-written human interest piece on one immigrant's life. Buckley's voice-over begins, "*She asked us to call her Tina González. Trusted us not to show her face.*" Viewers see a nearly pitch dark screen and must strain to see the outline of Tina's blacked-out figure working on a sewing machine. Next, in another excessively dark wide shot, viewers can just discern a bedroom. Tina is working on the sewing machine, and in the shadow a child may be perched on the bed. Buckley continues, Tina "*is in the US illegally. She has been for 15 years,*" as viewers see a close-up of Tina's hands working at the sewing machine.

The next scene presents heart-wrenching images of immigrants dashing across the San Diego border in broad daylight; several are running on or across a 10-lane freeway, accompanied by anxiety-triggering sounds of cars zooming by at full speed. Buckley narrates, "*She crossed by foot at San Ysidro like thousands before her and thousands since. She ran across the freeway with her husband and four young children.*" Among many family images, a frantic grandson tugs at his grandmother's wrist to urge her to move out of the rushing traffic. On the shoulder of the freeway, she must hitch her three-quarter-length skirt to clear a concrete barricade. Other clips show more families with children hurrying alongside speeding freeway traffic.

"*She made it to the fields and became a farmworker,*" Buckley intones, as viewers see workers in a field. The audience sees a close-up of her hands as he says, "*These hands picked countless cherries and pears and peaches and did the work, she says, that Americans didn't want to do.*"

The next shot has Tina silhouetted in the window of her bedroom. In translation she says, "*We, the workers, we clean the houses of the rich. We take care of the children of the rich. We sew the pants for these people. We bring fruits and vegetables to their table.*" The camera offers a set of shots (apparently filtered to reduce the color range) of her neighborhood of Los Angeles, which, Buckley says, "*few would consider desirable.*" Viewers return to her home, where again in digitized darkness she plays with her granddaughter, who is presumably in the grandfather's arms. Buckley notes that Tina "*still appreciates this country. An American flag hangs in her living room,"* as the audience sees the small flag on a mantle over Tina's shoulder. The footage is so dark that only a bit of the shine of her pulled-back hair can be made out. Buckley states, accompanied by corresponding visual images: *"She's worked in the fields of America, in its restaurants, in its garment industry."*

Buckley continues, *"It is a simple life with her husband and children and grandchildren. She came for a simple reason."* The camera returns to the window shot, and Tina says in translation, *"I wanted a better future for my children and my grandchildren."* In the darkness, viewers can finally make out the baby's face as Buckley says that Tina is not impressed by the president's proposal—after 15 years in the underground economy, a three-year work permit makes no sense: *"What she would like is legitimacy in a country that demands her labor."* Tina is given the last word: *"We want respect for civil rights because we're human beings."*

The second segment of the CNN story thus counterbalances Brown's censure of the presidential initiative with a potentially powerful human interest story. However, while Buckley compellingly tells the story of a woman who has courageously dealt with unauthorized immigrant life, his video editors undercut him. On the pretext of privacy, Tina's image was blacked out far beyond silhouette. At times even the outline of her face could not be perceived, visually "flattening" her in this segment.[8] This effect was intentional: video editors routinely modify such effects. For example, in a CBS story on Arizona's Proposition 200 (#117, discussed in Chapter 6), another unauthorized immigrant was also purposely silhouetted. However, the CBS video editors' treatment guaranteed Angelita's anonymity while still rendering her with far more subjectivity than CNN presented Tina. Absent an engaging visual portrait of his protagonist, Buckley's strong oral rendering of Tina's life was derailed at the network. Consequently CNN viewers were kept a safe emotional distance from Tina's story, which reduced sympathy and ultimately left Aaron Brown's original frame unchallenged.

We move next to NBC's reporting of the president's initiative, which in composition is similar to ABC's coverage in #3. We will see it offers more balanced coverage than CNN's #1, but develops polarizing visual oppositions.

NBC *Nightly News with Tom Brokaw,* #4

NBC also reported on the presidential initiative. Tom Brokaw is shown standing on the right side of the television screen in front of a full-screen semitransparent graphic. To his right, in the center-left of the television screen, is a video insert of President Bush speaking, accompanied by a large bold caption: "Immigration." Behind both the insert and Brokaw, a series of six video clips of Latino men and women working or crossing a border checkpoint fill the rest of the television screen. This graphically sophisticated establishing shot provides a rich visual accompaniment to Brokaw's introduction:

> *Now to the other big story on home front today. It's no secret that a big chunk of the American economy runs on illegal immigrants, most of them from Mexico and Central America. It's also no secret that Hispanic voters are an ever more powerful bloc in American politics. Those two realities converged today in a major speech by President Bush outlining a new plan for dealing with undocumented workers. It is the most significant step in the controversial area of immigration in years, and we begin tonight with NBC's David Gregory at the White House.*

Like the anchors at CNN and ABC, NBC's Brokaw and Gregory initially cast Bush's intention as an election-year political maneuver.[9]

While Brokaw uses both *illegal* and *undocumented* to characterize immigrants, Gregory is far less diffident. In Scene 2, he reports on the Bush administration's initiative as a human interest story. He begins with a midshot of a stout Mexican woman with strong indigenous features wearing a bright pink apron. Five shots of her follow as Gregory's voice-over identifies her: "*Like most women in Mendoza, Mexico, Sabina Estrada raises her family without a husband.*" She sits next to an old woman in the traditional black dress of Mexican widows. In a large plastic bucket Estrada kneads *masa*, 'corn dough,' as she prepares food. While creating deep sympathy for his protagonist, Gregory continues, Sabina's husband "*lives a secret life 1,400 miles away in Los Angeles, an illegal working odd gardening jobs,*" as NBC viewers see images of a North Hollywood freeway sign and a tracking shot of middle-class US residences taken from a moving vehicle, as Gregory calls her husband by the dehumanizing term, *an illegal*. In juxtaposition with sympathetic visuals of Sabina, the semiotic effect is to neutralize or normalize the dehumanizing of people, like her unseen husband, when they become immigrants.

Viewers return to central Mexico to see Estrada receive remittances at a bank teller window. Then Gregory says, "*At the White House today, the president said such families, who live separate lives for a better life, deserve help.*" NBC's camera now zooms in on George Bush making his address in the White House East Room. Before hearing from Bush, Gregory returns viewers to a Mexican main street with a middle-distant shot of pedestrians walking, with cars in the background and children on bikes in the front. He ends with a pair of middle close-up shots of Estrada hanging clothes and Bush delivering his speech, imbuing both persons with equivalent levels of subjectivity. The sound bite that NBC chose reflects Bush's best characterization of his initiative: "*Our nation needs an immigration system that serves the American economy and reflects the American dream.*" Thus, in this segment of the news story, the network frames the president's proposal as a matter of economic and humanitarian—not legal—considerations.

NBC's Scene 3 begins with an ankle-level shot of people moving along a sidewalk, which is the background for slides providing text information on the Bush plan. In large lettering the full-screen graphic caption reads "Temporary Worker Program" as Gregory intones, "*The White House is proposing a massive temporary worker program. It would give millions of undocumented workers spread across the US legal status for at least three years.*" He emphasizes the terms *massive, millions,* and *legal* as the background image changes. Viewers see a zoomed-in distance shot, which makes the 10-deep crowd of pedestrians headed toward the US/Mexico border crossing seem even more densely packed as they stand, unmoving, along a fenced-in sidewalk. The final shot shows people moving one at a time through a heavy-gauge-steel turnstile to cross the border. The next full-screen graphic background video replaces Mexicans with Anglo-American assembly-line workers, and the caption "Workers Rights." In voice-over Gregory notes that the proposal would give immigrant workers "*rights given US citizens, including a minimum wage and Social Security benefits, plus the ability to travel home without fear of being barred from returning to the US.*" From his original presentation in terms of family, Gregory reframes the presidential initiative in terms of a competition between Anglo-Americans and large numbers of immigrant workers.

Like CNN and ABC, NBC offers a set of critical evaluations. In Scene 4 Gregory notes: "*Mr. Bush insisted . . . the plan would not give illegal workers here now a leg up*" to citizenship, providing a video clip (that would repeatedly be broadcast over the course of the year) of the president saying: "*I oppose amnesty, placing undocumented workers on the automatic path to citizenship.*" NBC film editors offered their own visual criticism by displaying unflattering shots of day laborers loitering on street corners, then returning to the previous, 10-deep distance shot of pedestrians crossing the border checkpoint.

Gregory cites Bush provisions that liberals will find unacceptable, namely his insistence that unauthorized workers first leave the US to obtain permanent resident legal status. Cecilia Muñoz, identified only as "Civil Rights Advocate," is shown criticizing this provision.[10] Next Gregory states, *"Immigration reform is high-stakes politics for the White House. The president hopes to use the policy to broaden his support among Latinos, who could represent as many as 1 out of every 10 voters this fall,"* as viewers see Bush glad-handing a campaign crowd, the camera zooming in to the background to show a "Viva Bush" poster. Gregory continues by stating that proposing immigration policy reform *"has angered the president's core conservative supporters"* and broadcasting another Tom Tancredo three-beat sound bite. In the end, Gregory sums up that *"this immigration policy faces a tough fight on Capitol Hill. But politically, the president's advisers are betting he will get credit—for simply trying."*

The second segment presents a range of opinions on the proposal, opening with Brokaw in the NBC studio, in front of a blue screen featuring a California map captioned "IMMIGRATION" on the bottom. Video clips related to immigration are visible behind the map of California. Brokaw changes the metric to evaluate Bush's immigration proposal, stating: *"Undocumented workers, of course, can be found just about everywhere in this country, working in restaurant kitchens in Montana or carwashes in St. Louis, building stone walls in upstate New York. But California remains the epicenter for that population, and today's speech got mixed reviews in that state."*

NBC correspondent George Lewis describes a *"tent that the city of Los Angeles has put up as a makeshift hiring hall for day laborers, [where] a group of workers, most in this country illegally, watched the president on a local Spanish-language channel."* The perceptible apprehension on day laborers' faces in the presence of NBC cameras visually reinforces the illegality that Lewis expresses verbally. However, Lewis translates clips of interviews with two immigrants who are presented with ample subjectivity: Oscar Aguilar *"didn't like the idea [he] would be forced to go home after three years,"* while Nelson Moto thought the proposal *"did not go far enough"* toward regularizing their precarious legal status.

In contrast, the next scene consists of a quick series of seven shots of Latino immigrant workers that offers no subjectivity. Their faces are hidden in shadows or distance as the correspondent represents their numbers and economic impact, saying, *"Of the 8 to 12 million illegal immigrants in this country, almost half live in California. And they send money home, as much as $12 billion a year to Mexico. That is Mexico's second biggest source of revenue after oil."* Lewis provides an immigrant advocate, Robert Foss, who says, "*Immigrants contribute far more to the economic well-being of the United States than they consume in benefits,*" but he offsets Foss' statement by means of a voice-over that accompanies a shot of a busy Los Angeles boulevard filled with dark-skinned people:

> *But many Californians fear the impact of illegal immigration, calling it a drain on schools and social services. One reason they elected Arnold Schwarzenegger their new governor is that he promised to repeal a law granting driver's licenses to illegal immigrants.*

Lewis then shows Schwarzenegger showered with confetti, beaming on his election night. No Latinos appear on stage. Lewis' video team builds visual juxtapositions. A crowded street scene of Latino pedestrians is followed by a 1-shot of the governor at the state capitol as he proclaims, "*Rescinding that law was the right thing to do. And I thank you for your bipartisan support.*"

Lewis' video team continues to present visual contrasts, moving between an iconic shot of Schwarzenegger (in a dark suit with white shirt and solid tie) and four shots of a protest rally (held 10 years prior) of hundreds of Latino youth vigorously protesting Proposition 187, California's infamous referendum. Next, NBC once again shifts visual signs, from energetic placard-waving crowds (including a Spanish-speaking voice heard on a bullhorn, rallying the marchers), to a single dark-suited White man, the funder of Proposition 187. Ron Prince is shown speaking calmly in 1994. The news audience hears him say that Proposition 187 "*will be an opportunity for the people of California to say, 'We do not want more illegal immigration. We want this stopped.'*"

With historical footage NBC juxtaposes opposing narratives and visual contrasts. Lewis underlines the visual contrast at the end of his report. He stands still, a single White man, on Los Angeles' busy Broadway Street amid scores of Latino pedestrians moving past. Lewis sustains his professional objectivity by answering the question that Brokaw posed about Californians' view of the Bush plan: "*Mr. Bush may have a hard time promoting his proposal on immigration here in California. Conservatives are calling it a sellout; Latino groups are calling it half-baked.*"

While NBC's Lewis spoke about the irreconcilable opposition to Bush's plan, the accompanying semiotics of this second news segment display a visual and audio contrast. NBC presented Latinos and pro–immigrant rights groups as loud, restive, non-White, faceless multitudes while presenting their rivals with full human subjectivity—dignified White males in Brooks Brothers suits who maintain a rational and bipartisan position in the debate. NBC viewed Bush's initiative as primarily a political ploy to garner support from Latino voters. Following the structure of its multi-segment story, the network's stance on unauthorized immigration is that, while individual immigrant stories may be poignant, there are already too many immigrants and so federal policy should restrict their entry and control their disruptive presence.

Summing Up

The network stories on the January 7 presidential immigration policy initiative share several features: each consisted of multisegment reports that at points offered humanizing and dehumanizing imagery about immigrants; each quoted the same anti-immigration advocate; and each presented multiple framings of the initiative or of immigration policy reform. However, there were also notable differences. Each network had a recognizable message that it wanted its audience to remember. While ABC began by posing a key question about immigration—*Who has the right to be here?*—and Peter Jennings referred to Thomas Jefferson, the take-away answer was that human rights are a secondary issue. What matters is statute. So, since Bush's initiative was seen as a possible election-year ploy, ABC lamented that many decent, hard-working immigrants will continue to live in bad circumstances.

CNN's narrower question—*Who has the right to live and work in the United States, and by extension benefit from the protections provided by law?*—skirted the human rights issue. In spite of balanced reporting by correspondents, what was most salient about CNN's news report was how Aaron Brown commandeered the news story frame and rejected Bush's proposal out of hand. CNN's ultimate take-away message was that no immigration policy reform is better than anything that offers current unauthorized immigrants any legal protection.

Finally, NBC did not pose similar questions, because it judged (correctly) that Bush's announcement would not lead to a bill in Congress. Standing in front of a visually rich backdrop with an image of Bush over images of Latinos, Tom Brokaw characterized Bush's effort as a ploy to appeal to Latino voters. So NBC framed it primarily as a Beltway issue, insinuating that it should not to be taken seriously. However, NBC did not anticipate that immigration would become one of the country's more gripping policy issues in the coming years.

As for visual imagery, the networks invested significant resources in this high-profile news story. One purpose is pizzazz, visually enhancing what blasé viewers might consider just another presidential press briefing. Clarity is another purpose. This policy initiative involved a complex set of new information, which the newsrooms carefully organized to articulate network political messages in a number of ways.

One conventional observation about television news programming is that when anchors frame a story, they preempt later, alternative frames. Aaron Brown's performance is one extreme. However, throughout Chapter 2 we saw that this is not always the case. In #60, CBS anchor Dan Rather was visibly stunned by correspondent James Stewart's judgment that José Padilla was guilty. Moreover, on occasion, the anchor may simply be ignored. Later in this chapter we will see such an example, when correspondent James Hattori entirely disregards his anchor's opening query.

In these three stories, we find examples of how the visual elements enhance the verbal statement of the anchor, as when NBC's sophisticated visual effects were used to support Tom Brokaw's framing of the presidential initiative as a political stratagem. Visuals can be used to humanize immigrants, swiftly providing them with full human subjectivity, as when ABC's Terry Moran presented them in a sequence of close-ups. David Gregory narrated a human interest story that introduced viewers to Sabina Estrada, whose immigrant husband lives and works thousands of miles distant from her. While Sabina did not speak on camera, ABC's newsroom visuals nonetheless humanized her daily life.

But visuals can also reduce the viewer's perception of a person's humanity. The same NBC story stripped Latinos of their subjectivity with a zoomed-in distance shot showing them as dark-skinned masses. At two separate points in the story, NBC depicted these men and women moving to a border checkpoint like cattle in a funnel chute corral.

Even individual psychology can be intimated visually. In the shot that introduced Tom Tancredo to ABC viewers, Tancredo shivered as he walked without a topcoat in winter weather, visually rendering him to be a cold (hearted) man.

The visuals can also offer an independent subtext to the correspondent's spoken words, visual meanings not vocalized by the correspondent. NBC's George Lewis contrasted proponents and opponents in California in regard to national immigration policy reform. Lewis's spoken text was studiously neutral, but the visuals were not. The pro-reform advocates portrayed were raucous young Latino students who chanted slogans in the streets. Their adversaries were White men dressed in conservative suits who spoke in pressrooms or at podiums in calm (read: rational) conversational tones.

Finally, visuals can entirely undercut a message. While CNN's Frank Buckley narrated a compelling story about Tina González, a proud and resilient woman who lived most of her life in the shadows as she contributed to the nation's wealth, CNN video editors did not visually support Buckley's framing. They did not merely silhouette Tina's face to protect her from deportation, but blacked her out. While elements of her home were shown at an appropriate exposure, Tina's image was excessively underexposed. Even if the CNN camera crew took the original digital footage without recourse to a light meter, studio editing could have corrected this problem. This video editing reduced the probability that CNN viewers would identify with the protagonist of Buckley's story—unless they closed their eyes and just listened to his story.

Finally, videotape is a powerful multimodal medium, but a skilled speaker can still command a story's framing. Tom Tancredo always got across his message, in one case with tapping a pencil on a newspaper, repeating his message in an emphatic three-beat refrain. He made a memorable impression in part because he spoke with a simple cadence that was reinforced by paralinguistic signals.

In sum, the January 7 White House address abruptly made immigration deterrence a newsworthy issue. To conclude this chapter we will look at two stories that would not have run on network evening news before President Bush announced his immigration policy reform initiative. One is a sham story that should not have been broadcast at all—but that was broadcast twice. First, however, we look at a set of stories about the suburban sites where human smugglers drop off their human cargo to explore how the issue was covered in light of the president's initiative.

Phoenix "Drop Houses"

In early 2004, US Immigration and Customs Enforcement (ICE) officers and local police officers began arresting human traffickers accused of using suburban houses to hide groups of Mexican migrants.[11] Suburbs are typically far from the working-class neighborhoods with large Latino populations, and are less likely to attract the attention of US immigration agents. However, suburbs make good places to conceal illicit activity, since suburbanites are less apt to watch out for one another or know one another's business. Suburbs are tracts of detached single-family houses, often with fenced-in yards, at times set back from the street and equipped with electric gates that open by remote control. Smugglers and suburbanites alike can drive dark-window SUVs into closed garages, easily avoiding contact with any nearby residents. It is not unusual for suburbanites to live years without knowing the name of the person living next door, and monthly (much less yearly) interaction beyond a cursory wave or "hello" can be rare, since privacy is considered a right to be respected. Thus clandestine migrants can remain concealed in these "drop houses" until they pay the traffickers for their passage and are picked up by employers or families. In response, ICE agents developed new investigative tools.

NBC News Brief, #15

On February 12, one month after President Bush's stunning immigration policy reform announcement, NBC's Brian Williams anchored a 1-shot, 23-second, 54-word news brief on drop houses in Phoenix. Without graphic or video support, he gravely voices the news event as he frames the narrative:

> *There is word tonight of a <u>disturbing</u> discovery earlier today in a well-to-do suburb of Phoenix. About 160 illegal immigrants from Mexico and Central America crammed inside a single home in Mesa, Arizona. The immigrants— <u>men</u>, <u>women</u> and <u>children</u>—were discovered locked in bedrooms with <u>deadbolt</u> locks. Police arrested several men **believed** to be immigrant smugglers.*

Williams does not frame the story as involving criminal immigrants. Rather it is an immigrants-as-victims frame, starting with the alliteration, "<u>*disturbing*</u> *discovery*," to create anxiety and concern, rather than anger and resentment. Williams stresses the adjective. He also stresses each of the three types of people about whom the audience should be concerned: "*<u>men</u>, <u>women</u>, and <u>children</u>*," while the modifying word in "<u>*deadbolt*</u> *locks*" also emphasizes their imprisonment. His reporting style involves staccato phrasing and head gestures. As Williams delivers the phrase "*several men **believed** to be immigrant smugglers*," he nods his head as he says "***believed***," indicating he suspects their guilt.

However, his use of the word *disturbing* does not refer to the crime of trafficking human beings. Instead, these traffickers have trespassed the sanctity of a "*home . . . in a well-to-do suburb.*" Little matter that the crime scene was likely no one's home. What disturbs Williams is that the criminals defiled one of America's inviolable cultural spaces.

CNN News Brief, #24

Six days later, on February 18, CNN's Aaron Brown also reported on the Arizona drop houses. He uses less emotional language in the 2-scene, 6-shot, 56-word, 20-second brief, hence seeming to speak more objectively[12] than Williams:

> Before we go to break, a few other stories that made news today around the country, beginning in Phoenix, where authorities today discovered two houses harboring at least 100 undocumented immigrants between them. Two other so-called drop houses were also found in and around Phoenix in recent days, at least 288 illegal immigrants arrested in all, making this one of the busiest weeks in memory, according to immigration officials.

However, the CNN report is far from neutral, and objectivity is not a sufficient criterion to characterize the political message of the brief. While NBC's Brian Williams' narration referred to immigrants as victims, CNN's Aaron Brown refers to immigrants as both *undocumented* and *illegal*, thus involving two constitutive metaphors: IMMIGRANT AS CRIMINAL and IMMIGRANT AS UNDOCUMENTED.[13] In the 20-second, 2-scene, 6-shot CNN news brief, Brown's statement that *"at least 100 undocumented immigrants"* was the sole instance of the semantic source domain UNDOCUMENTED, which diminishes the immigrants' violation of federal law. However, in addition to mentioning *"288 illegal immigrants,"* six separate visual signs and four text captions refer to the IMMIGRANT AS CRIMINAL metaphor. The visual CRIMINAL imagery begins after Aaron Brown's establishing shot in the CNN newsroom. In Scene 2, the video of the news story is presented in the upper-left two-thirds of the television screen. The bottom-right third of the screen is taken up with the CNN logo, the teletype text of unrelated news stories, and the story title "Immigrant Bust." The first camera shot of this scene is a close-up shot of yellow crime scene tape taking up the bottom third of the screen space. The fluttering yellow tape takes up so much of the foreground that viewers can only presume that it sets off the nondescript house referred to by Brown as the *"so-called drop house,"* the scene of a crime.

In the second shot, tall White ICE agents escort detained Latinos across the screen, followed by a foregrounded police car and an ICE bus; then six Latino men, women, and children face the camera from behind a chain-link fence. The group is shown incongruously laughing at a time when they have apparently been arrested. In the fifth shot, ICE agents frisk five men leaning against the previously mentioned bus; this video has been taken through a chain-link fence, indicating that the CNN camera crew contrived to dramatize with camera angles the arrests they witnessed. A caption, "IMMIGRANT BUST," in capital letters, is shown in each of the four final video clips used. CNN graphics add a dynamic (moving) streak of color, underlining the caption and underscoring the caption's semantic content. Lastly, CNN news stories at times use low-volume dramatic background music to increase emotional gravity or heighten the suspense of reports. Such music was used here.

In sum, this news story was concise, but neither neutral nor objective. In addition to verbal information, CNN broadcast 12 CRIMINAL IMMIGRANT signs and 1 UNAUTHORIZED IMMIGRANT sign in its 20-second news brief. In Chapter 7 we will return to this news story to illustrate how television news viewers cognitively process information that comes to them in multiple semiotic modalities.

Second CNN News Brief, #28

Two weeks later, on March 3, CNN returned to the drop house news event with another news brief. This time Anderson Cooper anchored, stating:

> Some other stories from around the nation to tell you about right now . . .
> In Phoenix police discovered nearly 200 illegal immigrants inside an upscale property, about 100 to 150 people were inside the south Phoenix home and an additional 20 to 30 people were in a guest house on the same property. Officers went to the home after getting a call from a neighbor about suspicious activity.

As in the previous CNN news brief, the visual presentation was extensively developed. This short report (1 scene, 7 shots, 18 seconds) was part of a string of other news briefs, so it did not begin with a shot of Cooper. As in much CNN news programming, the videotaped imagery of the story occupied the upper-left two-thirds of the television screen. The other third of the screen was tied up with the looping teletype-style text headlines of other stories, the CNN logo, and the story title, "Immigrant Raid."

In comparison to Aaron Brown's, Cooper's spoken text and delivery are comparatively balanced. He voices only one criminalizing word, and twice refers to the immigrants as people. The story title caption and the videotaped images are also less inflammatory than those in the February CNN story. The seven camera shots are quick and diverse, first zooming in to men who are being guided into a truck, apparently being detained by ICE agents, followed by a shot of a Latina who is escorted by a female ICE agent. Viewers see a little boy of about four years old being led by the wrist by a man. Then the audience sees a female ICE agent leading a man and another small boy. The camera shifts abruptly to a very quick shot of a modest home—presumably where the immigrants were found.[14] The next shot zooms in close to a person's face through the window, possibly a visual reference to the suspicious neighbor who blew the whistle. Finally, CNN viewers see a poorly composed shot of ICE agents guiding people into a vehicle.

By this time, according to Arizona newspaper reports, ICE agents had "rounded up nearly 750 undocumented immigrants and arrested 20 suspected smugglers in 13 drop houses" in less than a month.[15] If anything, this CNN report underplayed the drama of the figures involved in the ICE operation on Phoenix drop houses, dubbed "Operation ICE Storm." Unlike Brown, Cooper did not focus on criminalizing but instead emphasized the large numbers of migrants (described as *"people"*) who were found in another *"home"* in a middle-class suburb, implying that human trafficking occurs not only in destitute parts of the world far from viewers' everyday reality, but in regular middle-class suburbs. CNN also refuted stereotypes by visually presenting children and women, visually demonstrating that families make up a significant part of immigration today. Finally, the newsroom's view on this news event apparently was in flux, since no single narrative is articulated.

CNN Feature-Length Story, #30

The next day, CNN ran a third story on the Arizona drop houses, this time on its series called "Segment 7." This 16-scene, 42-shot, 3-minute, 39-second story promised to amplify the network's posture on immigration policy in 2004. A library-like setting provides Anderson Cooper with greater visual gravitas than if he were speaking from the regular news anchor table. At the bottom of the screen runs the omnipresent CNN looping tickertape, and a story caption: "Human-Smuggler Crackdown." With comic-book simplicity, Cooper solemnly merges the serious and the silly:

> *The aim of the Homeland Security Act is to keep the bad guys out of the country and everyone else safe. Tightening security, the border's cracking down on illegal immigrants is one piece of the plan, certainly. Human smuggling rings in Phoenix have become a major target.*

CNN framed the story as a crime within a crime, an illicit enterprise that traffics in criminals. The CNN story is composed of scenes that alternate between rapidly changing many-shot sets of images and single-shot mid-camera scenes of Cooper to reinforce his authority as a correspondent.

Scene 2 is a quick, 8-shot sequence of video clips of the Phoenix coverage, with a wide distance shot of ICE personnel directing immigrants to a detention bus or van. Viewers see a manacled man, a mid-shot of three women detainees walking toward the vehicle, and a mid-shot of a dozen detainees walking to a waiting van, the previously shown image of a four-year-old child being led by the wrist, and another child of about seven poignantly lugging a suitcase twice his size. The visuals again underline the reality that unauthorized immigrants include families and children. Cooper's voice-over in this scene frames the story: "*In this raid, 1 of 17 in the last month, authorities discovered nearly 250 illegal immigrants crammed into two so-called drop houses in Phoenix, this on the heels of one of the busiest few weeks in history for human smuggling busts.*" With the words *raid, illegal immigrants, human smuggling busts*, two mentions of *authorities*, in addition to the title caption, he frames the news event as effective policing of illegal activity.

Scene 3 is a mid-shot of the Phoenix police chief, who proudly reports: "*In the last few weeks . . . we have found maybe 1,000 people in these safe houses . . . smuggled into the country.*" Scene 4 shows another bust in what seems to be a backyard. In voice-over, Cooper repeats the snappy name, Operation ICE Storm, "*the work of a new Homeland Security initiative.*" To assuage viewers who believe the federal government is doing nothing about immigration, the CNN newsroom reinforces the federal government's role in this apparently successful action by adding two lines to the running story caption:

Department of Homeland Security
Human-Smuggling Crackdown

In Scene 4 viewers see a mid-shot of a well-spoken Latino who is captioned "Michael Garcia, Assistant Secretary, US Immigration and Customs Enforcement," who tells CNN viewers about the increased personnel placed in Phoenix with this operation. In Scene 5 Cooper articulates CNN's explanation for these suburban drop houses in Phoenix in voice-over, as viewers see three ICE helicopter aerial shots of desert surveillance followed by a rattlesnake's-eye view of the desert: "*After 9/11, tougher border patrols in California and Texas forced illegal immigrants into the most dangerous and underpatrolled parts of the Arizona desert. Phoenix became the bottleneck and a lucrative smuggling operation sprang up.*" In Scene 6, Garcia returns to focus on the "bad guys," using nonhuman constitutive metaphors for immigrants, saying: "*Smuggling is being done by organized criminal enterprises. And the point is, in a particular time period, smuggling aliens across the border may be the most profitable thing to be doing.*" Next, Cooper addresses the smugglers' motives: "*More profitable than drugs, even, and it carries a lighter sentence. Smugglers can charge illegal immigrants up to $2,000 a head, cash on delivery.*"

CNN never provides viewers a full explanation of why smugglers enjoy a seller's market. For a fuller story, we turn to Daniel González, who wrote an article series on drop houses for the *Arizona Republic*:

> The proliferation of so-called drop houses in the Valley is a symptom of the booming immigrant-smuggling trade in Phoenix, which despite stepped-up enforcement at the border remains the nation's main hub for transporting undocumented immigrants from the U.S.–Mexico border to other parts of the country, experts say. "Organized smuggling of migrants from Mexico to the United States has mushroomed in the last 10 years, as a direct consequence of the U.S. strategy of concentrated border enforcement, which has significantly raised the physical risk of illegal entry," said Wayne Cornelius, director of the Center for Comparative Immigration Studies at the University of California, San Diego. "Smugglers are now necessary to minimize the risk of dying in the deserts as well as to evade detection by the Border Patrol," Cornelius added. "The smugglers' operations have expanded in response to the stronger demand for their services. The U.S. border-enforcement strategy has not been effective in deterring large numbers of unauthorized migrants from attempting entry, but it has made professional people-smugglers indispensable."[16]

Thus drop houses are a dashboard warning light, not the problem with the car. Migrants are desperate, and have no choice. If they live in the Caribbean, they must brave the ocean in little more than rowboats. If they live south of the border, they now face the pitiless Arizona desert. Since despair—not insanity—motivates them, they turn to smugglers to better their chances of survival. CNN's report addresses the superficial, not fundamental, reasons for increased smuggling.

Instead, CNN's Cooper elaborates on the cruelty of smugglers:

> *They may tell them, I'll charge you $1,500, but once they get them across, that price can go up to $10,000 . . . Illegal immigrants have been kidnapped, raped, and even murdered by smugglers. And then there's the gang warfare. Since*

it's getting harder for smugglers . . . they're finding it a lot easier just to steal another smuggler's group . . . This very scenario played out in broad daylight on a major highway near Tucson. Four people were killed in a shoot-out over human cargo.

The prurient element is stoked with stock footage of the dead Mexicans: "*The shoot-out on Interstate 10 last November clearly demonstrates the violence that these criminal smuggling organizations will go through to transport human cargo.*"

In the final scene Cooper reiterates his praise of US policing authorities: "*In the Phoenix area alone, law enforcement officials blame human smuggling rings for a 400% increase in violent crime. The authorities <u>are</u> cracking down*," he says, emphasizing the word *are*. Then the camera turns to a seemingly random Anglo-American man reiterating, "*It scares me. It scares me very much.*"[17] CNN then closes with shots of immigrants in a crouching run along an Arizona irrigation culvert, and Cooper says, "*And desperate immigrants are undeterred.*"

Fear is the primary message that CNN conveys; this problem threatens the viewer's own tract-home subdivision. The secondary message: the Department of Homeland Security has stepped up its policing. These messages provoke alarm in and then give relief to viewers; the story does not further understanding, passing over the fundamental reasons for immigration.

New Flood of Immigrants?
First NBC/Telemundo Report, #17

Many in Washington and across the country believed that George Bush's announcement on immigration policy would have unintended consequences. In a February 15 story, the NBC newsroom explored the possibility that his election-year political ploy would have a demographic downside.

Along the border between the United States and Mexico, federal agents are waiting to see if President Bush's new proposal to allow more so-called guest workers into the country will bring more people over the border <u>illegally</u>. That story tonight from Gustavo Mariel of NBC's Spanish-language network, Telemundo.

NBC anchor John Seigenthaler's wording may seem neutral, asking: Are more people crossing the border because Bush proposed reform? However, he reinforces criminality by emphasizing the word *illegally*. Moreover, he lengthened the syllables of the words *so-called*, hesitated just a beat before the euphemism *guest worker*, and sustained (not dropping/lowering) the intonational contour at the end of the phrase *into the country*. Since a fall of intonation at the end of a clause would have signaled that the assertion was normal, his intonational contour signaled skepticism or some other kind of incredulity toward Bush's initiative.

Seigenthaler posed a legitimate demographic question—if prematurely, since Bush had made his White House announcement only five weeks before. Seigenthaler's intonation hints that he expects increased immigration rates, so how NBC addresses this query will indicate what NBC means by investigative news. Its first move was to assign the piece to a Spanish-language affiliate reporter, Gustavo Mariel of Telemundo. At first nothing in the news story seems different. In Scenes 2 and 3, viewers see five shots of ICE agents arresting immigrants in mid- and wide shots that do not show anyone's face, reducing the perceived human subjectivity of both agents and immigrants.

However, Scene 4 moves to a novel setting for reporting on immigration. Viewers see a very wide interior shot of a clean, brightly lit, freshly painted three-story apartment complex from its central covered patio. The camera zooms in to an over-the-shoulder shot of a man surveying a dozen newspaper clippings, and then in to a headline: *Anuncian plan migratorio*, 'Migration plan announced.' As the correspondent will later note, this is La Casa del Migrante de Tijuana, the 'Migrant's House in Tijuana' (Baja California). However, the correspondent does not inform us if the migrant shelter is a government agency, a church-based project, or another kind of nongovernmental agency.

In voice-over Telemundo correspondent Mariel says: "*About a million people were caught trying to enter the US illegally last year. Some this year are coming for the first time, attracted by widespread coverage of President Bush's immigration proposal.*" Thus Mariel confirms Seigenthaler's expectation.

Scene 5 shows three shots of about 60 Latino men eating well and comfortably at the migrant shelter. Mariel singles out Ernesto Duarte, a very young man whose answer to an off-camera question Mariel translates: "*The president promised legal papers to all Mexicans, and I want to see if it's true.*" Taking it at face value, the reporter registers no surprise at Duarte's misunderstanding of Bush's proposed policy, nor does he probe further into the motives of Duarte or other men seated in the room.

Instead, in the next scene Mariel works to confirm that Duarte's misunderstanding is widely held by taking NBC viewers to the other end of the

2,000-mile US/Mexican border, to Matamoros, Tamaulipas. Here Mariel locates a second immigrant, Danilo Jiménez, who seems to say the same thing. Speaking in an understated low voice, Jiménez is a more mature and credible subject than Duarte. Mariel translates in voice-over that Jiménez *"heard on television about a new program to legalize immigrants, so he traveled all the way from Nicaragua."* These two people are Mariel's proof that *"along the border, many believe they're seeing just the beginning of a wave of undocumented migrants."*

Gustavo Mariel chose not to give details on Mexican newspaper clippings viewers saw pinned to the migrant shelter bulletin board or the televised Nicaraguan reports Jiménez mentioned. Thus NBC viewers have two anecdotal reports that Latin American news outlets are misrepresenting the White House proposal as *"a new program to legalize immigrants."* Mariel could have placed the smoking gun for recent increased immigration in the hands of Latin American news media. Breaking such a story with international implications would have been a tremendous coup for the Telemundo reporter. But he does not pursue this angle.

Instead, in Scene 8 Mariel continues to allege that the White House announcement has led to greater immigration rates, citing historical precedent: *"It happened before—after President Reagan declared amnesty for undocumented immigrants in 1986,"* as viewers see historical footage of Reagan. Mariel goes on to say, *"The numbers surged from 3 million then to an estimated 7 to 11 million now,"* without stopping to explain how an 18-year population increase can be compared to the purported increased immigration of a single month after a single news conference. His comparison bolsters his claim only by allusion. Further, while Mariel underscores that Reagan granted amnesty to unauthorized immigrants, he fails to note that Bush explicitly rejected amnesty.

Mariel ends his report with three more scenes, first with excerpts from a less-than-articulate immigrant rights advocate who tries to evade an off-camera question about possible immigration increases. In the final shots, Mariel replays stock footage of ICE agents covering the body of a dead migrant with a sheet. A seemingly staged enactment of immigrants marching along railroad tracks in broad daylight plays out. Having confirmed by means of specious reasoning that President Bush's proposal has led to an increase in illegal immigration, in voice-over Mariel finally makes an accurate statement: *"Only a month after President Bush announced his plan, the US Border Patrol says it's too early to tell what will actually happen this time."*

To his credit, Gustavo Mariel offers US viewers a series of personable views of immigrant men, with well-constructed mid-shots of two individuals who are named and whose voices are heard. He also provides US network viewers images of men who are about to immigrate. These men exhibit none of the anxiety and wariness that is often projected by news footage shot on the US side of the border. Network viewers rarely see unauthorized migrants comfortable in their own skin, undaunted by the specter of prosecutable legal status, unblinkingly facing the camera, and resolute as they prepare for their dangerous border crossing.

However, the most credible statement that Mariel makes comes only after he has totally undermined it. Moreover, his shallow understanding of the history of unauthorized immigration is demonstrated by his failure to consult migration experts such as Wayne Cornelius, Alejandro Portes, or Douglas Massey,[18] who might have provided his viewers a deeper historical understanding of the possible effects of the White House announcement. Finally, Mariel does not reveal a journalist's "nose for the story." He does not seek to corroborate the migrants' striking testimony that Spanish-language news sources are broadcasting misinformation, even though it would transform his pedestrian account into a breaking news story. Whether or not Jiménez' assertion can be verified, final responsibility for this poorly constructed news story falls on the NBC news editors who allowed its national broadcast. To their discredit, this story televised the answer they sought, without a valid basis of support.[19]

As it turned out, NBC was correct about one premise of the story; Bush's call for immigration reform would have huge unintended consequences. However, the effects of Bush's announcement (and his lack of follow-through) would not begin to appear until the first quarter of 2005. Then, after his reelection, so-called Minutemen would label him "traitor" and make their symbolic stand to defend the nation from what they believed was an immigrant invasion. By year's end the US House Judiciary Committee chair would move a bill, HR 4437, through the House to make it a felony to be an unauthorized immigrant worker, or for a citizen to help such an immigrant. In response, a new social movement of 5 million marchers would arise, calling for respect and immigrant rights in hundreds of cities across the country. Congress would not receive, much less pass, a comprehensive immigration reform bill. Instead, it would pass the 2006 Secure Fence Act, which authorized the construction of hundreds of miles of additional fencing along the US/Mexico border, as well as more checkpoints and advanced technology like satellites and unmanned aircraft, which further militarizes the border.[20] Finally, increasing numbers of frustrated state and municipal lawmakers, who waited in vain for national legislation, began to enact hundreds of regulations to allow local authorities to apprehend unauthorized migrants, in effect usurping federal authority.[21]

Second NBC Report, #48

NBC news editors addressed the question of immigration again on April 30 in a feature-length installment of the NBC "In-Depth" series. NBC correspondent James Hattori does not go into more depth, but instead offers viewers a more polished, longer, yet even more superficial, report than Mariel.

Scene 1 begins dramatically with an unusually wide shot of the entire newsroom stage, with anchor Brian Williams almost unrecognizable in the distance. Williams sits at the anchor desk with a full-sized backscreen that will show six video images. These images prefigure the story. The full backscreen footage includes men in hooded jackets with their hands on their heads, walking in the desert at night. A mid-shot silhouette of a barbwire fence zooming to a close-up and on to an extreme close-up of one barb on the barbwire is juxtaposed with a very wide shot of a line of people moving across an immense desert plateau. Visually, this 5-shot zoom to a single barb the size of Williams' head expresses the rise of criminality crossing borders, as he introduces the story:

> NBC News, "In Depth" tonight. The rise of illegal immigrants flooding across the Mexican border into the US. There's been a jump of 25% in just the past six months, which translates into as many as 2,000 illegal crossings a day. NBC's James Hattori explains what's driving this desperation.

Williams frames immigrants as a dramatically increasing criminal menace, describing thousands of daily "*illegal crossings*" and a "*flood*" of "*illegal immigrants*." He then charges Hattori to address a key issue that the networks frequently neglect, the source of immigrant desperation.

Hattori's report begins in Scene 2, which offers 12 camera shots that illustrate the cycle of unauthorized immigration. Shot 1 is taken from inside a border patrol truck driven by an ICE agent who points out features of the landscape. This is followed by a down-the-line shot of a border fence along the rolling hills of Nogales, Arizona, making evident the economic contrast of the Mexican and US sides of the border. Shot 3 shows border patrol officer Joe Penco, now out of his truck, asking in Spanish for documents from two individuals.

In voice-over Hattori says, *"This is part of this border right here in No-gales, Arizona; the 'Spring Rush' is on for border patrol agents like Joe Penco. Coping with an influx of Mexican workers seeking farm jobs."* As he states this, viewers see Shot 4, an ankle-level camera angle of immigrants moving away from the camera at dusk—the same staged footage used in Gustavo Mariel's story. The camera angle shows women who are not dressed for travel; one carries a baby with a hand-knit blanket hanging to the moth-er's knees for display, not trekking. In contrast, Shot 5 offers footage of im-migrants carrying heavy backpacks, purposefully moving along the desert trail in single file.

In the next shot Officer Penco explains the seasonal movement of im-migrants in terms similar to birds or deer, saying, *"Traditionally they re-turn in the spring months."* The migratory animal theme is repeated vi-sually in the next shot, an extreme wide angle on a group of immigrants moving across a desert plateau. An aerial shot taken from an ICE heli-copter follows 15 to 30 people moving across the desert in single file—the same long-distance shot used to introduce the story. Hattori's professional newscaster voice-over takes over from Penco: *"But after four years of de-cline, there's an apparent surge in illegal immigration."*

Now viewers see people climbing up and jumping from the top of the international border's 12-foot fence strung with barbed wire. Then view-ers see two people running headlong across a desert, as if being chased. Next a single ICE agent is illuminated by spotlights against the dark. The NBC audience can make out that she has custody of a group of immigrants squatting or seated on the desert floor. In the next shot viewers see and hear an ICE agent slam the padlocked door of an ICE van which closes on crouching figures inside. Hattori finishes his background: *"Nationwide, 530,000 people have been detained for trying to cross the border over the last six months, a 25% increase compared to last year. And more than half were picked up in Arizona."* The visual motif in Scene 2 dehumanizes im-migrant workers, describing a seasonal catch-and-release cycle of migra-tory animals. This motif becomes the assumed background information of this NBC story, onto which Hattori adds a narrative conflict: this year's seasonal increase is marked by many more immigrants.

Scene 3 establishes that officials corroborate NBC's claim that immi-grant crossings have increased, showing the border patrol commissioner in an office setting. His words are taken to support the NBC narrative. How-ever, the US border protection commissioner actually refers to apprehen-sions, rather than crossings: *"The border patrol is apprehending, on aver-age, close to 2,000 a day."* Scene 3 also reinforces the theme of a migratory cycle. Some will be caught by ICE agents and sent back to Mexico, where they will try to cross again.

Using the border patrol source, Hattori deftly develops a conventional narrative far more quickly than Mariel did in #17. The more experienced US news correspondent confidently disregards anchor Brian Williams' original query about the source of desperation, setting out a predictable narrative instead, with a simple plotline, a cast of two-dimensional characters, and a complicating conflict. Regular network news viewers will (tacitly) recognize the standard news narrative, where little new information can be expected and standard omissions are well defined. Viewers will not learn more than they already know about why people risk death to cross a desert, much less why their numbers have purportedly increased.

In Scene 4, in place of a preliminary answer to Williams' query, Hattori appears in a full-length body shot, arms outstretched to display the desert's expanse: "*This is why the border here is so porous: the wide-open, sparsely populated high desert that spans across much of southern Arizona.*" Hattori begins his narrative as viewers see a long shot of a Mexican town, then a series of wide and mid-shots of an unpaved main street, open spaces between buildings, and pickup truck traffic kicking up dust. We see Mexican men, only men, in the back of a pickup truck, loitering on a porch, or crossing an unpaved street with piles of rubble where sidewalks should be, and hear a single dog barking in this spaghetti Western scenario.

In Scene 5, Hattori delivers the centerpiece of his narrative in voice-over: "*In Sásabe, a small Mexican town just across the border, some believe there is a new, once-in-a-lifetime incentive to sneak into the US.*" This scene consists of three shots of an unnamed man who warily says: "*Creo que sí. Se van pa'allí . . .*" ('I think so. They [would] go there . . .') His guarded tone does not match Hattori's high-spirited free translation, which speeds along the narrative:

> *This man says if they really give them amnesty, it's better to live over there than here. He's referring to President Bush's proposal last January for a new guest worker program that would grant status to illegal migrants already working in the US.*

Before Hattori's voice drowns out the unnamed man's answer, the audience hears a bit of his minimal response. Conflicting body language suggests Hattori's translation may not be accurate. While Hattori stands legs wide and leaning forward to get more from his interviewee, the body language of the unidentified man and his companion remains guarded. The unnamed speaker leans cross-legged against a building and away from his interrogator; his arms are hidden behind him, as may be his real opinion. His companion's arms are also crossed, suggesting reserve.

The NBC correspondent punches home Mariel's thesis with a stronger lead-in: a *"new, once-in-a-lifetime incentive to sneak into the US."* By doing so, Hattori may be putting words into other people's mouths to claim increased migration in the past four months is due to Bush's proposal. Hattori implies that promised amnesty (which Bush explicitly disavowed) is the reason for the purported (and erroneous) 25% increase in immigration cited by Williams at the outset of this story.

Hattori passes over these incongruities and moves his story apace. Scene 6 opens with a ¾-shot of Bush speaking in the White House. NBC network news viewers then see the consequences of Bush's actions: a busy border town street with Spanish-language business signs and a crowd of brown-skinned shoppers.

Another cursory interview clip follows. An immigrant advocate is shown, saying, *"They feel that Bush will implement certain programs that will help the undocumented worker."* In the context of Hattori's claim that Bush's proposal encouraged more immigration, this vague comment may be taken as corroboration.

Scene 7 begins with a close-up of a US flag in the wind, fading to a US border port-of-entry building, followed by stock footage of two men stepping out of the trunk of a car and into border patrol custody. NBC returns to the footage of the female border patrol agent who apprehended people in the dark, and viewers see a group of men walking away from the camera in her control. Hattori begins to close his report by admitting (as did Mariel) that the most credible source of immigration statistics reads the evidence differently than he has: *"Border patrol officials say the spike in apprehensions began before the president announced his plan. They credit beefed-up enforcement in Arizona."* However, the take-away of the NBC correspondent's report is that the president's announcement has resulted in a dramatic increase in illegal immigration.

The last scene shows a Mexican flag in the wind against a backdrop of men working with pick and shovel: the dire economic conditions associated with the flag. The camera then returns to the border patrol agent introduced at the outset of this story. Joe Penco and Hattori walk in a two-shot, a news camera convention signaling personal affinity, as the officer responds to Hattori's off-camera query. Penco explains his view on the geopolitical reasons for immigration: *"The job market."* Hattori encourages Penco to continue with an audible *"Mm-hmm."* The ICE officer complies:

"Quality of life. That . . . that will probably always be there." The story ends with the classic policing shot, a border patrol officer scanning with binoculars, and a shot of the empty desert under border patrol surveillance.

While Hattori apparently composed this story to claim that Bush's immigration initiative led to more people crossing the border, this claim remained hard to verify. In contrast to Gustavo Mariel's interviews, Hattori's Mexican interviewee was reticent; even Penco offered an alternative account involving the seasonality of immigration. Only at the very end of his news story did Hattori offer the border patrol's best assessment that greater enforcement explains the increase in apprehensions, not a White House announcement. But the NBC correspondent would not be dissuaded.

Hattori's news story employed a standard narrative that sidestepped Brian Williams' opening reference to the source of immigrant desperation. The expert to whom Hattori defers was a border patrol agent, which is comparable to asking an infantryman why a battle is fought on one hill rather than another. The key observation is that once Hattori set up a standard narrative in Scene 2, everyday news viewers knew how Officer Penco would answer at the end of the news story, when asked why immigration occurs. The television news consumers of this story would tacitly recognize the standard trope. It might satisfy them. On the other hand, viewers may feel they learned nothing new. Or more critically, they may reject the trope and its implications. In the latter two cases, these unfulfilled viewers may eventually stop watching the evening news, which offers nothing new.

Conclusions

A review of the multisegment news reports of the president's immigration policy initiative revealed the range of uses of visual imagery to modify the frame and the take-away message of the news event. The visuals can humanize or dehumanize subjects and imply the psychology of individuals and groups. Moreover, these visuals can enhance the anchor's or reporter's frame, or they can offer distinct subtexts that may not be fully consistent with the reporter's narrative or entirely undercut the reporter's expressed message.

We compared NBC's and CNN's reporting on drop houses. NBC characterized the smugglers as criminals, while both immigrants and everyday Americans were their victims. The *"disturbing"* aspect of the story was that smugglers were now invading the American sanctum of suburbia, rather than arid border regions or non-White urban enclaves. CNN visually emphasized the criminality of both smugglers and their "*human cargo*," presenting local police and ICE agents as working heroically to restore the sanctuary of the American tract home. Even in the feature-length story, no explanation was offered about why suburban drop houses were now being used.

In two stories, NBC investigated whether or not unauthorized immigration increased following President Bush's pronouncement. Gustavo Mariel downplayed the response of ICE representatives, the officials most likely to know. Instead, he dutifully provided NBC and its viewers with the answer the newsroom apparently sought. While Mariel gave airtime to migrants who were moving north on the basis of purportedly misleading Latin American news reports, he did not follow up on this newsworthy lead, which suggests either that the claim could not be substantiated or that NBC was not interested in its veracity—only in its function as support for NBC's basic claim. When NBC sent James Hattori to once again address its initial query, he predictably came up with the same discredited answer, using a template news narrative that would only satisfy viewers who expect their evening news programs to confirm their deeply held preconceptions.

Our final chapter of close readings will study five feature-length news stories about Latino immigrants that can be considered network successes, because their narratives captivated their audience. These include both stories that will exasperate journalism scholars and some that will satisfy them. We will explore the differences in these network creations, which were produced with nearly equivalent resources.

CHAPTER 6

Feature-Length News Stories about Mexican Immigrants

To conclude our close readings of Latino news topics, in this chapter we present a handful of feature-length stories about immigrants. Their complexity offers network news viewers a richer set of conceptual structures with which to create a worldview about immigrants. These five stories offer several ways to compare story treatments. Three stories are about immigrants who cross the Mexican border. Two stories from the same network compare opposing political viewpoints on immigration policy, and three stories juxtapose different communities. Finally, two of these stories were reported by non-US correspondents.

NBC: Mexican Migrants in the Aftermath of a Hurricane, #83

Charley, the strongest hurricane to hit the United States in a dozen years, struck southwestern Florida with winds of 150 mph at peak intensity. This Category 4 hurricane left over $13 billion of damage in its wake.[1] Network television news crews followed Charley's trajectory for a week. When the winds died down, NBC ran a 5-scene, 27-shot human interest story on August 18 about the losses suffered by different Florida residents.

Brian Williams anchored the story, beginning with a standard midshot accompanied by a graphic insert in the upper-right corner of the screen. The insert, entitled "Hurricane Charley," shows red-and-black hurricane flags straining as people lean into the wind by a foaming sea. A full-screen video graphic of a Florida map then zooms in to the bottom-left side of the map (the Sanibel area) as Williams opens: *"An upscale community in the path of the storm was reopened today, and residents got their first chance to size up the damage to their luxury homes. . . . They are the lucky ones."*

As the map fades, Scene 2 begins with a predawn silhouette of a line of cars, a caravan of vehicles moving along a highway. NBC correspondent Don Teague is heard in voice-over: *"The 6,000 residents of upscale Sanibel were allowed to return early this morning."* A woman wearing shorts and a light top in the tropical heat comments with evident emotion, *"It's very bare. All the trees are stripped."* The camera moves outdoors to a big home and follows an older White woman's nervous inspection as she cries with relief, *"It's all here! We didn't lose anything!"* The camera zooms out to expensive, undamaged houses with Teague's voice-over: *"Officials credit strict building codes and money for saving Sanibel . . ."*

As he speaks the camera moves us to another location. We see the inside of a storm-wrecked mobile home, *". . . two things many migrant farmworkers caught in the hurricane's path don't have."* The roof and two sides of this house have been ripped open like an aluminum can; glaring daylight reveals a broken interior door, a battered fridge, and all the family's belongings tossed about, open to the tropical weather.

In Scene 3 we are introduced by voice-over to a young Latina, the principal subject of Teague's story: *"Elba García is a pregnant mother of two. She is married to a farmworker. Both are in the country illegally."* Four shots show her in the hurricane-destroyed property. Dressed in shorts and top, she carries her two-year-old daughter as she walks up the stairs of her trailer, the banisters hung with drying clothes. In a close-up, García pours water from a gallon plastic jug (implying no running water) and hands it to her daughter, who sits doll-like in a living room piled high with displaced belongings. Teague's voice-over continues: *"She needs help—water, food, shelter, money—things the government is providing but García can't ask for."* In an outside shot with her damaged home as background, García stands next to a Latino priest. She speaks in Spanish for a short time before a translator's voice drowns her out: *"I called FEMA,[2] and they asked me whether I was legal or illegal."*

Teague elaborates in Scene 4: *"Some services provided by FEMA are only available to families who can prove at least one member is in the country legally. The agency says it doesn't turn in illegal immigrants, but many simply don't believe it."*

The camera returns to García in a medium close-up, following her legs as she steps over debris next to her home, followed by a profile shot as she receives packages from a Red Cross truck. Teague continues, *"So families like García's are suffering. Her only relief from a Red Cross van and a lo-*

cal Catholic church, which is reaching out to migrant workers who have lost more than homes." The NBC visuals follow Teague's monologue closely, with a very wide shot of a large, open-air tent that is a food bank and a close-up of a Latina holding her child on her lap as the little girl eats.

The next shot is of the priest previously shown. A caption identifies him as Father Luís Pacheco of the St. Paul Catholic Church in Arcadia, Florida. He says, *"They pick oranges and there is no more orange season . . . no more tomato season . . . no more watermelon season. So the effect of the hurricane is not only physical. Their [livelihood] is gone."*

The final scene returns to the priest and García standing inside a mobile home bedroom. Teague's voice-over: *"For Elba García that means more hard times ahead and a harsh reality,"* as we see a close-up shot of García looking discomfited as she speaks through a translator: *"Even though we're illegal, we have certain rights."* The original contrast is then repeated, with two quick contrasting shots of a large undamaged luxury home and a crumpled trailer house. As Teague closes in voice-over, the camera shows a trailer park full of damaged homes. *"In a disaster that struck both rich and poor, some of the poorest won't get the help they need. Don Teague, NBC News, Punta Gorda, Florida."*

Teague's narrative gives full humanity and subjectivity to both the American and Mexican women. The correspondent evokes compassion for García and through her, for all unauthorized immigrants affected by Hurricane Charley. Teague's carefully choreographed text and video contrast the minimal effect of the hurricane on well-to-do citizens with the life-disrupting impact on families of unauthorized immigrants. Even the camera lighting reinforces the comfort of the wealthy, shaded in their cars, while the immigrants are displayed in intense tropical sunlight, seemingly more vulnerable to the elements. Teague's take-away message is that the federal government's inability to help immigrants in this natural disaster constitutes an inhumane policy.

NBC/Telemundo: Air Flight Repatriations, #89

On September 19, NBC anchor John Seigenthaler introduced an 8-scene, 36-shot story about an alternative method for deporting Mexican immigrants:

> *There's a $13 million experiment going on right now to permanently discourage the illegal crossing of the US-Mexican border. It involves giving illegal immigrants a one-way plane ticket home to the deep reaches of Mexico.*

Seigenthaler frames the story as a costly *"experiment,"* distancing the audience from the humanity of the immigrants as he repeats the word *illegal,* to solidify NBC's framing of Mexican immigrants as criminals. In the following scenes, however, the reporter is not an NBC correspondent, but rather Angie Sandoval, a correspondent for Telemundo, the Spanish-language network.

In Scene 2, the Telemundo news team immediately changes to an alternative, humane framing. In an English voice-over, correspondent Sandoval states, *"One by one they board the plane, Mexican citizens caught attempting to enter the United States illegally. Now they're on their way home."* Viewers see a series of five shots, beginning with a very wide shot of people boarding an airplane, followed by a mid-shot of Mexicans walking past a gauntlet of ICE agents, toward the plane. The third shot closes in from the angle of the first image, showing ICE agents on either side of the boarding ramp. This is followed by a shot of a young Mexican man walking up the ramp carrying a three-year-old in his arms. Smiling, the young man encourages the little boy to wave at the camera, humanizing the deportees. These scenes show equal numbers of men and women, all dressed in vibrant colors, which humanizes the deportees. Then Scene 3 opens with the statement of Gerardo Palacios, one of the deportees.

Sandoval translates, *"My goal was to get to the United States, but I failed."* Palacios' face registers resignation. By showing Palacios' emotions and allowing him to speak for himself, Telemundo deepens Palacios' humanity. In this medium close-up, which grants him full subjectivity, viewers see that his undershirt is partially exposed and his shirt is draped over his shoulders.

In Scene 3 Telemundo adds a third frame: ICE as humanitarian. And, since Sandoval also refers to *"a trial program . . . paid for by the US government,"* the nation by extension is also depicted as humanitarian.[3] A long-distance shot of the length of the airplane offers a view of the line of 40 or 45 deportees. The camera shifts to a close-up of Gerardo Palacios, walking on crutches on the tarmac between ICE agents. His exposed undershirt is explained by an intravenous line in his arm, indicating he was suffering serious dehydration when apprehended. A person holding the saline solution bag climbs with him. Next, in a near close-up, two men carry a woman up the ramp. To this point viewers see no handcuffs or wrist restraints, and NBC's criminalizing frame has been diminished in these two scenes showing that above all, immigrants are vulnerable human beings. Sandoval describes them as *"undocumented immigrants caught trying to cross the treacherous desert bordering Arizona and Mexico,"* presenting the desert itself, not the immigrants, as the villain.

The next scene begins with the Mexican consul stating with authority: "*The border between Arizona and Sonora is by far the one that has the highest mortality rate.*" The camera then returns to Palacios' face as Sandoval translates in voice-over once again: "'*We spent two days walking,*' he says. '*We turned ourselves in.*'" As he speaks viewers see a panoramic view of the desert of Arizona, then a full-screen graphic map of the US Southwest zooming in to a detailed map of southern Arizona and northern Mexico that illustrates the desert terrain. Stock footage is shown of a border patrol agent covering a body with a white cloth, and in a close-up, ICE agents attending to a corpse. The scene shifts to an airplane interview with an ICE spokesperson, who calls the flights a "*humanitarian effort*" to stop people from trying to illegally cross repeatedly, since smugglers have no regard for their safety. More stock footage of migrants walking in the desert at a low camera angle is shown in slow motion, visually suggesting hardship and strife, as their feet kick up dust.

While Telemundo correspondent Angie Sandoval elaborates the peril to which migrants expose themselves, she does not state that they cross the Arizona desert because ICE has closed down safer entry points, forcing people to cross the worst part of the desert during the height of summer. Instead, Sandoval states the consequence: 139 casualties in this 250-mile stretch of desert in the past year. She also notes, without attributing blame, that 80 immigrants have died in the past eight months.

In Scene 5, NBC viewers see the ICE holding facility, with shots taken through the chain-link fence. It is an open-air fenced-in facility the length of a football field, with a corrugated metal roof and Igloo watercoolers. A series of short close-up shots of individuals reinforce the idea of detention and heat. One video clip shows a man with his mouth open, looking stunned by the heat. Another man squints through the chain-link fence in the bright sun. A young woman holds a baby naked to the waist in the summer heat. The last shot follows people leaving the facility, moving to an ICE bus. Three border patrol agents control the door as men and women file out of the caged area into the bus.

The images in this scene are affecting. Detainees sit behind a chain-link fence in the Arizona summer desert. Sandoval's word choice describes the ICE detention facility as a "*center,*" not a prison, which suggests that migrants have a "*choice*" to take a bus ride just to the border or a plane ride to Mexico City or Guadalajara. Her tone suggests that these are pretty good options.

The crowded bus image is then replaced by an interior shot of passengers in the plane. In contrast to a less careful ABC report on a similar news item (#75), the Telemundo camera work employs adequate lighting in airplane interior shots to fully register passengers' facial features, which humanizes them.

In Scene 7, NBC viewers see other Mexican detainees after their international flight, in a Mexico City bureaucratic processing facility. Only now do viewers see correspondent Angie Sandoval. As people in line are being processed behind her, she bluntly states that American taxpayers are paying "*$50,000*" per flight. However, this decontextualized figure does not compare the equivalent cost of transporting the same people to the border multiple times by other means. Continuing, Sandoval's voice-over describes the costs of this *"flight service pilot program"* while the audience surveys images of a large room full of repatriated Mexicans.

At this point Telemundo offers its first critical assessment of the ICE program, in a shot of Andrés Rosental, formerly Mexico's ambassador to the UN. In answer to an off-air question if these flights will reduce repeat migration, Rosental is emphatic: "*No.*"

We turn now to Scene 8, which shows a hardscrabble Mexico City neighborhood. In a wide shot the camera first focuses on the shadows of two people reflected in muddy water. The camera pans up to a wide shot of the pair, a little girl and her father walking hand in hand along the road toward their home, stepping carefully to avoid the mud. An extreme long shot reveals that their neighborhood is a hodgepodge of tin and concrete homes, unpaved streets, and mud-caked sidewalks. Two scruffy dogs wander by as the camera centers a medium close-up on Benjamín, now holding his child in front of their apparently unfinished house.

Sandoval's voice-over accompanies these images: "*It is poverty that drives people—like Benjamín—back to the border. Repatriated by plane just a few weeks ago, he's ready to try again.*" As Sandoval translates, the camera captures his stoicism. He tenderly cradles his daughter, a two-year-old in a sparkling white dress with matching shoes, as he says: "*The need outweighs the risks.*" The scene closes with three shots of the desert wasteland, as the correspondent ends, "*This is why he and others will brave the dangers of the desert for a chance at a better life. Angie Sandoval for NBC News, Mexico City.*"

This story was rich and fulfilling because Telemundo used multiple framings to deepen both its political and human elements. The news team was especially sensitive and effective in its portrayal of the deportees. In the final scene, Benjamín, who had been flown home, was put at so much ease that he was candid about why he would soon face the desert again. Sandoval and her video editing team succinctly captured the crux of immigration in this loving father's statement that he must risk all for his daughter, and that he must leave her to cross again.

Still, there are important omissions. After speaking with the Mexican ambassador, correspondent Sandoval states that the ICE experiment is unrealistic, but she does not ask why the ICE undertook this *"experiment,"* explore the politics behind this *"humanitarian effort,"* or ask by what criterion the ICE will judge the program to be a success.[4] She only states that *"this door-to-door service"* is designed to slow the numbers of Mexicans entering the country. Depending on its operation and definition of success, this self-described humanitarian program may prove to be only a public relations display to mitigate the blame for the hundreds of desert deaths caused by US policies.

CBS: Contrasting Views of Arizona's Prop. 200, #117

On December 22, CBS anchor John Roberts introduced a 3-minute, 1-second feature-length news story about the effects of a new anti-immigrant law, the 2004 Arizona referendum Proposition 200.[5] The 7-scene, 46-shot news story begins with a conventional medium close-up anchor shot, with a dynamic, waving US flag graphic taking up the whole backscreen. Viewers see the CBS eye logo with the "Eye on America" series title as the story caption sets the story frame at the bottom right of the screen: "Illegal Immigrants." Roberts reinforces the frame, stating: *"A controversial initiative on illegal immigration became state law today in Arizona, at least for now, after a federal judge lifted a restraining order. But illegal immigrants aren't the only Arizonans who will feel the impact of the law."* He thus initially frames the story in terms of criminalizing immigrants, and new state laws that adversely affect all residents of the state.

Scene 2 begins with a high-desert winter scene of men working an agricultural field.[6] Correspondent Jerry Bowen cheerfully articulates a familiar refrain in voice-over: *"The only thing hotter than the peppers being picked along the Arizona side of the border with Mexico these days is reaction to Arizona's voter-approved Prop. 200, aimed at weeding out illegal immigrants, cutting off their public benefits, and sending them back home."* Scene 2 offers eight quick camera shots of Mexicans working in a field, the workers bundled against the cold. We see a close-up of hands picking chiles, a shot of another worker hoisting a container of peppers into a tractor bin, and then a shot from the top of the bin showing peppers nearly filling the whole trailer and more being thrown in. They must have been working a long time to fill it. A high-angle shot then captures a third worker crouched over the plants, with a following close-up of the peppers being gathered, bright red against the darkened leaves of the dead plants. Similar shots follow. Bowen's voice-over, *"weeding out illegal immigrants,"* complements the CBS anchor's original criminalizing frame with an IMMI-GRANT AS WEED metaphor. In this 8-shot scene, all the workers' faces are omitted. However, in this scene semiotic tension is created: Bowen and his newsroom verbally describe the laborers as civic weeds who use up public benefits, but viewers see productively engaged (hence decent and estimable) yet faceless farmworkers. This semiotic tension very likely will lead viewers to different readings of the immigrant workers' criminal or benign intent, in keeping with their political persuasion. Consequently, this opening scene is a noteworthy introduction to Arizona's immigration politics.

Next, in Scene 3, Bowen presents an especially appealing advocate for the anti-immigrant referendum: a mid-shot of a white-haired rancher, cowboy hat tilted back, with the Chiricahua Mountains in the background. He is introduced with a caption: "Walter Kolbe, Arizona Resident." The visual has the aesthetic quality of a Marlboro cigarette advertisement. This handsome old man speaks softly, in down-to-earth tones that make his uncompromising message seem only the more compelling: *"These people still flood across and they are ruining our health care system and they are ruining our schools."* Then, a 2-shot demonstrates Bowen's affinity with the rancher, as they walk together to examine evidence of migrant activity: a close-up of backpacks, another 2-shot of Bowen and Kolbe examining a water bottle, and a close-up of Kolbe holding the water bottle. Bowen's voice-over explains, *"From Walter Kolbe's backyard, you can see Mexico, and the backpacks and water bottles abandoned by the nightly wave of illegals crossing over."* Note his use of *illegal* as a noun, which is a journalistic usage that Latino journalists have criticized as inflammatory.[7] CBS ends this scene with a mid-shot of Kolbe in front of a picturesque mountain backdrop saying in a soft voice that quakes with anger: *"We were saying to our politicians, 'If you're against it, then do something. Stop this raping of our country.'"* The stunning backdrop and Kolbe's grandfatherly voice soften the racism of his discourse; he remains a sympathetic figure.

In Scene 4, CBS's Bowen sets up the foil to counterbalance Kolbe, the ideal advocate for Proposition 200. On a Tucson sidewalk, an undocumented mother is seen walking away from the camera with her daughter in hand. Bowen's voice-over sets the stage: *"It was 10 years ago that Angelita sneaked across to work as a housekeeper, a church volunteer, and to raise her family. Now, she's afraid to show her face."* The next shot is purposely darkened to hide her identity, since the referendum puts her at greater peril. Seated in a mid-shot overexposed profile against a brightly lit, curtained window in her home, she speaks in Spanish. CBS provides a woman's voice to translate: "*Ten years have passed, and I live in fear in a country that can send me back to Mexico—at any moment.*" Viewers then see her backyard, with deep shadows of her and a swing set, and a mid-view of her back as her daughter faces the camera. Angelita is dressed in jeans, white tennis shoes, and a white blouse; her hair is pinned up neatly. Bowen uses hunting imagery as he speaks about her: "*Angelita is in the Prop. 200 bull's-eye because she's still illegal. So is her oldest daughter.*"

Angelita's words are allowed to be heard before the voice-over translation, revealing that she is quite articulate in Spanish. From this shot of Angelita's back and the child on the swing set, Bowen's voice-over continues, "*Only her youngest girl is safe, a citizen born in the USA,*" as the camera zooms in to a mid-shot of the "safe" daughter. Bowen thus acknowledges the danger that unauthorized immigrants experience. Finally, returning to the darkened profile shot in her home, we learn that her older daughter (who is not a US citizen) has asked why the referendum passed: "*The oldest asks, 'Why? Why can't we be accepted as Americans, all of us?'*"

While Bowen clearly intended to offer Angelita as a foil to the sympathetic image of Kolbe, his spoken metaphors dissuade viewers from developing a similarly compassionate image of her. Bowen reiterates his own political stance by referring to Angelita as "*sneaking across*" and using criminal immigrant terms twice. Further, the CBS newsroom contributes to this unequal comparison. Among other editing choices, Angelita was not provided with the same kind of formal text caption that gives Kolbe his place as an "Arizona Resident," although she could claim this modest designation after living 10 years in the state. Since the scene revolves around her legal status, Angelita is not well placed to directly contest Kolbe. The innocent face and the guileless question of her daughters, however, indirectly rebuff the rancher's hateful statements.

Next, Scene 5 introduces a related topic as it sets up a comparison between Arizona health care professionals with different views of the referendum. However, once again the match up is unbalanced, showing the same newsroom semiotic bias that favors Proposition 200 advocates over its detractors.

In another 2-shot, Bowen walks in a hospital hallway with a White man, Jim Dickson, a "*hospital administrator.*"[8] Dickson is first seen answering, "*It's now about 500,000 a year,*" to Bowen's unspecified off-camera question. Rather than contextualize this statement, Bowen moves on with a voice-over: "*Hospital administrator Jim Dickson says soaring health care costs for illegals in border towns like Bisbee, Arizona, helped fan the fires of Prop. 200.*" While Dickson's figure remains entirely decontextualized, the implication is that this half-million dollars pertains solely to the hospital's annual cost of health care for unauthorized immigrants. Quick shots then show a panorama of the mining town clinging to the hillside, the town's welcome sign, and a pair of Mexican men walking along the street, before returning to a mid-shot of Dickson, who ominously says, "*It'll probably cause all the hospitals to close on the border if we don't start doing something about it.*"

Bowen also leaves Dickson's second assertion undeveloped, stating in voice-over: "*Prop. 200 doesn't just target illegals. State-funded workers, like the receptionists and doctors at this rural clinic, face fines and jail time if they don't turn in undocumented patients.*" The camera shows viewers a wide shot of a rural clinic, a mid-shot of its reception area, and close-up shots of a Latina in profile, who turns out to be one such rural doctor. In contrast to Angelita, in the previous scene, this Latina is identified with a caption as "*Dr. Peggy Avina, Chiricahua Community Health Centers.*"[9] During this close mid-shot of Avina, we hear her make only one statement. In response to an off-camera question, she declares, "*I won't do it! They'll have to arrest me, because I won't do it!*" Many law-abiding health care professionals share her apparent perspective on the new legislation, seeing no contradiction in this ethical stance, feeling obliged as doctors to safeguard their patients. Accordingly some Arizona health care professional organizations campaigned against the referendum.[10] CBS viewers do not learn if Dickson shares Avina's views; the news story editing only leads viewers to believe he opposes her.

In Scene 5, Bowen's contrast of the health care professionals is biased. He refers to immigrants as "*illegals*" three times as a noun when speaking with Kolbe. Bowen allows Dickson to claim that unauthorized immigrant costs will close all border hospitals without independently investigating the assertion or treating it as a personal opinion. Finally, Bowen also appears in 2-shots with Proposition 200 supporters Kolbe and Dickson, which conveys his solidarity with them, but not with Avina.

On the other hand, Bowen and the CBS editor who was credited for this story, Maria Nicoletti, constrain Avina's testimony. She is given no airtime to either explain her (possible) civil disobedience stance or dispute Dickson. In her opposition to Proposition 200 the Latina physician is shown to a national audience expressing only emotions and no rational arguments, while her political rival is permitted to articulate his views.

Scene 6 begins with a slow zoom of Bowen from mid to near close-up with the border fence at his back, saying: "*The move to block illegal immigration across this border triggered some surprising support. Nearly half of Arizona's Latino voters, 47%, voted for Prop. 200, voted for cutting off benefits to the newest arrivals from south of the border.*" The camera returns to those newest arrivals, the agricultural workers harvesting chiles.

Bowen's voice-over continues: "*The federal court's ruling today means the law can take effect immediately, but critics say it will be very costly if enforced . . .*" CBS viewers see an operating room of the Bisbee hospital and zoom in to a 2-shot of Jim Dickson and the correspondent, as Bowen's voice-over concludes: "*. . . especially if frightened illegals avoid health care to avoid being caught.*" We see a series of mid-shots and over-the-shoulder shots of Dickson, who says: "*As you have immigration across the border, diseases come. And so if the people who are here do not receive care, we cannot control the disease pattern.*" Here Dickson articulates a key drawback of this law, one more reason why physicians like Avila would defy the law. However, Bowen does not inquire whether Dickson would heed the health care provisions of Prop. 200 at the peril of the wider public.

In Scene 7 viewers see a few White people protesting in favor of Proposition 200 on a sidewalk as Bowen says in voice-over: "*Arizonans voted their frustration.*" The camera then returns to the telegenic rancher, William Kolbe, who softly threatens hostility: "*I'm afraid it's going to turn violent if somebody doesn't listen to us.*" The story ends with a shot panning the picturesque Arizona desert as Bowen says, "*With an appeal already in the works, this is one fight that is far from over. In Bisbee, Arizona, I'm Jerry Bowen for 'Eye on America.'*"

On paper, this extended news story seems like a balanced comparison of contending Arizonan opinions about Proposition 200, but the CBS news team tipped the scale. Viewers never see the faces of the agricultural workers whose work contributes to US society, while Bowen repeatedly characterizes the churchgoing mother of two as a criminal. Nor was the Latina physician allowed to argue her case. In contrast, proponents of Proposition 200 were granted complete subjectivity and were allowed to state their case fully. Moreover, in the final scene, the grandfatherly rancher warns of violence if his racist views are not respected. CBS gives the visually compelling Kolbe the final word—despite his message. In this episode of CBS's "Eye on America," thus, there is only a semblance of balanced reporting.

CBS: "Illegal Immigration—
What Does It Mean to You?" #77

In the next story, broadcast on August 5, we will compare Jerry Bowen's work to that of Bill Whitaker, another CBS correspondent who compared polarized views on immigration policy. John Roberts anchors again, opening the story by saying, "*One of the hot issues in this election year is illegal immigration. The positions taken by the presidential candidates could affect millions of people on both sides of the US/Mexico border. So what are the Bush and Kerry stands? Bill Whitaker reports tonight in our special 'Eye on America' series, 'What Does It Mean to You?'*"

CBS offers a complex, 20-second visual opening sequence that marks its signature series. As Roberts speaks, a shield-shaped video graphic insert to his right reads, "What Does It Mean to You?" in bold block print, accompanied by elephant and donkey political party emblems on bunting that is red, white, and blue. Behind the anchor and the shield, a dozen text streams spell out different political issues on a red, white, and blue screen that fills the background. The next shot provides another full-screen graphic in the middle of the light-blue screen: a circular logo with "'04" is surrounded by text reading "Campaign CBS News." The logo fades in the final shot to show a larger version of the first shield graphic, which now takes up the entire screen.

In Scene 2 the text of the previous full-screen graphic shrinks and drops to the bottom of the screen, forming a distinctive caption for the story that follows. Viewers first see a 2-shot profile of CBS correspondent Whitaker and a woman who is a key subject of this report, then an over-the-shoulder shot of Whitaker sitting with the woman's family on an outside picnic table. The audience hears Whitaker's voice-over: "*We first met Donna Tisdale in 1997, when her desert ranch along the border east of San Diego was being overrun by immigrants crossing illegally from Mexico.*"[11]

As Whitaker speaks, viewers see home video of a score of people moving past a barbwire fence at dusk. The first dramatic 2-second mid-shot seems to have been taken with a camera mounted on a fence post, since the people's profiles show anguish and fear as they rush to cross the fence. The footage is authentic. Since the audience does not hear verbal exchanges of individuals seen on the footage, it may be that CBS added a sound track of animals scurrying or people moving over broken ground to the silent footage to emphasize "*being overrun.*"[12] CBS's verbal, visual, and audio signs thus frame the immigrants' activity as animalistic. The next image (taken with a home video camera) is a very wide shot that shows immigrants running across a family ranch, with Tisdale's voice-over: "*Right here, imme-diately next to our house.*" Whitaker fills in for her, saying, "*She counted 9,000 that year, and shot home video to prove it.*" More home video follows, of seven immigrants running across a field, and then a clip from a 1997 CBS interview of Tisdale and her mother in which they state, "*We're suffer-ing from stress*" due to the immigrant crossings.

Scene 3 returns to the present day with a 2-shot of the correspondent standing at the wire fence next to Tisdale, whose appearance has hard-ened. Her once long hair is now cropped short, her face less open. A cap-tion confirms her as "Donna Tisdale, Rancher." The open desert, pre-sumably of Mexico, is seen behind them. As Whitaker asks, "*Have things improved in seven years?*" viewers see them in alternating medium close-ups. She says, "*The smugglers come and go at will. I don't really see any im-provement.*" As Whitaker visually registers surprise, Tisdale reiterates, "*I don't really see any improvement.*"

Whitaker says in voice-over, "*There is a difference. Now she carries a gun and more anger.*" The camera focuses on a close-up of Tisdale's pistol in a holster. Whitaker offers, "*They've got more border patrols—*" at which point Tisdale interrupts, "*Don't even need to go there! I'll tell you right now, peo-ple keep hiring illegals,*" as CBS provides another Tisdale home video clip of a man and woman running hand in hand. The camera returns to Tis-dale as she continues, "*When the smugglers come back through here and they thumb their nose at us and laugh, how do you think that makes us feel? . . . Neglected.*"

Whitaker signals his empathy for Tisdale's anger with a series of 2-shots. However, not content with a simplistic story line, Whitaker says, "*But this is a tale of two Americas.*" Scene 3 reveals a middle-class Latino home. The father, in a crisp white shirt and tie, stands over three children seated around a dining room table. With staged formality he leans to kiss two children and knuckle-tap the older son, and then prepares to leave for work as Whitaker says in voice-over, "*In 1984, Luís Vidas fled civil war in El Salvador and illegally crossed the US border near Donna Tisdale's stretch of desert.*" CBS then uses a cutaway shot, namely an inserted shot of barbed wire, to semiotically link Tisdale and Vidas.

Whitaker portrays Vidas sympathetically. In the next image, a mid-shot, Vidas is dressed as a janitor. Whitaker can be heard repeating Vidas' answer by saying, "*So, seven days a week?*" to which Vidas confirms visu-ally with a nod and repeating "***seven days a week***." This point is effectively made four times in two semiotic modes. In two subsequent shots, the CBS camera zooms in from a distance to reiterate the key assertion that Vidas is no criminal; he is a hardworking family man. Viewers first see Vidas working in a white shirt and tie as a waiter, and then in a profile shot walking beside a "*Los Angeles high-rise,*" where he works as a janitor.

The next shot is a close-up of an American flag and Salvadoran flag positioned next to each other, followed by a shot of Vidas' backyard. Whitaker describes Vidas' progress: "*After Ronald Reagan's amnesty, he became a US citizen, and now owns a house, a car, and his daughter is starting college,*" as the camera cuts to a quick profile shot of his daughter and the two flags. The summation shot returns to Vidas in his janitor shirt, captioned "LUIS VIDAS, Naturalized Citizen." Whitaker asks off-screen, "*So, you found your American Dream?*" Vidas answers affirmatively and ends with, "*But it was hard.*"

Whitaker consumed 60% of his story time to set up this stark contrast, stating that division on this issue between voters "*is so deep, no politician, no plan has been able to bridge it. But this year both presidential candidates promise a fix. One American's dream can be another's nightmare and the chasm dividing the two sets.*"

CBS viewers see a split screen with the series title "What Does It Mean to You?" and "Guest Labor Program" textually summarizing the correspondent's voice-over: "*This program expects temporary workers to return permanently to their home countries after their period of work in the United States has expired,*" with President Bush shown in the left screen. The half-screen shot of Bush expands to fill the TV screen as he emphasizes that guest workers must return home after their work period has expired.

This same format is then used for the Democratic candidate's proposal. The text side again summarizes Whitaker: "*John Kerry wants a guest worker program, too, but then would clear a pathway to legal residency and ultimately US citizenship,*" and the insert becomes a full-screen shot of Senator Kerry as the audience hears him speak. There is no applause in the background as he says, "*So that those who work hard and pay their taxes and raise their children have a right to share in America.*"

Viewers see Vidas in the next shot, standing and talking with Latino coworkers, followed by a 2-shot of Whitaker and Tisdale in front of the border fence. Whitaker summarizes, "*Vidas thinks Kerry's plan would help others like him. Donna Tisdale has heard it all before.*"

In a mid-shot Tisdale disdainfully says, "*Yeah, yeah, yeah. Political speak. Not buying it.*" The camera cuts and zooms in slowly on a desert foot trail leading straight to the fence they stand next to, as she says, "*You don't see an immigrant trail to the door of the White House, do you?"* Whitaker presses, *"Kerry. Bush. Any difference in your estimation?"* Contemptuously, she turns her head away and spits out, *"**No!**"*

Whitaker finishes in a voice-over in the final seconds as viewers see a pair of shots (presumably Tisdale's home footage) of a score of immigrants running across the desert landscape toward the camera at mid-shot level. The immigrants are aware of the camera. Some younger men playfully wave or feign lunges at the camera while running full-tilt. Viewers then see a shot of their backs as they run into the thick brush. Whitaker says, *"On immigration, frustration and demand for political action are high. Expectations . . . low."* A final source of Tisdale's frustration can be seen in the last shot. Forty or fifty immigrants walk in single file in front of the camera; few show any concern for the person shooting the footage.

This CBS story successfully illustrates the personal merit of many immigrants as well as the source of the hardening feelings and increasing rancor surrounding this contentious issue. Whitaker skillfully juxtaposes two fully fleshed out people, linking their half of the American dream or nightmare in his viewers' minds without setting the two people against each other. Tisdale is most angry with US politicians, while Vidas expresses no opinion of people like Tisdale and is overtly appreciative of his adopted country.

ABC/BBC: "Dangerous Crossing," #116

In our final social semiotic analysis, we offer a particularly accomplished news story, ABC/BBC's #116, as a contrast to NBC correspondent James Hattori's cookie-cutter report on Mexican migration (discussed in the previous chapter). Scene 1 begins with the standard mid-shot of ABC Sunday anchor Terry Moran at his desk. Behind him viewers see a digital screen map of the United States and Mexico, overlaid by the title "Dangerous Crossing" and a static image of a man, his face hidden in a hoodie, straddling a barbwire fence. Moran speaks gravely:

> *A Texas jury resumes deliberations this week in the trial of two men charged in a tragic and disgraceful episode of human smuggling. Nineteen illegal immigrants died in the back of a stifling truck last spring. The accused were allegedly transporting the immigrants across the Mexican border. As the BBC's Matt Frei reports for us tonight, the stream of immigrants is as constant as the dangers they face.*

The anchor thus introduces the story with two framings echoed by the background graphic, emphasizing the volume of immigration as well as the dangers faced by people who cross the border. Moran segues into the main story by referring to a trial involving *"human smuggling,"* thus representing immigrants as victims of *"tragic and disgraceful"* actions. "Dangerous Crossing" thus reiterates a humane framing of immigrants. However, this framing is weakened because Moran speaks only about *"illegal immigrants,"* and the image of a hooded man climbing the fence suggests criminal trespass.

In Scene 2 the audience sees two successive shots of two vans on a very wide dirt road in a vast desert, traveling toward the camera. The first shows them at a distance, the second much closer to the camera. BBC correspondent Matt Frei begins his voice-over by saying, *"Late afternoon and it's rush hour on a dusty road in Mexico."* While his words create a narrative dissonance because the vans are the only traffic on the road, the ABC audience gets no signal of humor or irony from his voice. The dissonance is reinforced as the vans travel further from the camera, and then more distantly still. Shot 5 is taken from over the hood of a police car at a Mexican checkpoint, as Frei says, *"Every one of these minibuses is heading to the US border. Twenty miles to go and there's a Mexican government checkpoint."* A van stops. As the van's engine idles and Mexican officials speak to the men in the background, Frei continues in voice-over as Scene 3 begins,

> *The passengers are unwilling to talk, caught between hope and fear. They come from every corner of Latin America. Some have paid $5,000 or more to a people smuggler to get this far. When night falls they'll sneak across the border into the US and what they hope will be a better life. They and thousands like them everyday.*

Over this succinct statement the camera presents five remarkable camera shots that portray the humanity of immigrant workers. The first is a close-up of three men in the van. Strong, dark indigenous faces return the camera's stare. Tension builds as the lens lingers 4 full seconds—a network news eternity—on three faces. It trains on them so long viewers recognize the regular blinking of the men's steady gaze. Unfazed by the camera, these unmistakably Latin American faces are more tightly centered by the beanies and heavy coats they wear to repel the winter desert cold. The second shot is even more closely framed on another young man. He also returns the camera's gaze for a while and then leans forward out of view. As the lens refocuses, the audience realizes another man is already gazing directly at the camera. For once, television news voyeur is caught off-guard: the viewer is the object of his gaze, not the reverse.[13] Another close-up of a stoic-looking man is followed by panning to a sixth passenger, who nods minimally to the overheard Mexican official's instructions without lifting his gaze from the camera. Reminiscent of Dorothea Lange portraiture, these compassionate video images are intensely rendered.

The next shot is more pedestrian, showing three rows of passengers sitting four across in the extended cab van. The audience has not seen these people before, and their looks range from apprehensive to indifferent. The camera moves to a near close-up on one of these travelers, a young woman who also defies the audience's voyeuristic intrusion. It then turns to a final person, a woman in her 20s, zooming in so tightly that viewers will note her perfect features and flawless skin. Her eyes shift back and forth from the camera to straight ahead, as Frei tells us she and the other passengers are caught "*between hope and fear.*" For 24 seconds the camera work insists that the news audience see these anonymous migrant workers as individuals, not as mere placeholders in the political debate.

Next, an over-the-shoulder shot shows a Mexican official standing outside of the van calling out "*Nada mas once,*" 'Only eleven.' Frei continues his voice-over: "*The Mexican officials no longer try to stop them. Instead, they hand out leaflets telling them how not to die in the Arizona desert.*" Mexican officials are shown performing a social welfare service, not a policing action. The viewers see two final point-of-view shots[14] of hands passing out and opening pocket-size fourfold leaflets with simple drawings and brief texts.

The camera crew has depicted these silent passengers with deep humanity and individuality, to an unusual depth of subjectivity for the US news-viewing public. This camera work was the networks' most consummate visual rendering of immigrants in 2004.

The next scene reframes the news story completely. It begins with a shot of a Hummer moving along a deep desert road and follows with a shot of the interior of the military vehicle. Conversation is heard between the BBC correspondent and the US border agents, clad in standard-issue camouflage fatigues: "*Fresh footprints.*" Frei's voice-over drowns out the conversation: "*The next morning, on the other side, what greets the US border patrol is evidence of a veritable stampede of illegal migrants.*" Here, the IMMIGRANT AS ANIMAL metaphor turns ICE agents into HUNTERS as Frei emphasizes "*veritable stampede.*"

In the next two shots, outside the vehicles the camera follows the same ICE agents to focus on scores of footprints in an arroyo. Border patrol agent Garrett Neubauer says, "*You can see the fingerprints where someone's crawled under.*" Three close-up shots follow the migrants' litter and personal effects, such as a pair of shoes and a Tweety Bird backpack, as Frei says in voice-over, "*Well-worn paths are littered with traces, precious personal belongings dumped because they've become too heavy.*" He thus refocuses attention on the immigrants' humanity by referring to their "*precious personal belongings,*" which include pages from a book, a toothpaste tube, and a child's backpack.

The juxtaposition of ICE military actions in search of ordinary humanity is an effective counterpoint. BBC correspondent Frei did not limit himself to a single discourse, in particular the quasi-official US news media discourse of IMMIGRANT AS CRIMINAL.[15] Frei freely used clashing metaphors in successive statements, from metaphors that portray immigrants as animals to a humane discourse of ordinary people jettisoning everything to try to stay alive in an unforgiving desert. The juxtaposition of imagery is disturbing and novelistic.

The following shot has Frei partially facing Officer Neubauer. In an awkward 2-shot they stand in a dry creek bed. The rock-strewn background could be a theatre of war as Frei asks, "*When you look at all this, do you feel that you're fighting a losing battle?*" Clearly fazed, Neubauer responds, "*Um, I don't know if I would say 'a losing battle.' Um, you know, we know that the, the volume of traffic is out there, but we also know that, um, the border patrol in general is doing a good job. We're stopping a lot of it, apprehending a lot of it.*"

Here Frei once again reframes the immigration story, this time in terms of a war in which civilians seeking work become invading combatants. Frei appropriates the discourse of ICE agents to depict them as military defenders of the US border. While Neubauer accepts Frei's framing, he is immediately caught by the journalist's sharp query, which pushes martial logic to its conclusion: without a foreseeable victory, war is defeat. Frei's team has rendered Neubauer as a likeable, down-to-earth person in manner and voice, even as the agent's war discourse dehumanizes immigrants, distancing them with the term *traffic* and the use of nonhuman pronouns for people: "*traffic . . . we're stopping a lot of it, apprehending a lot of it.*"

Another actor is then introduced into Frei's narrative to again reframe the viewer's perspective. The camera pans from a close-up of a cholla cactus, through the sun's glare to a panoramic view of the open, immense desert. The next shot is of a piece of litter, an empty plastic jug on the barren desert floor as Frei's voice-over intones: "*Forget about fingerprints or visas; here the biggest obstacle is the desert. Last year 600 people died of thirst crossing the border . . .*"

The shot of the plastic bottle cross-dissolves into a close-up profile of two young women, as Frei continues, ". . . *but even this isn't enough to deter the desperate.*" Then, in an over-the-shoulder 3-shot of the two young women, the news audience sees Frei seated on a low bank. He introduces the women in voice-over: "*In Phoenix, I met two sisters from Honduras. They crossed the Rio Grande last month and almost drowned.*" The camera offers a mid-shot of the correspondent, followed by a mid-shot of the two sisters. One woman gestures about the height of the water as the other narrates their story. Her face expresses disgust and a range of emotions, as her silent sister's face becomes impassive. Frei's voice-over translates her perspective: "*You know full well, there's no dignity in any of this. You come here to work and just to work. It's all about survival.*"

In this scene, Frei has shifted frames again to report an even more personal perspective on the dangerous crossing. His camera crew uses multiple angles and shots to enrich the viewers' sense of these individuals, making their near drowning an event of human consequence, not merely an interesting incident to make a rhetorical point. The term *dignity* was expressed only once in all Latino news stories broadcast on network evening news in 2004. In the face of ICE and other anti-immigrant discourses in the public sphere, it is telling that it fell to a foreign correspondent to explicitly remind US viewers of immigrants' humanity.

The story ends by returning to the Hummer parked on the top of a hill. The camera zooms out beyond it to the immense expanse of the desert, as Frei sums up in a voice-over, "*It's a game of cat and mouse, but the mouse is winning. Only one in three migrants gets caught. Matt Frei, BBC News, Arizona.*" In #74 (Chapter 4), NBC's Jeffrey Kofman also used the same catchphrase to refer to the spotty apprehensions of Dominican immigrants, whom he systematically characterized as criminals. In contrast, Frei has deliberately presented a series of different framings through the use of different metaphors of immigrants. First they are desperate humans, then hunted animals, an invading army, individuals fighting for their lives against the desert, and finally people calling for personal dignity. Of course, a 150-second news story cannot address every issue, such as the wider root processes of globalization that force people to immigrate, but Frei's range of framings and his rendering of the various protagonists are exceptional.

The camera work in this news story also emphasized the immigrants' humanity in ways that US camera crews rarely attempted. In particular, the immigrants' eye line in shots allowed for emotional identification with these human subjects. The camera position and use of close-ups offered individuated perspectives of several immigrants who otherwise remained anonymous; the people in the van were rendered with dignity and individuality, so viewers saw travelers on a perilous voyage, rather than floods and herds.

These multiple framings allowed viewers to see what immigration means to immigrants as well as to the ICE agents. The camera work offered exceptional subjectivity to individual immigrants, as well as a sympathetic rendering of ICE agent Neubauer, who was portrayed as a decent person who uses martial discourse, not a mindless soldier. As with the immigrants, the BBC showed viewers his individuality.

Conclusions: Semiotic Analyses of Network News Stories about Latinos

Here, we summarize the general findings gathered from close readings of individual news stories in this five-chapter section. We can make a few generalizations from our review of more than 40 network evening news stories from four networks. First, the professional journalistic quality of the stories about Latinos was uneven, across and within networks. While some news briefs were accurate, others—even those produced by the same network—distorted facts. Some longer stories were richly rewarding, while others employing similar network resources did nothing to accurately inform network audiences about Latinos. Finally, each network aired stories that should have been corrected before broadcasting, or that never should have been aired.

Second, with the exception of the presidential campaign stories that aired the views of political scientists and professionals, network newsrooms and correspondents constructed Latino news stories without the benefit of experts. In the 118 news stories broadcast in 2004, the networks did not consult sociologists, physicians, or historians who study the life experiences of Latinos. While this criticism might be construed as self-serving, instances of striking network ignorance could easily be avoided, even if the scholars consulted received no airtime.

Third, with the caveat that the number of stories is low, foreign news correspondents offered certain advantages over in-house correspondents. For example, both the Telemundo and BBC correspondents presented a more humanizing view of Latino subjects than did the national correspondents in similar news stories. These foreign correspondents used language about immigrants that was not limited to the conventional US public discourse of immigrants, and consequently were less likely to articulate stereotypes than their domestic colleagues.[16] In general, then, these "guest reporters" from foreign affiliates offered a more global, less parochial perspective on the topic at hand. The BBC's Matt Frei offered the ABC audience an exemplary news story, #116; one Telemundo report, #17, was poorly informed. We point out both specific examples of better and inferior stories in the following few paragraphs to exemplify general tendencies, not cherry-picked stories, from the complete set of stories from 2004.

Regarding visual reporting, excellent television journalism does not require cutting-edge videographics. While video newsrooms often add remarkable footage and illuminating graphics, generally contributing to good news reporting, in our review visual imagery was at times used to distract viewers from journalistic failings. The most visually creative stories included the least professional reports, such as the CNN paean about a dead soldier, #33, and the NBC story that rewrote an Olympian's life story to present her as a paradigmatic immigrant, #85. Nevertheless, the most accomplished news stories used visual imagery creatively and constructively. One example is the ABC story on another dead soldier, which visually rendered his sacrifice and the pathos of his mourning family with remarkable quality, #109.

In short, the networks' videographic tools were used effectively in both bad and good storytelling. In the stories discussed in the present chapter, we noted that ABC aired compassionate camerawork at a Mexican immigration checkpoint that rendered the human condition of desperate but not demoralized individuals. We also reviewed three multisegment news stories about George W. Bush's policy reform announcement, in which all three networks created well-crafted graphics to inform their audiences about the complex policy proposal. However, the multisegment CNN story of this news event, #1, aired footage that was so overexposed that an otherwise remarkable portrait of the immigrant was lost to viewers. Another CNN story, about Phoenix drop houses, verbally balanced humane and criminalizing discourses about unauthorized immigrants, but its visual composition overwhelmingly portrayed immigrants as criminals, #24. Finally, the most egregious report was CBS's indictment of José Padilla, #60. Since CBS did not counterbalance its sensationalizing videographics with even a rudimentary defense of the accused or critique of the allegations, the network effectively tried and convicted Padilla on national television.

Regarding the news content of reporting on Latinos during the presidential campaign in 2004, several news stories offered solid informative reporting. For example, one NBC story rejected the myth of Latino bloc voting, and another NBC story presented the issues that mattered to Latino voters (#82 and #90, respectively).

On the down side, the content of stories demonstrated that network personnel often work without basic knowledge about US Latinos. Network news writers conflated certain subgroups of Mexican Americans. Consequently, the only national economics news brief regarding Latinos, #27, was inaccurate; and the one news brief addressing Latino health, #80, on the vulnerability of Mexican American men to cerebral strokes, was needlessly alarming. Longer stories repeated stereotypes, such as the ABC story, #10, on using Spanish to lure Latino voters, and a less-than-penetrating "in-depth" story on the plight of Latino public schoolchildren, #51. Another was when CNN uncritically accepted the White House tall tale about its commerce secretary nominee, echoing Bush's description of Carlos Gutierrez' life as a rags-to-riches story, when a check of Gutierrez's biography would have swept the fable aside, #112. On occasion a network made the same mistake twice, seeking evidence of an increase of unauthorized immigration in response to President Bush's announcement on immigration reform. Immigration experts were not consulted, and even the judgment of ICE personnel was dismissed in a pair of disappointing stories, #17 and #48.

Another problem—which was not limited to reporting on Latinos—was a failure to sustain the journalistic principles of good practice. Although it was generally believed that Alberto Gonzales did not possess the pluck and mettle to stand down his career-long mentor, the president, on controversial constitutional matters, ABC did not inform its audience about the implications of the president's selection, #100. Instead, it cast Gonzales as an affirmative action hire as well as a Bush crony. Finally, the networks never explored the 50-year tradition of granting refugee status automatically to Cuban migrants seeking economic freedom (#11, #12, #34, #35, #106–#108), when other economic migrants are prosecuted for identical actions (#74, #105, #117).

Commentators from both the political right and the political left regularly criticize the ideological stance of network news reporting, with each claiming that networks favor the rival point of view. We reviewed all the reports about Latinos that NBC, CBS, ABC, and CNN broadcast in 2004. While some news briefs avoid a political posture, longer stories cannot preclude projecting story content through a political lens. We used a generous definition of a politically slanted news story: if the story presented a comparison of stances and the audio/video editing was largely balanced, we considered the story to be balanced. However, a news story was considered unprofessional if it presented a controversy without providing more-or-less equivalent airtime for rival positions, or if it undercut one position or group of people with demeaning messaging expressed in a secondary semiotic modality.

A few network stories were plainly left of center. One was the NBC story developed in collaboration with a Telemundo correspondent, reporting on a political rally held by DREAM Act students, #57. Another was the CBS news report on the movie "A Day without a Mexican," in which directors were allowed to freely articulate their pro-immigrant viewpoint, #49. In both, the views of the anti-migration representatives were presented very briefly, and in a context that belittled their opinion.

Right-of-center stories about Latino issues were far more common. The networks did not report neutrally on José Padilla (#2, #60). Several stories were crafted to fit archetypes of US superiority. CNN's story on the death of a Green Card soldier, #33, selectively reported facts to cast Lance Corporal Jose Gutierrez as the paragon immigrant soldier whose sacrifice honored the country that had given him so much;[17] NBC's story of the Cuban American triple jumper, #86, distorted the facts in order to present Pérez as an archetypal Cuban refugee who has been saved from her native Cuban prison by a compassionate US. There were also instances of ostensibly balanced stories that proved to be politically slanted. For example, in one superficially balanced CBS story on Arizona's anti-immigrant referendum, the correspondent symbolically stood with referendum advocates while denying the critics of Proposition 200 equal camera time or subjectivity, #117. Other stories that presented slanted political viewpoints by various means are treated elsewhere in this summary.

Our critical review of a year of Latino news stories, based on a rubric of journalistic standards that corresponds well to the Society of Professional Journalists' code of ethics, illustrates manifest network shortcomings. We have seen many poorly developed news briefs, some that are adequate, and a few that stand out as highly professional. The bad ones display basic ignorance about Latinos, exposing news writer viewpoints that do not differ significantly from a layperson's unfounded commonplace misunderstandings. Accordingly, these stories often fail to fully contextualize their claims and tend to rearticulate stereotypes.

In contrast, journalistically adequate briefs present news content accurately and with sufficient context to allow viewers to make apt interpretations. As a result, most stereotyping is eliminated. Finally, a merely adequate brief can become excellent if it offers appropriate additional information that elucidates the news content and educates the news audience. Here we list the characteristics associated with both simple (brief) stories and more complex (longer) network stories.

SIMPLE STORY
Bad
- Displays basic ignorance about Latinos
- Reinforces stereotypes
- Excludes contextualizing information

Adequate
- Is accurate
- Includes contextualizing information
- Does not stereotype
- Offers no information beyond news item

Excellent
- Informs beyond the news content

More complex stories also fall into bad, adequate, and excellent groupings. They employ all the simple story criteria, to which we add more scoring factors. The worst stories employ cookie-cutter narratives that can be recognized by their stock characters, recurrent narrative plots, and predictable resolutions. These narratives are not designed to inform the news viewer; at best they only confirm the viewer's preconceptions about the news topic. In poorly designed stories we also tend to find orphan statements or images, namely decontextualized statements that are open to excessively wide interpretation. Examples noted in our review include interviewee statements that seem to answer unidentifiable off-screen questions. As products of poor professional practice, orphans occur for many reasons. We surmise in some of our examples that orphan clips are spliced into a scene so a person's response appears to be the "right" answer, allowing a cookie-cutter narrative to flow uninterrupted.

COMPLEX STORY
Bad
- Cookie-cutter narrative—predictable plots and resolutions
- Editing leaves orphan statements
- Excludes a pro or con statement
- Editing discounts a position or demeans a person or people

Adequate
- Offers new information on a topic beyond the news content
- Provides subjectivity to one representative of each subject group presented

Excellent
- Interrogates stereotypes
- Multiple guiding metaphors or multiple frames
- Challenges cookie-cutter narrative

Adequate longer stories avoid the pitfalls of the poor stories. Given their extended length, they are able to offer viewers additional new information on the news topic to enrich the viewer's understanding about the Latino topic. While news briefs have little time to offer human subjectivity, it is a requirement in longer stories. News stories that aspire to more than pedestrian reporting practice therefore offer more kinds of related information to inform the viewership about aspects of Latino people and cultures. This can be done, for example, by verbally or visually contesting a stereotype in the course of a story. The best stories used multiple approaches to challenge predictable narratives. Our sample included rich stories that used multiple guiding metaphors or journalistic frames to tell stories about Latino men, women, and children in multiple aspects of US life. These different narratives encouraged viewers to reconsider uncritical or conventional views about Latinos, as well as other aspects of the world that may extend beyond personal experience. With excellent stories such as these, television news professionals fulfill their Fourth Estate responsibilities. In keeping with the Society of Professional Journalists' code of ethics, they cultivate a knowledgeable electorate who are better able to participate in the civil discourse necessary to sustain a strong democracy.

The chapters of this section offered a series of close readings of news stories to provide interpretations of individual news stories. In the following section, we move beyond interpretation to explanation. To this end, we bring together humanist theories about complex higher-order meaning formation. We employ the humanist insights in a cognitive processing model of how people make sense of televised multimodal discourse streams. We exemplify this new model with a small number of the news stories we have previously analyzed. Our goal is to explain how American television news consumers compose their understandings about the Latinos living among them.

HUMANIST THEORIES AND COGNITIVE MODELING OF TELEVISION NEWS READINGS

An ideology is always a derivative thing, and the primary thing is a mythology. People don't think up a set of assumptions or beliefs; they think up a set of stories, and derive the assumptions and beliefs from the stories. Things like democrat, progressive, revolutionary: these are comic plots, superimposed on history.

—NORTHROP FRYE[1]

In the previous section we used social semiotics to conduct intentional and symptomatic readings of 45 stories from the top 10 topics about Latinos that were broadcast by television network news programs to US audiences in 2004. Such stories become the basis for the national audience's understanding of today's Latino populations. Now we move away from interpretation to focus on the means by which viewers build social meanings about Latinos and immigrants.[2] Our explanation integrates recent cognitive modeling of television news stories, and venerable humanist accounts of how these stories make political ideology available to viewers.

We will focus on immigration, the major domestic topic associated with Latinos in the wider American consciousness. In 2004 immigration made up 28% of the network evening news stories about Latinos. For example, on March 4, CNN anchor Anderson Cooper related a story (#30) about unauthorized immigration, beginning with the following statement:

> *The aim of the Homeland Security Act is to keep the bad guys out of the country and everyone else, safe. Tightening security at the border, cracking down on illegal immigrants, is one piece of the plan, certainly. Human smuggling rings in Phoenix have become a major target.*[3]

As discussed in Chapter 5, for this story CNN news editors wove a sequence of 42 camera shots, with carefully selected footage, and a rich set of graphics around a 503-word spoken text to make a professionally crafted multimodal narrative. Cooper framed this story with terms such as *certainly* and *homeland security*, guiding the viewer's understanding of visual images of immigrant men, women, and children in federal custody. CNN's rich graphics, tables, captions, including the story caption "Human Smuggling Crackdown," make up a composite television news story. In the final section of this book, we ask: How does the audience interpret discursive multimodal news reports?

Foucault's Discourse

We set our work within the social theory of the historicist Michel Foucault. To explain the prevalent social order of the West, Foucault used the term *discourse*. He theorized that social relations are constituted and regulated in everyday social interactions in which people and things are named and discussed.[4]

While we might want to ask, What is discourse? Foucault points us away from such questions. Foucault argues that essentializing questions cannot be independently posed or answered, since they are generated within the institutional disciplines that lead to the question. He suggests it is more productive to ask: What comprises the discourse of the television news story? How is it produced? What are its social effects?

Foucault's notion of "discourse" encompasses whole epochs of Western civilization. It is constitutive in that discourses construct social structure. Disciplines (such as social science, mass media, or the military) have ruling discourses that are also regulative, providing the limiting parameters of social identities and social conduct. Within Foucault's formulation, people do far more than chat as they talk: they are discursively socialized to live their lives in terms of certain particular discourses and practices. These practices are not limited to speech, but all involve meaning-bearing components of social interaction.

Television news is arguably the most important commercial-mediated genre for the expression of subject-defining ideology, or the "common sense" that defines our lives in terms of knowledge beliefs, relationships, and identity, since it purports to present the pertinent facts of reality every day on the hour. Social semiotician Klaus Bruhn Jensen confirms this, stating, "News may be the prototypical genre of modern mass communication." He continues:

> By disseminating political, commercial, and other information to the general public, and by enabling the public to engage in reflexivity about society, the news media potentially contribute to the democratization of knowledge beyond the narrative and rituals of traditional societies. Symbolizing as well as serving new political practices from the eighteenth century onwards, the news genre thus offers the lowest common denominator for public debate, providing to the ordinary citizen, in Robert Park's terms, an "acquaintance-with" events and issues that modern science produces "knowledge-about."[5]

The news contrasts with situation comedies, dramas, or even so-called reality programs, which also articulate ideology, but which viewers consider to be genres of the imagination rather than mirrors of the actual.[6] Therefore news discourse is the source of systems of representations that members of a society widely take to most resemble reality. However, televised news stories by their very nature cannot mirror reality. Instead, they constitute an "imagistic discourse"[7] about Latinos. The previous five chapters of this book have given us reason to be concerned about the news media's dim and two-dimensional representations of Latinos. This is why we focus on this crucial source of information used by the US viewing public to formulate their understanding about our Latino population.

The questions we will begin to address are: What forms television news discourse? And what are its social effects? To operationalize a response to these questions we first undertook a social semiotic study (in terms consistent with Foucault's formulations) of the constitutive elements of television news. Speaking about newspapers, Gunter Kress asserted in Foucault's terms that texts build up particular possible worlds "through series of lexico-grammatical choices and differences played out in the text."[8] As an inherently multimodal discourse, television's evocative potential is far greater. A study of the social practice of television viewing will require tools that can accommodate visual sign of various types, spoken sign and other non-spoken audio sign, in addition to text (orthographic) sign.

Foucault's broad usage of the term *discourse* initially thwarted empirical investigations of his framework. Following Paul Chilton, in this book I work with a much more grounded notion of discourse, focusing on the "material content" of imagistic discourse, namely the alphanumeric symbols, visual images, and sounds of the televised material content of news stories that pass "back and forth between participants in dialogues and conversation, giving communicative cohesion, and providing a means for both consensus and conflict."[9] Since we sought to uncover the shared conceptual bases of US public worldviews on issues regarding Latinos, we looked to television news sources of such discourse as appropriate sources of public language and opinion. In the next two chapters, we will use immigration and immigration policy news stories to illustrate this integrated model.

In Chapter 7 I will explore the discourse of television news by looking at one key feature of the material discourse of television news: metaphor. We base our analysis on George Lakoff's cognitive theory about metaphor, sketching out the insights and limits it contributes to our enterprise. Then, we bring together our explanatory cognitive framework with the insights of humanist theories on how sign and story construct ideology. We will examine Calvin McGee's influential theory of rhetorical terms, *ideographs*, a small set of everyday words that are high-order abstractions of values that guide normative public commitments.

In Chapter 8, we also will explore Roland Barthes' semiotic concept of *myth*, a small set of second-order semiological signs, each of which is a "repository of a rarefied meaning" incorporating a history of a society's hopes, dreams, fears, and values. Finally, we draw on narratology to begin to address literary scholar Northrop Frye's notion of *archetypes*, a small set of story-types that have been used across time to define societal values. As we will see, these humanist elements fit well with our most recent scholarship on human cognitive processing, and can be applied to the formation of political concepts as they are expressed in television news reporting.

CHAPTER 7

A Cognitive Model to Incorporate Second-Order Signs

When a bit of talking takes place, just what is doing the talking? Just where are the words coming from? Some of the motivation must derive from our animality, and some from our symbolicity. Do we simply use words, or do they not also use us? An "ideology" is like a god coming down to earth, where it will inhabit a space pervaded by its presence.
—KENNETH BURKE[1]

Lakoff's Cognitive Theory of Metaphor

We begin with cognitive studies of imagery with metaphor. George Lakoff and his collaborators first elaborated a framework to explain the constitutive power of metaphor on the basis of written texts. Multimodal television news employs spoken intonation, visual graphics, video imagery, and nonspoken sounds, as well as orthography in the text of captions and titles; this requires a more robust framework of metaphor than one limited to text. As a base, however, Lakoff's cognitive theory has the advantage of having been fully elaborated by its proponents, and it has been subjected to critical appraisal.

Lakoff and his collaborators theorized that metaphor, above other structures of language, establishes the basis of people's everyday comprehension of social life. In this view, metaphor is a keystone cognitive structure that people use to make sense of behavior, relations, objects, and people, to the point that we often forget that these semantic associations are not natural, but socially constructed and conventionalized correspondences between one semantic domain and another.[2]

The fundamental claim of metaphor theory is that people do not primarily make sense of their surroundings in terms of logic and reason. Instead, images are a central part of human thought; people build their frameworks to understand the world by means of images. In text and speech, this image-formation function is expressed by means of metaphor. In other modalities, metaphor and image at times are one and the same. Humans use figurative language, particularly metaphor, as an essential tool to create abstract ideas. The cognitive empiricists[3] who have explored conceptual metaphor have found it to be nearly ubiquitous in human social organization, from science to song, and patterned in a way that indicates that the origins of the seemingly universal conceptual metaphors are in our bodies.[4] Lakoff has elaborated this epistemology, "embodied realism," over the past 30 years.[5]

In *Brown Tide Rising*, I concretely explored this aspect of cognitive science theory with an extensive empirical investigation of the conceptual metaphors found in seven years of newspaper texts. Using the newsprint of the 1990s, I examined the metaphors guiding the everyday understandings that Americans used, in this case, to make sense of the Latino population.[6] In the current book, I analyze the networks' multimodal news stories in terms of meaning making with a good deal of empirical detail, examining a rich array of the imagery that is presented to the American television viewing public and that informs their sense making of US Latinos. To do so, I return to the insight of cognitive linguists: metaphor establishes a significant basis of people's everyday comprehension of social life. My principal assumption is consistent with a constructivist view of social structure: in the absence of evidence of distinct hardwiring of human brains corresponding to different processes, constructivists assume cognitive uniformity across linguistic and nonlinguistic processes. Thus visual metaphor of various types[7] (and other sensory modes) operates in the same way as verbal metaphor. Commonplace conceptual metaphor and other tropes thus reflect the way human beings comprehend their social world.

Contemporary Cognitive Metaphor Theory

Much was written about the constitutive capacity of metaphor over the centuries before Lakoff and Johnson (1980) took up the subject; their work, however, woke social scientists and the wider public to prosaic (nonpoetic) metaphor when they theorized that metaphor, above other structures of language, establishes the basis of people's everyday comprehension of life.

Since then hundreds of studies have expanded our understanding of human cognition. We now understand that we build whole arrays of conceptual structures to make sense of the world beyond the body. People watching television employ sets of metaphorical primitives[8] of which they rarely take note.

Beyond these basic elements is conceptual metaphor, which humans build on the basis of our personal bodily experiences. As infants, our earliest kinesthetics provide the initializing precepts for preconceptual experience. For example, humans are born into a world subject to gravity, space, and time, whereas dolphins are not subject to gravity as humans are. Because of our bodily experience, we acquire worldly schemas that include a gravity-based up/down orientation, as well as dimensions and space, among many others. These schemas include movement, schema for grasping (since we have opposable thumbs), and schema for eating and sleeping and excreting. These and many more bodily frames of reference are the sources for analogical relations to abstract concepts. For example, the grasping schema leads to the metaphor CONTROL AS HANDLE, which can be expressed in a multitude of ways, such as "He's been grappling with quantum mechanics" and "I just can't get a grip on it."[9] As people mature and acquire the language of their communities, they rely on these schemata to formulate and verbalize the structural premises of both the societies that they inhabit and the world at large.

We will characterize the conceptual correspondence we call metaphors in an "X AS Y" format. The format displays the metaphor as a one-way mapping, Y → X, between two semantic domains: a SOURCE domain (y) and a TARGET domain (x). In an analogical process, the seemingly more "concrete" or embodied semantic content and relationships of the source domain are mapped onto the abstract target domain. Cognitive metaphors are not haphazardly distributed through the semantic fields of the English language, but are configured in a hierarchical array, from basic to abstract. The basic metaphors lay a cognitive foundation for higher-level everyday human understanding.[10] Lakoff demonstrates that a hierarchical structure organizes metaphors at distinct levels of abstraction, from foundational to conceptual and cultural.[11] Lakoff delineates the human topology of one semantic domain of one of our shared and yet most basic private experiences: the event.[12] Each and every occurrence of an event—whether a minor incident, a single episode in the course of a progression, or a world-shaking happening—all have been mapped out in terms of the semantic elements that we automatically draw upon to interact with the world. This fundamental part of people's way of talking about and constructing their

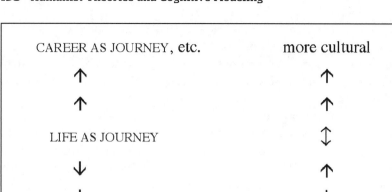

Figure 7.1. Conceptual metaphor hierarchy

world is conceptualized metaphorically. Its elements—state, change, process, action, cause, and purpose—are understood in terms of space, motion, and force. The mappings of the event metaphor in turn become the basis for higher-level cultural metaphors, as Raymond Gibbs has shown (see Figure 7.1).[13]

In the same way that the conceptual structure of the source domain is transferred onto the target domain in a simple linguistic expression of a metaphor, so the conceptual organization and its various and significant structures of the event structure metaphor are "inherited" by the conceptual metaphor LIFE AS JOURNEY. These structures in turn are inherited by higher-level metaphors, such as the NATION AS BODY, which leads to thinking of economics in terms of health, or NATION AS HOUSE and its corollary, IMMIGRANT AS INVADER.[14] The persuasiveness of metaphoric thinking is due in part to its basis in foundational human experience. The validity of the source domain experience, namely space, motion, and force, is beyond kinesthetic question. It is the embodied knowledge which people employ in daily life, the source domain experiences that, as Lakoff noted, we first learned as infants in our little bodies, and reinforce daily by living in these same, if somewhat larger, bodies. For these reasons Lakoff calls his theory of epistemology "embodied realism."[15]

We illustrate the use of metaphor theory on news media studies by summarizing a number of newspaper studies on the target concept, IMMIGRANT.

Metaphorizing Immigrants

The predominant conventional metaphor of US public discourse of the 1990s, IMMIGRANT AS ANIMAL,[16] was replaced with IMMIGRANT AS CRIMINAL by 2004.[17] This significantly transformed the nation's image of immigrants. Insofar as CRIMINAL is a more human metaphor than ANIMAL, the conceptualization shifts immigrants from being lowly animals to actual humans—albeit with violent volitions and immoral intentions. Now portrayed as criminals, immigrants remain the lowest form of humans. In one sense, it is an improvement, since immigrants are no longer characterized as lower forms of life.

For anti-immigration partisans, however, it was also a shift of political tactics, because while over the previous century they had been able to publicly excoriate immigrants with racist terms without repercussion, in the late 1990s their language increasingly diminished their moral standing in the eyes of the general public.[18] When the predominant IMMIGRANT metaphor shifted from ANIMAL to CRIMINAL, the terms of debate shifted away from immigrants' status as human beings to their legal standing. Advocates who favor the term *illegal* claim that unauthorized immigrants deliberately violate US law by crossing its borders, and when in the US continue to abuse the nation's social services. Therefore, they deserve punitive treatment. In contrast, their opponents favor the term *undocumented*, taking the position that most immigrants break minor laws in pursuit of a higher calling, to provide for their children. Hence Americans should treat immigrants with respect, protect them from exploitation, and welcome them into US society. Thus, in order to be fair, network news broadcasts should balance the metaphor-based discourse of their reports on immigration and other politically charged topics, since news reporters express normative evaluations when they predominantly use one of the contending discourses.

As noted in the previous five chapters, network anchors and correspondents consistently referred to unauthorized immigrants as *illegal immigrants*. The adjective *illegal* adds its semantic meaning to the concept of IMMIGRANT, namely a person who has come to this country from another place. The conceptual correspondence, or mapping of the semantic domain CRIMINAL onto the semantic domain IMMIGRANT, creates the metaphor IMMIGRANT AS CRIMINAL (Figure 7.2), which adds semantic domain characteristics associated with CRIMINAL, such as lawbreaking, dangerous, and violent, to the target semantic domain of IMMIGRANT. When immigrants are conceptualized as lawbreakers for crossing the national border without

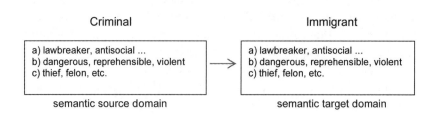

Figure 7.2. IMMIGRANT AS CRIMINAL metaphor

permission, all their contributions to the nation's social fabric are erased and forgotten, such as working, raising a family, and going to school.

This IMMIGRANT AS CRIMINAL metaphor is a conventionalized metaphor, that is to say, an established part of the conceptual system of American English speakers of this time period. Following cognitive metaphor theory, when such conventional metaphors are used, all their entailments (routine deductions following from the particular presuppositions of the source semantic domain) and implications are automatically invoked to make sense of the social world.

This was not just the usage of journalists. In a study of print media references of the same period, reporters quoted politicians who blurred the distinction between the actual civil misdemeanor of immigrants and far more serious crimes; for example, *"'I'm not for allowing illegals to stay in this country,' said Virginia Representative Virgil Goode: 'I think they should have to go back to their home countries.'"*[19] Politicians are not always statesmen. California representative Dana Rohrabacher (R) stated in response to a congressional debate on intelligence reform: *"This bill should be defeated because it has gutted the provisions in this bill that passed the House that were aimed at controlling this massive invasion we have of illegal immigrants into our country, and we are not going to have a secure America when we have millions and millions of illegal aliens coming here, many of whom could be terrorists."*[20] When politicians depict immigrants as a destructive presence, they do not distinguish the vast majority of immigrants who are law-abiding family men and women from the small percentage who commit serious crimes. This depiction of fundamentally decent people as criminals leads our thinking away from their contributions and motivations. It also passes over the role of US business interests and American consumerism in encouraging immigration.[21]

The IMMIGRANT AS CRIMINAL metaphor maps the structure of the semantic source domain, CRIMINAL, onto the IMMIGRANT target domain. Formal ontological mapping of metaphor allows speakers to use the same frame of reference to reason about immigrants that is commonly employed to reason about criminals. In this manner, speakers and listeners inadvertently apply to immigrants their semantic domain about criminals—their knowledge of what criminals are. Since this mapping is conceptual and not limited to the single phrase *illegal immigrant*, the power of such metaphoric mappings is robust and productive, and used in various semantically associated words and collocations, such as *sneak across the border*. Most disturbing, some network anchors used the noun, *the illegals*. The noun embodies the IMMIGRANT AS CRIMINAL metaphor, which reduces the individual to an exaggerated description of his or her ascribed immigration status, and excludes more germane associations of the immigrant, such as worker or even human being. Several national newspapers also used the noun; some even published front-page headlines with the dehumanizing noun, for example, the *Register-Guard*'s (Eugene, Oregon) "Plan for Illegals Sparks Anger" (the day following President Bush's January announcement), or the *San Francisco Chronicle*'s "Hospitals Won't Be Required to Report Illegals," or the *Washington Times'* ". . . While Arizonans Debate Illegals."[22] These 2004 headlines are only samples. Due to its frequent usage in the network news discourse, the CRIMINAL metaphor in all its instantiations was the predominant concept of immigrants transmitted to Americans.

In 2004, the CRIMINAL metaphor was one of two ways to conceptualize immigrants in US public discourse. On January 7 President Bush legitimized a more humane discourse about immigrants that was often signaled with the adjective *undocumented*. This usage maps immigrants to noncriminal notions such as of official documents and minor infractions of the law. This implication allows interpretations such as crossing the border in search of work, not crime. The implicit argument is that this human imperative takes precedence over statutes; since immigrants' intent and actions are not unethical, they are not criminals. Further, it allowed a reading that the immigrant crosses national boundaries to achieve a morally higher purpose, namely to feed his or her family by honest work. This discourse made the positive associations of WORKER available to news viewers, unlike the CRIMINAL metaphor.

Having described the two principal IMMIGRANT metaphor structures available to the public via the news networks in 2004, we now turn to the first humanist tradition that explored political power in public discourse. We will incorporate its insights as we elaborate our cognitive framework.

Ideograph Pairs Mark Societal Divides

Rhetorician Calvin McGee made a lasting impact on rhetoric studies when he asked where political power was located in rhetoric, what the source of its potency was, and what its substance was. He argued that it resided in a small vocabulary of everyday words that governs persuasive public discourse. McGee began investigating the source of the persuasive force of political language, building on the work of Kenneth Burke and a pithy observation by José Ortega y Gasset:

> Man, when he sets himself to speak, does so *because* he believes that he will be able to say what he thinks. This is an illusion. . . . Our thought, in large measure, is dependent on our language.[23]

Thus political suasion for McGee begins with a set of everyday words articulated in political settings. These are not dictionary entries with definitions that are set in stone, but are established in practice, what Ortega y Gasset describes as a "gigantic architecture of usages."[24] Practice within the public sphere is the key.

McGee points away from slogans and manifestos as the site of political power in rhetoric. Instead he considers the ordinary, taken-for-granted word that the public uses in everyday discourse. He defines the ideograph as "a high-order abstraction representing collective commitment to a particular but equivocal and ill-defined normative goal, . . . guid[ing] behavior and belief into channels easily recognized by a community as acceptable and laudable."[25] As his students Celeste Michelle Condit and John Louis Lucaites state, such ideographs "represent in condensed form the normative, collective commitments of the members of a public, and they typically appear in public argumentation as the necessary motivations or justifications for action performed in the name of the public."[26]

McGee originally characterized ideographs as a small set of vocabulary items such as *liberty, property, freedom,* and *equality,* and phrases such as *the rule of law.* These guide our thinking by imparting a design structure for "public motives." As McGee described it, all ideographs gain purchase on the public's understanding of the world because they have been used "vertically" across history, and currently are extensively used "horizontally" across a wide swath of public discourse. While McGee cites case law and other official sources as instances of vertical memory, he notes that "the more significant record of vertical structures lies in popular culture and history. This consists in part of novels, films, plays, even songs; but the truly influential manifestation is grammar school history, the very first contact most have with their existence and experience as a part of a community."[27] McGee also emphasizes contemporary usage: "But time is an irrelevant matter *in practice*."[28] The operative definition of an ideograph is its public usage during a particular time period in a particular setting.

Moreover, ideographs are understood only in relation to current usages of related ideographs. For example,

> "*equality*" is made meaningful, not within the clash of multiple usages, but rather in its relationship with "freedom" . . . One would not want to rule out the possibility that ideological disagreements, however rarely, could be simply semantic; but we are more likely to err if we assume the dispute to be semantic than if we look for the deeper structural dislocation which likely produced multiple usages as a disease produces symptoms.[29]

As a result, while scholars peruse history to gather examples of the expansion and contraction of ideograph meanings, a situation-based set of "ideograph clusters constantly reorganizes itself to accommodate specific circumstances while maintaining its fundamental consonance and unity."[30] Today linguists would call McGee's theory a pragmatic theory of political discourse: one based on usage rather than definition.

While McGee initially restricted ideographs to society's vocabulary of motives, a small set of words that guide or warrant behavior or public belief, he provided no watertight definition of ideographs, and explicitly excluded the language of political controversies, such as abortion, crime, or poverty. Still, McGee sought terms that people use to impart social value, which unite and "which separate us from other human beings who do not accept our meanings, our intentions."[31] This permeable nature suggests a wider set of ideographic terms since most language articulates social value. Scholars have since extended the notion of ideograph to photographs and other visual references, an exemplar of which is the 1945 Pulitzer Prize–winning photo of the raising of the US flag on Iwo Jima.[32]

The vertical and horizontal meaning-constructing processes that McGee described are descriptions of the influences governing the semantic shift of these terms. All manner of signs gather their effective definition in this manner, and contribute to public persuasion by the same process. While rhetoricians prefer categories and distinctions based on definition rather than interaction, a pragmatic theory of degrees of persuasion may well be warranted.[33]

Metaphor theory enhances McGee's insights. Consider the competing immigrant metaphors that constitute people's understanding of IMMIGRANT. Constitutive metaphors may be one of McGee's political hinge points in public discourse. Moreover, he noted that everyday public usage of pairs or clusters of ideographs provides their definitions. Thus *citizen* is an ideograph defined in relation to its opposite term, *immigrant*. Unsurprisingly, the definition of *citizen* across US history has varied significantly in tandem with *immigrant*, with the ebb and flow of immigration as a political issue in the public domain.[34] However, neither McGee nor his intellectual heirs have provided a cognitive basis for political persuasion, to which we now turn.

My team and I have conducted empirical studies of the role of news media in public discourse about these ideographs, which we have called "constitutive metaphors." First, we scrutinized a set of national newspapers published in 2004 to ascertain the relative frequency of these competing metaphors.[35] As gauged by the patterning of constitutive metaphors, US print journalists presented a political stance on immigration policy that was neither balanced nor neutral. A neutral presentation would have broadcast nearly equal numbers of the rival partisan adjectives, or would have used a nonpartisan alternative such as *unauthorized* to refer to immigrants.[36] The predominate use of the semantic domain CRIMINAL for IMMIGRANT made criminality part of the conventional conceptualization in the public discourse, which drove a psychological wedge between immigrants and the reading public. Since criminals are thought to have inferior moral characters and other failings, many people expressed the opinion that "these people"—apart from any other consideration—broke the law and should be prosecuted. By placing immigrant workers on par with felons, such public discourse was used to justify harsh penalties for peaceful unauthorized immigrants residing in the United States.

Ideographic pairs maintain everyday ideological divides between US Latinos and other Americans. Networks often fail to distinguish between Mexican Americans and Mexican immigrants when it is crucial to the report, as in #27, which left the impression that "Latinos" (an undifferentiated group) were taking too many American jobs. In empirical metaphor studies of newspaper stories, my team has been unable to locate statistically significant distinctions among subsets of Latinos.

On the other hand, consider how the news writers of one network made questionable distinctions between Mexican and Cuban undocumented immigrants. In #105, ABC anchor Elizabeth Vargas reproached as "***shocking***" a Mexican mother who placed her daughter in a piñata to cross a Mexico/US border checkpoint in a car.[37] In #12, however, another ABC anchor, Peter Jennings, did not mention the well-being of five Cuban children whose safety was far more seriously jeopardized when they were sent in a makeshift boat across 90 miles of open sea. While both the Mexican and Cuban parents undoubtedly risked their children's safety for greater economic opportunity, Vargas paralinguistically and prosodically disapproved of the Mexican parent's actions to national audiences while Jennings legitimated the Cuban migrants' efforts when he spoke of their ingenuity with admiration. In this standard differentiating pattern—an ideographic pair—networks characterize Cuban migrants (#11, #12, #34, #35, #106–#108) differently from non-Caribbean Latino immigrants, even when no evidence suggests that the migrants' motivations differed. The distinction is simply taken for granted. Such television news image making reinforces everyday images that socialize individuals by naturalizing their place in the social world, restricting people's lives and perspectives (both of Latinos and of the viewers).

Multimodal Metaphors for Immigrants

Televised news reports are more powerful than the newspaper in three ways. First, they are more salient because they center on the visual mode, the primary sense by which ocular-centric[38] Westerners interact with the world. Second, televised multimodal messages are semiotically more holistic than a printed message. Newspapers are limited to storytelling with text, graphics, and photos. Televised news additionally presents moving images and graphics, and sounds from sources visible on the screen as well as from sources not present in the news event, such as dramatizing sound effects, and mood music. Finally, television news draws a much larger audience.[39] The construction of such powerful multimodal messages in news stories is the object of our study. The televised news stories we describe create a holistic imagistic discourse (in terms of visual, audio, and text imaging) about Latinos that builds up the subject positions of Latinos for the US public.

To restate Foucault, the social order is constructed discursively, and individuals can only operate within the parameters of the discourses of power. Accordingly, individuals do not operate in society except in terms of societal discourses. Their participation in society involves being named and categorized into hierarchies (of normalcy, gender, health, class, morality, race, etc.), in short, subject positions. When a person participates in society, he or she employs societal discourse, becomes a subject, and undertakes certain established subject positions. The power of discourse, in Foucault's view, comes about because individuals cannot communicate meaningfully outside of this discourse.

To move from meaning making in newspapers to meaning making on television news, we elaborate Lakoff's work, expanding from the expressions of ideographic metaphors in the printed text to a full range of multimodal signs that make meaning. Thus, our study of audiovisual imaging, with which television news is constructed for viewing audiences, will begin with a key premise of cognitive theory, namely that social meaning is carried in constitutive metaphor.

Since cognitive scientists generally hold that the fundamental cognitive processes by which humans comprehend their social world are the same for all their senses, what goes for language should go, *mutatis mutandis*, for visual and other modal processes.[40] Most of the cognitive research on metaphor, however, examines speech and text. The study of visual metaphor remains far less developed, although Charles Forceville, a recognized leader of pictorial metaphor studies, indicates that nonverbal metaphor is receiving attention in advertising, art, film, political propaganda, and cartoons.[41]

Visual, Spoken, and Text Metaphors in TV News

The predominant meaning-making element of news articles is metaphor. Consider then television news, with its multiple types of meaning-making modes. Because of its larger audience and greater impact, we wanted to investigate the multimodality of television: the visual (camera shots of events), spoken text (including voice-overs), written alphanumeric texts (captions), graphics (from unadorned maps to complex visual renderings), nonvoice diegetic (e.g., gunfire recorded in battle) and nondiegetic (e.g., television program theme music) sounds.

My research team began our study of television's multimodal expressions of metaphors with a simple measure of quantity. Our original goal was to tally all the multimodal metaphors that appeared in the year's news stories about immigration that were broadcast by the four networks under question ($n = 33$). We immediately recognized that—much like newspapers—television news reports were replete with metaphors for all sorts of information. Our straightforward task turned out to be daunting, devouring more than 18 months of the resources of a team of 10 students working in independent pairs. The principal difficulty was that while newsprint metaphors have a clear Y → X structure that can be readily located in text irrespective of syntactic variation and referential complexity, locating nontext metaphors was much less clear-cut. We ultimately scaled back, limiting ourselves to locating, labeling, and counting only IMMIGRANT metaphors in all their semiotic modes for 20 television news stories. Our findings can be seen in Table 7.1.

We labeled 814 metaphors of the target domain IMMIGRANT in 20 television news stories, thus averaging 40.7 metaphors per story. In contrast, the *Los Angeles Times'* use of metaphor across seven years was 6.7 metaphors for all targets per story in the newspaper article ($n = 4,485$ text metaphors in 671 articles). Television metaphors are far more numerous because multiple sensory modes are articulated on the small screen, not just text metaphors. Story narrative can be succinctly stated through text or other metaphors, and television new stories are counted in tenths of seconds, not column inches.

In the television news stories, we counted on average 23 camera shots per news story, with at least one written or spoken text metaphor in each story. Although we noted that network news anchors regularly framed news stories with a verbal metaphor, visual metaphors appeared in 18 of the 20 stories. Visual metaphors were very frequent[42] but also the most salient, so they are the most powerful meaning-making mode. They have greater potential to make an instant, intense impact on a viewer than the same metaphor written on a piece of paper or spoken. However, we currently have no principled way to measure comparable salience of metaphors in different modalities.[43]

Multimodal Semiotic Cognitive Processing

As the importance of mapping the cognitive processing of metaphor became clear, cognitive theorists sought to replace the simple Y → X model with a more robust model that could track complex cognitive processes.[44] In television journalism, as well as everyday conversation, we needed to be able to account for how audiences process similar metaphors in different modalities, and how they process conflicting metaphors. To illustrate the cognitive processing required, we reproduced the full 56-word text of a

Table 7.1. Multimodal IMMIGRANT metaphor distribution in 20 news stories

	Metaphor Source	Metaphor Mode				Total	Total stories
		Visual	Textual	Spoken	Graphical		
more	PEOPLE	43	79	85	5	212	18
positive	VICTIMS	62	25	16	1	104	17
	WORKER	6	23	35	25	89	10
←	IMPOVERISHED	10	6	4	4	24	6
	DIVERSE	1	22	1	7	31	9
→	MASSES	52	13	1	13	79	15
	DYING	11	18	15	3	47	12
more	CRIMINALS	52	30	31	26	139	14
negative	ANIMAL	46	3	20	20	89	12
	Total metaphors	283	219	208	104	814	
	Total stories	18	20	17	15		

news brief, #24, in which CNN's anchor Aaron Brown strung together two sentences with clashing metaphors:

> *Before we go to break, a few other stories that made news today around the country, beginning in Phoenix, where authorities today discovered two houses harboring at least 100 undocumented immigrants between them. Two other so-called drop houses were also found in and around Phoenix in recent days, at least 288 illegal immigrants arrested in all, making this one of the busiest weeks in memory, according to immigration officials.*

The CNN news viewer perceived this 20-second, 2-scene, 6-shot report as a continuous digital information stream made up of semiotic stimuli in different modes: visual sign, nonspoken sounds, nonspoken texts, 56 spoken words, and meaningful graphics that do not involve letters or numbers. In his report, Aaron Brown mentioned a time, a location, various other groups of people, and also provided information regarding the relative newsworthiness of the event, among other features. All these kinds of information were projected to the news viewer in a complex multimodal stream.

In this example we will focus only on the images used to refer to immigrants, and exclude other people, places, or actions. Brown referred to immigrants once each as *"undocumented"* and *"illegal."* On the basis of previous empirical studies of mass media news about immigration, as mentioned earlier, we interpret these as referring to two metaphors: IMMIGRANT AS CRIMINAL and IMMIGRANT AS UNDOCUMENTED.[45] Moreover, in addition to *"288 illegal immigrants,"* his spoken descriptor, other nonspoken instances of the IMMIGRANT metaphor were found.

The visual imagery of the CRIMINAL semantic domain begins in Scene 2, after the anchor's establishing shot. Viewers see the whole story played out on the upper-left two-thirds of the television screen. The bottom-right third of the screen is taken up with the CNN logo, a running teletype string of text about unrelated news stories, and the story title "Immigrant Bust." Shot 1 of Scene 2 presents a close-up shot of yellow crime scene tape, filling the bottom third of the television screen space, presumably marking off an otherwise nondescript house as one of the *"so-called drop houses"* to which Brown refers.

In Shots 2 through 5, CNN shows ICE agents as they detain, frisk, handcuff, and otherwise arrest a number of Latinos, including women and children, as well as Latinos from behind a chain-link fence. Thus the CNN camera crew dramatized the arrests.

Next we turn to captions, the text labels that define people, places, and scenes. CNN provided the criminalizing caption: "IMMIGRANT BUST" in capital letters in a line below the anchor that defined the four final shots of the news brief. *Bust* refers to a police search without warning that leads to arrests and is most often used in reference to drug-related arrests. CNN further emphasized criminality with a dynamic line underscoring this caption each time a new shot played on-screen. Finally, throughout the brief, CNN editors added nondiegetic sound—sound from a source that is not present in the news event. CNN added dramatic music to heighten the report's emotional tension, as would be used in a television crime drama series. In this 20-second news brief we counted at least 12 instances of the IMMIGRANT AS CRIMINAL metaphor and 1 instance of the IMMIGRANT AS UNDOCUMENTED metaphor.

Along with other meaning-unit semantic domains, these are incorporated into the viewer's comprehension. A welter of metaphors are produced because CNN, like every other network, strives to keep the viewer's attention and pack in information by composing news stories with multishot scenes made up of many signs in various modalities.[46] As has been shown, CNN projected at least 13 distinguishable and contradictory IMMIGRANT metaphors. We now ask: What kind of cognitive processing is required for viewers to make sense of and construct meaning from CNN's news brief? How are multimodal semiotic signs incorporated into our thinking? By what procedure do viewers make meaning out of all this? Fifteen years ago, Gilles Fauconnier and Mark Turner proposed replacing the Y → X model with a general model for conceptual projection (what I will call "semiotic sign incorporation") to support a range of different cognitive operations, "including categorization, the making of hypotheses, inference, the origin and combining of grammatical constructions, analogy, metaphor, and narrative."[47] Their model captures a fundamental and general cognitive process, offering a flexibility and dynamism not captured by the original, unidirectional mapping. Fauconnier and Turner posited two additional cognitive spaces for real-time metaphor elaboration. One is a generic space, a location for articulating the higher-level relationships among the other blend-internal conceptual structures. This space also links input from different senses, such as visual and audio stimulus of related domains, so they can be treated accordingly. The second is called "blend" space, a place to incorporate conceptual elements of source semantic domains and target semantic domains of a metaphor.[48] Compare Y → X, the unidirectional two-space mapping, to the mapping shown in Figure 7.3,

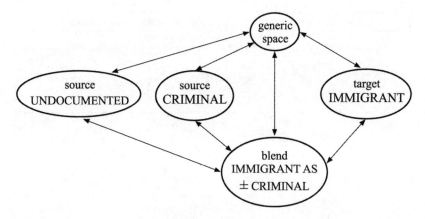

Figure 7.3. Cognitive blend (semiotic incorporation process) illustrated with two source domains for one target domain

a semiotic sign incorporation diagram that blends two metaphors, IMMIGRANT AS CRIMINAL and IMMIGRANT AS UNDOCUMENTED.

Since we lack direct access to basic cognitive processing, we cannot know how individual CNN news viewers processed this blend, but this is plausibly the first step of a multistep cognitive procedure. At the very least, we can propose that it will produce an initial plus-or-minus mapping, [IMMIGRANT AS [± CRIMINAL]], and that distinct visual and spoken signs for IMMIGRANT have been blended in this first stage of cognitive semiotic processing; therefore, various signs trigger the creation of a cognitive space that allows viewers to begin to make sense of what they perceive.

Line and Per Aage Brandt set Fauconnier and Turner's cognitive blend procedure, which in this book we call the "semiotics incorporation process" (SIP), into a more complete cognitive processing sequence that distinguishes three processes viewers use to create readings of news stories: data processing, pragmatics, and social value assignment.[49] In keeping with the purposes of this chapter, we have abridged their formulation. For illustration we will map the semiotic processing of the CNN story anchored by Aaron Brown on the Phoenix drop houses, #24 (see Figure 7.4). All variety of stimuli are entered, identified, classified, and organized in the SIP so viewers can mentally compose meaningful "readings" from them. However, concept buildup is in no way a simple transmission of units of information that viewers decode precisely and completely, and is especially complex for the multimodal stimuli of a televised news story since viewers

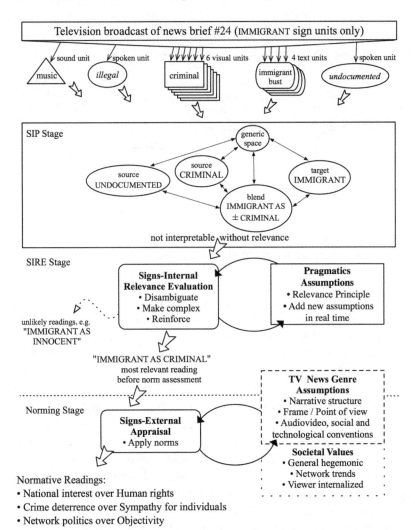

Figure 7.4. Cognitive semiotic processing of network news story signs (illustrated with #24)

employ a complex set of interpretation processes as they watch and listen to a news story. The viewer's final understanding of a news story is better understood as a "reading," rather than a "meaning," since the latter implies a decoding process.

Cognitive scholars posit that external factors have no influence in the SIP, which in Figure 7.4 is placed in a closed rectangle to indicate the isolation in which it produces blends. At this point in the process, no interpretation is yet available. Rather, any number of meaning-making elements are in competition, with much more cognitive work involving interpersonal relations and social value assessment needed in order to "read" these signs.

Cognitivists call the next two processing cycles "working the blend." The output of the SIP becomes the input to what Brandt and Brandt call the "signs-internal relevance evaluation" (SIRE) cycle. Here blends are evaluated for semantic relevance and how well they correspond to basic principles of interpersonal communication, or pragmatics.

In the SIRE cycle, newly generated blends are compared to certain standing pragmatics assumptions held to be part of all human communication.[50] The broad functions of the SIRE include disambiguating input, integrating and complicating semantic domains, and reinforcing content. Part of this reinforcing function is the weighting of different modes of closely related semiotic content. Discussing the relative salience of analogous signs expressed in different modes is well beyond the scope of this book. However, we must note that the salience of the multimodal signs that appear on a television news story in a complex and continuous semiotic stream involves various input and reception factors that are always important.

The crucial information stream factors are instantaneous and momentary relationships among various signs, as well as the accumulated content and built-up impact of sign values over the duration of a news story. The viewer's personal association with and knowledge about the news story topic are also crucial, as is attentiveness in the moment. Moreover, any one of these factors can override all other considerations on a given occasion.

In this chapter we will illustrate comparable salience by assigning numerical values to different sign units and making simple tallies of the combinations. In the CNN news brief, #24, we located nondiegetic sound, spoken, visual, and orthographic text signs (illustrated in Figure 7.4) for the semantic domain IMMIGRANT. So, to illustrate a key function of the SIRE, we will assign one unit of salience per sign of orthographic text, and two salience units per spoken sign, particularly when voiced by the anchor in an establishing shot. We assign three salience units to each visual sign. The greatest weighting is assigned to the visual because, in our ocular-centric society, this domain is often more salient than similar signs expressed in other modes. Since the preeminence of the visual mode in humans is rarely disputed, these absolute weightings are not arbitrary values. This is particularly the case in commercially produced mass-mediated news sto-

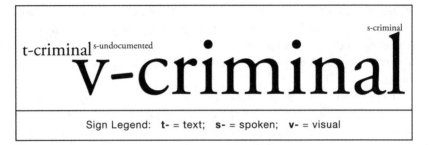

Sign Legend: **t-** = text; **s-** = spoken; **v-** = visual

Figure 7.5. Weighted visual display of IMMIGRANT AS CRIMINAL and IMMIGRANT AS UNDOCUMENTED metaphors in #24

ries, since their videographers create visual content with high production values to secure and retain the viewing audience's attention.

Making a simplifying assumption that all other factors are held in check,[51] we then add up the salience units. Thus in this CNN news story (#24) across all modalities, this formula yields 2 salience units for the IMMIGRANT AS UNDOCUMENTED metaphor and 24 salience units for the IMMIGRANT AS CRIMINAL metaphor. (See Figure 7.5, in which the size of the hyphenated words is proportional to the frequency and different mode weightings of the two metaphors.)[52]

In this CNN news brief, with its 1:12 ratio, only one of the two competing constituent metaphors is more salient. Thus, viewers will most likely read that immigrants are criminals, and dismiss the UNDOCUMENTED reading. The reading and weight of the ideographic metaphor IMMIGRANT AS CRIMINAL will be added to the growing set of semantic information being amassed and organized in the viewers' understanding of the Phoenix drop house news story content.

While contradictory semantic readings may be maintained in news stories, in this 20-second CNN news brief the lopsided ratio makes an ambiguous reading unlikely, irrespective of the ostensible balance of the anchor's spoken reporting. Consequently, alternative readings of the IMMIGRANT concept were likely rejected in the SIRE cycle, such as, for example, that some immigrants are guilty and others innocent, particularly the children shown in news footage.[53] For analytic purposes, the output blend of SIRE has not been assessed with social value information. It might be considered a presocial reading that will be completed in combination with a societal valuation process in the next stage.[54]

Up to now, we have followed the processing of only the IMMIGRANT concept of this news brief. In the next stage we will follow the reading of the news brief's full semiotic input. First, SIRE generates new information and new assumptions that become part of the pragmatic assumptions utilized later in the story and news program. Next, the feedback loop weighs different modes of closely related semiotic content and gathers general, genre-specific, and other assumptions that can be used to narrow and direct sign interpretation. In our case, the viewers tacitly operate to interpret the news story in terms of assumptions of network news programs that differ from situation comedies or police dramas. A cascade of other signs is also circumscribed in terms of sign-internal considerations, such as background information about the news story's topic.

In an obligatory aspect of news stories, and possibly all human social organization,[55] the SIRE feedback cycle organizes this cascading stream of blends into a narrative. Although reality is an endless, unfinished, and precategorical experience, humans break streams of consciousness into "stylistically-structured, morally-inscribed, and finite [chunks that have both] beginning and end."[56] At the micro level, Lakoff characterized the most basic metaphor used for private human experience as the "event," rather than a metaphor for the endless ongoing experience of life.[57] Similarly, news happenings are organized in terms of a particular setting, time frame, plot, set of characters, and actions. In this, the nondiegetic music of the CNN news brief plays its roles. Although composed of both rhythm and melody and spanning multiple camera shots, this music nevertheless functions as a single-sign unit. Its function is to add dramatic energy to the story and to weave together camera shot sequences.[58] Individual viewers actively and unconsciously compose their readings from the network's "mediated narrative,"[59] a story line composed of multimodal digital text that includes the anchor's spoken introduction, selected sequences of video clips and orthographic overlaps, visual images with voice-over, and dramatic music.

In this example, CNN's anchor and newsroom staff used time designations, place, and a set of actions performed by different groups of people and entities to interpret the facts about the Phoenix police action. News writers and video editors added descriptive color to certain bare facts and omitted other factual elements. The story is therefore established with a set of rhetorical directions accessible to the viewing audience. In a selection process called "framing" in communication studies scholarship, viewers use these cues to normalize the facts of the experience in terms of a sequence of events.[60] Cues for specific framings are given by elements of the visual, audio, spoken, and written signs of a news story.

In multimodal renderings of reality, such as televised news stories, it is useful to distinguish other aspects of framing from traditional literary terms that distinguish the senses. *Focus* (or *focalization*) refers to the quality of consciousness though which the story's events are seen.[61] Similarly, Abbott uses the term *voice* to refer to the "sensibility" through which we hear the narrative. Note the distinction between the 20 seconds of unbroken streaming stimuli that constitute the broadcast, from the narrative, which is always focalized, or framed.[62]

The SIRE cycle adds well-fitted new information onto previously held understandings about the topic, immigration. These assumptions accumulate as the news story progresses. The output of the SIRE is input to the signs-external appraisal, or norming cycle, where Brandt and Brandt posit that social meaning is fully integrated into the conceptual message. In Figure 7.4 these are again illustrated as separate cycles, but nonsequential processing is certainly possible. Here, the messages are assessed with societal values drawn from broad hegemonic discursive sources and television network discourse trends (such as mixing entertainment content into news stories, which used to exclude such content). Finally, cognitive theorists argue that the individual viewer makes sense of the mediated narrative in terms of his or her previously understood ways of thinking about the topic at hand, in this case, immigration. These normative assumptions can be unique to the individual and include the individual's views about television viewing, about network news programming, and about other topics associated with the news story.[63]

Although individual readings of the story depend on personal values and understandings, I propose that this news brief promotes three generally shared, normative readings: broad-scope, viewer-level, and institutional. On a broad level, CNN signals that US national interests are more important than the immigrant's personal moral/ethical imperatives. At the viewer's level, a concern for deterring crime is presented as more important than personal sympathy for individual immigrants. The CNN brief eschews so-called journalistic objectivity to render an explicit political perspective on the events in Phoenix.

This step-by-step cognitive processing procedure illustrates how individual viewers construct readings from a 20-second news brief. As Michael Schudson has noted, one source of the power of network news lies in its ability to offer information to viewers who do not have much independent experience relating to topics covered by the news.[64] However, the news media's power to constitute worldview is not limited to people who lack previous understanding of immigration; rather, its power saturates the everyday conceptualization of society and the world of all multimedia consumers.

Addressing Skepticism about Discursive Theory

We offered a detailed breakdown of the cognitive processing of a single news item using a set of assumptions that Schudson calls the "cultural model" of the news, which he aptly describes as offering "language in which action is constituted rather than the action that generates action."[65] Having done so, we agree, in his terms, that American journalists do not consciously "conspire" to "indoctrinate" their television viewers about immigrants and immigration.[66] Nevertheless, news viewers construct their worldviews on the basis of metaphors and narratives that newsrooms broadcast. Even when news editors do not take explicit political stances on topics, networks exercise power by articulating what Thompson calls "dominance relations"[67] in terms of, in Schudson's words, the "common sense" discourse of the public sphere, a "web of meanings and therefore web of presuppositions, in relation to which, to some degree, people live their lives."[68] In spite of his well-stated cultural account,[69] Schudson dismisses the explanatory claim of the discursive theory of journalistic suasion on the grounds that this power is "illusory . . . the visible tip of the iceberg of social influences on human behavior."[70] However, Schudson defines power in terms of federal policy issues, by measuring news media influence in terms of statistical changes in poll numbers. For example, he argues: "Sometimes the media exercise little or no measurable influence" on public opinion, since media coverage of the Monica Lewinsky scandal did not affect "public approval of President Clinton's job performance."[71] Although Schudson highlights particular instances that require greater consideration, these do not invalidate an observation accepted by the vast majority of communication scholars:

> The press plays a major role in public life, influencing citizens' focus of attention and providing many of the facts and opinions that shape perspectives on the topics of the day. . . . The public and policy makers in government at all levels also receive subtle but powerful messages about what is really important in the vast realm of public affairs. . . . This ability to focus attention on a few public issues . . . is the agenda-setting role of the press.[72]

Schudson is particularly skeptical of "notions such as 'agenda-setting,' 'hegemony,' and 'priming,' all [of which] refine but do not discard the concept of [media power source in social] indoctrination."[73] He unfavorably compares mainstream media's influence on society to the power of institutions such as churches: "a television set can never punish a child, but a teacher can, a parent can, a police officer can, a peer group can."[74] He thus argues that models of media power do not address the capacity of individuals to reinterpret, resist, or subvert media messages.[75] Instead he only grants real power to the president and "official sources," government employees who offer journalists tips and viewpoints.[76] In his model, people wield power, and the news is merely the "conduit" for their messages.[77] However, Schudson does concede the point that discursive practices are constitutive when he grants that the messages of official sources have the power to persuade the public. For him, the journalist is a cultural agent who "often unconsciously incorporates general belief systems, assumptions, and values into news writing."[78] Schudson discounts the power of the ritualized news recitation to socialize its audience:[79]

> The media offer only words and images, not love or hate, nothing but symbols, not aid, not notice, not attention, not sentience. They are part of culture, and culture, as anthropologist Clifford Geertz observed, is not itself "a power, something to which social events, behaviors, institutions, or processes can be causally attributed," but "a context, something within which they can be intelligibly . . . described."[80]

While Geertz is quoted correctly, his approach did not posit discourse as a mere backdrop for power. Geertz' ethnography is a social semiotics that considers a society's rituals as cultural "texts" that can be read for insights that are not self-evident. His classic study showed cockfights to be more than a pastime for the Balinese: "It is only apparently cocks that are fighting there. Actually it is men." Geertz' best known tagline fits well with our discursively centered approach: "The culture of a people is an ensemble of texts, themselves ensembles, which the anthropologist strains to read over the shoulders of those to whom they properly belong."[81]

I argue that people build their worldviews in interaction with mass media, specifically with the constitutive elements of discourse streams. As Lakoff, on the micro level, and Foucault, on a macro level, have argued, discourse carries the constitutive elements with which people construct their understanding of the world. It is perhaps surprising that Schudson remains skeptical about discursive analyses of news, since he approvingly cites Anderson's notion of "imagined community." In keeping with the discursive turn, Anderson argued that readers created the European national consciousness with the then-new technology of printing, established via a "rite" in which "each communicant" privately reads a newspaper, "replicated simultaneously by thousands (or millions) of others of whose existence he is confident, yet of whose identity he has not the slightest notion."[82] This "extraordinary mass ceremony" created the imagined community we call the *nation* that "exists in people's minds as objects of orientation and affiliation."[83]

The ubiquity and penetration of mass media in everyday life today would have been unimaginable at the end of the eighteenth century.[84] Now, at the beginning of the twenty-first century, Schudson notes four trends that I argue further reinforce the discursive power of television journalism to shape worldview. First, increasing professional intervention creates television news stories with "a more highly structured, thematic story, less wasted motion, less silence, and more rapid-fire editing."[85] Second, the need for intensified thematic coherence pushes television news to "tell a story" more than newsprint:[86] television is "far more coherently organized and tightly unified" than newspaper stories, which are written in an inverted pyramid format that allows readers to read only lead sentences for their gist. In contrast, television news stories require that the viewer watch a complete news segment.[87] Third, there is increasing inter-institutional news consensus. At the turn of the twentieth century, different newspapers did not run the same articles as rival organizations, even on the back pages, whereas today journalists comparatively assess each other's reporting on the same events, and assume that their audiences are aware of this competition.[88] Finally, today's news media display greater inter-textuality: actual journalist texts are shaped by reference, meaning, and even unacknowledged use of other texts. News writers borrow others' texts so extensively that news has become a more "widely distributed, seamless intertext"[89] at the same time that the range of its content has become more restricted.

Mass media's impact on today's socialization takes the form of individual viewpoints, assumptions, and attitudes that originate in the discursive patterning of the daily news and other mass media semiotic content streams. In particular, network news legitimizes the concepts, narratives, and story lines that they disseminate. Individuals who are exposed to—indeed are inundated by—the media internalize this imagistic discourse. This socializing discourse is also reinforced by other institutions (such as church, school, and the courts) to become crucial elements of the identities of members of their imagined communities.

CNN, like the other networks, works institutionally to legitimate itself in several ways, including by offering its extensive daily broadcasting operation and by structuring each news story and brief with the identifiable CNN format. It has two professional goals. First, it seeks to present the most important events of the day in a truthful manner. However, rather than admitting that any rendering of facts is filtered by a lens of interpretation, CNN takes the position that truth can be reported in a narrative. We will address this assumption of truth in the following chapter.

Second, CNN purports to present a balanced view on politically divisive issues. However, in our sample news brief, #24, CNN articulated the "common sense" about immigrants in a 20-second symbolic product. This product was constructed with a 12:1 ratio of semiotic units, overwhelmingly articulating one constitutive metaphor, IMMIGRANT AS CRIMINAL, over another, IMMIGRANT AS UNDOCUMENTED. This dominant metaphor existed in the public discourse, had been challenged by immigrant rights advocates over the previous 20 years, and was contested by President Bush, who offered an alternate metaphor in 2004. Yet CNN's news brief gave only lip service to the president's alternative, defining the social relations and subject position of the IMMIGRANT vis-à-vis the subject position of the PO-LICE. Over time, the criminality frame was primed among repeat viewers to be the most accessible interpretation of the facts of the news item. This encouraged the perception of immigrants as outlaws, subject to the actions of the police and ICE agents whose role in the narrative is to uphold the nation's rule of law. While coverage of the legal aspects of the immigration debates was certainly appropriate, CNN's journalism was not even close to balanced, because viewers were not encouraged to consider other narratives for immigrants. CNN's unwillingness to engage alternative images of immigrants, as well as alternative political viewpoints, suggests a minor modification in its catchphrase. Communicatively and politically, CNN is "the Most Trusted Frame in News."

We turn now to our final substantive chapter, where we will explore the potential of cognitive blending processing to illuminate the source of ideology in the myths and stories conveyed in everyday televised news.

CHAPTER 8

Adding Narrative to Semiotics: Myths That Underlie News Stories

I demonstrated in Chapter 1 that network news offers paltry few reports about Latinos. The semiotic readings of a set of these few stories illustrated that the networks present an exceedingly narrow vision of Latinos to the nation. When I explored a single topic, immigration, I found significant image and frame repetition. Given such restricted network news reporting, I am concerned that network ideology prejudices viewer opinions about Latinos. To this point, I have not directly addressed the narrative of television news stories. In this chapter, we will explore how narrative fits into the cognitive procedure presented in the previous chapter, and what it buys us.

Although narrative will not redeem network news reporting on Latinos, I will argue that narrative can provide a new and better criterion for American journalism than the criteria used for the past hundred years. To that end, in this chapter I will also address the standard journalistic claim that the best journalists strive to be objective in their news reporting. Objectivity demands that journalistic reporting be fair, factual, unbiased, and nonpartisan. I will argue that it is impossible to objectively report on a news event—but not because correspondents can't get their facts straight. Rather, it is because they tell a story about the facts. However, before I address objectivity, we will delve into narrative.

In this section's epigraph, Northrup Frye claims that stories precede ideas, and ideologies are derived from narratives. With the advent of cognitive modeling, we can provide the beginnings of an explanatory framework for the lightly empiricized scholarship on television news narrative. We will pursue Frye's view, demonstrating its consistency with cognitive modeling, to offer constructive criticism of US journalism. We begin our exploration of news narratives about Latinos by elaborating our blending process, by way of an exploration of visual semiotic theory and second-order signs processing.

Constellations of Multimodal Signs

The process of blending incorporates various sign types (visual, text, spoken) for news audience readings, that is, interpretations. The blending process incorporates non-metaphor semantic units as well as metaphors as a constellation of meanings. Figure 8.1 shows graphic renderings of such blend constellations.

The graphic representations of "on-the-fly" blends shown in Figure 8.1 illustrate how news viewers may construct their own readings of a news story subject. To begin we will draw on an instance we used in a previous chapter: the distinct metaphors of IMMIGRANT AS CRIMINAL and IMMIGRANT AS UNDOCUMENTED.

In Chapter 6, we reviewed a CBS news story (#117) about the effects of Arizona's Proposition 200. The semiotic content of one scene of this news story was as follows: CBS correspondent Jerry Bowen introduced viewers to an unauthorized immigrant woman in a single scene that began with Bowen's voice-over: *"It was 10 years ago that Angelita sneaked across to*

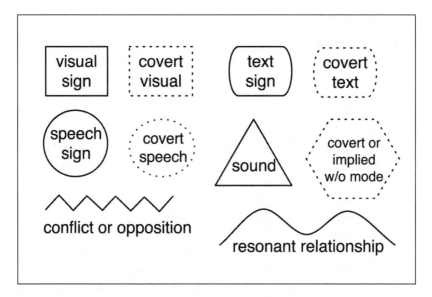

Figure 8.1. Legend of elements for multimodal blends

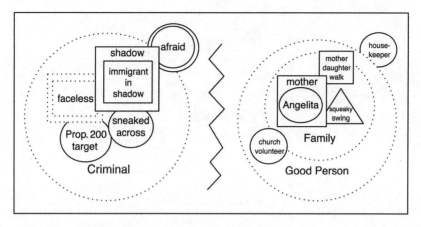

Figure 8.2. Constellations of two conflicting conceptualizations of Angelita, as depicted in one scene of #117

work as a housekeeper, a church volunteer, and raise her family. Now, she's afraid to show her face." This is followed by Angelita's own account (spoken in translation by an unnamed woman): "Ten years have passed, and I live in fear in a country that can send me back to Mexico—at any moment." Bowen then continues in voice-over: "Angelita is in the Prop. 200 bull's-eye because she's still illegal. So is her oldest daughter. Only her youngest girl is safe, a citizen born in the USA." The final words are Angelita's translated report: "The oldest asks: 'Why, why can't we be accepted as Americans, all of us?'"

This spoken account was accompanied on-screen by seven camera shots: first, a shot of the undocumented mother walking away from the camera on a Tucson street, with her daughter in hand, followed by a purposely underexposed shot in her house. In Shot 3 viewers can begin to make out, in an underexposed three-quarter close-up, the woman in profile. The low light exposure intentionally keeps Angelita's face hidden. A shot of her backyard follows, in which Angelita can be discerned playing with her daughter in the shadows on a swing set. Shot 5 begins with an over-the-back shot of Angelita, allowing viewers to see the little girl on the swing, and then pans to a mid-shot of the younger daughter. Here viewers are permitted to see the child's face, because she is an American citizen. The last two shots are a long shot of the whole backyard, facing into the sun so that Angelita's face is hidden, followed by an underexposed three-quarter close-up of Angelita in profile. Bowen offers no additional commentary to this scene, which is followed by an unrelated hospital scene in another town. See Figure 8.2.

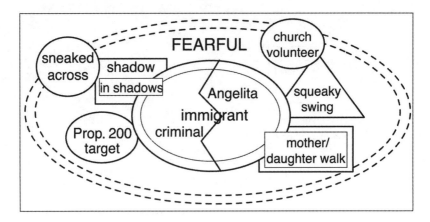

Figure 8.3. Alternative single constellation of Angelita

Angelita's scene articulates two complex and conflicting blends: a criminal immigrant versus decent mother of a family. The blend process explains how television audiences compose rich, complex semiotic assemblages on the fly. In this example, blends were composed from the semiotic information reported in one scene of a CBS news story about one person. The constellations were made up of the multiple but semantically related units of meaning.[1] The graphic representations of blends illustrate what kinds of readings were made available, and how news viewers might put these together on the fly as the news stories were told. However, the graphics in Figure 8.2 are meant only to offer one possible reading of each of the two blends.

Other arrangements are possible. A single constellation (Figure 8.3) is possible instead of two. This may begin to represent the painful personal feelings, bounded by fear, that people such as Angelita experience. However, it seemed unlikely that most news viewers would compose such an empathetic constellation as they viewed the news story. How individual viewers read, that is, mentally compose, such constellations depends on all of the internal and external sign considerations described in Chapter 7.

Visual Semiotic Modeling

To further understand these blends, we refer to one of the twentieth century's most influential theorists and practitioners, Roland Barthes.[2] When speaking about photographs, he argued for two tiers of semiotic signs, a more basic first-order "language" system and a more abstract "second-order semiological system" that he called *myth*.[3] Barthes' two-tier theory shares many aspects with later theories of visual semiotics. Theo van Leeuwen characterizes Barthes' first-order "language" tier as *denotative* (who or what is depicted), in contrast to *connotative* (what ideas and values are expressed through what is represented and the way in which it is represented).[4] Van Leeuwen and his colleagues advanced Barthes' framework with "social semiology," a system that I have found particularly useful to track the multimodal stream of signs flowing in a television news story.[5] In social semiotics, signs are resources (rather than a code), and semiotic expression opens up "meaning potentials"; that is to say, restricted fields of possible readings arise (rather than a single specific meaning), in our case, among news viewers.[6] Barthes' classic analysis of a single cover of an iconic French photo magazine, *Paris-Match* (similar to *Time* magazine), offers a sense of his visual semiotics:

> On the cover, a young Negro in a French uniform is saluting, with his eyes uplifted, probably fixed on a fold of the tricolor. All this is the *meaning* of the picture. But whether naively or not, I see very well what it signifies to me: that France is a great Empire, that all her sons, without any color discrimination, faithfully serve under her flag, and that there is no better answer to the detractors of an alleged colonialism than the zeal shown by this Negro in serving his so-called oppressors. I am therefore again faced with a [second-order] semiological system: there is a signifier, itself already formed with the previous system "a black soldier is giving the French salute"; and there is a signified "it is here a purposeful mixture of Frenchness and militariness."[7]

Barthes claims that the collection of denotative signs—an African soldier in a French uniform saluting an off-screen French flag—becomes a "sum of signs" that makes certain other readings possible. In this case, "French imperialism" becomes available to someone looking at the *Paris-Match* cover who has French cultural visual literacy. This bundle of first-order signs expresses one second-order sign. Barthes notes that many combinations of first-order signs can signal a second-order sign; however, the selection of particular imagery that stands for a second-order sign remains a deliberate and "motivated" choice, since each second-order sign is "open to the whole of History." This observation pertains to television news storytelling as well.

Barthes observed that when a second-order sign is read from the images on the magazine cover, the African soldier is reduced to a form that is used to communicate a concept. The life and history of the individual young man drains away and is ultimately lost to the *Paris-Match* reader, who reads the photo as a myth. Barthes' notion of myth as a "repository of a rarefied meaning," a small subset of concepts in which, as Howell puts it, "societies encode their hopes, dreams, needs, fears and cultural values even though they may take the overt form of other things, such as stories about dragons, heroes or wings made of wax."[8] Gillian Rose expresses this well:

> The contingency and the history of the meaning becomes remote, and instead a myth inserts itself as a non-historical truth. Myth makes us forget that things were and are made; instead, it naturalizes the way things are. Myth is thus a form of ideology. . . . But the myth is believable precisely because form does not entirely replace meaning . . . the interpretation of mythologies requires a broad understanding of a culture's dynamics.[9]

Certain aspects of Barthes' two-tier model have been rightly criticized. However, his key observation, which exemplifies how surface visual representations express more abstract concepts and a different class of semantic information, has not been displaced.

With only minor differences, McGee's ideographs operate in the same way as second-order signs. Ideographs are expressed as words or phrases, such as *equality*, that are written or spoken in only one form in newsprint.[10] In NBC's #48 and ABC/BBC's #116 news stories, the terms *illegal immigrant, border patrol agent*, and *border* are ideographs. In the multimodal medium of television, a wide range of combinations of first-order signs can signal the ideograph. Like myths, ideographs are first-order signs that have been elevated to second-order signals "representing collective commitment to a particular but equivocal and ill-defined normative goal."[11] The ideograph does not evoke merely a complex concept, but a full-fledged story.[12]

Making cognitive sense of Barthes' insight is the basic goal of the graphics in Figure 8.2. They depict the relationship between two constellations expressing a woman's social standing, discerned in the multimodal semiotic stream broadcast of a single scene of a CBS news story. The sum-of-signs, or second-order sign, analysis of this television scene thus might be stated as follows: US society maintains contradictory values toward Angelita, as a criminal and as an honest woman. One is the constellation (ultimately the social narrative) that she deliberately violated US law and is a criminal who deserves punishment. This is opposed by another constellation and social narrative that Angelita, like most unauthorized immigrants, is a good person who committed a minor civil infraction for the greater moral purpose of earning her daily bread and providing for her children.

Sum-of-signs analyses of visually complex stories can be informative. We can point to the coverage of José Padilla (Chapter 2). In #60 CBS methodically laid out the federal indictment against Padilla with rich graphics to visually assert that Padilla was a terrorist, making no effort to balance the coverage with Padilla's defense. CBS even visually blended Padilla's photo with one of a known terrorist to semiotically merge their identities. In 2004 the news media drained away the Chicago-born Latino's personal qualities from the public's understanding; his mug shot became a second-order sign for *"gang member turned terrorist"* and *"enemy combatant."* Meanwhile, during the same period two individuals who had been already convicted of terrorist acts, William Krar and John Walker Lindh, were not subject to such network news dehumanizing. They remained people in the public eye, not second-order signs for terrorism.

Two Examples of Sum of Signs

We will further explore sum-of-signs analysis in two news stories about immigrants that displayed high production values, using graphic representations of the blended multimodal sign constellations broadcast in them. Placing each sign in a cluster, or constellation, allows an assessment of its contribution to the whole. The complexity of individual concepts and the reiteration of elements (such as *immigrant, border,* and *border patrol agent*), as well as the resulting second-order signs, are more readily evaluated first scene by scene and then across the whole news story.

We return to two news stories we previously read closely, #48 and #116, to provide a scene-by-scene analysis of the semiotic elements that is summarized in Tables 8.1 and 8.2. The left-hand column offers a rendering of the blended constellations that were expressed, as if each scene were a single photograph. The right-hand column describes the semiotic elements of each scene, and the spoken and graphic text signs expressed during each scene. What we note immediately is that there are relationships between the constellations, which we take to be similar to Barthes' second-order signs, or concepts.

ABC/BBC Story (#116)

Table 8.1 breaks down story #116, a typical report on the drama of migration across the US/Mexican border (discussed in Chapter 6). In a minute and a half, BBC correspondent Frei presents a series of metaphors and different framings to characterize immigrants. First they are desperate humans, then hunted animals, an invading army, individuals fighting for their lives against the desert, and finally people who sacrifice their human dignity for mere survival. Accomplished news team camera work emphasizes the individuality and humanity of immigrants without sentimentality, allowing viewers to identify with their plight. Since this camera work occurs before immigrants are described as animals or as an army, these ensuing dehumanizing metaphors are mitigated. Frei and the camera crew also offer a compassionate portrait of the border patrol agent; in the end, the multiple framings in this story allow viewers to perceive with humanity what immigration means to these different subjects.

The second-order sign analysis (Table 8.1) of the ABC/BBC news story is as follows. The news story unfolds with the standard mid-shot of the anchor at his desk. Behind him viewers see a digital screen map of the United States and Mexico overlaid with the title "Dangerous Crossing," and a static image of a man whose face is hidden in a hooded sweatshirt straddling a barbwire fence. The visual images in Scene 1 are limited to the over-the-shoulder graphic labeled "Dangerous Crossing," while the anchor verbally introduces the subjects of the story as both *illegal* and *undocumented* immigrants.

This array of multimodal signs might best be understood as a relationship among three groupings of signs: the border, the immigrant, and the smugglers. The border and smuggler constellations are relatively simple. The border is dangerous and permeable; the smugglers' actions are inhumane. In contrast, the immigrant constellation is complex, involving a cluster of signs indicative of immigrants as human beings (moving, endangered, and dying), with the smugglers as their antagonists. The relationships between these immigrant signs and the smuggler signs are not in conflict; each cluster helps define the other. However, there is some dissonance with the remaining immigrant signs, which characterize them as criminal. The final second-order sign of this scene is "immigrants are human beings desperate to cross a border that is made dangerous by heartless smugglers."

The second-order sign derived from the constellation in Scene 1 is not as complete as the second-order sign "French imperialism" that Barthes discerned in the cover photo of *Paris-Match*. The constellation is drawn from only the first scene of a 10-scene televised news story, not a self-contained magazine cover. Next, I will describe each of the successive scenes and characterize the second-order signs that I believe are expressed in the news story. Scene 2 offers a cluster of signs showing Mexico as an unpaved, vacant desert, an uncivilized place patrolled by US border agents. An implied sign, therefore, is the US as civilized, juxtaposed to the uncivilized Mexico. In Scene 3, a series of close-up shots of the faces of immigrating Latin Americans, together with the correspondent's poignant description, further humanizes the immigrants, who are depicted as people exploited by smugglers, with the minibus seen as a shield that transports them from an uncivilized Latin America. Neither Scene 3 nor Scene 4 portrays these immigrants as criminals. In Scene 4, the constellation of signs depicts Mexican officials as humanitarians, not policing agents, and introduces another antagonist: the desert.

In Scene 5 an entirely new point of view is introduced and signaled with a shift of metaphors or ideographs. Here the border patrol agents are depicted as on a safari (only secondarily on a military mission) to track immigrants, who in turn are depicted as animals. This expedition is entertaining and fun for the hunters (they look for footprints and other traces of their prey). The ICE agents speak about them, and otherwise depict them, as migrating animals, *"a veritable stampede"* that is being hunted. In Scene 6 the camera and correspondent strip the immigrants of their human subjectivity. The correspondent's voice-over accompanies video images of a well-worn path *"littered with traces"* of *"precious personal belongings dumped, because they've become too heavy."* Here, the metaphor constellation clusters of IMMIGRANT and ICE AGENT define one another.

Any amusement associated with the safari expedition characterization is quickly replaced in Scene 7 with the deadly seriousness of war, as signaled by another metaphor change. The correspondent asks US border patrol agent Garrett Neubauer if the border patrol is "fighting a losing battle," to which Neubauer offers a hesitant response. Although there is no explicit reference to immigrants in this scene, a full constellation is implied (as illustrated in Table 8.1) of the IMMIGRANT AS ENEMY.

In Scene 8, close-up shots of cholla cactus and discarded water bottles articulate a juxtaposition of immigrant and desert in another war, one with thousands of casualties. The immigrant injury and death toll imagery—a battle with the relentless desert—suspends but does not replace the other battle with the border patrol.

Scene 9 presents an interview with and close-up shots of two Honduran

Table 8.1. Second-order sign analysis and semiotic constellations of #116 (ABC)

Semiotic constellation	Depiction and text
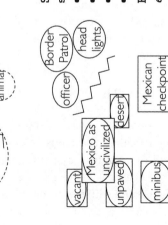	Scene 1: Minimal pan in to anchor at his desk. Background graphic of US/Mexico border map, and two photos of hooded men jumping a low fence. The story title "Dangerous Crossing" in large letters dominates the screen. Anchor: *"A Texas jury resumes deliberations this week in the trial of two men charged in a tragic and disgraceful episode of human smuggling. Nineteen illegal immigrants died in the back of a stifling truck last spring. The accused were allegedly transporting the immigrants across the Mexican border. As the BBC's Matt Frei reports for us tonight, the stream of immigrants is as constant as the dangers they face."* Scene 2: Van approaches from desert horizon and dissolves into Shot 3. (Dissolves symbolize time passing.) • Van now closer to camera. Dissolves into Shot 4. • Van moving away from camera. Dissolves into Shot 5. • Van on opposite horizon. • Van stops at Mexican checkpoint. Frei (voice-over): *"Late afternoon and it's rush hour on a dusty road in Mexico; every one of these minibuses is heading to the US border. Twenty miles to go and there's a Mexican government checkpoint."*

Scene 3: Tight close-up on man in van.
- Tight close-up on 2nd man.
- Tight close-up on 3rd man in van; pan reveals 4th man.
- Van interior wide shot reveals passengers.
- Tight close-up of woman; pans to reveal 2nd woman.

Frei (voice-over): *"The passengers are unwilling to talk, caught between hope and fear. They come from every corner of Latin America. Some have paid $5,000 or more to a people smuggler to get this far. When night falls they'll sneak across the border into the US in what they hope will be a better life. They and thousands like them everyday."*

Scene 4: Mexican officer inspects van.
- Close-up of leaflets handed to migrants.
- Extreme close-up of leaflets.

Frei (voice-over): *"The Mexican officials no longer try to stop them. Instead, they hand out leaflets telling them how not to die in the Arizona desert."*

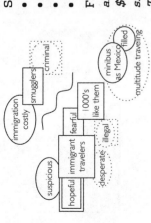

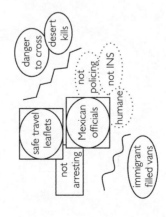

(continued)

Table 8.1. (continued)

Semiotic constellation	Depiction and text
	Scene 5: Full shot of border patrol Hummer.
	• 2-shot of agent and reporter.
	• Full shot of agent inspecting footprints. Camera zooms in to footprints close-up.
	• 2-shot of agents inspecting ground.
	Agent Neubauer: *"And you can see all along here."*
	Frei: *"So these are fresh footprints here?"*
	Neubauer: *"Right."*
	Frei: *"Oh yeah. The next morning on the other side, what greets the US Border Patrol is evidence of a veritable stampede of illegal migrants."*
	Neubauer: *"You can see over here, you can see the fingerprints where some-one's crawled under."*
	Scene 6: Close-up of backpack left behind, then pans to toothpaste packet.
	• Close-up of dusty discarded shoes.
	• Close-up of child's Tweety Bird backpack.
	Frei (voice-over): *"Well-worn paths are littered with traces, precious personal belongings dumped because they've become too heavy."*

Scene 7: 2-shot of Frei interviewing Agent Neubauer.

Frei: *"When you look at all this, do you feel that you're fighting a losing battle?"*

Neubauer: *"Um, I don't know if I would say a 'losing battle.' Um, you know, we, we know that the, the volume of traffic is out there, but we also know that, um, the border patrol in general is doing a good job. We're stopping a lot of it, appre-hending a lot of it."*

Scene 8: Close-up of cactus; pans to wide shot of desert.
- Close-up of empty water jug.

Frei (voice-over): *"Forget about fingerprints or visas; here the biggest obstacle is the desert. Last year, 600 people died of thirst crossing the border."*

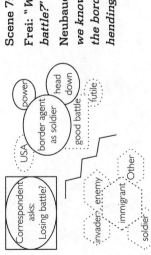

(continued)

Table 8.1. (continued)

Semiotic constellation	Depiction and text
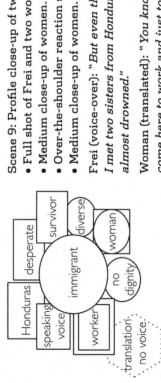	Scene 9: Profile close-up of two women. • Full shot of Frei and two women. • Medium close-up of women. • Over-the-shoulder reaction shot of Frei. • Medium close-up of women. Frei (voice-over): *"But even this isn't enough to deter the desperate. In Phoenix, I met two sisters from Honduras. They crossed the Rio Grande last month and almost drowned."* Woman (translated): *"You know full well, there's no dignity in any of this. You come here to work and just to work. It's all about survival."* Scene 10: Wide shot of desert zooming in to center, Hummer on right-hand side. Frei (voice-over): *"It's a game of cat and mouse, but the mouse is winning. Only one in three migrants gets caught. Matt Frei, BBC News, Arizona."*
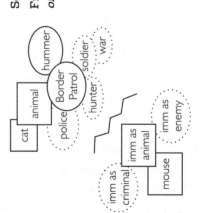	

sisters, in which they state that immigrating involves both danger and the loss of dignity. The concept of this scene is of immigrants as human, with the women allowed to express themselves. Finally in Scene 10, the camera depicts the futility of the border patrol's efforts in an immense desert as the correspondent speaks about a *"game of cat and mouse"* in which the immigrant is winning. This closing presents a contrast with the previous scene, in which the immigrants expressed no sense of winning the game.

NBC Story

Let us now compare the constellations of signs of this innovative and informative ABC/BBC news story to a news story from NBC. We discussed story #48, which has a conventional story line and predictable elements, in Chapter 5. NBC explored whether or not President Bush's immigration policy reform initiative had led to an actual increase in unauthorized immigration. The network gave this assignment to an experienced correspondent, James Hattori, and aired his feature-length piece in the NBC "In Depth" series. Hattori constructs a story asserting that Bush's initiative has led to more immigration, even though this claim cannot be verified. Hattori passes over a less dramatic, alternative explanation for apparent increases: seasonal labor patterns. The NBC correspondent moves his thesis forward with two truncated interviews, sidestepping the anchor's fundamental query about the economics fueling increased immigration—until the story's final scene. There, Hattori asks border patrol agent Penco about the (ultimate) source of this desperation, but the border patrol agent can only offer a superficial response.

The second-order sign analysis (Table 8.2) of the NBC news story follows. In Scene 1, the anchor poses the question: *What is driving this desperation?* Two constellations of signs are presented, the immigrant as both VICTIM and CRIMINAL, and IMMIGRATION AS AN INCREASING FLOOD. Scene 2 quickly presents the first answer to the anchor's query. It is not despair, but cyclical farmwork that draws a seasonal increase of workers. In this scene, the answer is shown through a pair of semiotic constellations. The Mexican immigrant is the core of one constellation, with links to four seasonal migration signs, six surge and influx signs, and Spanish-speaking workers. In this case, the second constellation (the border patrol officer who describes the immigrants) does not stand in conceptual opposition to the immigrant.

At the end of Scene 2, the NBC correspondent claims that 530,000 border patrol apprehensions have occurred in past six months. This

Table 8.2. Second-order sign analysis and semiotic constellations of #48 (NBC)

Semiotic constellation	Depiction and text
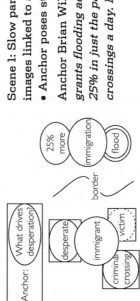	**Scene 1:** Slow pan in to anchor at desk. Backscreen flashes six video and photo images linked to anchor query, e.g., barbed wire, hooded men.
	• Anchor poses story topic question.
	Anchor Brian Williams: *"NBC News 'In Depth' tonight: the rise of illegal immigrants flooding across the Mexican border into the US. There's been a jump of 25% in just the past six months, which translates into as many as 2,000 illegal crossings a day. NBC's James Hattori explains what's driving this desperation."*
 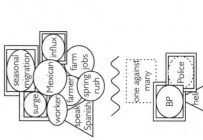	**Scene 2:** 12 shots.
	• Shot from inside a border patrol agent's truck.
	• Shot of snaking border fence.
	• Full shot of Agent Penco asking two men for documents.
	• 4-shot of people moving at a distance, ends with helicopter sound and shot.
	• Desert night shots of agents with captured migrants.
	Hattori (voice-over): *"This is part of this border right here in Nogales, Arizona; the 'Spring Rush' is on for border patrol agents like Joe Penco, coping with an influx of Mexican workers seeking farm jobs."*
	Penco: *"Traditionally they return in the spring months."*
	Hattori (voice-over): *"But after four years of decline, there is an apparent surge in illegal immigration. Nationwide 530,000 people have been detained for*

trying to cross the border over the last six months, a 25% increase compared to last year. And more than half were picked up in Arizona."

Scene 3: Standard ¾-shot of bureaucrat in staged office setting for official statement.

Border patrol commissioner: *"The border patrol is apprehending, on average, close to 2,000 a day."*

Scene 4: Full body shot of Hattori, arms outstretched to show "porous" desert.
- Long shot of dusty Mexican desert town.
- Traffic in unpaved downtown, men in back of pickup truck.
- Men on porch; men walking.

Hattori (voice-over): *"This is why the border here is so porous: the wide-open, sparsely populated high desert that spans across much of southern Arizona. And in Sásabe, a small Mexican town just across the border . . ."*

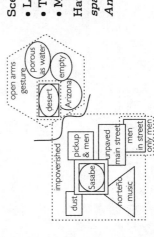

(continued)

Table 8.2. *(continued)*

Semiotic constellation	Depiction and text
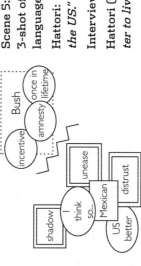	Scene 5: Close-up of Mexican man (interviewee) zooms back to compose a 3-shot of another presumed migrant and Hattori. Significant conflicting body language: Hattori leans forward; interviewees lean back, hands behind back. Hattori: *"Some believe there is a new, once-in-a-lifetime incentive to sneak into the US."* Interviewee (translated): *"I think so."* Hattori (voice-over): *"This man says if they really give them amnesty, it's better to live over there than here."*
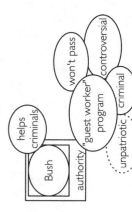	Scene 6: ¾-shot of Bush speaking in White House, zoom in to fade. • Long shot of border town sidewalk full of people. • Close-up of immigrant advocate in abbreviated interview. Hattori (voice-over): *"He's referring to President Bush's proposal last January for a new guest worker program that would grant status to illegal migrants already working in the US. They feel that, that Bush will implement certain programs that will help the undocumented worker. But Bush's proposal is controversial and likely won't be addressed by Congress this year."*

Scene 7: Cut to close-up of US flag, immediate fade to long shot of border port of entry.

- Quick shot of two people stepping out of car trunk into border patrol custody.
- Previously aired nighttime desert detention.

Hattori (voice-over): *"Also, border patrol officials say the spike in apprehensions began before the president announced his plan. They credit beefed-up enforcement in Arizona."*

Scene 8: Mid-shot of men loitering in Sásabe, Chihuahua.

- Mexican flag in wind and men working with pick and shovel.
- 2-shot of Hattori and Penco, who responds to off-camera query.
- Close-up of border patrol officer scanning with binoculars, to long shot of desert from agent's point of view.

Hattori (voice-over): *"What they can't combat, dire economic conditions in Mexico that draw so many to the US."*

Penco: *"The job market, quality of life, that, that will probably always be there."*

Hattori (voice-over): *"And always keep watchful eyes along the border. James Hattori, NBC News, Sásabe, Arizona [sic]."*

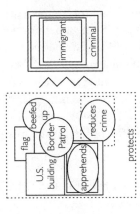

uncontextualized statistic is a lead-in to Scene 3, in which the border patrol commissioner states that this success has resulted from greater efficiency. However, he does not mention an increase in the flow of immigrants. Regardless, this commissioner's pronouncement sets up a twin-pole constellation defining the relationship of police and criminal, which is the second-order sign of the scene. It also confirms the claim (which will be repeated) that immigrant crossings have very recently increased.

In Scene 4, Hattori takes charge of the story by taking up an issue the anchor did not pose. He gestures with outstretched arms to a vast, empty high desert, stating that immigrants migrate because they face no effective barrier to the US. The desert is *"porous."* Multimodal images of a dusty Mexican town are displayed, including Norteño music and stray dogs crossing an unpaved main street. However, the image constellation does not merely depict Sásabe, Mexico, as a travelers' way station; the dusty town becomes a second-order sign of Mexico as the poor, backward world from which immigrants are escaping.

In Scene 5, Hattori says in voice-over that President Bush's immigration reform initiative has created *"a new, once-in-a-lifetime incentive to sneak into the US."* The correspondent receives nominal confirmation from an unnamed interviewee in Sásabe (*"I think so"*) in response to an off-camera question. The NBC viewer is encouraged to read into this a second-order sign that Bush's initiative encourages immigration.[13]

In Scene 6, that second-order sign is a triangle constellation of sign clusters including President Bush, his controversial guest worker program, and the Latino population. This triangle further supports the NBC correspondent's thesis: Bush's policy initiative, which *"would grant status to illegal migrants already working in the US,"* would encourage even more illegal immigration. The large criminal presence of undocumented immigrants is opposed by the border patrol in Scene 7. The border patrol is shown defending the US against criminal immigrants. Finally, Scene 8 defines the opposition with a cluster of signs that characterizes Mexico's permanent state of despair. Here correspondent Hattori walks side by side with border patrol agent Penco in a 2-shot, signaling empathy with the officer. Hattori then asks Penco the original question: What drives the immigrants' desperation? In this scene Penco's answer, economics, also expresses the pointlessness of border patrol's policing mission. The futility of the mission is the scene's second-order sign.

The sum-of-signs analyses of television news stories reveal rich constellations of readings and key relationships in each scene of these news stories. However, the sum-of-signs method does not capture the dynamism of news stories. The news story second-order signage was typically not an abstract term like *French imperialism*, but was a plot move or a juxtaposition. The sum of signs did not capture the qualitative differences between the two stories discussed—in short, the narratives.

Nevertheless, Barthes' structuralist analysis remains pertinent.[14] He analyzed culturally embedded signs hidden in plain sight. Like the American anthropologist Clifford Geertz, who learned to read the meanings of the Balinese cockfights, Barthes read his own Western European culture as an assemblage of semiotic texts that articulate social values and cultural forms.[15] Moreover, Barthes' myths, like McGee's ideographs, are everyday signs used in the daily discourse of a community of users. In this sense, collectivities of language users define and redefine these signs in "horizontal" synchronic use. These vernacular terms, which as second-order signs express higher-order abstractions of equivocal and normative concepts, are used to justify social classification and action. Before turning to narrative, the element of news stories that sums of signs do not capture, we will address the key and problematic criterion of American journalistic excellence: objectivity.

Critique of Journalistic Truth and Objectivity

One source of the everyday discourse of a society is its television news reporting. Just as French societal myths are expressed on French magazine covers, so US television news reports reflect the myths of US society. This view, that US journalism markets not only the day's events but also a conventional interpretation of the same, may strike the journalist as an unfair criticism, since objectivity became the touchstone of US journalism in the twentieth century and is generally considered a signal advance over the partisan reporting of earlier periods.[16] Objectivity mandates that reporting be fair, factual, unbiased, and nonpartisan. However, critics call this a chimera; its most ferocious detractors claim that while US journalism touts this principle, it favors the political views of government and corporate interests. In this view objectivity has been a fig leaf allowing corporate news to normalize an autocratic status quo and rationalize the oppression of weaker groups of people both domestically and internationally.[17] Schudson notes that the news-gathering process produces bias; apprentice journalists are selected and socialized to a restricted range of values; and the objective writing style can conceal bias.[18] Finally, the disinterested tone of newspaper writing has led to the normalizing of reporting of horrendous acts like genocide and lynchings.[19] However, in 1978 Schudson concluded that no new criterion has arisen to challenge, much less replace, this problematic "objectivity,"[20] and even today US journalists retain it as the standard of the profession. In my view, the source of the problem is systemic.[21]

It is impossible to report objectively about a news event. Philosopher of history Hayden White provides a sustained critique about another professional community's inability to give a truthful accounting of the day's events, in this case, nineteenth-century historians. The issue was not a matter of content; it was a matter of the form of narratives. To tell a story about the facts of an event, to narrate a story, fundamentally changes the relationship of the facts to people. White argues that before the raw facts of a historical event are reported, they are mere data points without orientation, social meaning, or truth value. However, to tell a story about the facts necessarily transforms them. Those meaningless points of information become coherent and normatively meaningful; only stories can be more or less true.[22] To make sense of these data points imposes values on them.

Moreover, we are talking about a fundamental element of human consciousness.[23] One aspect of being human is to tell stories. But narrative's omnipresence hides its distinctive features. The presumption of journalists is that competent correspondents can gather the facts of a news event and, by writing good copy, transparently transmit that knowledge to the news consumer. However, this professional conceit cannot avoid the structural constraints of human language and communication. Knowledge is constituted, not found whole. Similarly, people do not communicate by transferring whole messages from sender to receiver; they must compose readings of them.

Any effort by historians, and by extension journalists, to account for a day's events with "order and fullness" turns the raw facts of the event into a coherent story, or narrative.[24] Narratives assimilate objective facts into a subjectively written story. Since narratives have plots, White notes, historians end up writing history as romances, tragedies, comedies, satires, or epics. This certainly is the case for journalists as well. Narratives further impose the particular point of view of a community or "social center" on raw facts.[25] White asserts that the historian has a basic "impulse to moralize reality," that is, to place the facts of the event into an ethical schema that conforms to the social center.[26] Related to this urge is the journalist's tendency to present the day's events as an allegory to address the behavior of the people reading history.

Thus, while journalists may report the raw facts of a news item (for example, a car crash at a certain time and place), these facts are not socially meaningful or "true" until arranged into a narrative or story. Of course, many journalists (and scholars who are former journalists) acknowledge this. For example, Mark Allen Peterson has characterized some news stories as "discursive constructions," defining a story as "a narrative that makes a point, expresses a meaning."[27]

Journalists dealing daily with the real-world effects of tsunamis and train wrecks have good reason to operate with the view that they are reporting facts. Factual reporting is a badge of honor:

> Members of the Society of Professional Journalists believe that public enlightenment is the forerunner of justice and the foundation of democracy. The duty of the journalist is to further those ends by seeking *truth* and providing a fair and comprehensive account of events and issues.[28]

In reflective moments, moreover, when journalists should put aside the standard and essentializing claim that they mirror reality, they don't. For example Ettema, Whitney, and Wackman write, "Our focus on truth in journalism does not deny the ancient philosophical problems surrounding truth, but . . . we set aside this problem by assuming that *as a practical matter* there is truth to be known and told."[29] Unfortunately, regrettable professional consequences follow from denials that narrative takes preeminence over facts, and that truth is contingent.

In the rest of this chapter, we will offer suggestions and a new criterion that reconcile the "facts on the ground" (for example, babies are born; volcanoes erupt) and the indisputable reality that a news item is an amalgam of facts and story line. We will build on the observation that even digitally videotaping a live news event is subject to narrativization when, for example, one portion of the clip is broadcast while another is deleted. The choice of narrative directs the audience's interpretation of an event, giving the news its power over public perception. Communication scholars have long been impressed by the "priming" power of news, namely its ability to affect the public's assessment of political issues by selecting a narrative frame with which to present facts.

Defining the journalistic frame, however, remains a challenge. Schudson calls these frames "socially organized distortions" built into the routines of news gathering and writing: "Most subjectivity in news is not idiosyncratic and personal but patterned and predictable." However, in addition to the institutional processes that guide and narrow news gathering, there are conceptual constraints on news writing.[30] To this end, Todd

Gitlin called framing "little tacit theories about what exists, what happens, and what matters," and goes on to describe framings as "persistent patterns of cognition, interpretation, and presentation, of selection, emphasis, and exclusion, by which symbol-handlers organize discourse, whether verbal or visual."[31] The crucial element of framing is not the day-to-day operations of the institution, but wrapping a set of facts into a news report. In keeping with this discursive approach, Gamson and Modigliani offer their own definition of framing: "a central organizing idea or story line that provides meaning to an unfolding strip of events, weaving a connection among them."[32] Since framing is an essential feature of all news narratives, akin to the *focalization* of the narrative, I will now explore the characteristics of narratives.

Narrative Structure

The basic structure of a narrative, like the sign, is also a Peirce's triangle. We begin with the most concrete: the news report as it is displayed on the television screen, or what Abbott calls the "narrative discourse."[33] While others simply call it a "text," this does not do justice to the multimodal composition of a script of spoken words interwoven with a montage of camera shots, each made up of digitally recorded computer-generated graphics and/or a filmed choreography of movements and gestures by the correspondent and other people in a setting, all of which is edited by a team of professional journalists. This televised news report is simultaneously a text, a unit of mediated discourse, and a cultural artifact.

The "emplotment" or "narrative" is another point on the triangle.[34] Narratives have time-dependent beginnings and ends, and are composed of three parts: a plot (made up of characters, events, and things); a set of materials called a "description" that provides rhetorical directions for the narrative; and an argument, or point of view. Point of view is what Abbott calls the "quality of consciousness" through which viewers comprehend the events and characters. Sometimes it is useful to distinguish arguments expressed visually (*focus*) from those expressed by way of sound (*voice*).

Finally there is the story type, what Abbott calls the "master-plot" and what Northrup Frye referred to as the "archetype."[35] These are very old, traditionally recognized story lines that are rendered in any number of ways across wide swaths of humanity. "Cinderella," for example, is a traditional folktale about a persecuted heroine, embodying a myth element of unjust oppression and triumphant reward. This story type and its accompanying social meanings and values will be recognized, even if tacitly. The scholarship on myth and archetype in literature is immense.[36]

Narratology, the rich and subtle academic study of narrative, has focused on "poetic models of discourse featuring formalistic criteria of evaluation,"[37] rather than on social theory. Lucaites and Condit note that academic theories investigate the narratives, particularly of outstanding unique cultural products, through the lens of aesthetic expression, but only incidentally make reference to the social context in which these cultural texts were composed. Such formal literary analyses are part of substantive programs to explore the aesthetic creative process, but they are not particularly well equipped to reveal how our mass-mediated society uses formulaic televised news reports that purport to mirror the most significant events of the day.

Victoria Lynn Schmidt offers a serviceable typology of narrative in a book for aspiring writers, identifying five elements common to all narrative: conflict, dramatic situations, through-lines, master structures, and genre.[38] Narratives are built around *conflicts*. Schmidt notes that although narratives often employ more than one conflict, there is always at least one. For Schmidt, these conflicts are created, at their most basic, by at least one of about two dozen *dramatic situations*. All narratives have a *through-line*, namely a plot resolution in which the protagonist fails or succeeds at her or his objective. Any and all stories are constructed in terms of 1 of 11 plot structures that Schmidt calls "master-structures" and are also set into a *genre*. Since television news stories average about 90 seconds in length, they cannot go much beyond the basics. However, television news writers and editors still cast their news items in a genre, with straightforward story lines and dramatic setups. Schmidt's pared-down typology makes enough distinctions to explore television news narratives, beginning with a standard question: Why are some news stories predictable, while other aren't?

Narrative Analysis of Two Latino News Stories

I will return to the same two news stories about immigrants that were subjected to a second-order sign analysis earlier in this chapter, this time to analyze the stories in terms of their respective narratives, using Schmidt's typology. In the first, #48, NBC's James Hattori passes over less dramatic, more reasonable accounts to assert that Bush's reform initiative has led to increased immigration. The NBC news story has high production values and a seamless and swift story line. The second is the ABC news story,

#116, reported by BBC correspondent Matt Frei, who describes immigrants with a series of metaphors. This story is distinguished by humanizing camera work of both the immigrants and a border patrol agent; the story's narrative is more complex and requires more viewer attention than the NBC story.

NBC Story (#48)

In Scene 2, viewers meet the protagonist, border patrol agent Joe Penco, and learn (or recognize again) the through-line of the NBC narrative: Penco will be defeated in his role. The narrative thus begins with one conflict, what Schmidt calls a "situational conflict:" human-versus-nature. As Penco faces his antagonists, uncounted immigrants crossing into the country, NBC dehumanizes them with a long-distance camera shot. They are shown like so many migratory animals moving single file across a desert plateau, a characterization supported by a sound bite: *traditionally they return in the spring months.*" In Scene 5, a new conflict is introduced, this time between Penco and George W. Bush. Penco now faces a relational conflict with the president, who has proposed comprehensive immigration reform that NBC correspondent Hattori repeatedly argues has increased the number of immigrants.

Scene 6 reveals the other elements of the NBC narrative. The story genre becomes evident: a Western epic, with Penco as its hero.[39] In it, the protagonist will do his job (viewers see two would-be immigrants pulled from the trunk of a car) in spite of daunting odds (a camera shot displays a sidewalk entirely filled with Latino pedestrians and store signs in English and Spanish); the flood of immigrants has already changed the character of the US. To this point, the story could have taken another shape and genre, to become a crime story or personal drama. Moreover, the source of the NBC narrative drama is also apparent. Viewers can predict that Penco, the thwarted hero of this Western,[40] will strive against the impossible to protect his nation. The Western deals with "themes of honor, redemption, revenge, finding one's identity or place in life,"[41] and is exemplified in such film classics as Howard Hawks' *Red River.*[42] Viewers will also recognize that the NBC narrative is episodic: many border patrol officers along the nation's southern border undertake the same noble, yet futile, enterprise. The viewers will recognize, if only tacitly, that the border patrol agent's task has been made even harder with Bush's White House proposal, which allegedly gives a new incentive for more immigrants to come to the US.

ABC/BBC Story (#116)

The ABC/BBC story begins with the criminal trial of smugglers who allowed their "human cargo" to suffocate in sealed tractor-trailers. Two characters in the narrative are thus established: the protagonists are the immigrants and their antagonists are the smugglers. From prior knowledge of this social issue, viewers know the through-line: some protagonists will succeed, some will fail, and some will lose their lives. In Scene 1, then, viewers recognize a human conflict (what Schmidt calls a "relational conflict") between immigrants and the smugglers.[43] In contrast to the NBC news story, immigrants are rendered as humans. Scene 1 also makes the genre of the narrative clear. It is an adventure story, and this opens the possibility that it might be rendered as a treasure hunt or a voyage of discovery. According to Schmidt, this type of narrative has the structure of the feminine journey, which (in contrast to the masculine journey), "starts with the main character questioning authority, then gaining the courage to stand up for herself and finally embodying the willingness to go it alone and face her own symbolic death" in order to be transformed.[44] The dramatic conflict of the narrative is Schmidt's "daring enterprise."[45] In Scene 3, excellent camera work allows viewers to look directly into individual immigrants' faces and see their determination. However, the immigrants have not been given voice. In Scene 4, we meet the Mexican police, who turn out to be allies, not antagonists, of the immigrants. With their leaflets, the Mexican police try to warn the immigrants how to avoid death in the Arizona desert.

In Scene 5 we meet the anticipated antagonist of this standard journey narrative, border patrol officer Garrett Neubauer. However, at this point the story departs from a predictable plotline, because Scene 5 opens a second, totally different narrative with a full set of structural elements. Since the BBC news crew gives Neubauer his full measure of human subjectivity and allows him to speak, he turns out to be the likeable protagonist of his own narrative. Neubauer is not a two-dimensional character, since viewers tend to sympathize with him when they recognize his through-line: he will fail. Since in this scene the BBC correspondent tells viewers that Neubauer must confront "*a veritable stampede of illegal migrants*," an animal metaphor that dehumanizes immigrants, the second narrative presents its protagonist with a situational conflict with nature, not people. However, possibly because the first narrative has portrayed the immigrants in human terms, the second narrative does not become a Western, but a "human drama," which Schmidt minimally characterizes as "serious stories that portray realistic characters in realistic settings."[46] In Scene 6, the BBC correspondent and camera crew remind viewers that a human drama is playing out, pointing out that *"well-worn paths are littered"* with immigrants' *"precious personal belongings dumped because they've become too heavy"* as close-up images of everyday items appear, such as a pair of shoes and a child's Tweety Bird backpack.

Moreover, the dramatic source that propels this second narrative is not heroic self-sacrifice (as was the case with Penco in the NBC narrative). Instead, it is a "pursuit narrative" in which the protagonist strives to succeed, in this case, by arresting unauthorized immigrants.[47] In Scene 7 the BBC correspondent asks Neubauer whether he is fighting a losing battle. Neubauer's stumbling response confirms that he is aware of this inevitability in both his professional and narrative roles. Scene 8 focuses on the primary villain of the narrative: the Arizona desert. Thus, a new situational conflict is added to this already-complex journey narrative: immigrants must confront three antagonists: evil smugglers, stalwart border patrol agents, and implacable nature.

In Scene 9, the ABC/BBC news story finally gives the immigrants the opportunity to speak, balancing Neubauer's voice time. Viewers also come to see in these immigrants' narrative—what Schmidt calls a "feminine" journey—that immigrants do not achieve fulfillment. As one of the Honduran sisters explains: *"There's no dignity in any of this. . . . It's all about survival."* This scene also illustrates an instance of the situational conflict with nature, when she and her sister talk about nearly drowning when they crossed the Rio Grande. In Scene 10, Frei's narrative is summarized in the last statement of the news story: *"It's a game of cat and mouse, but the mouse is winning. Only one in three migrants gets caught."* The BBC story therefore presents Neubauer as the protagonist of a "vain pursuit" narrative, seeking to keep desperate people out of the country, not a tragic hero battling a relentless two-dimensional foe.

Seen in this way, both news stories display narratives based on recognizable story types. The NBC news story restates a classic Western epic plotline: border patrol agent Penco has been betrayed by his commander-in-chief even as he fights against an unlimited enemy force. This tragic hero embodies conservative American values of loyalty and honor, a genial everyman who embodies the frustration of viewers who feel oppressed or offended by the presence of unauthorized immigrants. Thus, by using a classic Western epic with a tragic hero, NBC narrates an ideologically slanted news story.

The ABC/BBC news story wove together two interdependent narratives: the immigrant's perilous journey and the border patrol officer's vain pursuit to stop people desperate to survive. The weave of two narratives mitigates the migrating animal metaphor, so the immigrants are not dehumanized; the portrayals of both the immigrants and the US border patrol officer are sympathetic. Because this news story presents cross-cutting narratives and provides humane renderings of the rival protagonists, it does not have a single ideological stance.

How Journalism Maintains Societal Myths

Of course, practicing journalists are quite willing to speak about conscientious use of narrative in news stories. Elizabeth Bird and Robert Dardenne note that in their everyday work, journalists focus on press freedom, fairness, impartiality, objectivity, and distinguishing fact from opinion. The view among well-seasoned correspondents is that events write themselves: "writer of fiction must invent. The journalist must not invent."[48] However, these views are not held by former journalists such as Mark Allen Peterson or Colleen Cotter. Peterson characterizes a recent wave of news stories deliberately woven together into a discursive construction: "Events taking place at different times in different places, with dissimilar actors and diverse objectives were reified into a single event, a global story about a clash of civilizational values between a rational Western world and an irrational Islamic 'other.'" Peterson notes that US journalists did not create the 2006 "Muhammad cartoon controversy" construct because it was violent or because they all believed that a confrontation of this sort had occurred, but because "standard US journalistic practices" encourage making the story relevant and true for local readerships using convenient framing tropes.[49] For Peterson, therefore, journalists use these narratives knowingly to sustain relevance with an audience.[50]

More fundamentally, following Hayden White, I hold that news reports are inherently narratives and that the longer pieces are often allegorical.[51] Allegory is an extended metaphor, a narrative conveying extraliteral meaning that restates collectively held political or psychological "truths." Among the Latino stories that we have reviewed in the previous chapters, allegories appear in news stories overtly at times (as in #33 on the death of a Green Card Iraq war soldier, or in #85 on Olympian Yuliana Pérez), or are a covert subtext of a narrative, as in #48.

To respond to the question opening Section II, *What forms television news discourse?*, I claim that television news stories are built on mythic story types.[52] In 2004 the networks aired 22 immigration stories, but with only three story types. In two the immigrant is portrayed as an antagonist—an invader or criminal. Only one story type, about the voyager, casts the immigrant as the protagonist.

Indeed, all television news stories are hung on at least one story type. Even a 20-second, 56-word news item is a narrative, as in CNN's #24.[53] However, the range of narratives about Latinos is remarkably confined; only a handful of story types are used.

Bird and Dardenne elegantly restate White's vision in reference to news stories: "The orderings and creations in narrative are cultural, not natural; news, like history, endows past events with artificial boundaries." They thus come very close to the position taken in this chapter: "Consider it as myth, a standpoint that dissolves the distinction between entertainment and information."[54] Finally, David Thorburn offers a similar analysis, describing television in sociological terms as a "consensus narrative" that "operates at the very center of the life of its culture, and is in consequence almost always deeply conservative in its formal structure and in its content," articulating "the culture's central mythologies . . . an inheritance of shared stories, plots, character types, cultural symbols, narrative conventions."[55]

Meaning in the Service of Power

In his classic work on news coverage of the anti–Vietnam War movement, Todd Gitlin argued that news reporting draws its political power not so much from informing viewers about the events and people of the day as from affirming viewers' preexisting beliefs about those events and people.[56] We now can point to the source of this power in foundational mythic story types that are ingrained into us as children and which continue to carry moral valuation and social ordering.[57]

Commercial mass media's discourses limit social identities and social conduct to create subjugated subjects. When journalists enact their professional practices, composing and broadcasting news reports, they reinforce the ideology of the standing social order, namely the institutional practices that sustain and legitimize power relations. Thus when CNN anchor Anderson Cooper performed his highly choreographed discursive practices,[58] supported by the CNN newsroom, to broadcast #30, the "Human Smuggling Crackdown" news story, CNN's ideological practices affirmed the nation's preexisting discourse about (Latino) immigrants, since only Latino people were shown. As Cooper's television viewers casually watch this multimodal news story, they also absorb this discourse. By doing so, they define certain "subject positions" that confine both the lives of Latinos in the wider US interactional context and the lives of television viewers themselves in terms of knowledge and beliefs, social relationships, and identities.[59]

Ideology is a system of representations, perceptions, and images that is constituted in specific everyday discursive practices that socialize individuals into social subjects who internalize a particular way of understanding their social world and their place in it. As noted earlier, ideology is a

> fundamental framework of assumptions that defines the parameters of the real and the self; it constitutes what Althusser calls the social subject's "'lived' relation to the real." . . . As a system of representations, ideology encourages people to "see" their specific place in their world as "inevitable, natural, and as a necessary function of the 'real' itself. This 'seeing' is as likely to be shaped through a relaxed fascination with the page or the screen as through any serious attention to political theory."[60]

Such frameworks of assumptions have always been enacted through traditional social organizations. Now media corporations also create symbolic goods out of discursive content, aesthetically enhanced mediated goods that wrap ideology-constituting imagery in compelling packages, to optimize their capacity to socialize the viewer.[61]

These representations organize social beliefs to the material and symbolic benefit of certain groups, granting them power over others by establishing and sustaining relations of domination.[62] John B. Thompson has called this "meaning in the service of power,"[63] citing five operations that articulate ideology in symbolic goods, such as national network news stories. The first operation is to *legitimate* with strategies that create narratives universalizing and rationalizing power relations, namely the network's primary message. The second is to *dissimulate* (to lie) by employing tropes, euphemisms, and false assertions that displace power relations and responsibilities. The third is to *reify* power relations, making false assertions about their naturalness and timelessness. The fourth and fifth are complementary operations: the fourth is to *fragment*, by differentiating populations with language that sustains power relations and by using strategies to "expurgate" the general US population of Latinos by framing them as the Other, while the fifth is to *unify* by enunciating symbols of unity among disparate groups.[64] All these strategies are illustrated in our news stories.

Among the Latino news stories we analyzed, a surprisingly direct example of dissimulation can be found in #27, when the editors of a network newsroom misquoted a *Wall Street Journal* article, falsely reporting that, in effect, Latinos were taking more than their share of jobs from (more deserving) Americans. More often, however, network news stories employ dissimulation in order to legitimate, rationalize, and reify social power relations. For example, the hallowed and often hollow myth of the American Dream was used repeatedly. However, it was not associated with the success of a working-class child of immigrants, but instead in #111 justified the rise to power of Secretary of Commerce Carlos Gutierrez, the scion of a wealthy Cuban immigrant family. I do not want to diminish Gutierrez' estimable deeds, but rather to illustrate the network's fabrications. In #33 a network reported on Lance Corporal Jose Gutierrez, an early casualty of the Iraq War and a "Green Card soldier," using the fable of the immigrant who willingly gave the final measure of devotion to his adopted country. On inspection, however, his willingness to go to his death on behalf of the United States was not self-evident. Finally, the networks used affirmative action to frame #100, which diminished the singular achievements of Alberto Gonzales.[65] In all these cases, the effect of news stories is to weaken Latino subject relations vis-à-vis majority-group White Americans.

My research team and I found complementary processes of fragmentation and unification in all 118 network news stories about Latinos. For example, in #97 Latinos were set aside and expurgated (cleansed) from the US social fabric when a network displayed the Spanish-language variety show *Sábado Gigante* as foreign and exotic, rather than similar to English-language analogues. Finally, in #117, a network directly juxtaposed Latinos and non-Latinos who had opposing views on immigration policy, but shortchanged the Latinos' airtime, making the rival anti-immigrant viewpoint appear to be the more rational stance.

As discussed in Chapter 7, one example of the discourse fragmentation operation involves the use of criminalizing terminology by network anchors and correspondents. Here the networks recurrently use the adjective *illegal*, a term that has been criticized as intemperate[66] and partisan.[67] The adjective puts distance between the presumably law-abiding news viewers and "those" workers. However, ABC's Peter Jennings and Terry Moran go further in #3 when they take up the vilifying language of Tom Tancredo (who was interviewed in #3) to refer to unauthorized immigrants with the noun *illegals*; CBS correspondent Jerry Bowen also repeatedly uses the noun in #117. Discursive fragmentation operations are not limited to the spoken word, but use the IMMIGRANT AS CRIMINAL metaphor very frequently in visual expression, a more forceful semiotic mode.

However, to be fair, the networks do not always keep Latinos at arm's length. The networks employed many instances of unification, incorporating Latinos into the American body politic. For example, CBS correspondent Bill Whitaker presented Latinos and non-Latinos in #77 on opposite sides of the immigration policy debate in a balanced manner; in #57 undocumented Latino high school graduates were simply portrayed as typical American teenagers; and in #14, #63, and #81 Dominican immigrants were not viewed as criminals but as economic refugees. Sometimes a short segment within a longer news story offered a unifying moment, such as in #3 when a day laborer faces the camera to proclaim in English: "*We're not terrorists.*" Network news editors also demonstrated that they could render immigrants as human even in polarizing circumstances, as in #24, when the humanity of children and families was projected as they were in the process of being arrested by ICE officers. However, this and most stories about Latinos were primarily negative.

Thompson's five operations boil down to two subject-positioning processes that articulate ideology in the case of Latinos on the network news: unify or fragment. The networks either build solidarity or divide. The networks rarely portrayed both immigrants and US Latinos with humanity, allowing audiences to recognize them as people just like themselves. Most of the time the networks did not allot Latinos this humanity, when they were portrayed, for example, as criminal, exotic, voiceless, and/or non-English-speaking. Such conflicting subject-positioning processes are sometimes expressed in the same story. For example, in #4, a Mexican woman is rendered with substantial subjectivity when the camera follows as she goes about her day while separated from her husband by a border and a thousand miles. However, the same news story at two separate points entirely dehumanizes Mexicans with images of them funneling like cattle into a border checkpoint, expressing the tacit take-away message that there are too many Mexicans in the United States. In such stories the negative messaging eclipses the positive.

There have been many calls over the years for network newsrooms to increase the numerical proportions of news stories on Latinos, as indicated in Chapter 1. However, numerical disparities are paired with even more significant representational disparities. My review of the discursive operations that help create mainstream American ideology perhaps can be reduced to a single question: Why don't networks consistently render Latinos with humanity, presenting them to the national television audience as people "just like you and me?" While such a move would eliminate a great deal of the fragmentation that distances Latinos from the hearts of the viewing public, it seems unlikely that networks will undertake such a shift of subject-position orientation. On the surface it would only require the backing of network executives and attentiveness in the network editorial room. However, to systematically humanize the portrayals of Latino subjects would require changing television news production practices. This would require reconceptualizing what a potential news story narrative is and reworking standard frames and boilerplate—in effect, revising news values.[68] As Cotter's recent ethnography of American print journalism reveals, the issue of retooling how television news stories are assembled would be substantial.[69] However, a more fundamental problem lies with the journalists themselves. These journalists, like Americans in general, seem to be of two minds about the place of Latinos in the rapidly shifting demographics of the nation. However, without a thorough reconsideration of their role as journalists, they will be unable to help others rethink their place in American society.

In Chapter 7 I analyzed how discourse organizes social beliefs for the material and symbolic benefit of some groups. The discourse grants some people power over others. In television news stories, social valuation does not have to be overt to function effectively in the scaffolding of fundamental story types. The story type scaffolding I have outlined allows us to answer the second question posed at the beginning of Section II: *What are the potential social effects of television news?* In the case of just one CBS news story, #117, the correspondent used spoken tropes and many other semiotic cues to typify Angelita (a modest church volunteer and working mother) as a criminal: Angelita is *"still illegal."* The juxtaposition of Angelita's family with rancher Walter Kolbe's commentary portrays her two children as *"ruining our schools,"* while the family's presence in Arizona is described as part of the *"raping of our country."* The correspondent describes the process in terms that render a specific social valuation: *"From Walter Kolbe's backyard, you can see Mexico, and the backpacks and water bottles abandoned by the nightly wave of illegals crossing over."* CBS correspondent Jerry Bowen explicitly recounts Kolbe's crime story, while he only indirectly refers to Angelita's American Dream narrative. The roles are clear. Walter is the victim; Angelita, the thief. Without a counterpoint story about the business interests who benefit from Angelita's labor or about the unjust restrictions imposed on Angelita's Arizona-born child, this segment of #117 is simply a crime story.

The narratives in news stories are processed within the cognitive framework described in Chapter 7. Like ideographs and other second-tier signs, each story is understood in terms of constellations of symbols. Note that since only a finite number of story types exist, regular television news viewers effortlessly capture a story type from its elements in news stories. This claim is shared by scholars working on different research agendas, including social semioticians and cognitive narrativists.[70]

Before cognitive modeling was developed, similar (if undertheorized) observations were made about the ways news stories evoke distinctive value orientations. For example, Paul Weaver stated that television news "does not so much record events as evoke a world. It is governed not by a political bias but by a melodramatic one."[71] Without reference to Frye's story types, communication scholars have made similar observations about the (American) myths that have developed over many generations. According to W. Lance Bennett, children grow up hearing folktales that are the basis of political myths. These are the stories about the "Founding Fathers, the slaves, western pioneers, European immigrants," to which we can add the Black Legend and the Alamo.[72] These dramatizations or allegories are meant to illustrate (White) American social mores such as honesty, industry, bravery, perseverance, and individualism,[73] which then become available for contrast with, for example, Mexicans (and by extension, non-Cuban Latinos), who are not attributed such values.

In the world conjured by news narratives, the adult audience can find "specific heroes and villains and deserving and undeserving people."[74] Audiences have a profound appetite for this type of invented history, which is restated daily by news narrative and which shapes its audience's "views of rationality, of objectivity, of morality, and their conceptualization of themselves and others." The appeal of the narrative is not "empirical" or factual; instead, the narrative demonstrates its "dramaturgical" power to embody the fears, hopes, and prejudices of the audience.[75] Hayden White believed the ultimate source of this power is that as children we learn that there is a lesson to be learned in history, beginning with our parents' depiction of the day's events. However, television presents many more versions of the finite set of story types that people use in their daily lives. As children, we incorporated these myths into our sense of who we are, to become competent participants of systems of laws, moralities,[76] social hierarchies, and subject positions. And as adults, we employ these values from internalized narratives to make sense of anything that we gather from a televised news item. White's idea works in tandem with Lakoff's observation that our most basic metaphor, the event, becomes a narrated event as soon as children comprehend language. The narrated event, then, is the original social characteristic.

These myths are rarely learned as complete stories that news viewers can fully recall at a conscious level. Instead, myths are assimilated through multiple inputs that "blend fact with fantasy and confuse history with legend."[77] Piecemeal referencing by metaphor or ideograph amplifies the power of the story type that news stories call to mind. Myth establishes its meaning through connotation rather than denotation,[78] draining individual stories of their literal and explicit meanings by "evaporating" denotation, to use Barthes' expression.

Since a given myth is rarely brought to the level of consciousness during a broadcast, it is intimated, not stated. Bennett notes that "the complete structure of myth remains hidden in ordinary political discourse . . . These forms are often the most profound carriers of insight in everyday life, [and] these forms also operate in politics to leave their impression in the deepest level of consciousness. . . . Only a few key symbols are needed to invoke a meaning and response."[79] Everyday journalistic narrative thus naturalizes the discursive constitutions of myth.[80] For this reason, the news-viewing public only obscurely understands the logic that links its mythic values to specific policy issues. This can be noted when incompatible, even contradictory, myths provoke similar levels of fervor among the same people. On those rare occasions when mythic themes are stripped from public discourse, very little substance remains. Since there is no cross-checking or comparison of the values implicated in myths, people express a tolerance for a range of possible outcomes in any policy decision, but they impose a rigid consensus about the limits of legitimate debate and acceptable policy.[81]

The form of television news makes it a more effective vehicle of myth management than other news media. Paul Weaver stated that television news tends to "tell a story" even more than newsprint, since televised news stories do not use the newspaper article's inverted pyramid compositional format.[82] The script of a typical television news story is "far more coherently organized and tightly unified than a newspaper," and has a "teleological drive to wrap things up." While the reader of a newspaper news item can choose to read only the lead sentence or paragraph and move on, television news stories are composed to be understandable only if viewers remain tuned to the whole news story.

Weaver went on to argue that television news goes beyond merely reporting an event, "to fix upon . . . whatever else seems a suitable theme in the circumstances.[83] Writing during the Cold War era, he argued that this thematic coherence "gives credibility to the idea that there exists in America a single, coherent national agenda which can be perceived as such by any reasonable and well-intentioned person."[84] Michael Schudson later wrote that grand narrative in television news had become "unsatisfying" in an age suspicious of grand narratives. However, 9/11 set the stage once again for grand narrative international reporting, as Peterson's study of the "Muslim rage" illustrates. Since network television journalists rarely attempt the task of explaining immigration as a consequence of ever-increasing globalization, 9/11 has become the backdrop for regularly evoked story types of the swarthy, criminal, immigrant invader. Claude Levi-Strauss would call this mythopoesis, the myth-making process, which van Leeuwen defines as a narrative process that defines actions as legitimate or non-legitimate, respectively warranting social reward or punishment.[85]

News reporting provides its audience with both a cognitive ordering of events and a moral ordering of responsibilities: "Events are not merely represented but rather made compellingly real because they are shown to belong to an order of moral existence that renders them meaningful."[86] Myths are the narrative models "for applying values and beliefs" from which public opinion arises.[87] Certain "tried and true" narratives are reassuring because ancient and simple formulas can be brought to bear to address new and complex problems. "In political discourse the narrative form is particularly vital because stock political plots . . . construct meaning to counter the ambiguity and to reinforce the ideological disagreements that pervade political communication."[88] Formulaic news stories therefore dissolve ambiguity and resolve possible points of new understanding into black-and-white replays of stories related to us in the past. "The intimate tie between accounts of events whose meanings are ambiguous and the reinforcement of ideology gives narrative its psychological appeal."[89]

Myth and story type allow us to believe we know the world and to accept the events as reported in the news, rather than individually work through the reports critically. While most seasoned journalists are aware of the allegories that they broadcast from the scene of a news event, if the average news viewer were to express doubt about a typical news report, it would likely be on some point of fact. Only the most egregiously slanted news story will force the viewer to question the whole news item, or interrogate the news item story type. Yet daily local and network television news provides scores of stories each day. Thus, television news offers its audience daily doses of the mythic elements that our society uses to sustain our understanding of its social relations,[90] at a cost. "The tragic price that the U.S. people pay for this distorted communication is the virtual absence of learning about world [and national] problems and new approaches to solving them. To the contrary, narrative closure results in the routinization of problem formation and resolution."[91]

Most students of the news have been astonished at one time or another at the American public's uncritical reactions to the day's events as presented on television news programs. But even the most sophisticated critic is susceptible, from time to time, to a news story suspended on a myth. One might wonder why we need myths at all, in the early twenty-first century. But we might as well wonder if ancient Greeks actually believed that satyrs walked on earth, or that the union of a god and a mortal really produced the minotaur. Paul Veyne reminds us of our own credulity when he points out that children can believe in Santa Claus even when they know their parents bring all the presents:

> Instead of speaking of beliefs, one must actually speak of . . . products of the imagination. . . . This imagination is not the faculty through dreams . . . we expand the fishbowl in which we live. On the contrary, it creates boundaries. Outside this bowl is nothing, not even future truths. We cannot make them speak. Religions and literatures, as well as politics, modes of conduct, and sciences are formed within these containers . . . Men do not find the truth; they create it, as they create their history.[92]

Myths are folk beliefs about a supernatural world that allow us to interpret the natural one. Our elders mesmerize us as children with bedtime stories about the world. We internalize the morals of these stories and remain subject to them throughout our lives. White did not condemn nineteenth-century historians for writing history, but he criticized their belief that they could write objectively. Journalists are likewise mistaken to believe that "objectivity" is attainable, much less to hold fast to it as their highest professional criterion of quality. Like historians, they cannot escape narrative, or fail to relate the day's events without a moral mantle. Journalists must recognize that when they report today's news using ancient story types, they write so that we, their audience, can be reassured that our bedtime stories still hold sway. Like the ancient Greeks, we remain in the thrall of myth.

CHAPTER 9

Conclusion

We need to re-cognize that the hegemonic does not dominate us from without but rather penetrates us, and therefore it is not just against it but from within it that we are waging war.

—JESÚS MARTÍN-BARBERO[1]

With its national reputation of legitimacy and trustworthiness and ever-increasing power to manipulate multimodal sign, network television re-articulates the nation's putative values directly to an audience who ritually watches the evening news. At its best, it can edify the American people. Our comprehensive review of a year of network news stories, however, demonstrates that reporting about Latinos is almost negligible and generally confined to inside-the-Beltway topics, in spite of an abundance of newsworthy stories. Moreover, the most sweeping longitudinal statement that can be made about network news reporting about Latinos is that nothing has changed in the past 15 years. The numerical and topic limitations and skewing lead American viewers to retain stereotypes. Given their deplorable performance, the networks' daily self-laudatory claims of trust ("CBS news: experience you can trust"), national scope ("More Americans get their news from ABC news than from any other source"), and leadership ("NBC: America's news leader"; "CNN: The worldwide leader in news") compel censure.

Indeed, Latino journalists regularly criticize the networks. As I write this in 2010, the National Latino Media Coalition, a civil rights media advocacy organization, released a report declaiming the decline of Latino presence in front of and behind the camera, in spite of network memorandums of understanding signed 10 years ago.[2] As expected, the networks chose to not cover the NLMC news conference.

Our 45 close readings reveal stories that gleam with a high production value veneer that conceals uneven quality. Some stories are inaccurate; others are flawed by newsroom unfamiliarity with Latino subjects; most perpetuate negative stereotypes of Latinos. While news briefs are almost always built around a single guiding metaphor or journalistic news frame, feature-length stories that employ a single frame are typically skewed. When a network news story uses a single guiding metaphor for politically charged issues, such as immigration policy, it is invariably inadequate and prejudges the debate. Video editors at times are apt to use their tools to tilt a news report politically. Because it is not likely that the networks will soon increase their payrolls with a good number of knowledgeable news writers and correspondents,[3] we offer rubrics to evaluate reporting quality of both news briefs and feature stories.

I share my normative standpoint with organizations such as the Society of Professional Journalists. It calls US journalism a "cornerstone of our nation and our liberty" that shores up "self-government [as] outlined by the U.S. Constitution" by providing "accurate, comprehensive, timely and understandable" news to keep "the American people . . . well informed."[4] The rival standpoint is that network news has no higher purpose than profit and political power. Since this book deals with discourse, I offer a discursive response to contest the latter countervailing trend.

One way to serve higher ends is to offer a better principle for news writing. Objectivity is an unachievable criterion, since facts cannot be reported objectively. However, as one of journalism's finest scholars noted over 30 years ago, no new ideal has arisen.[5] Yet, since narrative wields fundamental power to form and inform the world of the audience, it should become journalism's preeminent criterion for news writing. Such a criterion requires broad knowledge of metaphor, myth, and narrative, but will be a stronger evaluative metric since it is a scalar, not absolute, measure. Moreover, the number of story types is quite limited. Objectivity can then be demoted to a secondary tenet, to the level of concision and fact-checking. With a narrative-based criterion, journalists can better assess whether they compose news stories that enlighten or restrict their viewers' understanding of the world and their place in it.

Latinos and other minorities certainly recognize the limiting story types that network news regularly broadcasts to the nation, and we must remain mindful that our children—indeed all our nation's children—are particularly susceptible to the unawareness of which Martín-Barbero warns. Revealing that hegemony is not nature, but merely human convention, is the first battle. To our advantage, we now can draw on a wider variety of media resources than in the recent past.[6] However, the mainstream networks will no doubt redouble their efforts to capture the vast Latino market by broadcasting mirror images of the Latino, created in the media's own image. We must defy these twin figures that the public will come to presume, and which have the potential to become Latino self-images: the whitened figure who is indifferent to Latino injustice, and the brown-skinned criminalized Other.

Summary Table of 118 Television Network Evening News Stories about Latinos in 2004

Legend: Story reference number. Network, Date (Scenes), Camera Shots, Story Name, Thumbnail Summary

#1   CNN, January 7, 5 scenes, 50 shots, *Migrant Headache: President's Plan*: Like #3, this story covers Bush's migrant worker plan, providing an overview and oppositional opinions. It includes the personal story of one woman trying to support her family. Unlike ABC anchor, CNN anchor explicitly says that "if Bush's proposal is not amnesty, it's close to amnesty." See also #4.

#2   CNN, January 7, 2 scenes, 3 shots, *José Padilla Case*: The story focuses on the legal case. Padilla's personality, guilt or innocence, and loss of civil rights are incidental to the legal proceedings, which are characterized as potentially aberrant.

#3   ABC, January 7, 30 scenes, 44 shots, *Who Has Right to Be in US?* A report on Bush's new undocumented worker proposal states that all undocumented workers would get legal worker status (not citizenship) for three-year periods. The piece includes overview, footage of Bush, interviews with day laborers, and opposition to the proposal. ABC does not frame the plan as amnesty; compare #1.

#4   NBC, January 7, 13 scenes, 71 shots, *Bush's Immigrant Worker Plan*: Compared to #1 and #3, this pointedly links the "illegal workers" plan to US Latinos as a large voting bloc, suggesting this motivates Bush's plan. See also #6.

#5   ABC, January 11, 23 shots, *Bush Meets with Vicente Fox*: This story covers Bush's meeting with Mexican president Fox, which is characterized as a means of repairing their relationship. The story suggests that Bush's immigration policy initiative will help. The piece segues into a general story on the initiative.

#6   NBC, January 11, 15 shots, *Crossing the Line—Immigration Plan*: Like story #5, this piece centers on Bush's meeting with Fox as an opportunity to discuss Bush's new immigrant worker proposal and its significance for workers, the upcoming election, and the political landscape. See also #1, #3, #4.

#7   CNN, January 14, 17 scenes, 25 shots, *Tracking Illegal Aliens*: This human interest story focuses on a mother's concerns and fears about her and her family's prospects for remaining in the United States. The story also asks whether it is humane to use electronic ankle bracelets to track "illegal aliens."

#8   NBC, January 27, 16 shots, *Nydia Gonzalez Testifies*: Gonzalez, an airline operations specialist who received a 911 call on September 11, testifies at the 9/11 Commission. She is Latina.

#9   ABC, January 31, 8 scenes, 34 shots, *NFL Super Bowl and Hispanics*: This sports economics story examines the ways the National Football League is marketing to Latinos as a large untapped consumer bloc.

#10   ABC, February 2, 6 scenes, 20 shots, *Democratic Presidential Candidates Court Latino Voters*: This story outlines the efforts of Democratic candidates to court Latino voters in New Mexico and Arizona in order to win these "battleground states," as well as providing a brief overview of Latino voting patterns and significance.

#11   ABC, February 4, 1 scene, 5 shots, *11 Cubans in a Floating Buick*: This news brief provides a straightforward report on 11 Cubans who modified an auto into a seagoing vessel to travel to US shores. See #12.

#12   CBS, February 4, 1 scene, 6, shots, *To Freedom Road in a Floating Buick*: Reports on the same incident as #11. It frames Cubans as "remarkably" ingenious immigrants.

#13   ABC, February 7, 11 scenes, 22 shots, *Cuban Entertainers Barred*: On Bush administration's policy barring Cuban entertainers from receiving a Grammy Award in the US. The story trivializes the issue as a lost opportunity to "party." It does not contextualize the politics of entertainment.

#14   NBC, February 10, 4 scenes, 29 shots, *New Wave of Boat People—Dominican Immigrants*: This extended story outlines the risks of Dominicans trying to cross the Mona Passage to get to Puerto Rico on homemade boats.

#15   NBC, February 12, 1 scene, 1 shot, *160 Immigrants in One Phoenix House*: This news brief describes the "*disturbing*" discovery of 160 men, women, and children locked in an upper-middle-class house by smugglers. The story describes these immigrants as victims locked in bedrooms with dead-bolt locks.

#16   CNN, February 14, 1 scene, 1 shot, *Alex Rodriguez in Pinstripes*: This sports news brief summarizes a professional baseball trade moving Alex Rodriguez from the Rangers to the New York Yankees.

#17   NBC, February 15, 13 scenes, 26 shots, *Federal Agents on the Border*: The correspondent suggests that Bush's new immigration proposal has caused more people to immigrate. He offers no direct proof, and in fact the best indirect evidence indicates people crossing at rates similar to previous years.

#18   NBC, February 15, 26 shots, *Baseball and Money: A-Rod*: Baseball player Alex Rodriguez's trade to the New York Yankees "shocks" the sports world because of the sheer amount of money involved to add him to the Yankee roster. See #19–23.

#19   CBS, February 16, 26 shots, *Business of Baseball*: Like #18, this story highlights the expense of Alex Rodriguez's trade to the Yankees. This story offers more details (including the politics of the deal) than #18. Also see #16, #18, #20–23.

#20 ABC, February 16, 5 shots, *Baseball: Deal of the Century*: This story on the trade of Alex Rodriguez to the New York Yankees centers around the amount of money he will be making: more than $155,000 a game.

#21 CNN, February 16, 76 shots, *Baseball's A-Bomb*: This long story on the Rodriguez trade is framed around the New York Yankees as the team with the richest history, highest payroll, and the most revenue. The general details of the deal are highlighted. Compare #16, #18–20, #22, 23.

#22 ABC, February 17, 38 shots, *The Alex Rodriguez Story*: A second-day coverage of the A-Rod trade story. It is framed as "the rich getting richer," referring to both Rodriguez and the Yankees.

#23 NBC, February 17, 42 shots, *Alex Rodriguez*: Framed as economic news, the story covers the Rodriguez baseball trade, "calculating the cost in the real world" by breaking down the sums in a variety of ways.

#24 CNN, February 18, 2 scenes, 6 shots, *Immigrant Bust of Phoenix Drop Houses*: Authorities in Phoenix find four houses where they arrest a total of 288 "illegal immigrants." This story frames these activities as "one of the busiest weeks in memory according to immigration officials."

#25 ABC, February 20, 19 shots, *Enemy Combatant Padilla*: This story is framed around which legal rights citizens should retain in the age of terrorism. This extended statement about the US Supreme Court case highlights the fact that José Padilla's rights were suspended.

#26 CNN, February 20, 23 shots, *Enemy Combatant Case—Padilla*: CNN calls this an "extraordinary" case that the Supreme Court will hear. Unlike story #2, this story and #25 address Padilla's suspended rights. It can be compared to #25, since it questions how someone comes to be labeled an "enemy combatant."

#27 NBC, February 22, 1 shot, *Hispanics Are Taking American Jobs*: This weakly written and decontextualized news brief leaves the impression that (undifferentiated) Latinos are taking far too many "American jobs."

#28 CNN, March 3, 1 scene, 7 shots, *Phoenix Immigration Raid*: Reports on same incident as #24 but focuses on the nearly 200 immigrants found in one house.

#29 CBS, March 4, 1 shot, *New Immigration Rules*: This news brief credits the Bush administration with "easing" immigration rules to grant special visas to some Mexicans who frequently make short visits to border areas. The anchor's intonation is notably report style, not conversational.

#30 CNN, March 4, 16 scenes, 42 shots, *Human Smuggling Crackdown*: This extended story covers the discovery of 250 people in Phoenix drop houses (news briefed in #15, #24, and #28), exploring the money exchange, profitability, risks for immigrating people, and the federal program (Operation ICE Storm) to halt human smuggling.

#31 CNN, March 6, 4 shots, *Easing Border Crossing Restrictions*: Like #29, this news brief covers the granting of special visas to some Mexicans who frequently make short visits to border areas, but it is framed as a consequence of a meeting between US president Bush and Mexican president Vicente Fox.

#32   CNN, March 7, 19 shots, *Ernie Lopez—Vanished Boxer*: Once top boxer Ernie Lopez, who mysteriously vanished, resurfaces after a homeless stint, and is honored by the city of Los Angeles.

#33   CNN, March 20, 6 scenes, 42 shots, *A Marine's Story in Iraq*: This is a human interest story about a Guatemalan-born Marine who was one of the first killed in the Iraq War. He was granted posthumous US citizenship. His death is framed as a dignified death that honors the country that "gave him so much."

#34   ABC, March 25, 4 shots, *Cuban Immigrants Floating in Inner Tubes*: Like #12, this news brief describes the Cubans' "remarkable" determination to reach US shores by any means.

#35   CBS, March 25, 4 shots, *Coast Guard Rescue*: This story about Cubans immigrating on inner tubes is presented in a more straightforward manner than #34. It notes that while three migrants were rescued, five died en route.

#36   CNN, March 27, 3 shots, *Guardsman becomes a Conscientious Objector*: Story on an Iraq War conscientious objector who incidentally is Latino.

#37   CNN, March 27, 34 shots, *Freed California Felon Pamela Martinez*: Pamela Martinez, a released woman who served jail time on the three-strikes law, is required to return to jail because of a court mistake. Friends and supporters ask for clemency.

#38   ABC, March 28, 16 shots, *Latina Needing Clemency in California*: Human interest story about Latina who as a "third-strike" convict must fight for clemency. See #37.

#39   NBC, March 20, 20 shots, *Bush Courts Orlando Hispanics*: Bush visits Florida to court the most important group of swing voters. Like other stories on the attempt to gain Latino votes, the story focuses on candidates' superficial mastery of a few Spanish phrases, rather than on candidate political positions.

#40   CNN, April 6, 9 shots, *J. Lo's Mother Hits the Jackpot*: News brief about the Latina celebrity's mom winning a jackpot in a casino.

#41   NBC, April 7, 18 shots, *A Latino Marine's Death*: Imbedded in a longer story about the deaths of Marines, this story focuses on a mother, Ana Lopez, who lost her son in the Iraq War.

#42   CBS, April 14, 18 shots, *Latina Mother Dies in Car Wreck*: This story focuses on the outrage of a Latino family at authorities' failure to respond immediately after the family reported that two family members were missing. The family members—mother and child—were in a car accident that killed the mother; the child survived.

#43   NBC, April 15, 19 shots, *Southern California Child Survivor*: Continuing news item about child survivor (of a car wreck that killed her mother) is cast as a human interest story by focusing on the child's release from the hospital.

#44   ABC, April 17, 5 shots, *Latino Sex Offender Charged with Kidnapping*: This story reports that long-sought kidnapping victim Drew Sjodin has been found dead. The man charged with her death is a sex offender who happens to be Latino. Compare #45.

#45 NBC, April 17, 33 shots, *Kidnapping Victim Found Dead*: An in-depth story on the discovery of Drew Sjodin's body. As opposed to #44 this story recaps Sjodin's kidnapping and the search for her. The Latino sex offender who is charged is mentioned, but his legal situation is emphasized.

#46 CBS, April 19, 32 shots, *False Convictions to Murder*: A human interest story about intensively interrogated people who end up giving false confessions to crimes they did not commit. One such person is Joseph Lopez.

#47 CBS, April 25, 10 scenes, 45 shots, *Health Care for Uninsured Latinos*: This extended news story explores how hospitals charge uninsured patients more money for the same procedures performed on insured patients. CBS does not frame the piece around the patients' race, but all patients and the advocacy group are Latino.

#48 NBC, April 30, 8 scenes, 38 shots, *Immigrants Flooding across the Border*: To frame the topic, the anchor says that the correspondent will *explain* "what's driving this desperation." The correspondent does not focus on this question, instead claiming that Bush's new immigration policy has caused increased numbers, but offers no supporting evidence.

#49 CBS, May 5, 8 scenes, 44 shots, *A Day without a Mexican*: This story about the film of the same name includes interviews with the writers and actual movie footage. It offers significant subjectivity to the writers and their intentions in making the movie.

#50 CBS, May 15, 20 shots, *Torture Tactics—Interrogation Rules*: Contextualized by the recent torture of Iraqi prisoners, this story explores the experiences of past torture victims and questions the accuracy of information gained from tortured suspects, pointing out that many people will make things up in this situation. All people interviewed were people of color, including Orlando Tizán.

#51 CBS, May 17, 34 shots, *Residential Resegregation of Public Education*: This story about increasing school resegregation presents only the views of people who support busing to maintain integrated classrooms. The piece does not discuss the causes of school resegregation.

#52 CBS, May 21, 3 shots, *Latino Army Deserter*: This news brief (embedded in a longer Iraq War story) focuses on a conscientious objector, Camilo Mejia.

#53 ABC, May 22, 25 shots, *Latino Army Deserter*: Like #52, this news brief about conscientious objector Camilo Mejia is embedded in an Iraq War story. It also discusses other soldiers who have deserted.

#54 CBS, May 22, 36 shots, *Dead Iraq Soldiers from San Diego, Texas*: This human interest story focuses on the deaths of two young soldiers from San Diego, Texas, a small community that presumably is predominantly Latino. All the people interviewed are Latino.

#55 CNN, May 23, 21 shots, *Iraq Army Deserter Court-Martialed*: This news story is a longer and more in-depth engagement with Camilo Mejia (news briefed in #52 and #53). The story provides an overview of Mejia's court-martial and interviews his legal group to outline his defense.

#56 CNN, May 23, 56 shots, *Drill Sergeant Mr. Mom*: This human interest story contrasts the dual lives of a Latino staff sergeant who is a drill sergeant as well as the sole parent to his three children while his wife is serving in Iraq.

#57 NBC, May 23, 32 shots, *Undocumented High School Graduates*: This is a Telemundo human interest piece on DREAM Act students, who are unauthorized immigrants (carried to the US as young children). The piece follows their staged protest and a mock graduation, and spotlights one student who advocates granting the group the opportunity to gain US citizenship.

#58 CBS, May 25, 3 shots, *General Sanchez Replaced in Iraq*: This news brief covers the replacement of Rick Sanchez as the top military official in Iraq. The Department of Defense states that it is not because of the Iraqi prisoner abuse scandal but is a scheduled change in leadership.

#59 ABC, June 1, 21 shots, *Suspected Terrorist José Padilla*: This story highlights the fact that Padilla has been held for two years without charge or access to a lawyer, presenting both what the government alleges and interviews with people who believe his incarceration is unconstitutional. See #60–62.

#60 CBS, June 1, 6 scenes, 16 shots, *Suspected Terrorist José Padilla*: While the initial framing questions Padilla's incarceration (the word *allegedly* is used once), the story's structure presumes Padilla's guilt by implying the government allegations are facts. Compare #59, #61, and #62.

#61 CNN, June 1, 19 shots, *Declassified Information about José Padilla*: CNN presents the government allegations as fact, while overlooking Padilla's two-year incarceration without charge. Only briefly does the story give subjectivity to Padilla's lawyer, who states that the declassified information report reflects only the government's claims. Compare #59 and #62.

#62 NBC, June 1, 18 shots, *The Government's New Case against Padilla*: This story, like #60, mentions "alleged" accusations, but its predominant language and emphasis tend to indict him. Like all other network news stories on Padilla, it never inquires about Padilla as a person. Compare #59 and #61.

#63 NBC, June 16, 2 scenes, 4 shots, *Coast Guard Rescues Dominicans*: A news brief on a 40-foot homemade boat carrying 94 people from the Dominican Republic that capsized as the Coast Guard intercepted its "refugees." The Coast Guard could not save three people.

#64 CNN, June 24, 7 shots, *Cuban American Travel Rule Changes*: This news story outlines the responses to and effects of the Bush administration's decision to further restrict the travel of Cuban Americans to Cuba. Compare to #67, #68, and #70.

#65 CNN, June 26, 2 shots, *Kerry Goes after the Latino Vote*: A news brief on John Kerry's attempt to get the Latino vote by promising a prominent Latino group that he will save Latino jobs by ending outsourcing. See #66.

#66 NBC, June 26, 4, shots, *Kerry Goes after the Latino Vote*: This piece covers the same topic as #65.

#67 NBC, June 29, 8 shots, *Cuban American Travel Rule Changes*: This story covers the travel rule changes; compared with #68 and #70, it has slightly more focus on protesting Cuban Americans who dispute the new restrictions.

#68 ABC, June 30, 6 shots, *Cuban American Travel Rule Changes*: Brief report on rule changes.

#69 NBC, June 30, 32 shots, *General Rick Sanchez in Iraq*: The story focuses on Rick Sanchez, US forces commander in Iraq, with no reference to his ethnicity.

#70   ABC, July 3, 31 shots, *Travel Restrictions for Cuban Americans*: This story offers a far more in-depth engagement of the new travel rules than either #67 or #68. As more of a human interest and contextualized piece, it both gives voice to those who are negatively affected by the new restrictions and analyzes the political intentions of the Bush administration. All the networks covered this policy shift.

#71   CBS, July 4, 29 shots, *Republican Latinos—Voter Preference for Bush*: A profile piece of a young Latino man who espouses George W. Bush's values and identifies himself as a Republican. He is given ample air time to assert that Republicans policies best support Latino family values. No opposing view provided.

#72   CNN, July 5, 7 shots, *Cuban Crashes into Airport*: A news brief of a distraught ex-member of the Cuban Olympic wrestling squad who crashes his truck into an airport terminal.

#73   NBC, July 12, 24 shots, *TV Presidential Campaign (Hispanics)*: This story focuses on the spending of presidential candidates on campaign ads. Latinos are the only demographic group mentioned.

#74   ABC, July 14, 9 scenes, 33 shots, *Illegal Dominican Migrants*: Framed around the deaths of three Dominicans who attempted to reach Puerto Rico on homemade boats, this story explores the circumstances that push Dominicans to risk their lives trying to get to the US.

#75   ABC, July 17, 29 shots, *Flying Illegal Mexican Immigrants back Home*: Outlines government strategies to fly captured undocumented immigrants "deep into Mexico" on airplanes in attempts to deter them from returning. This story also explores the dangers of crossing the desert. Compare to #89.

#76   ABC, July 24, 23 shots, *Burying a Latino Soldier*: This news brief highlights the slightly controversial death of a Mexican national in US uniform, who ultimately received a 21-gun salute. Originally he was buried in Mexico, where the salute was not permitted. It is not made clear how the conflict was resolved.

#77   CBS, August 5, 41 shots, *Illegal Immigration—What Does It Mean to You?* Couched as an exploration of the personal consequences of hot political issues, this story offers interviews of a White ranch owner living in an area on the border where thousands of people cross, and a Salvadoran political refugee who crossed near her property. The story then explores the immigration policy proposals of both presidential candidates.

#78   NBC, August 7, 42 shots, *Sorrows of Illegal Immigrant Family*: This Telemundo story tells the tale of three children who died in a freak traffic accident. This human interest story highlights the inhumanity of US immigration policy.

#79   CNN, August 8, 5 shots, *Illegal Immigrants Busted in Texas*: News brief on immigrant smuggling where 60 people were found in a semi-truck.

#80   CBS, August 9, 1 shot, *Stroke in Mexican American Men*: A poorly written news brief that vaguely states that Mexican American men face a high risk of stroke. The report scares rather than informs.

#81   ABC, August 11, 5 shots, *Rescue of Dominicans*: Another news brief on the attempts of Dominicans to reach Puerto Rico. Story reports the "rescue" of 40 Dominicans who reported that 40 more had already drowned.

#82   NBC, August 11, 4 scenes, 29 shots, *Presidential Candidates Vie for Latino Voters*: This extended piece outlines the attempts of both presidential candidates to reach Latino voters and the issues that each side addresses.

#83   NBC, August 18, 5 scenes, 27 shots, *Hurricane Effects on Migrant Workers*: A report on Hurricane Charley's devastation, contrasting governmental support for residents of an upscale community and its lack of support for a woman who was thought to be an "illegal" immigrant.

#84   NBC, August 20, 49 shots, *"Old" Olympics Gymnasts—One Last Shot*: This human interest story follows two young US Olympians. One women is Cuban born; she came to the USA after rejection by the Cuban team.

#85   NBC, August 21, 6 scene, 38 shots, *The Olympic Story of a Cuban American Athlete*: This story describes how Yuliana Pérez (a long jumper raised in Cuba) made the Athens Olympics. NBC depicts her as escaping Cuba to fulfill the American Dream.

#86   NBC, August 23, 41 shots, *Latina Olympic Wrestler*: The personal story of Patricia Miranda's arrival at the Olympics, despite the concerns of her Brazilian father, whom she calls a "chauvinistic pig."

#87   CBS, August 31, 5 scene, 49 shots, *¡Gana la Verde! Reality Show*: Description of a Spanish-language television game show in which contestants (unauthorized immigrants) compete in dangerous events, hoping to win attorney support toward obtaining a US resident card.

#88   CBS, September 11, 23 shots, *Court Martial of Iraq Soldier in Abu Ghraib Scandal*: Story on Armand Cruz, who was court-martialed and discharged from the army because of his involvement in the torture of prisoners at Abu Ghraib. He is incidentally Latino.

#89   NBC, September 19, 8 scenes, 36 shots, *Experimental Plane Rides back to Mexico*: This Telemundo story outlines the $13 million INS project to discourage unauthorized border crossing by flying apprehended immigrants deep into Mexico's interior. It is framed as an INS humanitarian action. Compare #75.

#90   NBC, October 14, 6 scenes, 46 shots, *Latino Voters in Western States*: This story explores how Latino voters are "changing the landscape" of US politics in the western states. It covers many facets, from grassroots attempts to gain Latino votes to the issues relevant to Latinos.

#91   ABC, October 15, 39 shots, *Felipe Solis: Person of the Week*: This story highlights the museum curator of an Aztec art exhibition in New York. It is framed as an opportunity for Americans to become familiar with the history of their close neighbor, Mexico. The story briefly explores the history of the Aztecs.

#92   ABC, October 17, 4 shots, *General Rick Sanchez*: This story briefly mentions General Rick Sanchez in a longer news story on Iraq. It does not broach his ethnicity.

#93   NBC, October 23, 23 shots, *Colorado Latino Voters*: Embedded in a longer presidential campaign story, this story minimally mentions Latinos as a growing minority who might "take the red out of Colorado."

#94   NBC, October 25, 53 shots, *Latino Voters in Colorado Gubernatorial Elections*: This story covers the senate campaign between rivals Latino Democrat Ken Salazar and conservative Republican and beer scion Pete Coors.

Colorado is a "valuable piece of political real estate." No mention is made of political issues pertaining to Latinos.

#95   NBC, November 9, 14 shots, *Los Angeles Hostage Incident*: A man who briefly took a woman hostage at the city's Mexican consulate was shot and wounded by police. The woman was unharmed. NBC played up the terrorism angle, but police later said the man had demanded media attention and terrorism was not involved.

#96   CBS, October 28, 1 shot, *Fallen Latino Hero*: A brief tribute to fallen Iraq War soldiers, including William Salazar.

#97   ABC, October 29, 5 scenes, 18 shots, *Presidential Candidates on Spanish-Language TV*: This story highlights the power and importance of Latino voters by pointing to the appearances of US presidential candidates on *Sábado Gigante*, a popular variety show on Spanish-language TV.

#98   CNN, October 30, 43 shots, *Cuba and Israel—Issues in the Florida Vote*: This story discusses two ethnic groups, Cuban and Jewish Floridians, and outlines the historical and political importance of Florida in the presidential election. It focuses on Democratic attempts to win the "Cuban vote" by addressing issues that the Bush campaign neglects.

#99   CNN, October 31, 25 shots, *Latino Votes on Election Eve*: In a long story that summarizes the concerns of the candidates on the eve of the election, Latinos are profiled as one of many targeted demographic groups.

#100   ABC, November 10, 6 scenes, 26 shots, *Nomination of Alberto Gonzales*: President Bush nominates a Latino Texan to be attorney general. This story uncritically paraphrases Bush's portrayal of Gonzales as an example of the American Dream, although it raises doubts about Gonzales. Compare #101–#104.

#101   CBS, November 10, 19 shots, *Nomination of Alberto Gonzales*: Similar to #100, but offers a bit more detail about concerns regarding Gonzales' positions on issues such as torture in war. Compare #100, #102–#104.

#102   CNN, November 10, 27 shots, *Nomination of Alberto Gonzales*: The initial framing does not directly identify Gonzales' ethnicity, but suggests that he would be a "pioneer." The network allows the words of Bush and Gonzales to characterize Gonzales. The story raises concerns about Gonzales' past political stances. Compare #100, #101, #103, #104.

#103   CNN, November 10, 31 shots, *Nomination of Alberto Gonzales*: This second CNN story frames the nomination as a "political position," outlines the responsibilities of the US attorney general, and depicts the issues Gonzales will have to address. The story closes by asking whether Gonzales is prepared for the position. Compare #100–#102, #104.

#104   NBC, November 10, 19 shots, *Nomination of Alberto Gonzales*: In this story Gonzales is identified as Mexican American. Like #100 and #101, this story focuses on Gonzales in the context of the Latino community. The story then explores the controversy surrounding Gonzales, focusing on his acceptance of harsh treatment of prisoners classified as enemy combatants. Compare #102 and #103.

#105   ABC, November 12, 1 scene, 2 shots, *Girl Hiding in a Piñata*: A news brief on an unauthorized immigrant child found when authorities searched a car.

#106 ABC, November 15, 4 shots, *44 Cuban Dancers Defect*: This news brief notes that a Cuban dancing troupe defected, will be allowed to stay in the US, and will be granted citizenship in a year's time. (Other news stories state 43 defectors rather than 44.) Compare #107 and #108.

#107 CNN, November 15, 5 shots, *Cuban Dancers Defect*: This very brief report simply mentions that a group of Cuban dancers have defected. Compare #106 and #108.

#108 NBC, November 15, 6 shots, *Mass Defection of Cubans*: This extended story (compared to #106 and #107) frames the defection as "the biggest mass defection from a communist nation." This story pointedly contrasts American freedom to Cuban oppression.

#109 ABC, November 25, 7 scenes, 31 shots, *A Marine Hero in Iraq*: This is a well-crafted human interest story about Rafael Peralta, who sacrificed himself to save half his platoon. It addresses both the sorrow of his Mexican-born family and the gratitude expressed by a family whose loved one he saved.

#110 ABC, November 29, 5 shots, *Nomination of Carlos Gutierrez*: This brief story about the nomination of Carlos Gutierrez as US secretary of commerce is situated around a sensationalized account of his rise from driving trucks to becoming Kellogg's CEO. A brief comment from Gutierrez subtly reinforces the concept of the "American Dream." Compare #111 and #112.

#111 CBS, November 29, 4 shots, *Nomination of Carlos Gutierrez*: This story claims that Gutierrez came to the US as a "refugee from Cuba" and mentions his rise from truck driver to CEO. Compare #110, #112.

#112 CNN, November 29, 1 shot, *Nomination of Carlos Gutierrez*: In this brief, the anchor characterizes Gutierrez' rise as a "great story" and quotes President Bush as saying that "Mr. Gutierrez is the perfect example of the American Dream." Compare #110, #111.

#113 NBC, November 29, 2 shots, *New Secretary of Commerce Carlos Gutierrez*: A news brief that succinctly identifies Carlos Gutierrez as Bush's new secretary of commerce. Gutierrez is depicted as rising through the ranks of the Kellogg corporation.

#114 NBC, December 4, 25 shots, *Colombian Drug Lord Imprisoned*: This story covers the extradition of Gilberto Rodríguez Orejuela from Colombia to the United States. The story gives brief background of his rise to power and includes clips from the Justice Department and of the president referring to "justice" despite wealth.

#115 NBC, December 8, 30 shots, *Wounded Soldier Hugo Gonzalez*: A report on soldiers surviving previously mortal injuries, featuring Hugo Gonzalez.

#116 ABC/BBC, December 19, 10 scenes, 30 shots, *Dangerous Crossing*: This BBC story, though initially framed by the ABC anchor around immigrant smugglers on trial for the deaths of 19 people who suffocated in a truck, follows individuals who are crossing (or have crossed) the border. With several additional framings it details their tribulations and also gives subjectivity to both the immigrants and border patrol agents who regulate the border.

#117 CBS, December 22, 7 scenes, 46 shots, *Arizona Prop 200*: This extended story is focused on an Arizona referendum that cut off health care for unauthorized immigrants. The story profiles Arizonans who oppose the presence of "illegal" immigrants, health care workers who refuse to abide by the law, and people who have migrated.

#118   ABC, December 31, 2 shots, *US Redefines "Torture"*: This news brief connects the Justice Department's expanded definition of torture to the pending confirmation hearings of Alberto Gonzalez, who "helped formulate the Bush policy toward treatment of prisoners of war." ABC makes no statement about the nature of this policy.

Notes

Chapter One

1. Schudson 2002, drawn from Bernard C. Cohen's observation: "the press . . . may not be successful much of the time in telling people what to think, but it is stunningly successful in telling its readers what to think *about*." *The Press and Foreign Policy* (Princeton, NJ: Princeton University Press, 1963), p. 13.

2. Cable News Network (CNN), the American Broadcasting Company (ABC), the National Broadcasting Company (NBC), and the Columbia Broadcasting System (CBS).

3. My students included Adriana Arroyo, Albino Gámez, Alejandra Guzmán, Alejandra Padilla, Arturo Rangel Jr., Ashley Davidson, Brenda Pérez, Brenda Robles, Brian Sánchez, Cecilia González, Daniel Pizarro, Daniel Valencia Jr., Efraín A. Meléndez, Erik Preston, Eveline Bravo, Frieda Kellener, Ibet Serrano, Isabel Rojas, Jacquelyn Gómez, Javier Chávez, John González, Laurie Zabala, Layza López, Leo Cuadrado Jr., Maria Elena Vega, Marian Gabra, Mario Angel Escobar, Monique Cruces, Nancy Vera, Patricia Elizabeth Alfaro, Patricia Munguia, Robert Conrad, Roberto Vega, Rosa Maria Guerrero, Sandra Leticia Aguayo, Saray Navarro, Serena Estrella Villalba, Vanessa García, and Yvette Fraga. I also worked closely with two Occidental College students, Kai Azania Small and Rubén Antonio Farias, to analyze the 45 news stories that are presented in Chapters 2 through 6.

4. This research builds on the guiding work of Félix Gutiérrez (1977) and Federico Subervi. In the mid-1980s Subervi called for an integrated assessment of communication research on Latinos (Subervi-Vélez 1986). Thirteen years later Subervi noted that much of this basic research remained undone. We take up his call for scholarly "portrayals in news and entertainment media," which count among the five most pressing areas of communication policy research (Subervi 1999).

5. The Vanderbilt Television News Archive has served as a depository for network news research since 1968. Marshall Breeding, then director for Innovative Technologies and Research of the Vanderbilt University Library, graciously loaned us 25,178 records for the year 2004, and the following VTNA news story database fields: date, headline, network, duration, and abstract. An example of these fields (with one news story record) follows:

Network: NBC Evening News

Date: Friday, Jan 20, 2004

Headline: In Depth (Strokes)

Abstract: (Studio: Brian Williams) Series on strokes continued. (Cleveland: Robert Bazell) The advances in technology and medical techniques for limiting brain damage from a stroke featured; computer images shown. [Cleveland Clinic's Dr. Thomas MASARYK points out a blood clot.] [Neurosurgeon Dr. Peter RASMUSSEN says we're in the infancy of emerging treatment.] [Patient Patricia KETTLER recalls her stroke symptoms.]

Duration: 02:10

We did not use other VTNA fields or its bracketing and parenthesis coding system, which capitalizes all surnames. Like other archives, VTNA has a distinctive data structure and web-based retrieval system that permits certain research queries and disallows others. Given our need for specific story topic information, research assistant Robert Conrad wrote a MySQL program to create a story-topic index from the original VTNA data structure. The VTNA archive can be found at http://tvnews .vanderbilt.edu.

6. The terms used for the subpopulation category Women included *women*, *woman*, *mother*, *sister*, *female*, *girl*, *ladies*, *lady*, *daughter*, *wives*, and *wife*. For Latinos, terms included *Mexican American, Mexico, Mexican*; *Honduras, Honduran*; *Salvadorian, Salvadoran, Salvador*; *Guatemalan, Guatemala*; *Panama, Panamanian*; *Costa Rican, Costa Rica*; *Dominican*; *Haitian, Haiti*; *Cuban, Cuba*; *Puerto Rican, Puerto Rico*; *Latino, Latina, Hispanic*; *Central American, Central America*; *Caribbean*; *Nicaraguan, Nicaragua*; *Venezuelan, Venezuela*; *Chilean, Chile*.

7. As in the following VTNA news story record, in which the word *woman* triggered the tagging algorithm in spite of the absence of relevance to women's issues:

Network: NBC

Date: January 1, 2004, 5:36 pm

Headline: Middle East / Israelis vs. Palestinians / The Fence

Abstract: (Studio: Campbell Brown) Pope John Paul II's renewed call for peace in the Middle East noted. (Abu Dis, West Bank: Martin Fletcher) Growing concern over the wall Israel is building through the West Bank to stop suicide attacks featured; scenes shown. [Palestinian MAN, WOMAN complain about the separation of families and the difficulty in getting to jobs and services.] [Israeli STUDENT says there has to be a better way than to split a village.]

Duration: 02:30

8. For African Americans, however, a few celebrities and the legacy of the civil rights movement (particularly the 50th anniversary of *Brown v. Board of Education*) accounted for most of the news stories.

9. The Latin American cluster includes the Caribbean, Central American, Chilean, Costa Rican, Cuban, Dominican, Guatemalan, Haitian, Honduran, US Latino, Mexican, minority, Nicaraguan, Panamanian, Puerto Rican, Salvadoran, and Venezuelan groups, and excludes non-Spanish-speaking Brazilians.

10. Below is a record that the algorithm tagged as minority, African American, and Latino (as marked below in **bold**):

Network: CNN

Date: February 14, 2004, 9:21 pm

Headline: Auto Racing / Diversity

Abstract: (Studio: Carol Lin) Report introduced. (Daytona, Florida: Steve Overmyer) NASCAR's efforts to add more ethnic diversity to its slate of White drivers featured; details given about the "Drive for Diversity" training program for **minorities**. [NASCAR truck series driver Bill LESTER says NASCAR realizes that to be recognized as America's sport it needs to be reflective of the ethnic hue of this country.] [NASCAR COO George PYNE comments on the growing fan base of **African Americans** and **Hispanics**]. [NASCAR chairman Brian FRANCE says we're starting at the grassroots beginner level.] [NASCAR champion Darrell WALTRIP comments on advances in other sports.]

Duration: 02:20

11. The 100 most numerous topics of the 12,140 news stories (count, percentage) were as follows: Iraq (2,094, 17.25%); presidential campaign (1,249, 10.29%); health (597, 4.92%); terrorism (573, 4.72%); economy (556, 4.58%); human interest (346, 2.85%); President Bush (259, 2.13%); Middle East (242, 1.99%); September 11 (241, 1.99%); hurricanes (195, 1.61%); crime (184, 1.52%); business (166, 1.37%); USA (148, 1.22%); death (145, 1.19%); CA (144, 1.19%); space (142, 1.17%); Afghanistan (133, 1.1%); weather (120, .99%); Martha Stewart (116, .96%); gay marriage (112, .92%); Olympics (111, .91%); Supreme Court (106, .87%); Haiti (101, .83%); military (101, .83%); television (101, .83%); Russia (99, .82%); Saudi Arabia (95, .78%); Reagan (88, .72%); FL (87, .72%); Congress (74, .61%); religion (71, .58%); auto industry (70, .58%); gas prices (70, .58%); Pakistan (67, .55%); Britain (66, .54%); Iran (66, .54%); baseball (63, .52%); NY (63, .52%); Spain (61, .5%); Washington, DC (60, .49%); basketball (59, .49%); movies (59, .49%); holidays (58, .48%); CIA (57, .47%); consumer alert (53, .44%); Asia (51, .42%); person of the week (50, .41%); TX (49, .4%); Ukraine (49, .4%); food (45, .37%); Clinton (43, .35%); France (40, .33%); WA (40, .33%); colleges (38, .31%); environment (38, .31%); airlines (37, .3%); China (36, .3%); OH (35, .29%); politics (34, .28%); education (32, .26%); Sudan (32, .26%); Medicare (30, .25%); music (30, .25%); West (30, .25%); Guantánamo Bay (27, .22%); MA (27, .22%); North Korea (26, .21%); MD (25, .21%); Jackson (24, .2%); sports (24, .2%); WWII (24, .2%); African Americans (23, .19%); IL (23, .19%); air safety (22, .18%); GA (22, .18%); India (22, .18%); animals (21, .17%); football (21, .17%); Japan (21, .17%); photography (21, .17%); AZ (20, .16%); cycling (20, .16%); internet (20, .16%); guns (19, .16%); CO (18, .15%); Turkey (18, .15%); airports (17, .14%); computers (17, .14%); Israel (17, .14%); Libya (17, .14%); NJ (17, .14%); presidency (17, .14%); Social Security (17, .14%); horse racing (16, .13%); immigration (16, .13%); airplanes (15, .12%); Canada (15, .12%); Greece (15, .12%); Italy (15, .12%); NV (15, .12%).

12. To develop Table 1.3, our research team discussed various options, recognizing that alternative groupings of topics are available. We acknowledge that longer stories touch on multiple topics. Our team reviewed many individual stories to get a sense of the appropriateness of the subject matter distribution labels. Television news stories are not 100-word Associated Press blurbs, but multifaceted narratives composed by news editors. The longest of these stories have a rich background and provide a deep context that makes the stories lifelike and complicates our simple classification process.

13. The four aforementioned subject matter groupings tend not to overlap significantly with US domestic topics (11%) and human interest (4%). Differentiating these from the last set of subject matter groupings (natural disasters, 5%; sports, 4%; consumer related and entertainment, 3%) was more difficult, because the former displayed greater topic overlap.

14. The Caribbean cluster of stories combines stories attributed to the Caribbean, Cuban, Dominican, Haitian, and Puerto Rican subpopulations.

15. This is why we classified Guantánamo stories as Cuban rather than as terrorism stories.

16. E.g., Halloran, Elliot, and Murdock 1970; Gans 1979; Gitlin 1980.

17. See endnote 11.

18. In point of fact, it is as much a bureaucratic issue as it is a Latino issue, since nearly half of the nation's unauthorized immigrant population are individuals who have overstayed their tourist visas (http://pewhispanic.org/files/factsheets/19.pdf; retrieved 29 June 2011).

19. The cluster includes stories attributable to Central American, Costa Rican, Guatemalan, Honduran, Nicaraguan, Panamanian, and Salvadoran subpopulations.

20. "Menchu plans to join new Guatemalan government," *Milwaukee Journal Sentinel*, January 18, 2004, p. 8A; "Fifty years after coup, Guatemala struggles," by Marion Lloyd, *Boston Globe*, June 26, 2004, p. A4.

21. See endnote 11.

22. Gutiérrez 1977; Subervi-Vélez 1986; Subervi 1999.

23. Mastro and Robinson 2000.

24. Mastro and Stern 2003.

25. Oliver 1994.

26. Wible 2004.

27. Poindexter, Smith, and Heider 2003, p. 524. Subjectivity is a social psychology notion about the representation of the humanity of individuals and groups of people. It involves expressed human cognition, motive, and emotional affect. Television viewers perceive the humanness of an individual who is shown on news reports when they register these elements.

28. Mastro and Robinson 2000.

29. Oliver 1994; for an excellent overview, see Oliver 2003.

30. Oliver 1994.

31. Dixon and Azocar 2006; Dixon and Linz 2000a, 2000b, 2002; Dixon, Azocar, and Casas 2003. Students of media have long been aware of differential audience interpretations of controversial portrayals on television. Norman Lear, producer of the 1971 groundbreaking situation comedy *All in the Family*, presumed that the whole audience would recognize that the show's satire was designed to belittle the racist antics of Archie Bunker. However, Vidmar and Rokeach (1974) found that only less-prejudiced viewers judged Bunker's words and actions as objectionable and antiquated. Highly prejudiced viewers missed or dismissed the satire and believed that Archie's words and actions were creditable. We should not dismiss the impact of "reality-based" police programming on audiences.

32. Dixon and Linz 2000a, 2000b, 2002.

33. Dixon and Azocar 2006.

34. Mastro 2003.

35. Mastro, Behm-Morawitz, and Ortiz 2007.

36. Faber, O'Guinn, and Meyer 1987.

37. Schudson 2003, p. 87. Also see Wilson and Gutiérrez (1985) and Subervi-Vélez (1986) for assessments of minority representation in television two decades ago.

38. Lloyd 2006.

39. By 2006 over 58.4% of US homes subscribed to basic cable television services. The subscriptions were concentrated in middle-class households (www.market ingcharts.com/television/snl-kagan-cable-subscription-data-contradicts-fcc-chair-man-kevin-martin-2634/snl-kagan-cable-summary-data-2006jpg; retrieved 7 June 2011).

40. Suro 2004.

41. Schudson 2003, p. 71.

42. Schudson 2001, pp. 249–250; Knott 2005.

43. Schudson 2003, p. 30. However, Schudson was unconvinced of the utility of Entman and Rojecki's (2000) capstone study, which found that the news media overrepresented African Americans as criminals while underrepresenting them as crime victims. "It should be apparent that there is no agreement about what feature of reality would be the 'right' one for TV news to seek to mirror. It should also be apparent that the more one seeks some model of reality that describes the whole social scene, the less likely it is that standard news practices will lend themselves to its representation" (Schudson 2003, pp. 36–37). The point should be that journalism cannot mirror reality and tends to present hegemonic views of society. The findings of Entman and Rojecki should motivate network newsrooms to revise standard unjust practices.

44. Schudson 2003, pp. 29–31, emphasis in the original.

45. Schudson 2003, p. 31.

46. Schudson 2003, p. 105.

47. The gap in representation has not diminished significantly in the past 15 years. See also Navarrete and Kamasaki 1994; National Council of La Raza 1996; Méndez-Méndez and Alverio 2002; and Subervi 2004, 2005.

48. "Veteran fights different battle at home: Foreign-born ex-soldier finds U.S. citizenship an elusive goal," by Teresa Borden, *Atlanta Journal-Constitution*, September 15, 2004, p. 3F.

49. "GI may go from illegal to citizen," by Mark Bixler, *Atlanta Journal-Constitution*, February 6, 2004, p. 3A.

50. "Mother might face double loss: Woman whose son was killed in Iraq on verge of deportation," by Ann Imse, *Rocky Mountain News* (Denver), May 17, 2004, p. 6A.

51. "More Latinos turn out to the polls: Voter registration surpassed 10 million," by Leslie Berenstein, *San Diego Union-Tribune*, November 5, 2004.

52. "New census figures for presidential election show dramatic growth in Latino voting," June 9, 2005, press release of the William C. Velásquez Institute.

53. Patterson 2002.

54. "The Hispanic vote," *St. Petersburg Times* (Florida), November 28, 2004, p. 2P.

55. "Storefront clinics surge as Latinos seek low-cost care: Caregivers may lack state doctors' licenses, but they're in tune with traditional methods—and they speak Spanish," by Jennifer Mena, *Los Angeles Times*, May 2, 2004, p. B6.

56. "Mexican American communities offer health benefits to long-time residents," *Science Letter*, October 19, 2004, p. 1177.

57. "Health care needs diversity, says National Academies' Institute of Medicine," by Katherine S. Mangan, *Chronicle of Higher Education* 50(24), February 20, 2004, p. A11.

58. http://nces.ed.gov/programs/quarterly/vol_6/6_3/3_4.asp; retrieved 16 August 2006.

59. "Hub of hyper-segregation," *Boston Globe*, April 23, 2004, p. A23.

60. See, for example, "End school racial isolation," by Angelo Ancheta, *USA Today*, April 29, 2004, p. 11A; "Equal access to college," *Denver Post*, commentary by Carrie Besnette and Van Schoales, March 14, 2004, p. E-04.

61. Hill 2008.

62. "Legal industry still lacking in minorities," *USA Today*, September 9, 2004, p. 3B.

63. "UC to decide how to cut eligibility: Fewer Latinos, Blacks will get in," *San Francisco Chronicle*, July 13, 2004, p. B3.

64. "Too close for comfort," by K. S. Newman, *New York Times*, April 17, 2004, p. A15.

65. "Teen summit seeks to combat prejudice and violence in Houston schools," *Houston Chronicle*, November 9, 2004, p. B8.

66. "La Raza reports 'overrepresentation' of Latinos in U.S. jails," by Richard Woodbury, *La Voz* 30(45), November 3, 2004, p. 12. The 2004 NCLR report: "*Lost opportunities: The reality of Latinos in the U.S. criminal justice system*" (http://www.nclr.org/content/publications/detail/27587, retrieved August 13, 2006).

67. "Houses for undocumented immigrants," *La Voz* 30(41), October 6, 2004, p. 1.

68. "Lack of information stalls Mexican-Americans' dreams," *La Voz* 30(34), August 18, 2004, p. 30.

69. "Lack of information," p. 30.

70. "Supermarket janitors awarded $22.4 million in class-action suit: Big chains accused of failing to pay workers overtime," by Jason B. Johnson, *San Francisco Chronicle*, October 6, 2004, p. B3.

71. Representative stories are "A fruity success story," by Christine Granados, *Hispanic* 17(9), p. 62; "Empresas hispanas, de la supervivencia al crecimiento," *Mundo Hispánico* (Atlanta, GA) 25(706), December 23, 2004, p. A14; "'Sí se puede' dicen las mujeres," *El Latino* (San Diego, CA) 17(51), December 17, 2004, p. 29; and "Aida Santiesteban, el triunfo sobre ruedas," by Annette Lopez Muñoz, *Nuevo Herald* (Miami, FL), December 19, 2004, p. 11A.

72. "Cheese, Hispanic style: Specialty products are capturing growing chunk of market," by Linda Spice, *Milwaukee Journal Sentinel*, June 28, 2004, p. 1D.

73. "Diversas reacciones sobre Reagan," by Miguel Ángel Vega, *La Opinión* (Los Angeles) 78(267), June 8, 2004, p. 3A; "La otra cara de Reagan," by Roger Lindo, *La Opinión* (Los Angeles) 78(268), June 9, 2004. p. 3A; and "Ronald Reagan: Canoniza-

ción y amnesia social," by Max Castro, *La Opinión* (Los Angeles) 78(279), June 20, 2004, p. 3E.

74. "Una vela por Gloria: A candle for Gloria," by Cordelia Candelaria, *Frontiers* (Boulder, CO) 25(3), p. 1.

75. "Reynaldo Garza, 89, U.S. judge since 1961," *New York Times*, September 19, 2004, p. A44.

76. "Frank del Olmo, 55, Los Angeles journalist," by Douglas Martin, *New York Times*, February 20, 2004.

77. "Pedro Pietri, 59, poet who chronicled Nuyorican life," by David Gonzalez, *New York Times*, March 6, 2004, p. A13.

78. Pedro Pietri, *Puerto Rican obituary* (New York: Monthly Review Press, 1973).

79. "Puerto Rican obituary," *Monthly Review Press* 56(2), June 2004, pp. 48-55.

Section I

1. Geertz 1973, quoted by Roeh 1989, p. 166.
2. Schudson 2003, p. 2.
3. Tuchman 1976, quoted in Schudson 2003, p. 4.
4. Gripsrup 2000, in Schudson 2003, p. 14.
5. Hartley 1996, in Schudson 2003, p. 12.
6. Schudson 2003, p. 13.
7. Habermas' exemplar of civic life, nineteenth-century newspapers, was in the grips of capitalism. As newspapers became commodities, publishers began to use sensationalism to increase profits. Schudson describes Habermas as saying that capitalism "refeudalized" public life, even though capitalism had first shattered feudalism (Schudson 2003, p. 67).
8. Anderson 1983.
9. Schudson notes that Hegel saw newspaper reading as a substitute for morning prayers, and quotes Anderson as saying each reader "communicant" knows that "the ceremony he performs is being replicated simultaneously by thousands the existence of which he can be sure, yet of whose identity he has not the slightest notion" (2003, p. 68).
10. Schudson 1992, review of Thompson 1990.
11. Foucault 1980, pp. 92-108.
12. Foucault 1983, p. 208. *Discourse* for Foucault is socially constructed knowledge of some social practice, rather than the representations of the social practice. However, we can study the *discourse* of networks—institutionalized corporations which produce televised news reports—by studying their reports.
13. Please note that *ideology* does not refer to a rigidly held system of political ideas. Kavanagh appropriately contrasts theoretical concepts of thinkers such as Foucault or Althusser to the use of this word in commercial mass media news. In US print or television news, someone on the Far Left, such as Fidel Castro, or on the Far Right, such as Patrick Buchanan, will be identified as wishing to impose an extremist model on our mainstream moderate political system. News commentators

will say that this person "has" an ideology and may use it to disrupt a government or nation. The colloquial word *ideology* is then contrasted to political "pragmatism" or "common sense" (Kavanagh 1995, p. 306), implying that US politics and journalism travel a non-ideological middle way. Here we explore the ideology of this journalistic "middle way."

14. White 1990, p. x.

15. A comprehensive study of discursive meaning production would integrate dissimilar research programs, including the ritual of television watching; network newsroom institutional framing; the structure of the network television genre of news reporting, especially news story narrative; and televised media semiotics. Here we focus on the product of network newsrooms, leaving studies of audience ritual and effects to other researchers.

16. Stories were included if a Latino was in either the primary newsmaker role or the secondary newsmaker role for specific relevant issues. By "Latino," we mean someone of Latino/Hispanic heritage, including people of Latin America and the Caribbean if they are part of a news story originating within or directly affecting the United States. By "primary newsmaker role," we mean that one or more Latinos clearly played a central role in the creation, development, or resolution of a news issue being aired, with the topic of the story also being relevant to the Latino individual or his/her community, business, or organization. By "secondary for relevant specific issues," we mean the topic of the story is pertinent to Latinos and/or a Latino community (for example, affirmative action and civil rights). In this type of story, mention is made of how a legal case, law, pending legislation, etc., may affect diverse communities, including Latinos. This draws on Subervi 2004.

17. My sincere thanks go out to Kai Azania Small and Rubén Antonio Farias (undergraduates at Occidental College).

18. Abbott 2008, p. 235.

19. Lister and Wells 2001.

20. Jewitt and Oyama 2001.

21. This figure may be inflated. Of these 118 stories, up to 17 refer to individuals who are only incidentally Latinos, depending on one's judgment. I chose to be inclusive, retaining stories such as #44 and #45 (about a kidnap victim whose attacker apparently is Latino), #8 (about Nydia Gonzalez, who testified at the 9/11 Commission and may incidentally be Latina), and three stories about Rick Sanchez, commander of US forces in Iraq (#58, #69, #92). His ethnicity was not mentioned but is suggested because of his surname.

22. See Santa Ana 2003, pp. 249–258.

23. Smith-Maddox and Solórzano 2002, p. 71.

24. Iedema 2001, pp. 188–190.

25. Rick Iedema says, "In a scene the camera moves within one time-space, but is at the same time made up of more than one shot" (2001, p. 189).

26. We built on Lister and Wells' (2001) classifications, as well as those of van Leeuwen (2001), pp. 92–118.

27. Baum 2003; Baumgartner and Morris 2006, p. 341.

28. Tankard 2001, p. 101.

29. Gamson and Modigliani 1989, emphasis added.

30. Entman 1993, p. 52, excluding italics in the original.

Chapter Two

1. Quoted by Winslow 2008, pp. R1, R4.

2. Journalists call the political issues centering on the federal government, including foreign affairs, "inside-the-Beltway" issues, a reference to the freeway that circles the nation's capital.

3. I attempt to retain the spelling that Latinos use for their own names. Some prefer English orthographic conventions; others prefer Spanish ones.

4. The Defense Department defined an enemy combatant as "an individual who was part of or supporting Taliban or al-Qaeda forces, or associated forces that are engaged in hostilities against the United States or its coalition partners. This includes any person who has committed a belligerent act or has directly supported hostilities in aid of enemy armed forces." Legal scholar Ronald Dworkin (2008) points out: "It is unclear what limits the department might accept on what counts as 'supporting.'"

5. I want to thank Robert Castillo Cruz, who contributed many insights based on his review of an early draft of this chapter.

6. This book does not address the CNN running text that appears at the bottom of the screen in ticker-tape fashion, looping a set of headlines of the other news stories of the day. This looping text changes as the newsroom processes the latest information on the events of the day.

7. Schudson 2001.

8. The *medium close-up* is halfway between a mid-shot and a close-up. This shot shows the face more clearly, without getting uncomfortably close. The *mid-shot* approximates the field of vision of typical conversation, encompassing only the torso and head.

9. Thanks to Robert Castillo Cruz for these observations.

10. Caivano 1998.

11. Other networks carried more balanced reports of the federal indictment of Padilla. Over the course of 2004, the networks either reported on Padilla or on the Patriot Act, but did not weave the two topics together.

12. Four years later Anthony Lewis (2008) wrote: "A steady accumulation of disclosures, capped . . . by a Senate committee report and hearing, has made it clear that abusive treatment of prisoners was a deliberate policy that came from the top—the Pentagon, the Justice Department, and the White House. . . . We still do not know what was done to José Padilla, an American held for years in solitary confinement as an alleged enemy combatant and now reportedly suffering long-term psychological damage. . . . For more than two years Mr. Padilla was detained in a navy brig on the order of President Bush, without being charged with any offense and without access to counsel. He was kept in a cell with nothing to read except, for a short time, a copy of the Koran, and no sense of time or daylight and no interaction with anyone except his interrogators. When he was once taken to a dentist, his eyes and ears were covered to maintain the sensory deprivation."

13. Six years after then attorney general John Ashcroft alleged that Padilla plotted with al-Qaeda to detonate a radioactive bomb and President Bush proclaimed him an enemy combatant, a judge rejected the government appeal to sentence him to life imprisonment. Padilla was convicted of conspiracy to murder, maim, or kid-

nap persons overseas and to provide material support to terrorist groups, but US district judge Marcia Cooke said: "There is no evidence that [he] personally maimed, kidnapped or killed anyone in the United States or elsewhere. . . . I do find that the conditions were so harsh for Mr. Padilla . . . they warrant consideration in the sentencing in this case" (Williams 2008, p. A12).

14. A second, thinly reported case of domestic militancy may begin to reveal a pattern. In April 2003, the FBI arrested William Krar, a 63-year-old from East Texas. That year he pled guilty to possession of a weapon of mass destruction, "a sodium-cyanide bomb capable of killing thousands, more than a hundred explosives, half a million rounds of ammunition, dozens of illegal weapons, and a mound of literature." Like Lindh, Krar had a speedy trial. In January 2004 he was fined $29,600 and sentenced to 139 months in federal prison (http://www.justice.gov /usao/txe/news_release/news/krar_bruey_rivers.pdf; retrieved 23 April 2010). In contrast to the 2002 press conference where then-attorney general John Ashcroft announced the arrest of Padilla as a "terrorist," the US Justice Department never described Krar as a terrorist, in spite of his plans, his violent White supremacist, antigovernment views, and his fully functional chemical weapon (Axtman 2003). Citing the Krar case and others, Levitas stated (2002) that US law enforcement frequently employs a double standard, labeling some domestic offenders "terrorists" but characterizing White militia members as "criminals" (www.onthemedia.org /transcripts/2010/04/02/02; retrieved 23 April 2010).

15. Schudson (2003, p. 40) describes US news media tendencies to articulate statist discourse rather than a civil discourse independent of the government.

16. *B-roll* refers to supplemental visual footage that is interspliced among the main shots of a news story to enliven the visual narrative.

17. Appendix, #110 (ABC, 5 shots) and #111 (CBS, 4 shots).

18. http://biography.jrank.org/pages/3892/Gutiérrez-Carlos-M-1953-Corporate -Executive.html; retrieved 8 January 2008.

19. American journalism's milquetoast response to Bush initiatives, notably during the buildup to the Iraq invasion, has been explored in several book-length studies, including Bennett, Lawrence, and Livingston (2007).

20. LULAC (League of United Latin American Citizens) is the largest and oldest Latino organization in the United States. Since 1927, LULAC has advanced the economic condition, educational attainment, political influence, health, and civil rights of Hispanic Americans through community-based programs operating at more than 700 LULAC councils nationwide.

21. The SVREP "is the nation's largest nonpartisan Latino political machine." González does the "gritty, unglamorous work—mounting sign-up booths at bodegas, analyzing census tracts, training school-board candidates. But the results have been spectacular. When veteran community organizer González took over the group in 1994, only 5 million Hispanics were registered nationwide. Today there are 9.3 million. In the last presidential election, 81.5% of them cast ballots, compared with 88.5% of all voters" (Roosevelt 2005, p. 46).

22. Likewise, most of the video clips presented in these stories represent Latinos as laborers, farmers, construction workers, etc. There was little mention of diversity among Latinos of different origins, such as Mexicans, Central Americans, and South Americans, and only on occasion were contrasts made between first- and second-generation Latinos.

23. While the piece to which Clark bobbed was not a dance song, the Mariachi repertoire does include dance music, particularly for *baile folklórico*.

24. Perhaps unwittingly, Clark derided Spanish speakers. Jane Hill (1993) has characterized this kind of purposefully ungrammatical, derisive simulation of Spanish as "mock Spanish." This covertly racializing verbal practice functions to aggrandize whiteness and the English language by disparaging Mexicans and the Spanish language. Hill notes that while amused listeners will not accept that they are participants in a discourse that articulates racism, "it is impossible to 'get' Mock Spanish—to find these expressions funny or colloquial or even intelligible—unless one has access to . . . profoundly racist images of members of historically Spanish-speaking populations" (Hill 1998, p. 683).

25. President Bush ultimately took 40% of the Latino vote in 2004 rather than the 44% originally reported in major news media exit polls (Suro, Fry, and Passel 2005).

26. Vidmar and Rokeach (1974) and Gray (1995), among others, note that for many viewers, television shows that invoke stereotypes affirm racial prejudice.

27. Thanks to Sue Carter for this observation.

28. Roberto Suro is captioned "Election Analyst," an entirely inadequate characterization. In 2001 the veteran journalist became founding director of the Pew Hispanic Center, a research organization that produces "non-partisan statistical analysis and public opinion surveys chronicling the rapid growth of the Latino population and its implications for the nation as a whole" (http://www.pewhispanic .org/about-the-center/).

29. One *Sábado Gigante* regular segment involves a mock singing contest. El Chacal de la Trompeta stands behind each member of the audience who performs. El Chacal is quick to blow his trumpet to unceremoniously end a poor performance, which elicits derisive roars from the audience.

30. Between the 2000 and 2004 elections, Latinos accounted for 50% of the nation's population growth, with an increase of 5.7 million, but only 10% of the increase in the total votes cast (2.1 million new voters). This gap has widened in recent years: many Latinos are too young to vote, or are not citizens. Further, Latinos simply do not vote at the rates of Whites or Blacks. Only 18% of all Latinos (adults as well as children, citizens and noncitizens) went to the polls in 2004, compared with 51% of all Whites and 39% of all Blacks (Suro, Fry, and Passel, 2005).

31. See Baum (2003); Young (2004); Baumgartner and Morris (2006); Peterson (2008); and Santa Ana (2009) for discussions of the politics of "soft news" or what some people call "infotainment."

32. de la Garza et al. 1992.

Chapter Three

1. Jordan 2004.

2. Jordan 2004.

3. Jordan 2004, p. A2.

4. Jordan 2004, p. A2.

5. "Mexican Americans face far higher stroke risk than whites," *Mental Health Business Week*, September 4, 2004, p. 78.

6. In the course of this book, we will refer both to *subject positions* and to *subjectivity*. Subject positions are social network relations that are created in discourse, and *subjectivity* pertains to the network's presentation of the humanity of individuals and groups of people.

7. Thanks to Amelia Tseng for these observations.

8. The National Academy of Recording Arts and Sciences annually presents the Grammy Awards, the music industry's equivalent to the film industry's Academy Award, the Oscar.

9. This was not his first Grammy. In 2000 Ferrer won a Latin Grammy for Best New Artist. And his album *Buenos Hermanos*, in which producer Ry Cooder blended both southern gospel singers (the Blind Boys of Alabama) and an innovative accordion, won a Grammy for Best Traditional Tropical Latin Album of 2003.

10. The Department of Justice was verbally cited, and the United States Immigration and Naturalization Service insignia was used in the ABC graphic even though the INS ceased to exist under that name in 2003, when most of its functions were transferred from the Department of Justice to the newly created Department of Homeland Security. The transferred components include US Citizenship and Immigration Services, US Immigration and Customs Enforcement (ICE), and US Customs and Border Protection.

11. "As a cultural phenomenon, *Buena Vista* perpetuated misconceptions about Cuba, its music and its artists. The myth that Cubans had abandoned their traditional roots. That these Buena Vista performers were once the best in their day. That outsiders had to come and rescue a dying culture" (Gurza 2001, p. F6).

12. Ferrer passed away the following year, in August 2005.

13. Some Central Americans can receive "temporary protected" status that provisionally keeps them from being deported to their oppressive and genocidal home governments. In 1991 Congress awarded temporary protected status to Salvadorans, Nicaraguans, and Hondurans who had been in the United States since 1990, but not after February 2001. This allows qualifying immigrants to live and work in the US for a fixed period of time. The status was originally scheduled to expire for Salvadorans at the end of 1994, but has been extended in increments, most recently through September 2013.

14. In 2001 Tancredo introduced the Mass Immigration Reduction Act, which would have imposed an indefinite national moratorium on immigration, with the exception of spouses and children of US citizens. The moratorium would have remained in effect until it could be certified that fewer than 10,000 unauthorized immigrants had entered the country in the previous year. At that time, an immigration policy could be proposed, with the stipulation that the president and both houses of Congress must agree that the policy would have no adverse impact on domestic wages, housing, environment, or schools. In 2004, when this story ran, Tancredo's political star was only beginning to rise. In 2005 he would warn the nation about immigrants: "They're coming here to kill you, and you, and me, and my grandchildren," (quoted in Quillen 2005, p. B7). In 2007 Tancredo even sought the presidency, and in a GOP debate televised by CNN he said: "We're not just talking about the number of jobs that we may be losing, or the number of kids that are in our schools and impacting our school system, or the number of people that are abusing our hospital system and taking advantage of the welfare system in this country. . . .

What we're doing here in this immigration battle is testing our willingness to actually hold together as a nation or split apart into a lot of Balkanized pieces" (GOP debate at Saint Anselm College, 3 June 2007).

15. Hill 1998.

16. The redistricting plan adopted by the school board in March 2004 affected one-quarter of the district's 40,000 students, who would have to change schools (Malone 2004).

17. Malone 2004, p. 1.

18. Background information drawn from Pierce (2004).

19. The backstory includes a $40 million deficit (created by overestimating the number of schools needed to be built as the student body shrank) that forced the loss of 600 teachers, and a policy that would "put all the White, middle-class kids in the gleaming new buildings, close good schools and isolate all the struggling students (mostly poor and not White) together in the older buildings" (Bailey 2004, p. 16).

20. While neither principals nor assistant superintendents set school district policy, the principal is legally responsible for the safety and education of the children who attend the school site. Both administrators interviewed are required to follow board policies. It should be noted that the CBS news team was remarkably careful to respect Cabrera's and Ponce's limited accountability. CBS did not mention why it did not air the board's explanation.

21. In fairness, the pending lawsuit was first published after CBS broadcast its story (Malone 2004).

22. Cavanagh 2005, p. 4.

23. Note the response of some parents: "As a member of Legislation for Education Accountability Right Now . . . Marie Wiermanski . . . thinks forming a new school district [splitting from U-46] will help the community of Wayne control its own destiny." Wiermanski also pointed to problems at the large schools her sons attended. "The bar was lowered academically at Ellis Middle School because they had so many children where English was a second language," she said. "Instead of having children strive for a higher level of education, it was a lower level" (Pierce 2004, p. 3).

24. Many have described the gap. For example, Haycock (2003) stated, "Between 1970 and 1988, the achievement gap between African American and White students was cut in half, and the gap separating Latinos and Whites declined by one-third. . . . Since that time the gaps have widened." By 2003, by the end of high school, Latino students had math and reading skills that were comparable to those of White middle school students (The Education Trust 2003). In 2003, only 53% of all Hispanic students graduated from high school on time, compared to 78% of Whites; only 20% of Latino students left high school prepared for college, compared to 40% of Whites; and of students entering college, only 7% were Latinos, while 76% were White (Greene and Winters 2005).

25. In 2000, while the aggregate population of school-age children since the 1990 census "had increased by 12 percent, the population of [English language learners] ELs grew by 54 percent. Sixty percent of ELs in the United States were Spanish speakers" (*National Education Association* 2007).

26. Gans 1979, p. 168.

27. Annually proposed since 2001, the DREAM Act (Development, Relief and

Education for Alien Minors) is a federal legislative remedy for undocumented students who were brought to the United States as minors and who have attended and completed elementary and secondary education in the US. In *Plyler v. Doe* (1982) the US Supreme Court determined that these students are entitled to public elementary and secondary education. However, federal law does not take into account that they were minors, hence not to blame, when they crossed US borders without appropriate documentation. Consequently, they are not provided special consideration for citizenship or higher education when they reach majority age, after high school graduation. While the DREAM Act would provide those paths, the 2004 version would not have made these students eligible for federal financial aid. As of 2012, this legislation has not become federal law.

28. Balancing "ideological blackening" of immigrant students (see Lee 2005 and Ong 1996).

29. Review of these stories led us to provide a rubric distinguishing between appropriate and inappropriate editing: if listeners cannot determine what the off-camera question was that elicited the broadcast response, excessive editing has occurred. Excessive editing allows skeptical viewers to presume that some kind of misrepresentation (whether malicious, inadvertent, or benevolent) is being broadcast.

30. In Spanish, "Chapín fallecido en Iraq." *Chapín* is a Guatemalan colloquial term meaning 'someone from Guatemala.'

31. CBS news (20 August 2003), "The Death of Lance Cpl. Gutierrez." This CBS website report cites an earlier *60 Minutes* segment on Gutierrez and the approximately 38,000 other "Americans in uniform" who were not US citizens.

32. By the fifth anniversary of the war, over 20,000 noncitizens still served in the US military, and "the Pentagon has recorded 142 non-citizen fatalities in support of operations in Afghanistan and Iraq" (Pickerton 2008, p. A1).

33. http://www.cbsnews.com/stories/2003/04/23/60II/printable550779.shtml; retrieved 6 March 2008.

34. The 2003 advertising cost per new recruit neared $1,900. The navy acknowledged, "Family income [is] the most important variable . . . Enlistment rates are much higher when income is lowest." Hence the focus on lower-class adolescents. Poor communities bristle with armed forces billboards. Ethnic website marketing now promotes "El Navy" to the Latino community, with substantial advertising in hip-hop magazines (Saulnier 2004).

35. Simon 2003.

36. Schudson (2003, p. 188) noted that television news, in particular, shifts its presentation in accordance with cultural traditions, so editors and anchors will likely modify the text and delivery of some news items to acknowledge a national holiday.

37. Newspaper articles on Peralta were often built around the history of his immigration status, such as the one entitled "From Illegal to Immortal."

38. Soon after this broadcast, Peralta was nominated for the Congressional Medal of Honor. The exhaustive investigation into Peralta's background for his nomination for this award was longer than the typical three years. Meanwhile, he remained in the national spotlight with a History Channel report (www.history enespanol.com/espanol/elhonor/aoh_videos.jsp), and several magazine articles beyond military presses, notably the *National Review*. On Memorial Day 2005, Pres-

ident Bush referred to Peralta, saying he "understood that America faces dangerous enemies, and he knew the sacrifices required to defeat them" (Cole 2008). In
late 2007, an assistant secretary of the navy said that the Pentagon had approved Peralta's nomination (Cole 2008). Ultimately, Peralta's nomination was not approved.

39. See Molina-Guzmán 2010, 2000; Molina-Guzmán and Valdivia 2004, among
many others.

40. Pérez' mother was accidentally killed in her San Diego home during a neighborhood altercation when Yuliana was three years old. Tom Spousta noted that Yuliana had not seen her father, Juan Carlos Martínez Vallez, "since she was five, but
knows he lives somewhere in the United States" (Spousta 2001, p. D6). This is Sanders' first reporting inaccuracy.

41. Kai Small commented (personal communication) that Sanders' statements
are contemptuous of Cubans, reducing the Cuban people's life experiences to their
economic circumstances.

42. Spousta, the *New York Times* reporter, is far more precise: in 2001, "Pérez no
longer trains barefoot so as not to wear out her only pair of shoes, which she occa-
sionally did in Cuba." Kai Small (personal communication) had an additional take:
Sanders represents Cubans as desperate. He is condescending toward Cubans who
do not share American values. His tone demeans the lives of ordinary Cubans as it
glorifies US lifestyles. Without denying that some Cubans experience real poverty,
Small noted that Sanders speaks as if all Cubans were unable to provide solutions
for themselves. For his self-satisfied US audience, Sanders treats Cubans as having
no ability to rise above mere survival. As privileged social interrogators, news correspondents should denounce Cuban poverty, but should not deny humanity to the
Cubans. Sanders allows his US audience to ignore their government's role in Cuban
poverty and promotes pity as a quality of a good person; he does not call for intro-
spection or action to rectify an unjust state of affairs.

43. Sanders uses hyperbole when describing Pérez as "destined for greatness."
World-class athletes competing at the international level are never destined to win;
they only have the potential to succeed. Winning is a matter of an abundance of natural talent, single-minded determination, years of effective training, good health,
and sheer luck.

44. Like the US, Cuba is known for its powerful Olympic training program and
uses it to promote its image domestically and internationally. By 2000, however,
Cuba had "suffered the defection or departure of over 100 athletes to other countries." For the 2004 events, the International Olympic Committee dictated that an
athlete "who switches nationalities must wait three years to compete for the new
country." However, athletes with dual citizenship could choose to compete for the
country of their choice. Longman states: "Pérez believed she was not allowed to
compete outside Cuba for fear she would not return" (Longman 2000, p. D6).

45. Since the details about Pérez' views do not support the NBC metaphor,
Sanders omits what Pérez readily acknowledged; she "credits Cuba's respected jump
coaches for teaching her how to train, but bristles at the way she was ostracized and
dropped from the national sports program" (Longman 2000, p. D6).

46. See Gergen 2005. It is not surprising that NBC did not present Cuba's viewpoint. We might gather the official point of view from a 2000 *New York Times* article, where journalist Jere Longman (2000) quotes Cuban Olympic Committee pres-

ident José Ramón Fernández: it is fair to refuse Pérez further support, "taking into consideration . . . the fact that the people of Cuba generate the funds and other resources for the preparation of our athletes and provide training facilities, education, medical services and meals at no charge" (pp. D1, D6).

47. The CUBA AS PRISON visual metaphor reinforces the athlete's statement that she had to give up her US citizenship in order to compete in the 2000 Olympic Games. The key for NBC is that Pérez viewed US citizenship as superior to her Cuban citizenship. Sanders' voice-over intonation, the images characterizing Cuba as a prison, and the omission of background information about the citizenship requirement all reinforce this interpretation.

48. Quoted in D'Hippolito, Joseph's undated Frontpagemag.com.

49. Spousta 2001, pp. D1, D6.

50. Spousta 2001, p. D6.

51. Spousta 2001, p. D6.

52. Gergen 2005, p. A56.

53. Peterson 2007, p. 248.

Chapter Four

1. Appendix, #1, #3, #4, #5, #6, #7, #11, #12, #14, #15, #17, #24, #28, #29, #30, #31, #34, #35, #48, #49, #57, #63, #74, #75, #77, #78, #79, #81, #87, #89, #105, #106, #107, #108, #116, and #117.

2. Fernández and Pedroza 1982; Ono and Sloop 2002; Santa Ana 2002.

3. Santa Ana et al. 2007. There are two possible reasons for this temporary balance. First, the president of the United States spoke compassionately about unauthorized immigrants in his January 7 speech, which legitimated a humane discourse in the public sphere. Second, the immigrants themselves and their supporters took to the streets in 2006 with immense, disciplined, and peaceful marches. In many respects Bush's rhetoric of immigrants as decent human beings legitimizes a previously countercultural rhetoric. This act agitated political conservatives, who wanted to sustain the prevalent archetypes of IMMIGRANT AS CRIMINAL, ANIMAL, MENACE (Santa Ana et al. 2007). For a while in 2006–2007 there was a public-sphere battle over the appropriate imagery (what Calvin McGee [1980] has called "ideographs") of immigrants. The conservative imagery IMMIGRANT AS CRIMINAL dominates public discourse today.

4. With notable exceptions such as Chávez (2001), Travis Dixon and Linz (2000a, 2000b), and Peterson (2007) in the European setting.

5. In 2006 the vote was 157 to 2. Many major human rights organizations, including those inside Cuba, have called for an end to the blockade.

6. The 1980 Mariel Boatlift was an exodus of 125,000 Cubans who left from Mariel Harbor in Havana over a period of six months. It started with an abrupt decline in the already-shaky Cuban economy. As its internal crisis deepened, the Cuban government declared that anyone who wanted to leave was free to go. Cuban Americans in Florida organized the exodus, in an agreement with Fidel Castro. The Floridians' political coup became a nightmare when inmates of Cuban jails and psychiatric hospitals were found to be among the exiles. By mutual agreement of the US and Cuban governments, the boatlift ended in October 1980.

7. For 2007, the Department of Homeland Security reported that 11,487 Cubans entered the US over the Mexican border, 4,825 successfully crossed the Florida Straits, and 2,861 were caught and returned to Cuba by the Coast Guard (Grillo 2008).

8. Thanks to Sue Carter for pointing out this symbolism.

9. Vargas pronounced the Spanish word *piñata* with an entirely English pronunciation. Vargas is the daughter of a Puerto Rican colonel in the US Army and an Irish American mother. Her childhood was spent at various international military bases. If she speaks Spanish, her pronunciation disaffiliates her from Latino ethnicity and reaffirms "neutral" (i.e., Anglo-American) network professionalism.

10. Republican US congresswoman and Cuban exile Ileana Ros-Lehtinen requested that the seagoing Buick not be sunk, but that it be saved as an emblem of the Cubans' love of freedom. The executive director of the Cuban American National Foundation (CANF) also said his group had appealed to the US Department of State "in hopes they would give some humanitarian consideration" to the unauthorized immigrants apprehended aboard, who included five children. The CANF called the attempt "a product of incredible ingenuity that is embarrassing to the regime" (cbsnews.com/stories/2004/02/04/world/main598019.shtml; retrieved 17 April 2008).

11. There are just two cases where the US news media discussed the effects of immigration and immigration policy on children. One is the case of Elián González, a telegenic Cuban child who became the center of an international custody court case. See Banet-Weiser 2003 and Molina-Guzmán 2006. The other circumstance is the case of unaccompanied children traveling across Mexico on the tops of trains, seeking their parents in the US (Nazario 2006) and, more recently, *Which Way Home* (a 2009 documentary by Rebecca Cammisa).

12. Others do not consider this Mexican mother's actions to be reprehensible. In fact, for one visual artist, Julio César Morales, it "reveals the resourcefulness of immigrants trying to cross the border illegally by exposing them in their hiding places, such as [in his painting of] the little girl inside a piñata, through transparent water-color illustrations" (Gurza 2008, p. E1). Also see Magaña and Short (2002) for a comparison of how US politicians discursively construct Cuban and Mexican immigrants.

13. In 2004 the Bush administration imposed two changes in Cuban policy. One limited the number of visits Cuban Americans could make to Cuba to once every three years instead of once a year. The second restricted the amount of money they can take to Cuban relatives. These policies set off a row that was covered by three news briefs and one longer news story. See Appendix A, #64, #67, #68, and #70. Flights to Cuba are legal only for Americans of Cuban descent; the US prohibits travel to Cuba by other American citizens.

14. At the time the population of Cuba was 11.3 million, compared to 8.8 million for the Dominican Republic and 8.3 million for Haiti. The largest group of Caribbean migrants captured in 2004 by the Coast Guard was Haitians ($n = 1,929$). The Coast Guard figures were cited without source (WPBF.com, 2004). We excluded news stories of Haitians from our 2004 sample of news stories, since they are generally not seen as Latinos.

15. Cited in #74.

16. Gans 1979, p. 43.

17. Here we see the conflict between enduring values in the news reporting that Gans (1979) identified, between "the preservation of freedom of the individual" (p. 50) and the "corrosive influences . . . of immigration" (p. 205) of racialized people.

18. Santa Ana 2002, Chapter 3.

19. Close-ups focusing on the terrified faces of individuals would not serve the purposes of the Coast Guard, who likely seek to document the whole episode for nonjournalistic purposes.

20. Dominican immigration to Puerto Rico reaches back to the 1960s, when middle- and upper-class Dominicans began to leave in response to national and international political pressures. In 1962, Juan Bosch, a prolific writer exiled during a military regime, was swept into the presidency in the first free election in the country's history. Bosch promulgated a new constitution guaranteeing rights for farmers, the working class, unions, mothers, pregnant women, the homeless, children, and the illegitimate. He broke up *latifundias*, the large landed estate or ranches of the elite, and limited the power of the industrialists and the military. After seven months in office, a military junta overthrew Bosch; in turn it faced an insurrection demanding Bosch's reinstatement. However, the US invaded the Dominican Republic in 1963 to prevent Bosch from returning to power. To prevent further civil war, the US then issued visas to the potential opponents of the US-backed regime. In succeeding decades, Dominican immigration to Puerto Rico was led by the managerial and professional sectors. Skilled workers such as mechanics, masons, seamstresses, and nurses were also attracted by Puerto Rico's higher wages, as the Dominican peso was frequently devalued. Emigration increased with the economic crises of the 1980s. Emigration also increased during the 1990s, a period of strong, sustained economic growth; Duany (2005) attributes this to extreme income disparities. A severe economic crisis in 2003 led to another surge of emigration.

Chapter Five

1. Bush 2004.

2. Noted in CNN's 7 January report, entitled "Migrant Headache," Appendix, #1.

3. Santa Ana, 2012.

4. Gutiérrez 1995; Santa Ana 2002; O'Brien 2003. For a commentary, see Santa Ana 2006b.

5. The "gaze," namely the eye line and facial expression of the televised person looking into the camera, creates a social relationship with viewers that does not occur if the person does not face the camera directly (Jewitt and Oyama 2001, pp. 141–43).

6. The National Association of Hispanic Journalists (NAHJ) has repeatedly denounced the use of the term *illegal* as a noun, as well as other demeaning descriptions and depictions of immigrants (see, e.g., http://www.nahj.org/2010/04/nahj-denounces-unfair-depiction-of-immigrants-and-people-of-color-in-boston-herald/; retrieved 9 October 2010).

7. Barrett 2004.

8. Abbott 2008, p. 133, cites E. M. Forster's description of characters with no depth or complexity as "flat." The CNN newsroom blacked out Tina, the visual equivalent of "flattened."

9. In Chapter 2 we reviewed #82 (correspondent David Gregory), which debunked the Latino voting bloc fable.

10. At the time of the news story, Muñoz was vice president for policy at the National Council of La Raza.

11. "Law-enforcement officials say drop houses have existed for years. But in the past they were found in lower-income, mostly Latino neighborhoods in the Valley [i.e., Phoenix metropolitan area], where neighbors often turn a blind eye. 'They are usually stacked like *pollos* (chickens) in a damn hen house,' [Phoenix police detective Tony] Morales said. 'A lot of people don't care. They just turn their back.' But smugglers, in an effort to elude police, increasingly are renting houses in upscale neighborhoods to harbor undocumented immigrants" (González 2004, p. A1).

12. Schudson 2003, pp. 47–50. Brian Williams' relatively objective language is undercut by the visual messages, which repeatedly present the immigrants as criminals.

13. See Santa Ana 2002; Santa Ana et al. 2007.

14. By appearances it is not an upscale property, but a modest stucco-faced house that needs a paint job and has no landscaping except for two spindly trees. However, the *Arizona Republic* newspaper stories about drop houses of this time period describe one as "a once-handsome home on a golf course," stating that "immigrant smugglers increasingly are renting houses in upscale Valley neighborhoods" (González 2004, p. A1).

15. González 2004, p. A1.

16. González 2004, p. A1.

17. González again elaborates: "In areas where drop houses have been discovered, neighbors say their sense of security has been shattered. 'This was a very private secluded oasis that no one even knows about. That's changed. We close our doors, our garages. We don't feel safe anymore,' said Kathy DeSanto, 38, whose house was searched by police after several people escaped from the drop house in a country-club area of northeast Phoenix" (2004, p. A1).

18. Cornelius is director of the Comparative Immigration Studies Center at the University of California, San Diego; Portes is director of the Migration and Development Center at Princeton; Massey is co-director (with Jorge Durand) of the Mexican Migration Project at the Universidad de Guadalajara.

19. In 2000, the ICE apprehended 1,643,679 unauthorized immigrants along the Southwest border. These Department of Homeland Security (DHS) statistics are based on the fiscal year 1 October 1999 to 30 September 2000. In subsequent years, ICE recorded fewer apprehensions. In fiscal year 2003, ICE registered a 26% increase in apprehensions (1,129,282). The agency notes that this figure remains far below the 2000 record (Dougherty, Wilson, and Wu 2005). Thus when NBC reports an "increase" (as they did on 15 February), or "a 25% increase" (as they did on 30 April), the network was referring to fiscal year 2003, before the president made his 7 January 2004 announcement.

There were no creditable statistics for the quarter-year period on which NBC reported, since statisticians require longer time frames to detect reliable trends. Passel and Cohn (2008) estimated that the "inflow" of unauthorized immigrants to the US averaged 800,000 a year from 2000 to 2004, and then fell to 500,000 a year from 2005 to 2008, "with a decreasing year-to-year trend." The DHS estimated that 11.6 million unauthorized immigrants lived in the United States at the beginning of 2008, compared to 10.5 million in January 2005, and 8.5 million in 2000 (Hoefer, Rytina, and Baker 2008). It provides no estimate between 2000 and 2005. Between 2000 and 2008, the unauthorized population increased by 3.1 million, or 37%. The DHS deduces that the unauthorized population increased by 390,000 annually.

20. See Santa Ana et al. (2007) for a depiction of the news media's 2006 response to the Bush initiative.

21. Between 2004 and 2008, municipal and state governments enacted 300 laws in 43 states requiring government workers to verify the legal status of residents and/or allowing local authorities to apprehend unauthorized migrants. Philip Kretsedemas describes these laws as an appeal to the "territorial paradigm of national sovereignty that equates the integrity of the nation with the ability to control its borders" (2008, p. 553).

Chapter Six

1. Charley would be only the second of four big hurricanes that would strike Florida that year. In 2004, the people of the Caribbean region would experience greater total cyclone energy and suffer more deaths and damage from these monster storms than in any previous recorded year.

2. FEMA, Federal Emergency Management Agency.

3. NBC's favorable framing of the ICE air flight repatriation matches other NBC portrayals of public institutions, such as the Coast Guard open-sea rescues of Dominicans or the ICE apprehensions in suburban drop houses. NBC may tend to give public institutions the thumbs up, but it clearly criticized the legislated limit to governmental humanitarianism in the aftermath of Hurricane Charley.

4. This was not the first such experiment. Kelly Lytle Hernández (2006) describes the history of the INS (which was absorbed into the ICE) during another period of intense activity, the infamous Operation Wetback. To deter quick return of deportees between 1943 and 1954, the INS made formal arrangements with Mexican officials to forcibly relocate deportees (particularly unauthorized braceros, who were called "chronic offenders") to points further south than the border by several means. In the 1940s and 1950s between 600 and 1,000 trains were used to send deportees deeper into Mexico, to the cities of Monterrey (Nuevo León), Torreón (Coahuila), and Jiménez (Chihuahua). Trains were cost-efficient, according to INS funding reports. For a time the INS also conducted daily airlifts to the central Mexican states of San Luís Potosí, Guadalajara, and Guanajuato. It airlifted 34,000 deportees in 1951 and 51,000 in 1952 (Hernández 2006, pp. 429–430). History thus reveals that the 2004 program was not an "experiment."

5. Proposition 200, an Arizona referendum, passed in November 2004 with 56% of the vote. The measure, which became part of the state constitution, requires indi-

viduals to produce proof of citizenship before they register to vote or apply for public benefits. Under it, public officials (including teachers, doctors in state clinics, and
municipal police) can be charged with a misdemeanor if they fail to report noncitizens who apply for state benefits, and citizens can sue those public officials who have
allowed unauthorized immigrants to receive state benefits.

6. Of special interest are newsroom credits for this news story that appear briefly
in the second scene: producer, Marsha Cooke; editor, Maria Nicoletti; and camera,
Tony Borrello. Such identification is rare for network news pieces.

7. National Association of Hispanic Journalists (March 2006). Santa Ana et al.
(2007) compared the use of the conflicting terms (*illegal* versus *undocumented*)
within the body of US newspaper articles for two large samples of article. These
terms have become code words for opposing political positions on immigration policy. The term *illegal* criminalizes immigrant workers. And, while the adjective *illegal* currently tends to be the common-use term of newspapers, politically conservative partisans have appropriated it expressly to emphasize the unlawfulness of
unauthorized immigration as they call for greater punitive measures to limit immigration. The term *undocumented* highlights the legal detail of paper permissions for
immigrant workers seeking a livelihood. Liberal and progressive partisans who emphasize benevolent considerations for current immigrant workers and their families
prefer this term. On these grounds, in an opinion piece, Santa Ana (2006b) claimed
that news writer overuse of one term constituted political partisanship, and that
journalists cannot claim that word use is merely a matter of standard journalistic
stylistic criteria: common use and concision.

8. At the time of the broadcast, Dickson was the chief executive officer of the
Copper Queen Community Hospital in Bisbee, Arizona.

9. At the time of the broadcast, Avina was a family physician who provided spe-
cialized care for HIV/AIDS patients in the Bisbee clinic, and served as an emergency room physician at Copper Queen Community Hospital, where Dickson was
CEO. At that time, Avina traveled throughout Cochise County to provide health
care in isolated communities.

10. For example, the Arizona Hospital and Health Care Association, an association of health care workers at all levels, contributed $50,000 to oppose Proposition
200 (Jordan 2008).

11. Credits for this news story were listed as follows: producer, Eleanore M.
Vega; editor, Frank Walters; camera, Hank Schroeder, Les Rose, and Hunter Bloch.

12. The sound track may be of other Tisdale clips, because she narrates what she
is filming in other clips.

13. The gaze set up by camera work establishes social and power relations between the camera and the viewer. Kress and van Leeuwen described a power relationship set up when the camera's representation of a human sets up a "direct gaze"
to a viewer. The subject (actually a screen image of a person) becomes an interac-
tant with the viewer. A level gaze denotes equality, while other directions of gaze
are symbolic. If the subject is looking up toward the camera, the subject is inferior.
If the subject is looking down, he or she is superior. When the gaze is directed at the
viewer by the correspondent, politician, or other sophisticated practitioner, it can
create a "mobilizing look" that offers information or makes demands of the viewer.

Viewers also have a "controlling" gaze that makes them voyeurs, as when they take on a so-called tourist gaze, which creates exoticized ethnic Others (Kress and van Leeuwen 1996; Lister and Wells 2001).

14. A point-of-view shot presents an object to the audience from the viewpoint (angle and distance) from which the subject of the story would see that same object.

15. Schudson 2001.

16. Armando Morales (1971, p. 289) distinguishes between unconscious thoughts (usually repressed) and preconscious thoughts, such as stereotypes (readily available or identifiable). Also see Bargh and Morsella 2008.

17. *Paragon* is a term used by George Lakoff and quoted in Harrell (2010).

Section II

1. Quoted in Saluskinszky 1987, p. 31.

2. The UCLA undergraduate research team who made this chapter possible included Robert Conrad, Vanessa García, Jacquelyn Gómez, Layza López, Efraín A. Meléndez, Brenda Pérez, Erik Preston, Arturo Rangel Jr., and Brenda Robles.

3. Reporting the discovery of 250 people in Phoenix drop houses, this extended story explored the risks and profits of trafficking in people, as well as the federal program (Operation ICE) to halt human smuggling.

4. Foucault 1980, pp. 92–108. Subject positions correspond to "macro-categories" in empirical sociolinguistics (Eckert 2000).

5. Jensen 1995, p. 74.

6. Parenti 1986.

7. Parenti 1986; also DeLuca 1999, p. 19.

8. Cited in Luke 1996, p. 17.

9. Chilton 1996, pp. 37–38.

Chapter Seven

1. Burke 1968, p. 6.

2. Lakoff 1987, pp. 207–208. Also see Lakoff and Johnson 1980, 1999; Lakoff and Turner 1989; Lakoff 1993.

3. Goatly (2007) is an excellent recent representative.

4. Gibbs 1994; Santa Ana 2002, Chapter 2.

5. Lakoff and Johnson 1980, 1999; Lakoff 1993.

6. In *Brown Tide Rising*, a full-scale empirical study of newspaper discourse, I argue that 4,485 metaphors spread throughout the material content of the *Los Angeles Times* (671 articles published over seven years) constituted US public opinion and a widely shared US public worldview. I specified in empirical detail (including 20 tabular summaries) how newspaper discourse reproduces and reinforces an unjust US social order, which debases Latinos as a group.

7. Forceville (2007, p. 16) distinguishes four types of pictorial metaphor: those which straddle two modalities or channels, e.g., language and images, and those which are only cued by visual means.

8. In order to understand the images that are broadcast on the small screen, cognitive theorists use "image schema" as well as basic schemata such as the "container," especially for the projection of the spectator into the film and the small screen; "part/whole" schema, for example, in camera shot/news story or scene/news story analytics; and "link" schema, to connect various parts of film together with continuity editing, establishing shots, and analytic cut-away shots. Simons (1995) applied these primitives, such as center-periphery schema and source-path-goal schema, to analyze Dutch political language campaigning.

9. Goatly 2007, p. 15.

10. Goatly 1997, p. 41.

11. Lakoff 1993.

12. Lakoff 1993, p. 219.

13. Gibbs 1994, p. 152.

14. Santa Ana 2002, Chapter 7.

15. Lakoff 1987. Lakoff uses a compendium of conceptual metaphors to bolster his claim that a solution exists for the standard epistemological conundrum posed by objectivism (we know the world directly since we all can touch it) and subjectivism (all we have is radical conceptual relativism since no one has unmediated access to reality) in a brand of experientialism (our infantile bodily experiences are the universal basis for a basic metaphorical language we share).

16. Santa Ana 2002, Chapter 3.

17. Santa Ana et al. 2007. Jacobson (2008) locates a sociological basis for the shift of predominant constitutive metaphor for IMMIGRANT from the ANIMAL metaphor in the 1990s to the CRIMINAL metaphor of the first decade of the twenty-first century.

18. See West 1993, p. 106.

19. Reported on Fox News (8 January 2004), "Bush Immigration Reform Plan Draws Criticism" (www.foxnews.com/story/0,2933,107707,00.html; retrieved 25 June 2011).

20. Quoted in a transcript of "CNN in the Money," aired 8 December 2004 (edition.cnn.com/TRANSCRIPTS/0412/08/cnnitm.01.html; retrieved 25 June 2011).

21. Gans 2008.

22. news.google.com/newspapers?id=NFNWAAAAIBAJ&sjid=uesDAAAAIBAJ&pg=5721,1496195&dq=plan+for+illegals+sparks&hl=en; retrieved 25 June 2011; Zachary Coile (19 May 2004), Chronicle Washington Bureau, http://www.washingtontimes.com/news/2004/sep/25/20040925-102817-8725r/; retrieved 25 June 2011.

23. Quoted in McGee 1980, p. 7; italics in the original.

24. Quoted in McGee 1980, p. 8.

25. McGee 1980, p. 15.

26. Condit and Lucaites 1993, xxii–xxiii.

27. McGee 1980, p. 11.

28. McGee 1980, p. 12.

29. McGee 1980, p. 14.

30. McGee 1980, p. 14.

31. McGee 1980, pp. 7–8.

32. Edwards and Winkler 1997.

33. Solid linguistic theories of scalar semantic implicature have been developed. See, for example, Papafragou and Musolino 2003.

34. Newton 2008; Ngai 2005. Indeed, Ono and Sloop (2002), critical rhetoricians who have built on McGee's insight, have provided a powerful analysis of the rhetoric of California's Proposition 187.

35. In the LexisNexis newspaper database, a search of the root word *immigra-* yielded 460 articles. By one measure, 200 newspapers used the adjective *illegal*, while only 16 newspapers used the adjective *undocumented*. Another measure demonstrated the same skewed proportions. These 460 articles used the root word *immigra-* a total of 1,582 times. While 12.6% of all references of the root word were preceded by the adjective *illegal*, the adjective *undocumented* preceded only 1% of them.

36. Santa Ana et al. 2007, Table 2.

37. "The girl—who's about 4 or 5 years old—was meticulously sealed inside but she was able to breathe. The girl's mother was curled up inside the car's trunk, and her brother, who's about 9, was underneath the collapsed back seat" (www.mega games.com/node/1032800; retrieved 26 June 2011).

38. Rose 2001, p. 7.

39. In 2006, the top three national newspapers had a combined daily readership of 5.4 million, whereas the top three network news programs had a combined viewership of 25 million. Indeed, the nation's 20 top-selling newspapers sell only about 13.6 million newspapers each day. See *USA Today*, "Newspaper sales dip, but websites gain," May 9, 2006.

40. Fauconnier and Turner 2002.

41. Forceville's literature reviews indicate that Simons (1995) has discussed nonverbal metaphor in political propaganda (Kaplan 1990, 1992); Messaris (1997) and Forceville (1994, 1996, 1999b, 2000) have discussed nonverbal metaphor advertising; Rozik (1994) in cartoons; Kennedy (1993) and Danto (1993) for drawing; Forceville (1988) and Carroll (1994) have discussed pictorial metaphor in surreal paintings; and Whittock (1990) and Carroll (1996) have discussed nonverbal metaphor in film. Forceville recommends Kennedy (1982, 1997), Sedivy (1997), and McGuire (1999) for their general reflections on pictorial metaphor; see McNeill (1992) and Cienki (1998) for suggestions on gestural metaphor, and Seitz (1998) for a review of studies pertaining to nonverbal metaphor.

42. Smith (1979, p. 80) found in a 1978 sample of 317 news stories among 20 televised news programs that no visual symbols appeared in 97 of these stories. His finding conflicts with ours, but his thinly described account makes it difficult to account for the discrepancy.

43. Kress and van Leeuwen (1996) demonstrated that the manipulation of the mode of signs made them more prominent and led to viewers attributing these signs with greater or lesser importance. See Jewitt and Oyama 2001, pp. 150–151.

44. See Goatly (1997) for a critique of unidirectional mapping.

45. Santa Ana 2002 and Santa Ana et al. 2007.

46. Schudson 2002, p. 107.

47. Fauconnier and Turner 1994, p. 1.

48. "Conceptual projection from one mental space to another always involves projection to 'middle' spaces, whether abstract and 'generic,' or richer 'blended'

middle spaces. Projection to a middle space is a general cognitive process, operating uniformly at different levels of abstraction and under superficially divergent contextual circumstances. Middle spaces are indispensable sites for central mental and linguistic work" (Fauconnier and Turner 1994, p. 1).

49. Brandt and Brandt 2005.

50. Brandt and Brandt call this stage of cognitive processing the "relevance space," or "relevance evaluation procedure," based on Sperber and Wilson's (1995) theory of human communication. Their basic idea is that humans seek the greatest possible cognitive effect for the smallest possible processing effort. In their theory of pragmatics, Sperber and Wilson make certain general assumptions (e.g., all utterances or semiotic stimuli occur in context and convey certain implicatures). The principle is that all communication is articulated with the manifest intent to communicate, even though understanding is not guaranteed. Thus both speaker and hearer presume that the messages are both relevant and economically stated for meaning processing.

51. Since salience additionally depends on repetition, accumulated assumptions, conceptual coherence, and cross-modal resonance or dissonance.

52. This Wordle™ "word cloud" gives greater prominence to words that appear more frequently in our chosen source: the multimodal metaphors for IMMIGRANT in the CNN news brief. The prefixes refer to semiotic mode: v = visual, t = text, s = spoken. We used the following salience scale (visual = 3, spoken = 2, text = 1) to display differences in semiotic mode salience. We exclude the music sign, which may not be attributable to the immigrant target domain, but certainly contributes to the news story meaning. Berger (1972) notes that a denotational meaning of an image can be overlaid with connotations via background music. The spoken sign "*undocumented*" appears above the prefix of the visual sign. The spoken sign "*illegal*" is found above the final letter of the visual sign. www.wordle.net, generated 30 March 2010.

53. Another rejected reading: immigrants do not intend to hurt others and primarily seek work, so the severity of their infractions is akin to misdemeanors like jaywalking, rather than to felonies such as armed robbery.

54. The pragmatic assumption evaluation process operates automatically. However, adults' meta-pragmatic awareness can disrupt the reflex function at this hinge point, permitting skepticism about news viewing as well as other, general political perspectives.

55. Barthes 1966, 1975; White 1984; Ochs and Capps 1996.

56. White 1984.

57. In contrast to the relative ease with which people disrupt the automatic pragmatic relevance processes, individuals must make greater efforts to disrupt the narrativization process, e.g., by way of meditation or with psychopharmaceuticals.

58. This nondiegetic music is not a semantic domain sign, but a narrative-level sign, an issue we begin to address in the following chapter.

59. Abbott 2008, p. 20.

60. Abbott 2008, p. 44.

61. Abbott 2008, pp. 123–125.

62. Abbott adds *argument* to plot and description in his division of the third part of narrative. But he also refers to focalization, perspective, and voice. He (2008,

p. 199) cites Jerome Bruner, who distinguishes argument (an appeal by procedure to establish a proof) from narrative (an appeal to "verisimilitude" and lifelikeness). So, argument can be incorporated into a narrative, and often is in the news.

63. Gillian Rose (2001) notes that W. J. T. Mitchell posed fundamental questions about the study of visual culture. Although we operate almost effortlessly in a world that has a preeminently visual culture, Mitchell believes that scholars cannot answer questions such as How do pictures work? What's the relation of pictures to language? How do pictures operate on observers? and How do pictures operate on the world? We can begin with one kind of answer: Humans process linguistic and visual perceptions with the same low-level (prelinguistic) cognitive tools, as well as higher-level cognitive strategies in a sort of feedback loop, while creative language (such as poetry) and photographs are interpreted with richer arrays of social knowledge.

64. Schudson 2003, p. 13.

65. Schudson 2002, p. 265.

66. Affirming Schudson's (2002, p. 265; 2003, pp. 19–26) view, which rejects the conspiracy and indoctrination views of American journalism.

67. Thompson 1991, p. 60.

68. Schudson 2002, p. 266.

69. Such as, a major source of the power of the media lies "in its power to provide the forms in which the declarations appear. News . . . has a relationship to the 'real world' . . . the world is incorporated into unquestioned and unnoticed conventions of narration, and then transfigured, [making it] no longer a subject for discussion but a premise of any conversation at all" (cited in Ettema and Glasser 1988, pp. 8–9). However, Schudson's claim is that "news is not fictional, but it is convention. Conventions help make messages readable . . . Their function is less to increase or decrease the truth values of the message they convey than to shape and narrow the range of what kinds of truths can be told" (Schudson 1982, pp. 98–99). While Schudson's argument is far more nuanced, at base there is an assumption of truth.

70. Schudson 2003, p. 19.

71. Schudson 2002, p. 265. Regarding the policy changes of the Vietnam War, for example, he quotes historian George Moss that media influence on public opinion was "peripheral, minor, trivial, in fact, so inconsequential it was immeasurable" (2003, p. 20).

72. McCombs 2005, p. 156. Also see Croteau and Hoynes 2002.

73. Schudson 2002, p. 23.

74. Schudson 2003, p. 25.

75. See for example, de Certeau (1984) on individuals' "tactics" to bypass institutional "strategies" to control the space of individuals, and Martín-Barbero's (1993) analyses of viewer resistance to Latin American *telenovelas* ('soap operas'). Schudson (2003, pp. 24–25) provides as an example "how prejudiced people read racially loaded sitcom humor one way [while racially] tolerant people take the same jokes to have that opposite meaning." For an alternative view of mass media humor, see Santa Ana (2009).

76. Schudson considers these people to be the "deep, dark secret of the power of the press . . . exercised not by news institutions themselves but by the sources that feed them information" (2003, p. 134).

77. Schudson 2003, p. 21. This conduit metaphor for communication is prob-

lematic. Instead, linguists espouse the view that recipients actively construct readings of multimodal stimuli (Reddy 1979).

78. Schudson 2002, p. 249. But he believes journalistic discourse accounting "can explain too much," basing his claim on the fact that even though journalistic coverage on homosexuals over the past 50 years is far less marked as deviant, a "universal cultural anxiety about anomalous [sexual orientation] categories" persists (p. 261). In contrast, I do not claim that mass media are the only sources of discursive socialization, but rather that family and other face-to-face communities also socialize via discourse, and that mass media discourses are the most widely shared streams of discourse.

79. Couldry 2003.

80. Schudson 2003, p. 24.

81. Geertz 1973, p. 452; Couldry 2003.

82. Anderson, 1983, p. 39, quoted in Schudson 2003, p. 68.

83. Schudson 2003, p. 68.

84. "The mail-coach system had several effects . . . the more rapid standardization of culture, as publications homogenized the countryside. London's first daily newspaper, the *Daily Courant*, was founded in 1702. . . . There were six dailies by the 1730s, fourteen morning papers by 1790 . . . There were fifty provincial papers by the 1780s . . . They were devoured eagerly by their readers. Only a few thousand people might actually buy a successful provincial paper, but they would share the paper with others or read it aloud to coworkers and friends. Whether it happened at the coffee shop or workplace (as . . . where a blacksmith's shop shuts down to hear the news), the reading of the newspaper was an event" (Olsen 1999, p. 184).

85. Schudson 2003, p. 107.

86. Schudson 2003, p. 108, where he quotes A. Paul Weaver.

87. Weaver 1976.

88. Schudson 2003, p. 109.

89. Schudson 2003, p. 110.

Chapter Eight

1. There are several caveats. In this figure we did not represent the saliency weightings of different sign types. Some of the implied but unstated concepts are represented with dotted lines, such as the obvious effort to hide Angelita's face from viewers. This facelessness can be read with meaning that is likely associated with the criminal immigrant constellation; it offers no meaning to the good person constellation. On the other hand, the *afraid* meaning units (expressed two times) might be arranged on either constellation. I believe that the two constellations contribute to the story in an oppositional relationship. In other stories, pairs and multiple constellations combine in resonant relationships.

2. van Leeuwen 2001, pp. 92–100.

3. Barthes [1957] 1972, pp. 109–131.

4. van Leeuwen 2001, pp. 92–118.

5. Jewitt and Oyama 2001; Iedema 2001.

6. Jewitt and Oyama 2001; Iedema 2001. In the 1950s, Barthes (for example)

tended to write about semiotics as if were a code by which single meanings could be discerned.

7. Barthes [1957] 1972, p. 116 (italics in the original). *Tricolor* refers to the French flag.

8. Howell 2003, pp. 101–102.

9. Rose 2001, p. 91.

10. However, the articulation of an ideograph can occur in other semiotic modes in television.

11. McGee 1980, p. 15.

12. Bennett and Edelman 1985, p. 165.

13. Another way for the viewer to read this scene integrates the interviewee's too-brief avowal and body language to cast doubt on Hattori's claim. This requires the viewer to watch the news story attentively, with some level of skepticism.

14. Barthes later addressed the postmodern critiques of structuralism, on which his semiotics was built. In the 1960s Derrida tried to subvert structuralism, noting that de Saussure built his semiotics like he did his linguistics, in terms of binary oppositions. Since signifiers acquired meaning through their differences, Derrida claimed that without a baseline meaning, the so-called transcendental signified, structuralism had no bedrock on which to build its meaning edifice. Derrida's premise was that since meaning somehow ought to be denoted in a dictionary of some sort, this thesis fails because it admits no change. For practicing linguists, however, Derrida's critique has no purchase. Throughout the poststructuralist era, most linguists continued to maintain that semantic drift is an abiding feature of language use and that semiotics is a ceaseless process of renewal and change across a finite network involving all the users of a language or a semiotic system. Much later Derrida himself noted that the structuralist assumption of a fundamental meaning, while an illusion, was a "necessary illusion" (Callinicos 2004). In opposition to Derrida, structuralists can still claim that elements of language are paired and opposed elements to ascertain meaning in an "infinite play," as Derrida described it. Rather than a failing, this is an indispensable element in language change; linguists affirm and revel in the infinite play of each and every human communicative exchange, a slow motion dance that retraces strands of the social web of meanings that are negotiated one at a time in each communicative interaction. See Jensen (1995), as well as Daylight (2011).

15. David Thorburn notes that the "story-systems" of television "present even greater challenges to adequately 'thick' description than the immense complexities in understanding a Balinese cock fight as Clifford Geertz would have us understand it." While Geertz "offers powerful arguments for the centrality of aesthetic perspectives in the reading of all forms of ritual, urging us to bring to the cockfight the same respect for complexity and the same attentiveness to dramatic ritual as we bring to a reading of *Macbeth*," Thorburn notes that "the forms of narrative, at least the most coherent and significant of them are more taxing still in their claims on the interpreter, because they do not merely embody cultural assumptions and values, they consciously articulate, examine, and judge such matters themselves" (1988, pp. 58–59).

16. Schudson 1978, p. 6.

17. Herman and Chomsky 1988.

18. Schudson 1978, p. 182.

19. Mindlin 1998.

20. Schudson 1978, p. 193.

21. In addition to the erroneous belief that objective truth can be discovered in a news event, another criticism of journalism is the "myth of the mediated center" (Couldry 2003, p. 2)—that the mass media speaks from the center of the social world. This is increasingly difficult to justify in our internet-connected society, but seems to be sustained; Gans, for example, found that journalists do not pay much attention to their public, but write and broadcast for their professional peers (Gans 1979, p. 229–32; Cotter 2010, pp. 88–109).

22. White 1980.

23. Barthes writes: "Narrative is present in every age, in every place, in every society; it begins with the very history of mankind and there nowhere is nor has been a people without narrative. All classes, all human groups, have their narratives, enjoyment of which is very often shared by men with different, even opposing, cultural backgrounds. Caring nothing for the division between good and bad literature, narrative is international, transhistorical, transcultural: it is simply there, like life itself" (1966, p. 1; 1975, p. 237).

24. White 1987, pp. 1–25.

25. As Schudson says, news is "a dominant force in the public construction of common experience and a popular sense of what is real and important" (2003, p. 13).

26. White 1984, p. 14.

27. Peterson 2007, p. 248.

28. My emphasis: http://www.spj.org/ethicscode.asp; retrieved 15 May 2010.

29. Ettema, Whitney, and Wackman 1987, italics in the original.

30. Schudson 2003, pp. 33, 34, and 19, respectively.

31. Gitlin 1979, quoted in Schudson 2003, p. 35.

32. Gamson and Modigliani 1987, quoted in Schudson 2003, p. 216.

33. Abbott 2008, pp. 18–19.

34. White 1984, p. 7. Abbott also calls the narrative the "instrument of power" (2008, p. 40). Drawing on Russian formalists, Mieke Bal (2004) refers to narrative as "fabula."

35. Abbott 2008, p. 46. Marsh (2003) notes that Holman's *The Handbook of Literature* defines *myth* as "an anomalous story or stories having roots in the primitive folk-beliefs of races or nations and presenting supernatural episodes as a means of interpreting natural events in an effort to make concrete and particular a special perception of human beings or a cosmic view" (Holman 1980, p. 282). Frye's own definition of *archetype* is as follows: "A symbol, usually an image, which recurs often enough in literature to be recognizable as an element of one's literary experience as a whole" (1957, p. 365).

36. Scholarship on myth and archetype in television news, on the other hand, remains limited. Among the few studies, see Kolbenschlag 1976; Lincoln 1999; Lule 2001, 2002; Marsh 2003.

37. Lucaites and Condit 1985, pp. 90–91.

38. Specifically, all narratives have

1. one of five dramatic "through-lines," or plot resolutions (the main character succeeds, is defeated, abandons his goal, has an undefined goal, or the reader creates the goal);
2. one of six types of conflict, namely relational (human vs. human), situational (human vs. nature), inner (human vs. self), paranormal, cosmic, or social;
3. at least 1 of 20 "genres," with subcategories: action, adventure, children, comedy, creative nonfiction, crime, diary, drama, historical/epic, horror, inspirational, musical, mystery, suspense/thriller, gothic, political, persuasive, romance (of which there are 10 subcategories), Western, and science fiction;
4. 1 of 11 plot progressions, including roller coaster, replay, fate, parallel, episodic, melodramatic, romance, and journey;
5. at least 1 of the 55 paired "dramatic situations" that are the basic circumstances in the story that set up the narrative conflict (some examples are conflict with God and supernatural occurrence; mistaken judgment and intuitive judgment; and vengeance for a crime and rehabilitation. (Schmidt 2005)

Schmidt takes pains to demonstrate that rich and memorable stories use combinations of these five elements; for example, a single narrative may exhibit multiple conflicts. Schmidt applies her typology to the works of novelists such as Dumas, Steinbeck, and Vonnegut; playwrights from Euripides to Ibsen; and filmmakers such as Woody Allen and Steven Spielberg. Since television news stories average about 90 seconds in length and do not have the luxury of serpentine story lines or the more realistic complex dramatic situations, news writers and correspondents produce stories that whittle down reality to "the basics." Schmidt's typology can be used to better understand the narratives of television news stories.

39. The American Film Institute describes the Western as a genre that "embodies the spirit, the struggle and the demise of the new frontier. Brimming with subtext and mythology, westerns offer iconic images of a time gone by and perhaps a time that never was. A man of action with an unspoken code of honor, the western hero faces gun-toting opponents, hostile natives, lawless towns, the harsh forces of nature, and the encroachment of civilization. But the westerner keeps going, drawn to the freedom of the open plains and the promise of a new life" (www.filmsite.org /afi10toptennoms5.html; retrieved 3 May 2010).

40. Schmidt's (2005) dramatic situation no. 39.

41. Schmidt 2005, p. 26.

42. An anonymous American Film Institute writer wrote that *Red River* is an epic journey (cf. *The Odyssey*) fraught with external dangers, threats, tests of strength, and tensions between "its two strong-willed, conflicting leaders: a hard-nosed, bitter, ruthless commanding father" (John Wayne) and his men, defiantly led by his adopted son (Montgomery Clift). By the film's conclusion, the cattle herd is delivered to market "on the new Chisholm Trail, and the two men are reconciled after a brutal brawl" (www.redriverdbeltbuckle.com/history.html; retrieved 3 May 2010).

43. Schmidt 2005, p. 15.

44. The feminine journey "is based on the *Descent of Inanna*, one of the oldest

recorded myths in history. Think *Wizard of Oz*." Schmidt contrasts this with a masculine journey in which the hero begins in his version of the perfect world, but is thrust into a situation that forces a decision. The inward decision leads to a feminine journey that he has to undertake a number of times to get right. Schmidt gives the example of the *Epic of Gilgamesh*. The external decision usually brings destruction, as in *Moby-Dick* (Schmidt 2005, pp. 75–76).

45. Schmidt's dramatic situation no. 17.

46. Schmidt 2005, p. 23.

47. Schmidt's (2005) dramatic situation no. 10, pp. 131–133.

48. Bird and Dardenne 1988, p. 67, citing Hersey.

49. Peterson 2007, p. 248.

50. Bennett and Edelman offer a more pessimistic view: journalists use "stock political narratives" to "disguise and digest ideology" while representing "themselves as passive or objective reporters of the world around them" (1985, p. 159).

51. White 1984, p. 22.

52. This observation about the mythic news narratives has been made since television news broadcasts became established in the mid-1960s. Over 30 years ago, Sharon Lynn Sperry noted that television news articulated a "controlling narrative," which I take to be a hero story type (Lawrence and Timberg 1979, p. 321). Paul Weaver (1981) later observed that television news narratives of political winners and losers employed a competition story type. John Lawrence and Bernard Timberg looked at three similar hijackings in the 1970s: the 1975 Mayaguez incident, in which the Cambodian Navy seized an American merchant ship; the 1976 flight forced to land in Entebbe, Uganda; and the 1977 Mogadishu hijacking of a Lufthansa flight. Lawrence and Timberg argued that only one of these incidents was widely covered, because it evoked what they called the American captivity narrative. Of the three incidents, only this one met the "popular mythic expectations" that made it newsworthy. Only the Entebbe incident garnered international attention and led to several books and film and television documentaries. Lawrence and Timberg noted that the popular mythic expectations included a polarized moral world, evil villains, poignant victims, and superhero rescuers who save (nearly) everyone with nary a scratch to themselves, as they humiliate the bad guys. Lawrence and Timberg argued that the more a news event conforms to preexisting features of a culturally relevant myth, the more likely it will be considered newsworthy. James Ettema and Theodore Glasser explored the narrative form in investigative reporting of victims and guilt, noting that such journalism resembles the "social melodrama genre of popular fiction." Ettema and Glasser also noted that the "theme" of news stories might be generalized. I concur, reading "theme" as story type: "Indeed, form is a theme, perhaps even *the* theme, of the news story." Ettema and Glasser concluded that news narrative form is "fundamentally metaphorical" in that individual news stories refer to a primal theme or story type (1988, pp. 8, 11, italics in the original).

53. Newspaper briefs sections may be instances of *chronicles*, namely chronological listings of separate news events that are not woven into a narrative. These news items form, over the years, a list of events that are not linked into a narrative that articulates the possible connections among them. Television news briefs, however, are narratives, as can be seen, for example, in CNN news brief #24, previously discussed.

54. Bird and Dardenne 1988, p. 70.

55. Thorburn 1988, p. 57. Also see Roger Silverstone's thesis: "Television is the contemporary expression of myth. Its forms—news, documentary, serial drama— each and together, are at work on politics, science, the private, the strange, the challenging, offering accounts of the world with one aim in view: to give pleasure, to give reassurance" (Silverstone 1988, p. 35).

56. Herbert Gans provided a specific example of this generalization: "Marches and demonstrations are, from one point of view, protest activities, but the news almost always treated them as potential or actual dangers to the social order" (1979, p. 53).

57. Individuals who are visually and media literate will interpret second-order signs broadcast on a television network news program in terms of story type. However, there is another source of power that we cannot address here. Watching a news program alone in our living room is also a social practice in which we participate with social consequences, as large as when eighteenth-century townsfolk would share a provincial newspaper by reading it aloud to each other (Olsen 1999, p. 184).

58. Couldry 2003.

59. Foucault 1980, p. 97.

60. Kavanagh 1995, p. 311.

61. This socialization is not automated, however slick the packaging or inattentive the audience. Martín-Barbero (1993) argues persuasively that as commercial mass media has produced an increasingly sophisticated product, many viewers' critical faculty has correspondingly grown more able to evaluate it. He points to the times people have creatively usurped corporate media messaging to compose counterhegemonic responses. This occurs on occasion, but cannot be said to occur uniformly across the population. Organic critics who creatively subvert the commercial packaging of ideology are a small subset of any population.

62. Thompson 1991, p. 56.

63. Thompson 1984, p. 7.

64. Thompson 1991, p. 60.

65. While the successes of an exemplar of the American Dream are his or her own, the merit of the success of a recipient of affirmative action can always be questioned. Upon being nominated US attorney general (#100), Gonzales called his achievement an example of the American Dream, which it was. However, all four networks characterized it as an affirmative action appointment. Consequently, Gonzales' successes were never considered totally his own, since patronage is intimated, while any failures are his to bear alone, and imply that the doubts about his merits were warranted.

66. National Association of Hispanic Journalists (2006); Santa Ana et al. (2007).

67. Santa Ana 2006b.

68. Cotter 2010, particularly chapters 4 and 8.

69. Cotter (2010) offers an insider's view of American print journalism. It begins with an apprenticeship that socializes neophytes to a professional ethos that is linked to a well-defined set of rules of news writing and reporting. Changing the profession-directed ethos and institutionalized procedures will require significant energy. Network television newsrooms will also resist making changes to story design and development.

70. For the latter, see Aldama (2010).
71. In Lawrence and Timberg 1979, p. 322.
72. "Black Legend." Also see Horwitz 2006. For the Alamo, see Flores 2003; Morán González 2009.
73. Bennett 1980, p. 168.
74. Bennett and Edelman 1985, p. 159.
75. Bennett and Edelman 1985, pp. 157–159.
76. White 1984, p. 12.
77. Bennett 1980, p. 168.
78. Again, the denotation of a word is its explicit dictionary definition; the connotations are the associations that a word brings to mind.
79. Bennett 1980, p. 170.
80. Knight and Dean 1982, p. 145.
81. Bennett 1980, p. 169.
82. In Schudson 2003, p. 108.
83. Weaver 1976, p. 283.
84. Weaver in Adler 1981, p. 292.
85. van Leeuwen 2008, p. 106.
86. Schudson 2003, p. 181.
87. Bennett 1980, p. 168. Also see Schön 1979.
88. Bennett and Edelman 1985, p. 158.
89. Bennett and Edelman 1985, pp. 157–159.
90. Gripsrup 2000, in Schudson 2003, p. 14.
91. Bennett and Edelman 1985, p. 169.
92. Veyne 1983, pp. xi–xii. The ancient Greeks considered what we call their mythology to be part of their history, from the one-eyed Cyclops to Athena bursting from Zeus' head fully grown and dressed for war. They accepted as fact stories about Perseus, who battled fantastic creatures like the Medusa, stories about incest or rape leading to heroic offspring, and allegorical stories, such as that of Prometheus. It would have been as unthinkable for them to disavow the Trojan War as we the convenient fictions about the Revolutionary War. See Foley (2005).

Chapter Nine

1. Martín-Barbero 2000, pp. 47–48.
2. National Latino Media Coalition 2010.
3. The National Association of Hispanic Journalists has repeatedly decried the "lack of a meaningful increase in Latino journalists and journalists of color" in recent years, in spite of network statements of concern and ventures such as the NAHJ Parity Project, which effectively prepare students of color for careers in journalism (www.nahj.org/nahjnews/articles/2006/april/asne.shtml; retrieved 7 December 2010).
4. www.spj.org/mission.asp; retrieved 5 December 2010.
5. Schudson 1978, p. 193.
6. In particular, Latinos can draw on the Spanish-language networks for needed perspective.

References

Abbott, H. Porter. 2008. *The Cambridge introduction to narrative*. 2nd ed. Cambridge: Cambridge University Press.

Adler, Richard P., ed. 1981. *Understanding television: Essays on television as a social and cultural force*. New York: Praeger.

Aldama, Frederick Luís, ed. 2010. *Toward a cognitive theory of narrative acts*. Austin: University of Texas Press.

Allan, Stuart. 1998. News from NowHere: Televisual news discourses and the construction of hegemony. In *Approaches to media discourse*, ed. Allan Bell and Peter Garrett, pp. 105–141. London: Blackwell.

Anderson, Benedict. 1983. *Imagined communities: Reflections on the origin and spread of nationalism*. London: Verso.

Andreas, Peter. 2003. A tale of two borders: The U.S.-Canada and U.S.-Mexico lines after 9-11. In *The rebordering of North America? Integration and exclusion in a new security context*, ed. Peter Andreas and Thomas J. Biersteker, pp. 1–23. New York: Routledge.

ASNE (American Society of Newspaper Editors). 13 April 2008. Newsrooms shrink: Minority percentage increases slightly. www.asne.org/files/08Census.pdf. Retrieved 16 April 2008.

Axtman, Kris. 29 December 2003. The terror threat at home, often overlooked: As the media focus on international terror, a Texan pleads guilty to possessing a weapon of mass destruction. *The Christian Science Monitor*. http://www.csmonitor.com/2003/1229/p02s01-usju.html. Retrieved 23 April 2010.

Bailey, Chris. 1 February 2004. Don't enjoy questions about U-46? Don't read any further then! *Chicago Daily Herald*, p. 16.

Bal, Mieke. 2004. *Narratology: Introduction to the theory of narrative*. 2nd ed. Toronto, Buffalo, and London: University of Toronto Press.

Banet-Weiser, Sarah. 2003. Elián González and "the purpose of America": Nation, family, and the child citizen. *American Quarterly* 55(2): 149–178.

Bargh, John A., and Ezequiel Morsella. 2008. The unconscious mind. *Perspectives on Psychological Science* 3(1): 73–79.

Barrett, Grant. 2004. *Hatchet jobs and hardball: The Oxford dictionary of American political slang*. New York: Oxford University Press.

Barthes, Roland. [1957] 1972. *Mythologies*, trans. Jonathan Cape, New York: Hill and Wang.

―――. 1966. Introduction à l'analyse structurale des récits. *Communications* 8(1): 1–27.

―――. [1970] 1974. *S/Z*. New York: Hill and Wang.

―――. 1975. Introduction to the structural analysis of narratives. *New Literary History* 6(2): 237.

Baum, Matthew A. 2003. Soft news and political knowledge: Evidence of absence or absence of evidence? *Political Communication* 20: 73–190.

Baumgartner, Judy, and Jonathan S. Morris. 2006. The Daily Show effect: Candidate evaluations, efficacy, and American youth. *American Politics Research* 34(3): 341–367.

Bell, Allan, and Peter Garrett, eds. 1998. *Approaches to media discourse*. London: Blackwell.

Bennett, W. Lance. 1980. Myth, ritual and political control. *Journal of Communication* 30(4): 166–179.

Bennett, W. Lance, and Murray Edelman. 1985. Toward a new political narrative. *Journal of Communication* 35(4): 156–171.

Bennett, W. Lance, Regina G. Lawrence, and Steven Livingston. 2007. *When the press fails: Political power and the news media from Iraq to Katrina*. Chicago: University of Chicago Press.

Berger, John. 1972. *Ways of seeing*. London: Penguin.

Bird, S. Elizabeth, and Robert W. Dardenne. 1988. Myth, chronicle and story: Exploring the narrative qualities of the news. In *Media, myths, and narratives: Television and the press*, ed. James W. Carey, pp. 76–86. Sage Annual Review of Communication Research #15. Newbury Park, London, and New Delhi: Sage.

"Black Legend." 2011. *Encyclopædia Britannica Online*. www.britannica.com/EB checked/topic/67986/Black-Legend; retrieved 3 September 2011.

Bové, Paul A. 1995. Discourse. In *Critical terms for literary study*, ed. Frank Lentricchia and Thomas McLaughlin, 2nd ed., pp. 50–79. Chicago and London: University of Chicago Press.

Brandt, Line, and Per Aage Brandt. August 2005. Cognitive poetics and imagery. *European Journal of English Studies* 9(2): 117–130.

Bryson, Norman, Michael Ann Holly, and Keith Moxey. 1994. Introduction. In *Visual culture: Images and interpretations*, ed. Norman Bryson, Michael Ann Holly, and Keith Moxey, pp. xv–xxix. Middletown, CT, and London: Wesleyan University Press.

Burke, Kenneth. 1968. *Language as symbolic action: Essays on life, literature and method*. Berkeley and Los Angeles: University of California Press.

Bush, George W. 7 January 2004. *President Bush proposes new temporary worker program*. Remarks by the President on Immigration Policy, Washington, DC. www .whitehouse.gov/news/releases/2004/01/20040107-3.html. Retrieved 19 March 2007.

Caivano, José Luis. 1998. Color and semiotics: A two-way street. *Color Research and Application* 23(6): 390–401.

Calafell, Bernadette M. 2001. In our own image?! A rhetorical criticism of Latina magazine. *Voces: A Journal of Chicana and Latina Studies* 3(1/2): 12–46.

Callinicos, Alex. 2004. Obituary: The infinite search. *Socialist Review.* www.socialist review.org.uk/article.php?articlenumber=9101. Retrieved 28 April 2010.

Carlson, Marvin, ed. 1990. *Theatre semiotics: Signs of life.* Bloomington: Indiana University Press.

Carroll, Noel. 1994. Visual metaphor. In *Aspects of metaphor,* ed. Jaakko Hintikka, pp. 189–218. Dordrecht: Kluwer.

———. 1996. A note on film metaphor. In *Theorizing the moving image,* pp. 212–223. Cambridge: Cambridge University Press.

Casas, Michael C., and Travis L. Dixon. 2003. The impact of stereotypical and counter-stereotypical news on viewer perception of Blacks and Latinos: An exploratory study. In *A companion to media studies,* ed. Angharad N. Valdivia, pp. 480–492. Malden, MA: Blackwell.

Cavanagh, Sean. 16 February 2005. Families accuse Illinois district of discrimination in redistricting. *Education Week* 24(23): 4.

Center for Media and Public Affairs. 2 June 2000. Elián story makes the biggest splash. Report by the Center for Media and Public Affairs. http://www.cmpa.com/PressRel /Archive/2000/2000.11.22.%20Media%20Feeding%20Frenzy%20in%20Florida .pdf. Retrieved 10 September 2005.

Chávez, Leo R. 2001. *Covering immigration: Popular images and the politics of the nation.* Berkeley: University of California Press.

Chilton, Paul A. 1996. *Security metaphors: Cold War discourse from containment to common house.* New York: Peter Lang.

Cienki, Alan. 1998. Metaphoric gestures and some of their relations to verbal metaphoric expressions. In *Discourse and cognition: Bridging the gap,* ed. Jean-Pierre Koenig, pp. 189–204. Stanford, CA: CSLI Publications.

Cole, William. 22 January 2008. Marine may finally get Medal of Honor: Mother of hero who smothered grenade gets call that signals a final decision is near. *Honolulu Advertiser.com.* http://the.honoluluadvertiser.com/article/2008/Jan/22/ln /hawaii801220364.html. Retrieved 15 April 2008.

Condit, Celeste, and John Louis Lucaites. 1993. *Crafting equality: America's Anglo-African word.* Chicago: University of Chicago Press.

Cornfield, Michael. 1988. The Watergate audience: Parsing the powers of the press. In *Media, myths, and narratives: Television and the press,* ed. James W. Carey, pp. 180–204. Sage Annual Review of Communication Research #15. Newbury Park, London, and New Delhi: Sage.

Cotter, Colleen. 2010. *News talk: Investigating the language of journalism.* Cambridge and New York: Cambridge University Press.

Couldry, Nick. 2003. *Media rituals: A critical approach.* London and New York: Routledge.

Croteau, David, and William Hoynes. 2002. *Media/society: Industries, images, and audiences.* 3rd ed. Thousand Oaks, CA: Sage.

Danto, Arthur C. 1993. Metaphor and cognition. In *Metaphor and knowledge,* ed. Frank R. Ankersmit and J. J. A. Mooij, pp. 21–35. Dordrecht: Kluwer.

Daylight, Russell. 2011. *What if Derrida was wrong about Saussure?* Edinburgh: Edinburgh University Press.

de Certeau, Michel. 1984. *The practice of everyday life,* trans. Steven Rendall. Berkeley and Los Angeles: University of California Press.

de la Garza, Rodolfo, Ángelo Falcón, F. Chris García, and John A. García. 1992. *Latino national political survey, 1989–1990*. Philadelphia: Temple University, Institute for Social Research.

DeLuca, Kevin Michael. 1999. *Image politics: The new rhetoric of environmental activism*. New York and London: Guilford Press.

Dixon, Travis L., and Cristina L. Azocar. 2006. The representation of juvenile offenders by race on Los Angeles area television news. *Howard Journal of Communications* 17: 143–161.

Dixon, Travis L., Cristina L. Azocar, and Michael Casas. 2003. The portrayal of race and crime on television network news. *Journal of Broadcasting and Electronic Media* 47(4): 498–523.

Dixon, Travis L., and Daniel G. Linz. 2000a. Overrepresentation and underrepresentation of African Americans and Latinos as lawbreakers on television news. *Journal of Communication* 50(2): 131–154.

———. 2000b. Race and the misrepresentation of victimization on local television news. *Communication Research* 27: 547–573.

———. 2002. Television news, prejudicial pretrial publicity, and the depiction of race. *Journal of Broadcasting and Electronic Media* 46: 112–136.

Dougherty, Mary, Denise Wilson, and Amy Wu. November 2005. *Annual Report. Immigration enforcement actions: 2004*. DHS Office of Immigration Statistics. Washington, DC: Department of Homeland Security.

Duany, Jorge. 2005. Dominican migration to Puerto Rico: A transnational perspective. *Centro Journal* 17(1): 242–269. City University of New York, Centro de Estudios Puertorriqueños.

Dworkin, Ronald. 14 August 2008. Why it was a great victory (Boumediene v. Bush). *New York Review of Books*, p. 18, footnote 4.

Eckert, Penny. 2000. *Language variation as social practice: The linguistic construction of identity in Belten High*. Oxford: Blackwell.

The Education Trust. 2003. *Latino achievement in America*. www2.edtrust.org/NR/rdonlyres/7DC36C7E-EBBE-43BB-8392-CDC618E1F762/0/LatAchievEnglish.pdf. Retrieved 1 November 2010.

Edwards, Janice L., and Carol K. Winkler. 1997. Representative forms and the visual ideograph: The Iwo Jima image in editorial cartoons. *Quarterly Journal of Speech* 83: 289–310.

Entman, Robert M. 1990. Modern racism and the images of Blacks in local television news. *Critical Studies in Mass Communication* 7: 332–345.

———. 1992. Blacks in the news: Television, modern racism and cultural change. *Journalism Quarterly* 69(2): 341–361.

———. 1993. Framing: Toward a clarification of a fractured paradigm. *Journal of Communication* 43(4): 51–58.

Entman, Robert, and Andrew Rojecki. 2000. *The Black image in the White mind*. Chicago: University of Chicago Press.

Ettema, James S., and Theodore L. Glasser. 1988. Narrative form and moral force: The realization of innocence and guilt through investigative journalism. *Journal of Communication* 38(3): 8–26.

Ettema, James, Charles Whitney, and Daniel B. Wackman. 1987. Professional mass communicators. In *Handbook of communication science*, ed. Charles H. Berger and Steven H. Chaffee, pp. 747–780. Beverly Hills: Sage.

Faber, Ronald, Thomas O'Guinn, and Timothy Meyer. 1987. Televised portrayals of Hispanics: A comparison of ethnic perceptions. *International Journal of Intercultural Relations* 11(2): 155–169.

Fauconnier, Gilles, and Mark Turner. 1994. *Conceptual projection and middle spaces.* Report 9401 of the Department of Cognitive Science, University of California, San Diego. Manuscript.

———. 2002. *The way we think: Conceptual blending and the mind's hidden complexities.* New York: Basic Books.

Fernández, Celestino, and Lawrence R. Pedroza. 1982. The Border Patrol and news media coverage of undocumented Mexican immigration during the 1970s: Quantitative content analysis in the sociology of knowledge. *California Sociologist* 5(2): 1–26.

Fernandez-Sacco, Ellen. January–February 2002. Review of *Approaches to Understanding Visual Culture. Afterimage.*

Finnegan, Cara A. 2003. *Picturing poverty: Print culture and FSA [Farm Security Administration] photographs.* Washington, DC: Smithsonian Books.

———. May 2004. Review essay: Visual studies and visual rhetoric. *Quarterly Journal of Speech* 90(2): 234–256.

Flores, Lisa A. 1996. Creating discursive space through a rhetoric of difference: Chicana feminists craft a homeland. *Quarterly Journal of Speech* 82: 142–156.

———. 2003. Constructing rhetorical borders: Peons, illegal aliens, and competing narratives of immigration. *Critical Studies in Media Communication* 20: 362–387.

Flores, Lisa A., and Marouf A. Hasian. 1997. Returning to Aztlán and La Raza: Political communication and the vernacular construction of Chicano/a nationalism. In *International and Intercultural Annual, Vol. 20: Politics, Communication, and Culture,* ed. Alberto Gonzalez and Dolores V. Tanno, pp. 186–203. Thousand Oaks, CA: Sage.

Foley, John Miles, ed. 2005. *A companion to ancient epic.* Hoboken, NJ, and San Francisco: Wiley-Blackwell.

Forceville, Charles. 1988. The case for pictorial metaphor: René Magritte and other Surrealists. In *Vestnik IMS 9,* ed. Aleš Erjavec, pp. 150–160. Ljubljana, Slovenia: Inštitut za Marksistične Študije.

———. 1994. Pictorial metaphor in advertisements. *Metaphor and Symbolic Activity* 9(1): 1–29.

———. 1996. *Pictorial metaphor in advertising.* London/New York: Routledge.

———. 1999a. The metaphor COLIN IS A CHILD in Ian McEwan's, Harold Pinter's, and Paul Schrader's *The Comfort of Strangers. Metaphor and Symbol* 14(3): 179–198.

———. 1999b. Metaphor in moving images. Paper given at the Sixth International Cognitive Linguistics Conference, Stockholm.

———. 2000. Compasses, beauty queens and other PCs: Pictorial metaphors in computer advertisements. *Hermes: Journal of Linguistics* 24: 31–55.

———. 2004. When is something a pictorial metaphor? In *A course in pictorial and multimodal metaphor.* http://projects.chass.utoronto.ca/semiotics/cyber/cforce ville2.pdf. Retrieved 10 November 2010.

———. 2007. Multimodal metaphor in ten Dutch TV commercials. *Public Journal of Semiotics* 1(1): 15–34.

Foucault, Michel. 1980. *Power/knowledge: Selected interviews and other writings, 1972–1977*, ed. Colin Gordon. New York: Pantheon Books.

———. 1983. The subject and power. In *Michel Foucault: Beyond structuralism and hermeneutics*, ed. Hubert Dreyfus and Paul Rabinow. Chicago: University of Chicago Press.

Frye, Northrop. 1957. *Anatomy of criticism: Four essays*. Princeton, NJ: Princeton University Press.

Gamson, William A., and Andre Modigliani. 1989. Media discourse and public opinion on nuclear power: A constructionist approach. *American Journal of Sociology* 95: 1–37.

Gandy, Oscar H. Jr. 1998. *Communication and race: A structural perspective*. New York: Arnold Press.

Gans, Herbert. 1979. *Deciding what's news: A study of CBS Evening News, NBC Nightly News, Newsweek, and Time*. Evanston, IL: Northwestern University Press.

———. 2004. *Democracy and the press*. New York and Oxford: Oxford University Press.

Gans, Judith. 2008. *Immigrants in Arizona: Fiscal and economic impacts*. Tucson: Udall Center for Studies in Public Policy, University of Arizona.

Geertz, Clifford. 1973. Deep play: Notes on the Balinese cockfight. In *The Interpretation of Cultures*. New York: Basic Books.

Gerbner, George, Larry Gross, Michael Morgan, and Nancy Signorielli. 1994. Growing up with television: The cultivation perspective. In *Media effects: Advances in theory and research*, ed. Jennings Bryant and Dolf Zillman, pp. 17–42. New York: Erlbaum.

Gergen, Joe. 18 October 2005. Yuliana Perez makes jump from despair to Games. *Newsday*, p. A56.

Gibbs, Raymond W., Jr. 1994. *Poetics of the mind: Figurative thought, language and understanding*. Cambridge: Cambridge University Press.

Gitlin, Todd. 1980. *The whole world is watching: Mass media in the making and unmaking of the New Left*. Berkeley: University of California Press.

Goatly, Andrew. 1997. *The language of metaphors*. London: Routledge.

———. 2007. *Washing the brain: Metaphor and hidden ideology*. Amsterdam and Philadelphia: John Benjamins Publishing Company.

Goldstein, Evan R. 15 August 2008. Who framed George Lakoff? A noted linguist reflects on his tumultuous foray into politics. *Chronicle of Higher Education Review* 54(49): B6.

González, Daniel. 4 March 2004. Feds aid drop-house crackdowns. Nearly 750 caught in 23 days. *Arizona Republic, p. A1.*

González, David. 2006. Televisión y frontera: El espacio audiovisual en Tijuana. In *Los medios de comunicación en Baja California*, ed. Manuel Ortiz, pp. 143–156. Mexicali, Mexico: Universidad Autónoma de Baja California and Porrúa.

———. 2007a. Aquí, allá y en todas partes: Las audiencias juveniles en la frontera norte. In *Un mundo de visiones: Interacciones de las audiencias en múltiples escenarios mediáticos y virtuales*, ed. Guillermo Orozco, pp. 117–131. Mexico City: Instituto Latinoamericano de Comunicación y Educación.

———. 2007b. El sueño americano en México. *Televisión y audiencias juveniles en Tijuana*. Mexicali, Mexico: Universidad Autónoma de Baja California.

Gray, Herman. 1995. *Watching race: Television and the struggle for Blackness*. Minneapolis: University of Minnesota Press.

Greenberg, Bradley S., and Pilar Baptista-Fernandez. 1980. Hispanic-Americans: The new minority on television. In *Life on television: Content analyses of U.S. Television drama*, ed. Bradley S. Greenberg, pp. 3–12. Norwood, NJ: Ablex.

Greenberg, Bradley S., Michael V. Burgoon, Judee K. Burgoon, and Felipe Korzenny. 1983. *Mexican Americans and the mass media*. Norwood, NJ: Ablex.

Greenberg, Bradley S., Dana Mastro, and Jeffrey E. Brand. 2001. Minorities and the mass media: Television into the 21st century. In *Media effects: Advances in theory and research*, ed. Jennings Bryant and Dolf Zillmann, pp. 333–352. Mahwah, NJ: Erlbaum.

Greene, Jay P., and Marcus A. Winters. 2005. *Public high school graduation and college readiness: 1991–2002*. New York: Manhattan Institute for Policy Research.

Grillo, Ioan. 18 January 2008. A deadly turf war over Cuban illegals, *Time*. www.time.com/time/world/article/0,8599,1704913,00.html. Retrieved 16 April 2008.

Gurza, Agustín. 12 July 2001. Buena Vista. A rift opens between two men behind the popularization of Cuban music: Should it look backward or forward? *Los Angeles Times*, F6.

———. 6 April 2008. Chicano art, beyond rebellion. "Phantom Sightings: Art after the Chicano Movement" provides a rare showcase at the Los Angeles County Museum of Art. *Los Angeles Times*, E1.

Gutiérrez, David. 1995. *Walls and mirrors: Mexican Americans, Mexican immigrants, and the politics of ethnicity*. Berkeley: University of California Press.

Gutiérrez, Félix. 1977. Chicanos and the media: Bibliography of selected materials. *Journalism History* 4(2): 34–41, 65–67.

Hall, Stuart. 1980. Encoding/decoding. In *Culture, media, language*, ed. Stuart Hall, Dorothy Hobson, Andrew Lowe, and Paul Willis, pp. 128–138. London: Hutchinson.

———. 1997a. Old and new identities, old and new ethnicities. In *Culture, globalization and the world-system*, ed. Anthony D. King, pp. 41–68. Minneapolis: University of Minnesota Press.

———, ed. 1997b. *Representation: Cultural representations and signifying practices*. London: Sage.

Hall, Stuart, and Paul du Gay, eds. 1996. *Questions of cultural identity*. Thousand Oaks, CA: Sage.

Hallin, Daniel. 1986. We keep America on top of the world. In *Watching television*, ed. Todd Gitlin, pp. 9–41. New York: Pantheon.

Halloran, James D., Philip Elliot, and Graham Murdock. 1970. *Demonstrations and communication: A case study*. Harmondsworth: Penguin.

Harrell, D. Fox. 2010. Toward a theory of critical computing: The case of social identity representation in digital media applications. *CTheory: An International Peer-Reviewed Journal of Theory, Technology and Culture*. http://www.ctheory.net/articles.aspx?id=641. Retrieved 10 September 2010.

Haycock, Kati. 2003. Closing the achievement gap. *Educational Leadership* 58(1): 6–11.

Herman, Edward S., and Noam Chomsky. 1988. *Manufacturing consent: The political economy of the mass media*. New York: Pantheon Books.

Hernández, Kelly Lytle. 2006. The crimes and consequences of illegal immigration:

A cross-border examination of Operation Wetback, 1943 to 1954. *Western Historical Quarterly* 37: 421–444.

Hill, Jane H. 1993. "Hasta la vista, baby." Anglo Spanish in the US Southwest. *Critique of Anthropology* 13: 145–176.

———. 1998. Language, race, and White public space. *American Anthropologist* 100(3): 680–689.

———. 2008. *The everyday language of White racism*. Malden, MA, and Oxford: Wiley-Blackwell.

Hoefer, Michael, Nancy Rytina, and Bryan C. Baker. 2008. *Estimates of the unauthorized immigrant population residing in the United States: January 2007*. Office of Immigration Statistics, Policy Directorate, U.S. Department of Homeland Security. http://www.dhs.gov/xlibrary/assets/statistics/publications/ILL_PE_2007.pdf. Retrieved 10 January 2010.

Holman, C. Hugh. 1980. *A Handbook to literature*. 4th ed. Indianapolis, IN: Bobbs-Merrill.

Horwitz, Tony. 9 July 2006. Immigration and the curse of the Black Legend. *New York Times*, p. A23.

Howell, Richard. 2003. *Visual culture*. Hoboken, NJ, and San Francisco: Wiley-Blackwell.

Iedema, Rick. 2001. Analyzing film and television: A social semiotic account of *Hospital: An Unhealthy Business*. In *Handbook of visual analysis*, ed. Theo van Leeuwen and Carey Jewitt, pp. 183–204. London, Thousand Oaks, and New Delhi: Sage.

Jacobs, Lawrence, R., and Robert Y. Shapiro. March 1996. Toward the integrated study of political communications, public opinion, and the policy-making process. *PS: Political Science and Politics* 29(1): 10–13.

Jacobson, Robin Dale. 2008. *The new nativism: Proposition 187 and the debate over immigration*. Minneapolis: University of Minnesota Press.

Jacoby, Susan. 2008. *The age of American unreason*. New York: Pantheon.

Jahlly, Sut, and Justin M. Lewis. 1992. *Enlightened racism: The Cosby Show, audiences and the myth of the American Dream*. Boulder, CO: Westview Press.

Jasinski, James. 2001. *Sourcebook on rhetoric: Key concepts in contemporary rhetorical studies*. Thousand Oaks, CA: Sage.

Jensen, Klaus Bruhn. 1995. *The social semiotics of mass communication*. London and Thousand Oaks, CA: Sage.

Jewitt, Carey, and Rumiko Oyama. 2001. Visual meaning: A social semiotics approach. In *Handbook of visual analysis*, ed. Theo van Leeuwen and Carey Jewitt, pp. 134–156. London, Thousand Oaks, and New Delhi: Sage.

Jordan, Miriam. 23 February 2004. Latinos take the lead in job gains: Hispanic workers receive higher proportion of posts in construction, services. *Wall Street Journal*, p. A2.

Kaplan, Stuart Jay. 1990. Visual metaphors in the representation of communication technology. *Critical Studies in Mass Communication* 7(1): 37–47.

———. 1992. A conceptual analysis of form and content in visual metaphors. *Communication* 13: 197–209.

Kavanagh, James H. 1995. Ideology. In *Critical terms for literary study*, ed. Frank Lentricchia and Thomas McLaughlin, pp. 306–320. Chicago and London: University of Chicago Press.

Kennedy, John M. 1982. Metaphor in pictures. *Perception* 11: 589–605.

———. 1993. *Drawing the blind: Pictures to touch.* New Haven and London: Yale University Press.

———. 1997. Visual metaphor in contest. *Semiotic Review of Books* 8(2): 2–5.

Knight, Graham, and Tony Dean. 1982. Myth and the structure of news. *Journal of Communication* 32(2): 144–161.

Knott, Alex. 8 April 2005. The "fourth branch" of government. *AlterNet.* http://www.alternet.org/story/21702. Retrieved 8 August 2008.

Kolbenschlag, Madonna C. 31 July 1976. The evening news: Qualitative assessment and systematic analysis. Paper presented at the annual meeting of the Association for Education in Journalism, College Park, Maryland.

Kress, Gunther, and Theo van Leeuwen. 1996. *Reading images: The grammar of visual design.* London: Routledge.

Kretsedemas, Philip. 2008. Immigration enforcement and the complication of national sovereignty: Understanding local enforcement as an exercise in neoliberal governance. *American Quarterly* 60(3): 553–573.

Lakoff, George. 1987. *Women, fire and dangerous things: What categories reveal about the mind.* Chicago: University of Chicago Press.

———. 1993. The contemporary theory of metaphor. In *Metaphor and thought,* ed. Andrew Ortony, 2nd ed., pp. 202–251. Cambridge: Cambridge University Press.

———. 1996. *Moral politics: What conservatives know that liberals don't.* Chicago: University of Chicago Press.

———. 2004. *Don't think of an elephant: Know your values and frame the debate.* White River Junction, VT: Chelsea Green Publishing.

Lakoff, George, and Mark Johnson. 1980. *Metaphors we live by.* Chicago: University of Chicago Press.

———. 1999. *Philosophy in the flesh: The embodied mind and its challenge to Western thought.* New York: Basic Books.

Lakoff, George, and Mark Turner. 1989. *More than cool reason: A field guide to poetic metaphor.* Chicago: Chicago University Press.

Lawrence, John Shelton, and Bernard Timberg. 1979. News and mythic selectivity: Mayaguez, Entebbe, Mogadishu. *Journal of American Culture* 2(2): 321–330.

Lee, Stacey J. (2005). *Up against whiteness: Race, school and immigrant youth.* New York: Teachers College Press.

Levine, Elana. 2001. Constructing a market, constructing an ethnicity: U.S. Spanish language media and the formation of a Latina/o identity. *Studies in Latin American Popular Culture* 20: 33–50.

Levitas, Daniel. 2002. *The terrorist next door: The militia movement and the radical right.* New York: Macmillan.

Lewis, Anthony. 25 September 2008. Official American sadism. *New York Review of Books* 55(14).

Lincoln, Bruce. 1999. *Theorizing myth: Narrative, ideology and scholarship.* Chicago: University of Chicago Press.

Lister, Martin, and Liz Wells. 2001. Seeing beyond belief: Cultural studies as an approach to analyzing the visual. In *Handbook of visual analysis,* ed. Theo van Leeuwen and Carey Jewitt, pp. 61–91. London, Thousand Oaks, and New Delhi: Sage.

Lloyd, Mark. 2006. *Prologue to a farce: Communication and democracy in America.* Urbana: University of Illinois Press.

Longman, Jere. 19 August 2000. Olympics: For defectors from Cuba, rough political waters: Cuba's objections may keep kayaker and others out of games. *New York Times*, p. D6.

López, Ronald W., and Darryl D. Ennos. 1974. Spanish-language only television in Los Angeles County. *Aztlán* 4(2): 283–311.

Lucaites, John Louis, and Celeste Michelle Condit. 1985. Re-constructing narrative theory: A functional perspective. *Journal of Communication* 35(4): 90–108.

———. 1990. Reconstructing <equality>: Culturetypal and counter-cultural rhetorics in the martyred Black vision. *Communication Monographs* 57: 5–24.

Luke, Allan. 1996. Text and discourse in education: An introduction to critical discourse analysis. *Review of Research in Education* 21: 3–48.

Lule, Jack. 2001. *Daily news, eternal stories: The mythological role of journalism.* New York: Guilford Press.

———. Summer 2002. Myth and terror on the editorial page: The *New York Times* responds to September 11, 2001. *Journalism and Mass Communication Quarterly* 79(2): 275–294.

Magaña, Lisa, and Robert Short. 2002. The social construction of Mexican and Cuban immigrants by politicians in mainstream newspapers. *The Review of Policy Research* 19(4): 78–94.

Malone, Tara. 21 March 2004. A look at foundation's work elsewhere may indicate what's in U-46's future. *Chicago Daily Herald*, p. 1.

———. 7 August 2004. U-46 lawsuit remains unfiled. Attorneys for Elgin, school district agree talks may still be beneficial. *Chicago Daily Herald*, p. 3.

Marsh, Charles. 30 July 2003. Deeper than the fictional model: Structural origins of literary journalism in Greek tragedy and Aristotle's poetics. Paper presented at the 2003 Association for Education in Journalism and Mass Communication Conference, Kansas City, Missouri.

Martín-Barbero, Jesús. [1987] 1993. *Communication, culture and hegemony: From the media to mediations*, trans. Elizabeth Fox and Robert A. White. London: Sage.

———. 2000. Transformations in the map: Identities and culture industries. *Latin American Perspectives* 27(113): 27–48.

Martínez, Thomas M. 1969. Advertising and racism: The case of the Mexican American. *El Grito: A Journal of Contemporary Mexican American Thought* 2(4): 3–13.

Mastro, Dana E. 2003. A social identity approach to understanding the impact of television messages. *Communication Monographs* 70(2): 98–113.

Mastro, Dana E., Elizabeth Behm-Morawitz, and Michelle Ortiz. 2007. The cultivation of social perceptions of Latinos: A mental models approach. *Media Psychology* 9(2): 347–365.

Mastro, Dana E., and Amanda L. Robinson. 2000. Cops and crooks: Images of minorities on primetime television. *Journal of Criminal Justice* 28(5): 385–396.

Mastro, Dana E., and Susannah R. Stern. 2003. Representations of race in television commercials: A content analysis of prime-time advertising. *Journal of Broadcasting and Electronic Media* 47(4): 638–647.

McCombs, Maxwell. 2005. The agenda-setting function of the press. In *The Press*, ed. Geneva Overholser and Kathleen Hall Jamieson, pp. 156–168. Oxford and New York: Oxford University Press.

McGee, Michael Calvin. 1980. The "ideograph": A link between rhetoric and ideology. *Quarterly Journal of Speech* 66(1): 1–16.

————. 1990. Text, context, and the fragmentation of contemporary culture. *Western Journal of Speech and Communication* 54(3): 274–289.

McGuire, John Michael. 1999. Pictorial metaphors: A reply to Sedivy. *Metaphor and Symbol* 14(4): 293–302.

McNeill, David. 1992. *Hand and mind: What gestures reveal about thought.* Chicago and London: University of Chicago Press.

Méndez-Méndez, Serafín, and Diane Alverio. 2002. *Network brownout 2001: The portrayal of Latinos in network television news.* Report prepared for the National Association of Hispanic Journalists, Washington, DC.

Messaris, Paul. 1997. *Visual persuasion: The role of images in advertising.* Thousand Oaks, London, and New Delhi: Sage.

Mexican Americans face far higher stroke risk than whites. *Mental Health Business Week*, September 4, 2004, p. 78.

Mindlin, David T. Z. 1998. *Just the facts: How "objectivity" came to define American journalism.* New York: New York University Press.

Molina-Guzmán, Isabel. 2000. Spanish Caribbean women images. In *Routledge international encyclopedia of women*, ed. Cheris Kramarae and Dale Spender. New York: Routledge.

————. 2006. Covering ethnic conflicts: Tracing the discourses of race, ethnicity and difference in the local press. *Journalism: Theory, Practice, Criticism* 7(3): 281–299.

————. 2007a. Mapping the academic terrain of US Latinas/os in the general-market and Latina/o media. In *The experiences of Latinas/os in the United States*, ed. H. Rodriguez, R. Saenz, and C. Menjivar, pp. 199–208. New York: Springer.

————. 2007b. Discourses of disorderly bodies in the Elián story. In *From bananas to buttocks: The Latina in popular film and culture*, ed. Myra Mendible, pp. 219–242. Austin: University of Texas Press.

————. 2008. Policing the Latina/o Other: Latinidad in prime-time news coverage of the Elián González Story. In *Latina/o communication studies today*, ed. Angharad N. Valdivia, pp. 115–135. New York: Peter Lang.

————. 2010. *Dangerous curves: Latina bodies in the media.* New York: New York University Press.

Molina-Guzmán, Isabel, and Angharad Valdivia. 2004. Brain, brow or bootie: Latina iconicity in contemporary popular culture. *Communication Review* 7(2): 203–219.

Montalvo, Daniela, and Joseph Torres. 2006. *Network brownout report 2006: The portrayal of Latinos and Latino issues on network television news, 2005.* Washington, DC: National Association of Hispanic Journalists. http://www.scribd.com/doc/27291832/2006-NAHJ-Network-Brownout-Report. Retrieved 9 November 2010.

Morales, Armando. 1971. The collective preconscious and racism. *Social Casework* 52: 285–293.

Morán González, John. 2009. *Border renaissance: The Texas centennial and the emergence of Mexican American literature.* Austin: University of Texas Press.

Mumford Jones, Howard. 1963. Review. *Political Science Quarterly* 78(4): 597–599.

National Association of Hispanic Journalists. March 2008. NAHJ urges news media to stop using dehumanizing terms when covering immigration. Calls for stopping the use of "illegals" as a noun, curbing the phrase "illegal alien." http:// www.nahj.org/nahjnews/articles/2006/March/immigrationcoverage.shtml. Retrieved 6 January 2012.

———. 14 April 2008. NAHJ disturbed by figures that mask decline in newsroom diversity. http://www.nahj.org/nahjnews/articles/2008/April/ASNE.shtml. Retrieved 26 February 2010.

National Council of La Raza, Center for Media and Public Affairs. 1996. *Don't blink: Hispanics in television entertainment.* Washington, DC: Author.

National Education Association. December 2007. Special education and English language learners. In *Focus on Hispanics.* Washington, DC: National Education Association.

National Latino Media Council. 2010. Television networks fail Latinos in diversity performance. http://www.nhmc.org/content/nlmc-press-conference-television-networks-fail-latinos-diversity-performance. Retrieved 7 December 2010.

Navarrete, Lisa, and Charles Kamasaki. 1994. *Out of the picture: Hispanics in the media. State of Hispanic America 1994.* Washington, DC: Policy Analysis Center, Office of Research, Advocacy, and Legislation.

Nazario, Sonia. 2006. *Enrique's journey.* New York: Random House.

Nelson, Thomas E., Rosalee A. Clawson, and Zoe M. Oxley. 1997. Media framing of a civil liberties conflict and its effect on tolerance. *American Political Science Review* 91(3): 567–583.

Newton, Lina. 2008. *Illegal, alien, or immigrant: The politics of immigration reform.* New York: New York University Press.

Ngai, Mae M. 2005. *Impossible subjects: Illegal aliens and the making of modern America.* Princeton, NJ: Princeton University Press.

O'Brien, Gerald V. 2003. Indigestible food, conquering hoards, and waste materials: Metaphors of immigrants and the early immigration restriction debate in the United States. *Metaphor and Symbol* 18(1): 33–47.

Ochs, Elinor, and Lisa Capps. 1996. Narrating the self. *Annual Review of Anthropology* 25: 19–43.

Olivarez, Adriana. 1998. Studying representations of U.S. Latino culture (Constructing (Mis)Representations). *Journal of Communication Inquiry* 22(4): 426–437.

Oliver, Mary Beth. 1994. Portrayals of crime, race and aggression in "reality-based" police shows: A content analysis. *Journal of Broadcasting and Electronic Media* 38(2): 179–192.

———. 2003. Race and crime in the media: Research from a media effects perspective. In *A Companion to Media studies*, ed. Angharad N. Valdivia, pp. 421–436. Malden, MA: Blackwell.

Olsen, Kirstin. 1999. *Daily life in 18th-century England.* Santa Barbara, CA: Greenwood Press.

Ong, Aihwa. 1996. Cultural citizenship as subject-making: Immigrants negotiate racial and cultural boundaries in the United States. *Current Anthropology* 37(5): 737–762.

Ono, Kent, and John Sloop. 2002. *Shifting borders: Rhetoric, immigration, and California's Proposition 187.* Philadelphia: Temple University Press.

Papafragou, Anna, and Julien Musolino. 2003. Scalar implicatures: Experiments at the semantics-pragmatics interface. *Cognition* 86: 253–282.

Parenti, Michael. 1986. *Inventing reality: The politics of mass media.* New York: St. Martin's Press.

Passel, Jeffrey S., and D'Vera Cohn. October 2008. *Trends in unauthorized immigration: Undocumented inflow now trails legal inflow.* Washington, DC: Pew Hispanic Center.

Patterson, Thomas E. 2002. *The vanishing voter: Public involvement in an age of uncertainty.* New York: Alfred A. Knopf.

Pease, Edward C., Erna Smith, and Federico Subervi. 2001. Connecting newsroom attitudes towards ethnicity and news content. The News and Race Models of Excellence Project–Overview. http://www.poynter.org/content/content_view.asp?id =5045. Retrieved 11 November 2010.

Peterson, Mark Allen. 2007. Making global news: "Freedom of speech" and "Muslim rage" in U.S. journalism. *Contemporary Islam* 1: 247–264.

Peterson, Russell L. 2008. *Strange bedfellows: How late-night comedy turns democracy into a joke.* New Brunswick, NJ: Rutgers University Press.

Pickerton, James. 19 March 2008. Thousands of immigrants in U.S. military: They're drawn by pay, benefits and patriotism. *Houston Chronicle*, p. A1.

Pierce, Gala M. 1 November 2004. Wayne residents weigh leaving U-46: Proponents say split will boost property taxes, improve education. *Chicago Daily Herald*, p. 3.

Pieterse, Jan Nederveen. 1992. *White on Black: Images of Africa and Blacks in Western popular culture.* New Haven and London: Yale University Press.

Pinker, Steven, and George Lakoff. March–May 2007. Mind games: Does language frame politics? Steven Pinker versus George Lakoff. *Public Policy Research*, 14(1): 59–71.

Poindexter, Paula M., Laura Smith, and Don Heider. 2003. Race and ethnicity in local television news: Framing, story assignments, and source selections. *Journal of Broadcasting and Electronic Media* 47(4): 524–536.

Pollock, Griselda. 1988. *Vision and difference: Femininity, feminism, and the histories of art.* London: Routledge.

———. 1994. Feminism/Foucault–Surveillance/sexuality. In *Visual culture: Images and interpretations*, ed. Norman Bryson, Michael Ann Holly, and Keith Moxey, pp. 1–41. Middletown, CT, and London: Wesleyan University Press.

"Puerto Rican obituary." 2004. *Monthly Review Press* 56(2): 48–55.

Quillen, Ed. 26 July 2005. Preventing wars, the Tancredo way. *Denver Post*, B7.

Rabaté, Jean-Michel. 1997. Roland Barthes. In *The Johns Hopkins guide to literary theory and criticism*, ed. Michael Groden and Martin Kreiswirth. Baltimore: Johns Hopkins University Press. http://litguide.press.jhu.edu.

Reddy, Michael J. 1979. The conduit metaphor: A case of frame conflict in our language about language. In *Metaphor and thought*, ed. Andrew Ortony, pp. 284–310. New York: Cambridge University Press.

Roeh, Itzhak. 1989. Journalism as storytelling, coverage as narrative. *American Behavioral Scientist* 33(2): 162–168.

Roosevelt, Margot. 22 August 2005. Antonio Gonzalez: The get-out-the-vote guy. *Time*, p. 46.

Rose, Gillian. 2001. *Visual methodologies: An introduction to the interpretation of visual materials.* London, Thousand Oaks, CA, and New Delhi: Sage.

Rozik, Eli. 1994. Pictorial metaphor. *Kodikas/Code* 17: 203–218.

Saenz, Michael K. 1992. Television viewing as a cultural practice. *Journal of Communication Inquiry* 16(2): 37–51.

Saluskinszky, Imre. 1987. *Criticism in society: Interviews.* New York and London: Methuen.

Sánchez, Leo A. 1973. Treatment of Mexican Americans by selected US newspapers, January–June 1970. Master's thesis, Pennsylvania State University.

Santa Ana, Otto. 2002. *Brown tide rising: Metaphors of Latinos in contemporary U.S. public discourse.* Austin: University of Texas Press.

———. 2003. Book review of *Shifting borders: Rhetoric, immigration, and California's Proposition 187. Aztlán: A Journal of Chicano Studies* 28(2): 249–258.

———. 2006a. Imaging Latinos: Semiotic analyses of the 2004 network Television news. Panel paper given at American Anthropological Association annual meeting, San Jose, California.

———. 15 May 2006b. Journalists aren't vigilantes, so why do they talk like them? *Hispanic Link Weekly Report,* 24(20).

———. 2009. "Did you call in Mexican today?" The racial politics of Jay Leno immigrant jokes. *Language in Society* 38(1): 23–45.

———. 2012. U.S. crisis reporting on mass protests and the depiction of immigrants in the 40 years after the Kerner Commission Report. In *Migrations and the media,* ed. Kerry Moore and Terry Threadgold, pp. 93–117. New York: Peter Lang.

Santa Ana, Otto, Layza López, and Edgar Munguía. 2010. Framing peace as violence: U.S. television news depictions of the 2007 Los Angeles police attack on immigrant rights marchers. *Aztlán: A Journal of Chicano Studies* 35(1): 69–101.

Santa Ana, Otto, and Sandra L. Treviño, with Michael Bailey, Kristen Bodossian, and Antonio de Necochea. 2007. May to remember: Adversarial images of immigrants in U.S. newspapers during the 2006 policy debate. *Du Bois Review: Social Science Research on Race* 4(1): 207–232.

Saulnier, Natasha. 10 December 2004. *Recruiting at any cost: How the Pentagon keeps the new recruits coming.* CommonDreams.org (http://www.commondreams.org/cgi-bin/print.cgi?file=/views04/1210-20.htm). Retrieved 6 March 2008.

Schmidt, Victoria Lynn. 2005. *Story structure architect: A writer's guide to building dramatic situations and compelling characters.* Iola, WI: Writer's Digest Books.

Schön, Donald A. 1979. Generative metaphor: A perspective on problem-setting in social policy. In *Metaphor and thought,* ed. Andrew Ortony, pp. 137–163. New York: Cambridge University Press.

Schudson, Michael. 1978. *Discovering the news: A social history of American newspapers.* New York: Basic Books.

———. 1982. The politics of narrative form: The emergence of news conventions in print and television. *Daedalus* 111(4): 97–112.

———. 1992. Review of John B. Thompson's *Ideology and modern culture: Critical Social Theory in the Era of Mass Communication. Contemporary Sociology* 21(1): 106–108.

———. 2001. The objectivity norm in American journalism. *Journalism: Theory, Practice and Criticism* 2(2): 149–170.

————. 2002. News, public, nation. *The American Historical Review* 107(2). http://www.historycooperative.org/journals/ahr/107.2/ah0202000481.html. Retrieved 27 August 2011.

————. 2003. *The sociology of news.* New York and London: W. W. Norton.

Sedivy, Sonia. 1997. Metaphoric pictures, pulsars, platypuses. *Metaphor and Symbol* 12(2): 95–112.

Seitz, Jay A. 1998. Nonverbal metaphor: A review of theories and evidence. *Genetic, Social, and General Psychology Monographs* 124(1): 121–143.

Silverstone, Roger. 1988. Television, myth, and culture. In *Media, myths, and narratives: Television and the press,* ed. James W. Carey, pp. 20–47. Sage Annual Review of Communication Research #15. Newbury Park, London, and New Delhi: Sage.

Simon, Bob. 20 August 2003. The death of Lance Cpl. Gutierrez: Simon reports on non-citizen soldier. CBS. http://www.cbsnews.com/stories/2003/04/23/60II/printable550779.shtml. Retrieved 6 March 2008.

Simons, Jan. 1995. Film, language, and conceptual structures: Thinking film in the age of cognitivism. Unpublished PhD diss., Department of Film and Television Studies, University of Amsterdam.

Smith, Robert Rutherford. Winter 1979. Mythic elements in television news. *Journal of Communication* 29(1): 75–82.

Smith-Maddox, Renée, and Daniel G. Solórzano. 2002. Using critical race theory, Paulo Freire's problem-posing method, and case study research to confront race and racism in education. *Qualitative Inquiry* 8(1): 66–84.

Sperber, Dan, and Deirdre Wilson. 1995. *Relevance: Communication and cognition.* 2nd ed. Oxford: Blackwell.

Sperry, Sharon Lynn. 1976. Television news as narrative. In *Television as cultural force,* ed. Richard Adler and Douglass Cater, pp. 129–146. New York: Praeger.

Spousta, Tom. 11 July 2001. Track and field: Twists, turns and triple jumps. *New York Times,* p. D6.

Subervi, Federico A. 1994. Mass communication and Hispanics. In *Handbook of Hispanic Cultures in the United States: Sociology,* ed. F. Padilla, pp. 304–357. Houston, TX: Arte Público Press.

————. 1999. The mass media and Latinos: Policy and research agendas for the next century. *Aztlán* 24(2): 131–147.

Subervi, Federico A., Joseph Torres, and Daniela Montalvo. 2004. *Network brownout 2004: The portrayal of Latinos and Latino issues in network television news, 2003.* Austin, TX, and Washington, DC: National Association of Hispanic Journalists.

————. 2005. *Network brownout 2005: The portrayal of Latinos in network television news 2004, with a retrospect to 1995. 1999.* Report prepared for the National Association of Hispanic Journalists, Washington, DC.

Subervi, Federico A., and Heidi Eusebio. 2005. Latino media: A cultural connection. In *Hispanic marketing and public relations: Understanding and targeting America's largest minority,* ed. Elena del Valle, pp. 285–325. Boca Raton, FL: Poyeen Publishers.

Subervi, Federico A., and Dana Rios. 2005. Latino identity and situational Latinidad. In *Hispanic marketing and public relations: Understanding and target-*

ing America's largest minority, ed. Elena del Valle, pp. 29–46. Boca Raton, FL: Poyeen Publishers.

Subervi-Vélez, Federico A. 1986. The mass media and ethnic assimilation and pluralism: A review and research proposal with special focus on Hispanics. *Communication Research* 13: 71–96.

Suro, Roberto. 2004. *Changing channels and crisscrossing cultures: A survey of Latinos on the media*. Washington, DC: Pew Hispanic Center.

Suro, Roberto, Richard Fry, and Jeffrey Passel. 27 June 2005. *Hispanics and the 2004 election: Population, electorate and voters*. Washington, DC: Pew Hispanic Center. www.pewhispanic.org. Retrieved 27 August 2008.

Tan, Alexis. 1978. Evaluation of newspapers and television by Blacks and Mexican-Americans. *Journalism Quarterly* 55: 673–681.

Tankard, James W. 2001. The empirical approach to the study of media framing. In *Framing public life: Perspectives on media and our understanding of the social world*, ed. Stephen Reese, Oscar Gandy, and August Grant, pp. 95–106. Mahwah, NJ: Erlbaum.

Thompson, John B. 1984. *Studies in the theory of ideology*. London: Polity Press.

———. 1991. *Ideology and modern culture: Critical social theory in the era of mass communication*. Stanford, CA: Stanford California Press.

Thorburn, David. 1988. Television as an aesthetic medium. In *Media, myths, and narratives: Television and the press*, ed. James W. Carey, pp. 48–66. Newbury Park, NJ: Sage.

van Leeuwen, Theo. 2001. Semiotics and iconography, in *Handbook of visual analysis*, ed. Theo van Leeuwen and Carey Jewitt, pp. 92–118. London, Thousand Oaks, New Delhi: Sage.

———. 2008. *Discourse and practice: New tools for critical discourse analysis*. Vol. 2. New York: Oxford University Press.

van Leeuwen, Theo, and Carey Jewitt, eds. 2001. *Handbook of visual analysis*. London, Thousand Oaks, and New Delhi: Sage.

VanSlyke Turk, Judy, Jim Richstad, Robert L. Bryson, Jr., and Sammye M. Johnson. 1989. Hispanic Americans in the news in two southwestern cities. *Journalism Quarterly* 66: 107–113.

Veyne, Paul. 1983. *Did the Greeks believe in their myths? An essay on the constitutive imagination*, trans. Paula Wissing. Chicago and London: University of Chicago Press.

Vidmar, Neil, and Milton Rokeach. 1974. Archie Bunker's bigotry: A study in selective perception and exposure. *Journal of Communication* 24(1): 36–47.

Villalba, Serena Estrella. 2006. African Americans, Mexicans and Asian Americans in the news: A closer look at the reports of subpopulations on CNN, ABC, NBC and CBS. *2004 network news stories indexing of 12,000 stories from the Vanderbilt Archive*. UCLA research paper.

Weaver, Paul. 29 August 1976. Captives of melodrama. *New York Times Magazine*, p. 164.

———. 1981. TV news and newspaper news. In *Understanding television: Essays on television as a social and cultural force*, ed. Richard P. Adler, pp. 277–293. New York: Praeger.

West, Cornel. 1993. *Prophetic fragments: Illuminations of the crisis in American religion and culture.* Grand Rapids, MI: Eerdmans Publishing.

White, Hayden. 1980. The value of narrativity in the representation of reality. *Critical Inquiry* 7(1): 5–27.

———. 1984. The question of narrative in contemporary historical theory. *History and Theory* 23(1): 1–33.

———. 1987. The value of narrativity in the representation of reality. In *The content of the form: Narrative discourse and historical representation*, pp. 1–25. Baltimore: Johns Hopkins University Press.

———. 1990. *The content of the form: Narrative discourse and historical representation.* Baltimore: Johns Hopkins University Press.

Whittock, Trevor. 1990. *Metaphor and film.* Cambridge: Cambridge University Press.

Wible, Scott. 2004. Media advocates, Latino citizens and niche cable: The limits of "no limits" television. *Cultural Studies* 18(1): 34–66.

Williams, Carol J. 23 January 2008. Padilla gets unexpected sentence. *Los Angeles Times*, p. A12.

Williams, Raymond. [1974] 1992. *Television: Technology and cultural form.* London: Fontana.

Wilson, Clint C. III, and Félix Gutiérrez. 1985. *Minorities and media: Diversity and the end of mass communication.* Beverly Hills, CA: Sage.

Wilson, Clint C. III, and Félix Gutiérrez. 1995. *Race, multiculturalism, and the media: From mass to class communication.* Thousand Oaks, CA: Sage.

Winslow, Art. 10 February 2008. Dumbing down America. Book review of Susan Jacoby's *The Age of American Unreason. Los Angeles Times*, pp. R1, R4.

WPBF.com. 29 March 2004. Cuban refugees' boat for sale on eBay. http://www.wpbf.com/news/2957340/detail.html. Retrieved 17 April 2008.

Young, Dannagal Goldthwaite. 2004. Late-night comedy in election 2000: Its influence on candidate trait ratings and the moderating effects of political knowledge and partisanship. *Journal of Broadcasting and Electronic Media* 48(1): 1–22.

Zelizer, Barbie. 1990. Achieving journalistic authority through narrative. *Critical Studies in Mass Communication* 7: 336–376.

Credits

I would like to acknowledge the publishers that have given their formal permission to reprint in this book excerpts of their copyrighted material authored by the following writers or produced in their newsrooms:

American Broadcasting Company, for permission to reproduce extended excerpts numbering 2,360 words from eight American Broadcasting Company news stories that were broadcast in 2004. ©*ABC News*, 2004. Used with permission. Permission does not imply endorsement.

Roland Barthes, excerpt from *Mythologies* by Roland Barthes, translated by Annette Lavers. Translation copyright ©1972 by Jonathan Cape Ltd. Reprinted by permission of Hill and Wang, a division of Farrar, Straus and Giroux, LLC.

Roland Barthes, excerpt from *Mythologies* by Roland Barthes, published by Jonathan Cape. Reprinted by permission of The Random House Group Ltd.

Roland Barthes, excerpt from *Mythologies*. By permission of Editions du Seuil. ©1972 Editions du Seuil.

Cable News Network, for permission to reproduce excerpts totaling 1,544 words from five news stories that were broadcast in 2004. By permission of the Cable News Network. ©2004 by Cable News Network.

Columbia Broadcasting System, for permission to reproduce extended excerpts numbering 1,869 words from seven news stories that were broadcast in 2004. By permission of the Columbia Broadcasting Company. ©2004 by Columbia Broadcasting Company.

Daniel Gonzalez, for excerpts from "Feds aid drop-house crackdowns: Nearly 750 caught in 23 days," published on March 4, 2004, in the ©*Arizona Republic*. Used with permission. Permission does not imply endorsement.

Miriam Jordan, for excerpts from "Latinos take the lead in job gains: Hispanic workers receive higher proportion of posts in construction, services," published on February 23, 2004, in *The Wall Street Journal*. Reprinted by permission of *The Wall Street Journal*, Copyright ©2011, Dow Jones and Company, Inc. All Rights Reserved Worldwide. License number 2713721446942.

National Broadcasting Company, for permission to reproduce extended excerpts numbering 2,448 words from nine news stories that were broadcast in 2004. By

Index